PAUL GREEN

JOHN HERBERT ROPER

Paul Green

Playwright of the Real South

THE UNIVERSITY OF GEORGIA PRESS   ATHENS AND LONDON

The paper in this book meets the guidelines for permanence and durability of the Committee on Production Guidelines for Book Longevity of the Council on Library Resources.

© 2003 by the University of Georgia Press

Athens, Georgia 30602

Set in Carter and Cone Galliard by Bookcomp, Inc.

Printed and bound by Maple-Vail

Printed in the United States of America

07 06 05 04 03 C 5 4 3 2 1

Library of Congress Cataloging-in-Publication Data

Roper, John Herbert, 1948–

Paul Green, playwright of the real South / John Herbert Roper.

p. cm.

Includes bibliographical references and index.

ISBN 0-8203-2488-4 (alk. paper)

1. Green, Paul, 1894–1981.   2. Dramatists, American—20th century—Biography.   3. Social reformers—United States—Biography.   4. Southern States—Intellectual life—1865– 5. Southern States—In literature.   I. Title.

PS3513.R452 Z84 2003

812'.52—dc21

2003002759

British Library Cataloging-in-Publication Data available

IN MEMORIAM
SAM RAGAN

CONTENTS

ACKNOWLEDGMENTS

All errors of fact are my responsibility.

I wish to acknowledge a number of people who kindly helped me on my way:

Malcolm Call, who kept me at these tasks by whatever means necessary, and Nancy Grayson, who saw the project through to the end after Malcolm retired.

All members of the Paul Green Foundation, especially its president, Dr. Laurence Green Avery. All members of the Kelly Library at Emory and Henry College, especially former director Thelma Hutchins and reference librarians Jane Caldwell, Patty Greany, and Claudine Daniel, and archivist Robert Vejnar and "Mr. Fix-It" David Baber. All members of the North Carolina Collection, but especially its longtime director, Dr. H. V. Jones, and my friends Harry McKown and Keith Longiotti. All members of the most important place in Chapel Hill, the Southern Historical Collection, but especially Richard Schrader and John White. Anonymous referees at *Southern Cultures*. Ron Bayes. Glenn Blackburn. Paul Blaney. Sally Buckner. Augustus M. Burns. Lynne Cheney and the people of the National Endowment for the Humanities, who provided a generous grant for a year of research leading to the production of this biography and an edited set of wartime poems. Bruce Clayton. Ciro Dawsey. Jimmy Dawsey. Bart diPietro. Joy Dunbar. Lisa Price Eskridge. William Friday. Diane Gallagher. Eugene Dominic Genovese. Erma Green Gold. Ellen Harris. Joseph A. Herzenberg. Fred Hobson. Walter C. Jackson. John Lang. Sarah McKee. Felicia Mitchell. John Morgan. Sean Noel. Nathaniel Parks. Rita Perry. Richard Pfau. Allan Pickrell. Michael Puglisi. Eugene Latimer Rasor. John Shelton Reed. Saint Andrews Press for permission to quote from poems by John Charles McNeill. Stephen Smith. Terry Smith. Mary Snotherly. Angelia Denise Stanley. Shelby Stephenson. George J. Stevenson. Jennifer Stewart. Charles Sydnor Jr. Charles S. Watson. Harry Watson. Steven Wheeler. Joel Williamson. Brian Wills. C. Vann Woodward.

Last, and most important, Samuel Talmadge Ragan, who insisted that I take on this project, and who lived a life that showed how to fight for the right.

Previously published articles and other versions of material in this biography are:

"Confessions of a Chapel Hill Liberal." *Southern Cultures* 6 (2000): 112–20. Sections are quoted or paraphrased with permission of editors.

"Introduction" and "Notes on the Poet Soldier." From *Paul Green's War Songs: A Southern Poet's History of the Great War, 1917–1920,* edited, with an introduction, by John Herbert Roper. Rocky Mount, N.C.: North Carolina Wesleyan College Press, 1993. The introduction (pp. xi–xix) and the interpretive essay (pp. 91–165) are copyright 1993 by John Herbert Roper. Brief sections of poems are quoted with the permission of the director of the North Carolina Wesleyan College Press.

"Paul Green and the Southern Literary Renaissance." *Southern Cultures* 1 (1994): 75–89. Sections are quoted or paraphrased with the permission of the editors.

"Paul Turns Pro." *Sandhills Review* 46 (1994): 85–105. Sections are quoted or paraphrased with the permission of the editors.

John Charles McNeill, "Sunburnt Boys," "Autumn," "The Ploughboy at New Year," and "Old Spring Hill." In *The Pocket John Charles McNeill,* edited by Grace Evelyn Gibson. Laurinburg, N.C.: St. Andrews College Press, 1990. Brief quotations appear with the permission of the director of the St. Andrews College Press.

INTRODUCTION

This biography is the story of a liberal, and it is meet and right to say what the word means, at least for Paul Green in his day in his Old North State. The famous categories established by Condorcet are at the heart of it and are thus at the start of it: people are perfectible, people are individuals and have dignity as individuals, people are equal, people are rational, people are good, and people will progress (Green was more likely to say *advance*). But these categories are fully acceptable among most modern persons, and they lack ideological weight or drive in any recent political or social dispute. No, what defined liberalism in Paul Green's South was integration. If you could accept racial integration at all levels, including the social level and most particularly including the sexual level of miscegenation, then you were a real liberal. Nor was it passive acceptance, but rather something to be worked at—and worked at hard. In the words of a northern journalist emigrated from Fascist Italy, a real liberal was someone always on "special assignment," and no human being was ever more self-consciously on assignment than Paul Green.[1]

He was grand. He liked hard work of all sorts, and he could be seen playing tennis, chopping firewood, and pulling maintenance on his tractor when he was quite old. He misunderstood some ideas, and he was not really an intellectual; but he certainly caught hold of and expressed ideals, and he was a genius at the task of showing ideals in conflict in a way that sharpened focus on the larger issues. Long before Paolo Freyre brought us the phrase *consciousness raising,* that is what Paul Green was doing. The hardships of youth in a poor place and adulthood in a poor time were traced in the self-conscious grandness of his fashion. He dressed himself in expensive suits, he built a handsome estate allusively named Windy Oaks, and he betrayed the most foolproof sign that he was a man who had "made it" without actually being accepted by the real elite: he borrowed money in order always to have the biggest and newest Cadillac.

It was easy to see the speck in his blue eyes. Everything was going away from him in 1974. His dramatic art was passé, even ridiculed by the new cognoscenti at his own university. The political campaign against damnable Jim Crow had been won so thoroughly as to be forgotten, even and especially by the still-living old segregationists who now lied and claimed to have been working quietly "behind the scenes" all along. Black pride, soul movement, Afrocentrism, and all the other strains of black separatism confused and eluded him. His wife, Lib, and his favorite sister, Erma, occasionally mocked him, albeit always gently, and they said that his "favoring" and "fancying" women in his dramas and in his politics and elsewhere was not true feminism, not even the liberal's beginning of wisdom, but at least in part simply his physical attraction to the bodies that he made the objects of his affections.[2] Once defiantly a pro in filial revolt, now he was almost an amateur in a world of pros. And of course he was himself the patriarch now, no less dominant—and no less domineering—over the young writers and actors in his own community than had been the plantation paterfamilias who once made Summerville his place of sport back in Green's native Harnett County, in eastern North Carolina.

But the shrewd critic of 1974 or of a later day must needs acknowledge the mote in the beholder's eye. This man cared. This man had taken courageous steps. This man took risks. Real intellectuals had missed the prize in the sky to which he pointed, however awkwardly; now a later generation of real intellectuals noted that the prize was always there and marked how clumsily Paul Green had moved toward it. Better artists had been encouraged and even inspirited by him, and the list was interesting and varied. There were the obviously accomplished protégés Betty Smith, who wrote the artistically and commercially successful plays *A Tree Grows in Brooklyn* and *Joy in the Morning,* and John Ehle, who wrote fine novels such as *The Journey of the August King* and who also wrote that matchless memorial to Chapel Hill's civil rights movement, *The Free Men.*[3] There were also the feminist writers Frances Newman and Sara Haardt, now rediscovered by a new generation, who in their own day had been championed in Paul Green's magazine *The Reviewer,* which he ran on nerve, courage, sporting blood, and pennies. The southern literary renaissance, now studied within an inch of its historical life, had involved people like Thomas Wolfe and Sherwood Anderson and Richard Wright, who in their time considered Green fully an equal. And on Broadway and off Broadway, epochal revolutionists like Kurt Weill and Eugene O'Neill and Lynn Riggs had regarded him as worthy coworker, while that judgment had been ringingly affirmed by the leading critics of an ancient era, Burns Mantle, Brooks Atkinson, and Barrett Clark. Even in Hollywood, a place that he scarcely understood and certainly a place that scarcely understood him, even there stars Bette Davis and Franchot Tone and Will Rogers were happy to work with him and delighted to speak the lines he wrote for some of their most memorable characters.

Indeed, even that thing most easily maligned, even his outdoor drama productions, some of which were occasionally syrupy celebrations of a middle class comfortable and safe in their suburbs after World War II, even these yet bore a risk, for his first and best one, *The Lost Colony,* prodded the audiences of attorneys and realtors and accountants and brokers to think about their relationship with Lumbee Indians—Indians who were obviously also partly African American. No serious-minded social scientist concedes any physical or "blood" relationship between Lumbee Indians and the Roanoke Island settlers of the sixteenth century, but Paul Green insisted that it was all possible. In any case, he insisted on the metaphorical blood relationship between red, black, and white in a South that only pretended to be segregated. Paul Green believed in the integration of all things, and he specifically defended miscegenation, the untalked-about physical mixing of the races. This is by far the most radical position taken by white southerners, and especially in the era of the 1920s and 1930s.

The name Paul, carefully chosen by his mother, was entirely appropriate, for he would find and then take the faith of liberalism all over the empire of the New South New Rome. It was the biblical Paul who first used the image of the prize in the sky that became so crucial to the entire civil rights movement and thus crucial to the Chapel Hill liberal.[4] So too it was appropriate that his old professor Horace Williams commanded the chosen student named Paul to *take a new view of religion* and then teach it to the Carolina boys. Paul Green, without entirely intending to and certainly in ways very different than his mother or his old professor had planned it, did both of these things.

This study cannot pretend that Paul Green was a major artist, for he was not. Nor can it claim for him a greater mind than he had. And it cannot make him flawless. Nevertheless, the study is dedicated to something that this Chapel Hill liberal was trying to say, however awkwardly and in however time-bound and dated a way. The prize is still there in the sky, and we do well to turn ourselves in its direction.

The prize is racial integration, and we should remember that our brilliance, our gracefulness, our superior intelligence, our technological expertise, as well as our unmatched abilities to focus on our personal feelings, do not move us one step closer to that prize than did the admittedly stumbling and even spasmodic strivings of a man who dared to be ridiculous in the right cause. Paul Green epitomized liberal reformism of a day in a particular place. He expressed it in *The Lost Colony*. He declared it in his campaigns, with actions, with speeches, with letters to the newspapers, with letters to prominent people, with dreams *advanced* aloud.

PAUL GREEN

I : A HARNETT BOY

1894–1916

He was born Paul Eliot Greene on 17 March 1894 in Harnett County, in the sandhills of eastern North Carolina.

There are complexities and confusions of identity right from the start. The family was a large one, and it was rambling. William Archibald Greene had had three children by his first wife, Elizabeth Spence, and then she had died and he had remarried, taking to his side Bettie Lorine Byrd, who bore him six more children, of whom Paul was the third. Elizabeth Spence Greene's children were thus much older than Bettie Byrd Greene's children, and the first set of children were more like uncles and aunts than half brothers and half sisters of the younger set. The eldest of Elizabeth's children, John, would later and unsuccessfully attempt to serve as the new fatherly head of the farm after William Archibald Greene's death. At the same time, Bettie Byrd Greene's children were so numerous and so spread out in ages that her eldest, Mary, became a surrogate mother, especially for Paul, when Bettie died suddenly and unexpectedly in 1908.

Even the spelling of the baby's name involves confusion and conflict. As the careful scholar Laurence Green Avery notes, the family names are disorderly in spelling, and several of the children spelled their names more than one way. Indeed the family's very surname is spelled as often *Green* as *Greene* in correspondence, in the U.S. census, and in surviving Presbyterian church records. Only marriage to Elizabeth Atkinson Lay in 1922 would bring at least a little order to such things, as Lib, the tough-minded and beautiful red-haired Yankee, demanded that her new husband be *Paul Eliot Green*.[1]

Harnett was sandhills mixed with some of the black waxy loam generally seen in the broad inner coastal plain of eastern North Carolina. The upper valley of the Cape Fear River was cut across the county by that brown stream, which emptied itself into the Atlantic Ocean some ninety miles south and east. There was also the Little River, and both these bodies of water fertilized the Harnett soil with rich deposits carried from sources in the piedmont to the north and west. Too, this was low-country land well east of the fall line, and the rivers were easily navigable, since they flowed slowly to the sea down the slightly tilted plane of the region, where elevations seldom topped four hundred feet above sea level. The young boy could watch Buies Creek, the Little River, and the Cape Fear River, and he could sense what his mother read aloud to him and what he liked to recite, *The rivers run into the sea, and the sea is not full.*[2]

When this mother read, this son listened, and he still heard her long after she was gone. Bettie Greene was tall and lithe with "sunny" hair and with luminescent pearl-gray eyes that haunted her son until his final day. Her features were finely chiseled, delicate, and indeed almost fragile. She was not built physically or emotionally for the work of the farm, and in some ways she was the antebellum lady, a high and fine and unattainable vision that floated just beyond a man's grasp.[3] Claiming descent from *the* Byrds of Virginia, she thereby claimed as well the legacy of the English country lady, her identity unalloyed by other national or ethnic influences in a land—and in a marriage—of rough and rebellious Scots who liked to throw logs and kick and gouge each other in sweaty and grimy contests.

For her son and for the artistic daughters Caro Mae, Erma, and Gladys, Bettie Lorine Greene was an instructor in basic reading and also in singing, banjo picking, piano playing, poetry, and other artistic expressions.[4] She instructed, too, in the spiritual, all aspects of which were very closely connected, even organically joined, with things artistic—and this in a land where some of the exiled Highland Scots still banned music and other artistic expression from church services and from church sanctuaries. She was Calvinist in the sense that she firmly believed a predestined fate awaited a chosen group, a small Gideon's band who were to lead the people to the Lord's justice. And for all the weakness of her physical heart and the fragility of her bodily frame, she was hard as adamantine and unbending as the rare Harnett hardwood oak tree in her belief that Paul Greene was so chosen and must be taught to lead in art and in justice.

This compelling sense of mission for the chosen son she expressed in song and poetry and in pictures, all of it designed to lift up the boy's eyes so to see the right way already appointed for him. She was thus Calvinist in the central points that only a few could lead and that these were elected by no less than God and assigned paths of leadership that the chosen few were supposed to discover and then follow (the very Calvinist Episcopal *Book of Common Prayer* that the mature man would read Sundays in his church put it, "that we may . . . do all such good works as thou hast prepared for us to walk in"[5]).

Yet Bettie Greene was most unlike the prevailing Scots Presbyterians in the region, for she was evangelical, that is, she dealt in things of the spirit and she found God at a personal level, sometimes in nonrationalist and even emotional ways. Although many evangelical congregations were also fundamentalist— that is, adhering to a strict reading of the literal word of the Bible—she was in no sense a fundamentalist. It is sometimes forgotten that, in the old saw, all fundamentalists are evangelical, but not all evangelicals are fundamentalist; and Bettie Greene was significantly in that latter group. The Greene family had been very involved in the creation of three traditional and nonevangelical Presbyterian churches in Harnett County, but she never attended these. Often she and her children attended the Pleasant Union Baptist Church, and the children were educated by the tutors who were attached to that church's school, Paul Greene being especially influenced by the teacher Vassar Matthews. However, Bettie Greene was often restless at the Pleasant Union Church too, and she often took Paul to other churches, especially during revivals. At those meetings, if the minister adopted a hard-edged and judgmental approach instead of a broadly spiritualist one, then she carefully sheltered her son, as the mature man often recalled it in some bittersweet memories of revivalists who could really "roar" their disapproval of sin.[6]

Bettie Greene did not come to her theology casually or by some accident. Her father was the Reverend William Byrd, who preached with distinction in the upper valley and claimed to be the ninth generation in descent from the William Byrd of the same name who founded the most famous dynasty in Old Virginia. The Harnett minister was remembered by his grandson as the most intelligent man in the upper valley and also as a man who was tenacious and unrelenting in theological disputes. Above all, Grandfather William Byrd was intent on the value of an education, especially including good schooling for his daughter Bettie. While the mature playwright sometimes liked to remember himself as being much like his Grandfather Byrd, he also generally added the caveat that he hoped he had more will and ambition than his maternal ancestor.[7]

By contrast, the paternal ancestors provided plenty of will and ambition—if nothing like the level of intelligence ascribed to the Reverend Byrd. The mature man remembered his father, William Archibald Greene, as a "stirring man" hot to make his mark in the little world of the valley. The playwright wrote so often and so affectingly of the desperately poor that New York publicists and theater people sometimes assumed that he came from poverty himself. Such assumptions always angered the mature man, and for the very good reason that his father's family had always stood just beneath the top rung of the very high fence of class status in eastern North Carolina.[8] The area was Scots territory and self-consciously Celtic, and the descendants of the Highlanders built the first churches, planted the first tobacco and cotton, brought in the first slaves, and established themselves firmly in political, economic, and—more than those— moral control of things in the nineteenth century. When Paul Greene was born at the end of that century, change was afoot, and there were losses for some of the elite and those just beneath the elite, including for William Archibald Greene; but it remained the case that good land measured wealth, that control over black labor demonstrated power, and that membership in the Presbyterian churches signified authority, even if one's broadcloth was growing shiny at the elbows and threadbare.

The Buies Creek bottomland where the Greenes set their stake was originally called Neill's Creek, and William Archibald's father and grandfather each owned at least ten slaves and at least three thousand acres there. Such holdings put them in the planter class, but not into the elite. The family recollections are firm that John Greene, patriarch of Buies Creek on the eve of the Civil War, fully intended to move upward into the "big planter" elite by buying more land and more slaves and raising more cotton during a boom time that set in for cotton growers after the economic downturn of 1857. Like a good Scots Presbyterian, John Greene put his children, including his daughters, through school, although he had to pay for such an education himself in the absence of publicly supported schools in the upper valley of the Cape Fear River.[9]

The Civil War broke apart all such dreams, for John Greene and the other planters striving upward in the sandhills. At the same time it opened up grand new dreams for the fourteen former slaves of the Greenes, and from an early age Paul Greene would be keenly aware of this double vision among southerners concerning the loss of the war and the ending of slavery. Family memories, from Mary Green Johnson and from Paul Green in his mature years, describe John as tired and broke at the end of the war. The official records show that the Greenes of Buies Creek still retained more than three thousand acres of bottomland, though of course the price of cotton had dropped precipitously since the main buyers in England had found new suppliers in Mexico and Egypt.[10]

John Greene died in 1866, leaving behind his wife, Flora Catherine Greene, and three sons who stayed on the farm, including Paul Greene's father, William Archibald, who was fourteen years old in 1866. Although there was the older namesake John Greene who could have taken over the Buies Creek lands, it was the tall, stirring teenager who did so, and by 1870 the census indicates that William Archibald Greene was running the farm and the household, which included his mother, Flora Catherine, and at least three younger children. The family still held some one thousand acres, and William Archibald had sharecroppers, both white and black, who in that cash-starved era "paid" to work the Greene land with a share of the cotton they harvested. The boy patriarch also had renters, white and black, who were able to find enough cash to pay for the use of his land and thus escape the considerable stigma of being sharecroppers.[11]

Times were still tough in the upper valley of the Cape Fear at the end of the century, but the stirring man William Archibald had made a good marriage, to a Byrd, and he had prospects as bright as anyone else thereabouts. He was tough, he was tall, he could work tirelessly, and he was talented enough to do many different tasks on the farm and elsewhere. More important, he had strong sons and strong daughters as well as sharecroppers and renters, all of whom worked hard in his fields. He could, and he did, *roar* his disapproval of shoddy farm work, but he also could walk across his fields at dusk in the luminescent pearl-gray light and look across a thousand acres of well-tended white short-staple cotton and golden "bright-leaf" tobacco, all of it fringed by scientifically managed pine forests for the new paper industry. And just beyond the forest with its pungent pine-straw bedding were other farming households of big and loose-knit families, and interspersed among these neighbors were Calvinist churches, some calling themselves Presbyterian, some calling themselves Baptists, but all quite Calvinist. Most important of those church buildings was one that lay only a brief walk through the piney woods, the Pleasant Union Baptist Church, which included a school built and maintained by the churchgoers. In that building William Archibald's seven children could be educated, much as a similar school had educated him and his ancestors' children. When Paul Greene came into this valley in 1894, his father thus considered it to be a good place that could get better, even as his mother considered it a place of some loneliness and sadness that should be escaped, and both emotions would remain forever inside the man formed by that union of considerations and genetics.

Papa Greene's approach to the Pleasant Union school and church was different from his wife's, but it was also different from everyone else's. He was far ahead of his neighbors in his insistence on scientific farming, which could only be attempted by educated farmers managing educated workers. Despite his great prowess at raising cotton, William Archibald rotated other crops through, including tobacco, which in that era was actually thought to be harmless. He let a portion of the land lie fallow for a season, he raised livestock on other portions, and he raised for harvest yellow pine and scrub oak. Too, he sent out his sons John and Paul and Hugh to make turpentine, tar, and pitch from the yellow pine in the wooded periphery of his cotton lands.[12] The stirring man had a successful farm, although he saw and handled no more cash than his neighbors saw and handled; and he pushed his children to work and to study hard.

Yet his notion of education was practical and applied, and he grew fretful when Paul, Gladys, Caro Mae, and Erma spent long moments in philosophical speculation, poetry reading, or creative writing. Above all, he was suspicious of long periods of contemplative reflection. The favored child, Paul, was given to "the blues" and to "melancholia" in his youth, in what was likely the harbinger of more serious clinical depression that would assault him much later. When such spells descended, Papa Greene was displeased and called for the physical exertions of farm labor as an antidote, but Paul's mother (and later his surrogate mother, his sister Mary) took him to her side and sang and soothed and stroked his hair and defended him against the angrily roaring patriarch.[13] When the melancholia lifted, Paul was encouraged to recite poems and stories to his enthusiastic mother and sisters. He was encouraged as well in his dream of attending college in order to study fine arts and the humanities. That dream certainly led to further difficulties with Papa Greene, who wanted higher education but doubted the value of studies grounded in speculation and contemplation.[14]

As for church, Papa was said by his daughters Mary Green Johnson and Erma Green Gold to be far ahead of his times, for William Archibald put no great store in organized religion, especially as organized by the local Protestants; and yet he was spiritualistic, if not naturalistic, in his own way. Since education in the upper valley was so closely linked with the Protestant clergy, Papa often had a minister or a tutor boarding at the Greene home, and these visitors generally "took" or "cottoned" to Paul at once, urging him to recite and otherwise perform for them. Papa was generous with such guests, whether they were traveling through or were boarding in partial exchange for 120 days of instruction at the Pleasant Union school. Yet he made no bones with any of them about his preference for the practical, his distrust of the intellectual, and his disinclination to worship in the Protestant rituals of the time and place, that is, camp meetings, tent revivals, or even quiet prayer meetings of small "intentional" groups. If Papa recognized God, then his divine being must have been, in the son playwright's matchless phrase, "a field god" inspirited with and embracing an organic relationship with the very soil and crops and animals of the upper valley of the muddy and unremitting Cape Fear River.

Much was good and much was bad on the Buies Creek bottomland, and there was as much of tension as there was of "pleasant union" in the lives of all the Greene children. Then in 1908 came a complete upheaval. The beautiful matriarch collapsed, apparently of a burst aneurysm, and she did not stir, or even breathe. The chosen son with the name Paul was chosen for another mission. He was told to go to a neighboring farm for help. It is doubtful that a local doctor could have done much, since time was of the essence and the local doctors could arrive only by mule-drawn buckboard or even by foot. It is even more doubtful that a neighboring farmer with no practical medical training could have done much good. In fact, his mother was probably gone beyond saving before the boy was ordered out on his errand.[15]

Nevertheless, Paul Greene did not think these things through. He was an athlete, he had long legs and good endurance, and he would run the race like Paul the apostle, exactly as his mother had chosen to name him. He did not even pause to fasten his shoes properly, and as he tore through the woods, one shoe came off. Rather than delay to refit the shoe, he ran along, one shoe on and one shoe off, in painful hop-along style that would be funny in a different circumstance. He got to the neighboring farm quickly, however awkwardly; the neighbor came promptly—and nothing could be done. Bettie Greene was gone.[16]

The memory of that hobbling, futile race to accomplish nothing remained with the surviving son for six more decades. He dreamed about it, he talked about it, he obviously thought about it. His own children grew bored with the seriocomic melodrama, but it is clear that he never grew bored with it, likely because he never achieved peace with himself over it. Always a deeply conflicted man, he was sent into some of his profoundest internal conflicts by this strange episode.[17]

It is an oddly affecting story with an oddly compelling image. The boy was as stirring as his father, but it was not the cotton fields that stirred him. It was his mother's plan for him. He did not care that he looked ridiculous on his run, and he never would care how he looked once he accepted a mission. And it was hard to get others, not excluding his own children, to understand the depths of his passions. It is the first recorded proof that he was to be a reformist who would race for a prize that others could never see.

Family history repeated itself in some ways. In a previous generation in 1866 John Greene had left the farm and was thus unable to fill the role of family patriarch; instead, the stirring teenaged William Archibald had done so. Now, in 1908, John Greene, son of William Archibald and Elizabeth Spence Greene, could make his bid to run the family on behalf of the tiring patriarch Papa Greene, who had just lost his second wife. It was a time of economic difficulties in the rural South, although a time of growth and prosperity elsewhere, even in Carolina in the piedmont cities of Greensboro and Charlotte and in the upper-valley cities of Fayetteville and Goldsboro. But William Archibald was not ready to have John run everything, or even most things, and the children of Bettie Lorine were not at all beholden to his claims of authority. Tensions grew apace, as two demanding paternal figures called for redoubled efforts by the strong sons of Bettie Greene, Paul and Hugh. John, as did John before him in another century, left, apparently for Texas; unlike John before him, this one would come again.[18]

No matter who was the commanding patriarch, the one thing Paul and Hugh could do was work. The two grew tall, if a bit rangy and rawboned, Paul eventually topping six feet in height and weighing 186 pounds of farm-boy muscle; and this in an era when few were so tall. The two liked the fieldwork, and they enjoyed competing with each other. It was in picking cotton that Paul excelled, and family members and friends recall with a smile his moving down the rows, often wearing heavy knee pads so that he crawled with a straight back instead of with the famous stooped crouch of his powerful Papa Greene and the other workers in the upper valley. His arms were long, and he was as good with his left as with his right as he scudded through the fields, both hands furiously at work and yet delicately, too. Family and personal memory records that the boy won a Harnett County cotton-picking contest one autumn harvest season; and other memories recall the pleasure that he took all his life in farm work. *Cotton picker* was a title he selected early and held onto for a big part of his identity.[19]

There was also baseball, and Paul Greene excelled in that popular Carolina pastime. He could hit the ball hard, and he could field well, but what he could really do was pitch. He threw the ball hard and fast, and, though it strains credulity, he could pitch with either hand, as is attested by teammates.[20] He earned money as a semiprofessional, appearing on and against town teams and mill teams in Erwin, Dunn, and Lillington and other places in the upper valley where baseball was played, and played well, by the farm boys and the mill hands. The money was useful, because this Greene intended to study at the state university in Chapel Hill, and to do so he would need to pay his full fare of tuition, room, and board and, if possible, leave Papa something in compensation for the loss of the Greene farmlands' best cotton picker.[21]

It is not recorded how much Paul Greene actually liked playing baseball. Occasionally he grew weary of it, and sometimes he seemed to be playing strictly for the money, or in the army, under direct orders. Certainly he was good at it, and certainly he played hard, whether out of pure joy or out of solemn obligation.

There were other ways to earn money, and Papa was pleased to see his son diversify his skills and then develop those new skills. Paul Greene learned how to keep the books for the farm's accounts and for town businesses. In those often lengthy oddments of time between the exhaustions of the chopping/weeding season and the exhaustions of the season of harvest, he could go to Lillington and keep the books for businesses there, earning a decent fee for those off-the-farm chores. These earnings, plus the semiprofessional baseball pay, began to make a sum that the boy could offer for tuition at the state university in Chapel Hill.[22]

Yet as he began to discuss these possibilities, he came to see how he was angering Papa. An academy had been established near the Greene farm by the Reverend J. A. Campbell, and this Buies Creek Academy featured the moral instruction of the Baptist minister who was headmaster and instruction in creative writing by Hubbard Fulton Page. Campbell had founded his academy, today's Campbell University, in 1887. A fellow with a high forehead, classic facial lines, a trim moustache, and elegant wire-rim reading glasses, Campbell looked the part that he was, that is, a tough, intelligent, pragmatic, and resilient administrator. When his academy burned to the ground on 20 December 1900, the minister organized his students to raise money and to do much of the actual construction work of rebuilding. Within a year, a new Buies Creek Academy stood on site, now with four literary societies for debate, discussion, and presentation, and with laboratory facilities for natural and mathematical sciences. Campbell intended nothing less than that his academy be transformed into an accredited baccalaureate college, a goal that he did in fact realize.[23]

Papa Greene found in Campbell his kind of man, and he was pleased that, by 1914, his son Paul Greene was certified to teach subjects including the natural sciences in public schools and in church schools of the valley. Now the family had one who could draw professional fees for teaching and bookkeeping while also farming. When the boy brought up the subject of university training, Papa talked with Campbell, who arranged a full scholarship at Wake Forest College, a Baptist institution then located in Wake County near the city of Raleigh.[24]

None of this was to Paul Greene's liking, although there was much that he enjoyed at the academy, including the sessions with Hubbard Page and the enduring friendship of a literary society fellow, Josiah Bailey, who would later become state senator and a prominent ally in the cause of outdoor symphonic drama. However, when Campbell announced plans to arrange for him to study at Wake Forest College, Paul grew rebellious. He dropped out of his Sunday school classes, where he once taught enthusiastically, and he let it be known rather noisily that he fully accepted Charles Darwin's explanation of human evolution in the *Origins of Species,* which was quietly taught at Buies Creek Academy. Campbell wanted his science instruction to be practical and up-to-date, but none of the Baptist leaders wanted a lot of public discussion about Darwinian theory, since the academy was still committed to a literal interpretation of the two Genesis accounts of creation. Too, Paul Greene spent more and more time swapping manuscripts with Page, whom he credited "as the teacher who awoke in me a feeling for life and the people whom I have seen living it." At Page's urging, Paul Greene walked among all the peoples of the valley, especially including the black people of the sharecropping farmlands, and he listened to and wrote down their songs and their stories.[25]

In fact, Paul Greene created an author/character, Harvey Easom, who "recorded life" in Little Bethel, the name of a real place nearby that he took for an imaginary town composed of elements of Lillington and Buies Creek. With Page encouraging him, he began an ambitious regime of keeping a "real" diary of his doings and a Harvey Easom "H. E. Diary" that was fictional. He filled the pages of both with observations of real and imagined people, and with poems "written by Harvey Easom" as well as poems written by Paul Elliot Greene. Most of the "H. E. Poems" drawn from the "H. E. Diary" feature characters who have an actual counterpart in the farm communities and mill villages of Buies Creek, Lillington, Little Bethel, the almost-deserted Summerville (once the center of planter elegance), and Dunn and Erwin.[26]

Teaching Darwinian evolution as well as the basic reading, writing, and arithmetic in Buies Creek, keeping the books in Lillington, farming the bottomland, playing semiprofessional baseball in the valley, writing poetry, and collecting folklore all around. It was a lot to do, even for one who had been "intentionally" instructed by his mother that he had been given great talents in order to use all of his talents: "To you has been given the secret of the Kingdom of God. . . . Take heed what you hear; the measure you give will be the measure you get."[27]

For all his sense of mission and for all of his great energies, Paul Greene was wearing himself out, and his sister Mary could see that exhaustion.

Mary Greene could see something in addition to the boy's exhaustion. There was a mysterious infection that caused her brother's right arm to swell up grotesquely and painfully. No one in the family knows why the infection started, or even when it first became painful, because the hard-working young man evidently suffered with the problem silently until it became too obvious for others to ignore. The local physician, Joseph McKay, could find no cure or treatment and suggested that Papa Greene seek the help of one of the few neurologists then practicing in the United States. Dr. Walter Edward Dandy of the relatively new Johns Hopkins University medical school (founded in 1893) in Baltimore was the closest such specialist, the others being in San Francisco and Boston. While Papa Greene pinched his pennies and watched the books closely, he was in no sense penny wise and pound foolish, especially where the chosen son was concerned.[28]

Around 1914 or 1915, Papa Greene took his son up to Baltimore for the neurological surgery and therapy. Dr. Dandy cut out damaged tissue, worked on damaged nerves and inserted a silver plate into his long right arm. This scar the mature man would show people, especially his children, and he always emphasized—with that poetic eye for the concrete particularity of detail—that the plate under the scarred surface was not steel but silver. During recuperation and therapy, Paul Greene learned how to write with his left hand, and it may be that his left-handed baseball-throwing prowess developed as a consequence of the operation rather than before it. Papa Greene was relieved that his son recovered fully, and he would send his son to Dr. Dandy in Baltimore again, as that son would one day send a daughter to Dr. Dandy. Although Papa Greene and Paul Greene would fret about bills, and despite the way that Paul Greene could wax poetic about the romance of the simple farm, each man was fully committed to finding the best health care available from the top specialists. And each man was always willing to pay the bill for such services no matter how cash-starved and land-poor the family was.[29]

Papa Greene's kindness and caring knew no bounds, but his sense of a proper education certainly did. Delighted that the Reverend Campbell could arrange a scholarship at Wake Forest College, Papa Greene talked with his son about the two years of study—and a possible return to manage things in Buies Creek. But Paul Greene revealed to Papa that he wanted to attend the state university, and particularly so in order to study philosophy with Horace Williams and to make a serious study of North Carolina literature, both apparently suggestions from his mentor Hubbard Page. Hearing such plans, Papa Greene was outraged. Philosophy and literature, abstract speculation and soulful mooning about, were exactly the kinds of activities that Papa found so useless as to be a menace to the scientific running of the farm. More especially, he recalled that Campbell and most holy men of the upper valley were warning parents to keep their impressionable children away from Horace Williams, perpetrator of "Yankee skepticism," although Williams's Gates County accent was as broadly eastern as Papa's own. Papa was no churchgoer, but he had no truck with Yankee skepticism. Besides, unlike the full-fare scholarship proffered at Wake Forest, Carolina was all expense, and it might take four full years to accomplish the baccalaureate degree in two fields. [30]

This time there was more serious quarreling than before, and Paul Greene delayed his college studies for another academic year, but only with a smoldering resentment. When a new planting season had come round in 1916, he pressed Papa Greene for permission, and some money, to go to Chapel Hill. This fight was very bitter, and Mary Greene had to intervene, invoking the memory of the beautiful matriarch to calm both men. John Greene, back from his travels, and Hugh Greene and the girls all promised to do more work to make up for Paul's absence from the farm—and the boy himself promised to work at all his jobs, bookkeeping, semiprofessional baseball playing, and farming, in the winter and summer interim periods between academic quarters. [31]

Papa Greene was intensely displeased, the more so since the whole family stood arrayed against him and his will. He relented before the inevitable, but only in a way that let Paul Greene know that a serious personal break was occurring. The chosen son was going to the Hill with no kiss of blessing from his father.

2 : CHAPEL HILL

1916–1917

What kind of school was Carolina?

What kind of place was the Hill?

The state university and Chapel Hill, these intertwined communities of the central piedmont, both awaited the sandhills boy and a couple of hundred others matriculating from burgs and crossroads and a few modest towns in the diverse regions of the nation's most rural state. "Socdolager!" exclaimed the eastern farm boys. Greene wrote the word in his diary. What did it mean? It meant nothing, but it meant everything; it was a sign of membership in a special group on a special mission. It meant that no translatable words could capture his joy: using *socdolager* let a boy show that he understood something that he could never explain unless it was to someone else who was here, and if someone else was here, then there would be no reason to explain. Greene was overwhelmed by the historic buildings and the professors with their training and the accomplished older students and the town filled with shrewd professionals. *Socdolager.* And there were the extracurricular things: concerts to attend, for music here was not a matter of farmers dressing up their daughters twice a year for an ensemble. Debates, with two different learned societies, each of them loaded down with talented cosmopolites from Charlotte and Raleigh as well as boys more like Greene, from Asheville and Scotland Neck, Cullowhee and Currituck, Brevard and Ahoskie. And the really extracurricular: drinking clubs and fraternal organizations, sports teams and places downtown to meet girls, lots of girls, even though, or perhaps because, the university dormitories were strictly for boys, as were the classrooms, save for a few graduate programs and an occasional junior or senior town-dwelling female who walked in to "sit" a few classes. *Socdolager.*

In the first week on campus, Greene ran through his cash quickly in several all-night drinking and skirt-chasing sprees, and he awoke with pounding head and coated tongue and fuzzy vision. The Scottish Greenes would not have been surprised, and of course neither would the pastor of the Pleasant Union Baptist Church, the Reverend Tom Long with his prim beard and stiff resolve and his plain-Baptist fundamentalist suspicions. But Bettie Lorine Greene would have been surprised, and Paul Greene confessed all to sister-mother Mary Greene, not without some left-handed pride in his hell raising. Indeed, hard drinking and attention to skirts would be features of his life from this point on. He would work hard and then play hard. For now, however, in this new scene, he vowed to be more of a student and less of a playboy. He sent for more money, for blankets, for proper bed-sheets, and he listed the academic things that he would do. To Mary Greene, and to himself, he vowed to get serious now that classroom instruction had actually commenced.[1] All of it, including the skirts and the songs and the booze, was still inexplicably *socdolager,* but it was the *socdolager* other, the lecterns, the library alcoves, the arboretum, the debating clubs, the music clubs, the literary societies, that he would explore now.

It is almost impossible to overstate the extreme idealism with which Greene approached the university in Chapel Hill in this Indian summer of 1916. Of course, the sacrifices and circumstances of those additional years of hard work had prepared him in unique ways for college. Even the hardest-working and most plain-living university student lived a life of no little comfort when contrasted with the lives of farmers and rural schoolmasters, and Greene frankly looked forward to some relief from the physically demanding labors of the Harnett countryside. But there was something else even beyond these things: the challenge of teaching before he himself had had a real opportunity to learn much had made him all but ravenous for the chance to use a real university library, not to mention the feast he envisioned about the processes of studying with learned men of scholarly expertise and cosmopolitan experiences. The university slogan, *Lux libertas,* "Light and freedom," Greene took with full seriousness.

Lux libertas. Socdolager.

A cynic could well have asked if the game was really worth this candle, for UNC's light was not then conspicuous even in this most dimly lit regional corner of American higher education. The student body was counted by the hundreds, the faculty by the dozens, in an era when state universities, especially in the upper Midwest, were ten times larger—and enrollments were changing slowly in Chapel Hill while growing rapidly elsewhere. More, there were fundamental questions of quality, for there seemed a willingness and even an eagerness to let the same Carolina families proceed with the same stultifying curriculum and policies, all designed more to produce a kind of a gentleman with a patina of the classics rather than a genuine humanist with serious commitments to study the larger and deeper questions of life. As noted by the southern-born New York theater critic Montrose Jonas Moses, who was intimately familiar with UNC in this era, the classics were then used by graduates of such schools to exclude rather than to engage the majority of the citizens in matters of policy. There was, in fact, a clubbiness, a damning self-satisfaction in much of the campus and community, perhaps best expressed by Chapel Hill's equivalent of a dowager aunt, Cornelia Phillips Spencer, who once pointedly lectured at a newly arrived Yale-trained philosopher, "We don't want any Yankee skepticism down here."[2]

For all that, change was not impossible at UNC, as ably demonstrated by the career of the very target of Spencer's sling on the occasion of his arrival in 1891: her intended "bag" was Henry Horace Williams, the very man Hubbard Fulton Page wanted his student Paul Greene to study with—and the very man the Reverends Long and Campbell had warned Papa Greene about. This Horace Williams was a man armed not only with skepticism learned from Yankees but also with a full array of more traditionally southern techniques: he disarmed Spencer's entrenched opposition by convincing her that he was, after all, one of us, too. Having been summoned to tea by the "lady who rang the bell" to reopen UNC after its closing during Reconstruction, Williams realized that he was in trouble for a public remark of his. Speaking as a student at a Boston Youth Forum discussion about religion and society, he had held his tongue firmly in cheek and said for the record that he had been astonished to learn that Jesus Christ was not a Methodist and not even an American. If news of such attitudes had set Spencer in opposition to him, then Williams's life in Chapel Hill could become quite a miserable experience, since the dowager did indeed set the tone for the social lives in this small and isolated community.

But there was more, since she was also a dowager in the older sense of the word, one who brought, albeit somewhat indirectly, the power of wealth and legitimating family blood into this "marriage" of university and political families. She was daughter of a UNC professor, sister of two others, mother-in-law of a fourth, and a dame of the Carolina Presbyterian enclave that dominated town and gown; moreover, she was influential enough, and sometimes mean-spirited enough, to see that her friends and relations on the school's board of trustees could allow significant financial pressures to visit this struggling new department of philosophy with its developing "secular" curriculum. In that era UNC's lack of money and other resources was always a real factor that could be called upon to rationalize almost any action or, more often, to rationalize any given *inaction*. Knowing that the stakes were this high, Williams must have been more nervous than village myth declares him to have been as he sipped his tea and awaited the start of the games. At last came her first thrust about Yankee skepticism, and before he could parry, she thrust again: "We want you to title your course 'Christian Philosophy.'"

"All right," Williams replied quickly; but then he added significantly, "on one condition: you will have to agree to have your son-in-law call himself a professor of Christian mathematics." Mercifully, Mrs. Spencer laughed and allowed the course—and the professor—to pass through. In fact, she herself nurtured the mythic qualities of this exchange, thereby encouraging an early acceptance of Horace Williams as an authentic type who should be permitted enough freedom of movement to become a real scholar.

Thus sanctioned, he began his teaching, emphasizing argumentation and pointed questioning in his own version of the Socratic method. Thomas Wolfe, who studied alongside Greene, has caught the image of Horace in the classroom:

> Erect, with arm akimbo on his hip, he stood, his domed head turned out toward the light: sixty, subtle and straight of body, deep-browed, with an old glint of hawk-eyes, lean apple-cheeks, a mustache bristle-cropped. That face on which the condor Thought has fed, arched with high subtle malice, sophist glee.
>
> Below, benched in rapt servility, they waited for his first husky word. Eugene [the student narrator] looked at the dull earnest faces, lured from the solid pews of Calvinism to the shadowland of metaphysics. And now his mockery will play like lightning around their heads, but they will never see it, nor feel it strike. They will rush forward to wrestle with his shadow, to hear his demon's laughter, to struggle solemnly with their unborn souls.[3]

Horace Williams indeed had chosen the right approach for dealing with the dowager, partly because it won her to his side but also because it helped to build the legend about himself that he would nurture until adoring students, as Wolfe does here, took up that task for him. Southerners do not like straightforward conversation in most cases, but Williams could have told a simple thing to Spencer and to Wolfe's concerned students fresh from their solid Calvinist pews: he did teach Christian philosophy, albeit with a great distrust of most sects organized into self-conscious churches. His graduate research thesis was a close textual analysis of the New Testament letters to the Hebrews, traditionally attributed to the apostle Saint Paul. His analysis, after the fashion of the era's emerging "higher criticism" of biblical and sacred texts, convinced him that Paul of Tarsus was not the author of these documents, because the style of expression and the substance of the message were both from a later era. That might not pass muster with Spencer's friends, but it is hardly skepticism, for Williams the scholar, wishing to learn from the revealed wisdom, was eager to know exactly what Saint Paul did say. It is the believer's passion to unfold the truth that Williams brought to this study. In class he called for nothing less than a "new Isaiah," someone to rekindle the ancient passions and use them in new ways for God's work in modern times.[4]

Deeply spiritual, Williams in his graduate days at Yale University had absorbed the late German romanticism of Georg Wilhelm Friedrich Hegel, and he would remain faithful to Hegelian idealism throughout his long career. The notes he took on Hegel in a seminar in 1883 reappear in different versions until the end of his professorial days in the late 1930s. As a Yale graduate student, he made for himself the project of translating Hegel's *Philosophy of Religion,* and it is interesting that all through his graduate-school notes and his professor-days lecture notes, he often wrote in German about Hegel, something he did not do for the many other German-speaking philosophers from Leibniz to Schopen-hauer whom he also taught and studied. It was the energy and the passionate sense of mission in quest of the inspiriting ideal that Williams learned from Hegel, and that was what he passed along so affectingly to his many students from 1890 to 1940.[5]

In fact, the students did not see the feared Yankee skepticism in Williams. Of skepticism they saw precious little in such an idealist and romantic, and nothing at all of the Yankee. Born in 1858 in Gates County in the far northeastern corner of Carolina, Horace had grown up in the Chowan River basin of the Albemarle Sound. This was a land of the unspoiled natural habitat, the Great Dismal Swamp; and it was also a land with a human history, for the rebellious slave Nat Turner in August of 1831 had struck for freedom not far away, in Southampton, Virginia; and after the fight Turner and his small band had hid out in the vast swampland until captured by the "vigilance" patrollers. It was farming country, still good land, but after the Civil War all crops, even including the once-reliable cotton and tobacco, brought poor prices. By the 1870s the plentiful woodland had attracted a season of entrepreneurial attention from timber men and from sawmill operators, and Williams left home and went off to New Haven with images of the shays—the slow-moving, wood-burning, geared locomotives that hauled wood to mill for sawing. In talking with his students, the majority of whom were, like Paul Greene, from the country, the professor could make Hegel into something of a homespun easterner warming his hands at the stove in the feed store and talking about the state of the local crops. Williams's lecture notes are witty, colorful, and memorable; but he was never able, indeed not willing, to write effectively for publication, and his one textbook and his abortive project for a second one are dull, oddly organized, hard to follow, and quite different in kind from the sparkling classroom lecture notes.[6]

Almost at once he became famous on campus, but soon he faced still another challenge, albeit one from someone less important to UNC than Spencer was. A professor, perhaps a bit jealous of Williams's popularity with students, inquired testily if it were not true that students "sass you." "Do they now?" Williams put it in reply. "But you know, I sass them right back." These stories, charming in one sense, demonstrate the kind of quick but still eminently respectful riposte for which Williams was distinguished, but the nature of each story is also quite troubling. If greatness is a measure of how much water is displaced by a personage, then Williams was great in this community by virtue of these two splashes alone; but how small a volume of water there must have been there in Williams's first decade of teaching in Chapel Hill![7]

Fortunately, Williams between 1891 and Paul Greene's arrival in 1916 gained precious elbow room for the ideas of hard questioning by inquiring minds, and so too did other fine scholars who came to the campus with similar expectations. At last, sometime in the 1910s, these more challenging instructors found a working plurality of students ready to join in meaningful dialogue. When Greene did matriculate, Edwin Almiron Greenlaw, Harry Woodburn Chase, Robert Diggs Wimberly Connor, William Chambers Coker, and Archibald Henderson had joined Williams on the faculty. One thing about a small faculty was that the addition of a mere handful of talented and innovative people could dramatically improve instruction on the campus, as each of these men did. More important, former Horace Williams student Edward Kidder Graham had become president of the university in 1914 and was providing an intelligent and carefully articulated intellectual and moral direction for the school.

For this struggling university, the future lay in Graham's little black book, a palm-sized notebook in which the president wrote down his plans. He built well in these pages, and scholars who have examined the development of the modern UNC are as impressed with his plans as were the appreciative coworkers among the contemporaneous faculty and staff, 1914–17. Graham certainly intended to continue serving the region, as Carolina and the newer North Carolina State Agricultural and Mechanical College (then generally styled State College) already were; but he wanted more than the current level of service. [8] Carolina before 1914 was training professors and attorneys and engineers and teachers and ministers and bankers and other professionals and business leaders who came from a particular class of people and who subsequently worked for the interests of those same people. The tone was high, with the classics and moral philosophy primary, and Montrose Moses' complaint must be measured carefully because of the fine instruction in the classics provided there. But there was very little that could be considered practical; it never served the common Tarheel, and even some members of the elite, specifically those managing the textile industry and the newer farming, considered themselves ill served by UNC.

Although some of the latter needs, certainly those of new farming and textiles, were met at State College in Raleigh through advanced courses in chemical and electrical engineering and applied technological research and development, that school was often disdained as the "Cow College" or as "West Wake County Tech." And even the avowedly populist sentiments of the Watauga club, which had produced State College, were fading in Raleigh by 1914: the lower middle class had a tough time on either campus, Carolina or State, and the working class was far to seek, unless you counted the janitorial and kitchen and grounds crews. Graham wanted to serve a wider range of Carolinians, and with an education that was at once practical and moral.

Of course, the universities of the upper Midwest were there as an example, with the University of Wisconsin as the most prominent among this sort of public school. Yet, for Graham, even Wisconsin was a little suspect since it sometimes politicized its research and even personalized the politicization on behalf of Governor Robert LaFollette. Such abuses could compromise the mission of the modern scholar who wanted to serve both the whole public and the muse of some discipline. A tough critic, this otherwise unassuming man Graham. The criticism always was there, albeit implied rather than directly spoken, and he insisted that the University of North Carolina be a real university of helpfulness to an entire nation by developing its own citizen scholars. Even the midwestern behemoths with their undeniable accomplishments were not his exemplar; he was reaching for something different altogether, something sui generis and hard to outline, even in that little notebook.

However preposterous Graham's goals might sound to us decades later, his effect on the Hill in his own day was immediate, and his words and gestures were always considered to be fully credible. *It could happen right here,* and Why not *now?* said the mentor Williams, who had survived so much. And Williams, now with substantive administrative support, set about to create a curriculum and to provide the other resources to teach and train professional, and secular, philosophers. *Yes,* echoed the newcomers Greenlaw, Chase, Connor, Coker. Thus Greenlaw worked to create a modern English department, assisted by the polymath Archibald Henderson, biographer and correspondent of George Bernard Shaw as well as mathematician and moral philosopher. Coker set demanding standards for instructing and conducting laboratory-science research, despite complaints from students, some influential alumni, and even scientists at other colleges in the region that this work was too demanding for southern pupils. Historian Connor for his part was busy developing a good state archives, but he helped also to build a real history program on the Hill. And Chase, a philosopher of education and a psychologist, immediately began to demonstrate the high qualities of his own leadership in all areas of curriculum and policy, becoming Graham's academic dean of this faculty that intended to do so much.

This was the spirit that Paul Greene caught during his long-delayed freshman year of study. Keep it firmly in mind that, in the academic year 1916–17, President Graham's plans were by and large only plans in a small notebook. Remember too that, with the exception of Henderson and Williams, the figures prominent in this faculty were not then very prominent anywhere else. Chapel Hill and Carolina were not much noticed on the national scene. The university was closer to Cornelia Phillips Spencer's ideal of a gentleman's regional center than to Graham's ideal of a scholar's center of service to a larger public. Only with hindsight can we see that the institution and the community were in the chrysalis phase of intellectual and moral evolution. Others passing through beheld a somnolescent town and undistinguished gown: Chapel Hill lacked the colonial glory of Williamsburg, and its university claimed neither the grand memories of the College of William and Mary nor the present greatness of the University of Wisconsin. It was to Edward Kidder Graham's credit that he kept alive in his scholars a belief in their own potential and a will to act on that belief, for a less romantic assessment of things could certainly have produced if not despair then a resigned submissiveness to the fact of mediocrity.

Greene passed his qualifying examinations without much trouble and received permission to take at least one English course normally reserved for sophomores. For the three academic quarters of this freshman year, his schedule was decidedly a humanist's: Greek, Latin, French, and six courses in English, with a mere two sessions of mathematics to exercise the other side of his brain. This student was not a classicist, however, despite the nod to Greek and Latin. His diary notes and his correspondence home both indicate that he enjoyed French while only tolerating the "dead" languages; in any case his real love was literature, and specifically North Carolina literature. He studied dutifully and built a good record, but his real work went into writing poems and short stories. He wrote them for class assignments, he wrote them for the student literary magazine, he wrote them for formal and informal student groups, he wrote them for the family back home, he wrote them for his diary. It was in this first season at Carolina that he began the systematic regime of diary writing and copybook exercises, all of which he would carry on until his final day.[9]

With some initial grumbling, he joined in the undergraduate sports. Football and basketball were not then the dominant sports they would become at Carolina, for *the* sport in 1916 was baseball. The distant gods of the professional major leagues, Ty Cobb and Tris Speaker and Home Run Baker and Shoeless Joe Jackson, rumored though they were to be willing hostages of gamblers, were given their due reverence; but genuine passions were spent on local amateur teams. And the profoundest passions were invested in the most local of all. Not only were the boys rabidly interested in the university varsity team, but they also were enthusiastic about freshman-class and sophomore-class and upper-class baseball squads not connected in any way with the varsity club. Plainly, no boy with Greene's build and skills could rightly decline the invitation to play; and, when he did play, his own competitive nature was always stirred into effect. Soon these Chapel Hill classmates, like the boys back at Erwin Mill, Duke Mill, Angier, and Lillington, were bearing the tales of the big skinny kid who pitched with either hand and who knocked the leather off the ball when it was his turn at bat.[10]

Although Greene disliked the excessive talk about his ambidexterity and his fastball, his diary shows that the sport satisfied more than a few needs felt if not spoken. As always, there is a story in the making here, and, as always, it has a twist. This most accomplished of raconteurs created and then acted out his own stock baseball-diamond character, the strong, silent batsman; but on the pitcher's mound, the Paul Greene character was different yet again: the incommunicative wizard throwing pitches from odd angles with either hand and posing a hazard as much to his uninformed catcher as to the opposing batters. For all of Greene's protestations to the contrary, there must have been some real talent there, given the interest in him from semiprofessional, college-club, and armed-forces teams. Still, there also must have been limits to that talent, for there is no record of any interest by the varsity Tarheels, who were content to battle State and Wake Forest with their existing squad of less colorful hitters, fielders, and pitchers.[11]

There were other touches expected of the *regular fellow*. Despite all the allure of studying alongside cosmopolites and boys from farther regions of Carolina, he consciously kept up his hometown and local ties. He joined the Buies Creek Club and the Harnett Boys Club, serving as recording secretary for the latter. Each club numbered only a baker's dozen members, and obviously there was overlap between the two. What exactly they did is unclear, but the members did keep track of one another throughout college and during the war years, which drew most of them away from campus. Later in this freshman year Greene would again go out successfully in search of girls, but this time with nothing stronger for fuel than soft drinks. When his money ran low and nothing was forthcoming in the mail from Buies Creek, he could always borrow from Henry Speas, UNC class of 1879, a Harnett native called "Cousin Henry" by the boys from the county. This Cousin Henry could speak eloquently of fiscal and other responsibility while lending at 25 percent. This was a favor provided all the college boys from Harnett, and to be both broke and in debt to Cousin Henry was part of a regular fellow's identity, at least for the sandhills regular fellows.[12]

These things were of course diversions, however special, and, if carried on too long, they became annoying to the young man with big plans and with other things on his mind. From time to time, Greene avoided the company of the Harnett Boys and the baseball club so that he could wander alone. As at home, he had the same spells of melancholia first observed fretfully by his sisters; and during those spells his face showed his need for solitude, what with his brows furrowed and his gaze darkly inward. Eventually he would be treated for clinical depression, but in his youth family and friends simply observed that he "had the blues" and needed to be left alone. During some of those spells he wrote poems. And sometimes the writing was so therapeutic that he would go find a friend to read to. Often too, he read aloud, especially the *Rubáiyát of Omar Khayyám,* as translated by Edward Fitzgerald, and anything by Edgar Allan Poe or Alfred, Lord Tennyson. One classmate in particular, Allan Dunn, shared these literary passions, and the two often slipped away from the ball field and the card games and the library to walk the shady streets of compact old Chapel Hill and to recite verses from the *Rubáiyát* and to talk eagerly in their special way about that work.[13]

Although 1916 was a little late in the day for this, Paul Greene and Allan Dunn were not unusual in forming their own sort of cult around Omar Khayyám. Throughout the United States, from the late nineteenth century, small groups gathered, especially at universities and especially among those in late adolescence, to talk in their own special way about the *Rubáiyát.* Likely, they were talking as much about the soulful rebelliousness resonating with the Celtic translator Edward Fitzgerald as they were about the words of an eleventh-century Persian who may have been a Sufi, or a prophet, or a hedonist, or the heretic the contemporaneous Moslems judged him to be. It is not a hard thing to find the attractiveness in the four-line stanzas with their compelling rhythm: whoever this medieval figure was, he was telling his readers to enjoy the beautiful things now, for they are beautiful precisely because so fragile and so short lived. He was telling them that the moral authority and spirituality were immanent, inside any two of them, rather than general and transcendent over the ages. And the pleasures, especially the sensual pleasures, enjoyed in youth were not sinful, but even self-sanctified. What a different thing to hear for those who as children were goaded along by unbending presbyters and already-saved elders to postpone, if not forego, the body's urgings. Too, the university could oppress just as much with its own demands, since its professors were dismantling the words and sometimes ruining the music in the phrases to search for and judge the meaning; and even the college boys themselves were taking a once-simple pleasure like baseball and making it into a solemn duty. The critical analysis of the rational inquiry so central to Western thinking was just everywhere, and certainly it was deep down in Paul Greene himself, and probably in Allan Dunn too. But here was a chance, the chance itself beautiful because evanescent, to enjoy a thing purely as a thing to enjoy.[14]

Even the very university endeavors for which Paul had sacrificed were bracketed as an irrelevance:

> Myself when young did eagerly frequent
> Doctor and Saint, and heard great Argument
> About it and about: but evermore
> Came out by the same Door as in I went.[15]

Both the Chapel Hill sages and the Harnett countryside saints

> who discuss'd
> Of the Two Worlds so learnedly, are thrust
> > Like foolish Prophets forth; their Words to Scorn
> Are scatter'd, and their Mouths are stopt with Dust.

All of this left Paul Greene and Allan Dunn with the clear signal:

> Ah, make the most of what we yet may spend
> Before we too into the Dust descend.

And from there the freshmen could move inexorably to the two most quoted injunctions, almost anti-injunctions: "Ah, take the Cash, and let the Credit go"; and

> A book of Verses underneath the Bough,
> A Jug of Wine, a Loaf of Bread—and Thou. [16]

Whether Cousin Henry Speas's 25 percent credit or Archibald Henderson's great Shavian argument, whether the Reverend Tom Long's bitter draught or Professor Horace Williams's sweet cup, "the wine of Life keeps oozing drop by drop, / The Leaves of Life keep falling one by one," and "Thee and Me" would soon be gone as well, a pity to lose even that brief moment together. Such sentiments, expressed with women, often would lead Greene into passionate lovemaking, and there is in the brief note about Allan Dunn an erotic quality that would also fit in with a homoerotic part of the cult of Omar Khayyám as it was in the English public schools. Yet Greene, who usually marked, albeit discreetly, with veiled and coded phrases, the particularities of his lovemaking, makes no further note; and he and Allan Dunn are left in the diary record and correspondence as boys in the university wilderness and without wine, protected, perhaps even from each other, by their shared verses. [17]

There were still other reasons for Greene to reach for and hang onto the *Rubáiyát.* The sandhills populism and the sandhills tunes and tales of the old Celts were also organically part of the *Rubáiyát,* at least as he read Fitzgerald. Greene often spoke of a thread, that is, the *thread of tradition* that students unroll after themselves and so make their excursion into the unknown. This *held thread* was the only measure by which they could tell how far they had come—or how to get back. And this little volume for several years gave him an especially firm grasp on that thread. [18]

Fitzgerald was Irish, not Scottish, but the celebrants of things Celtic could always look past the long path of ethnic and religious warfare between the Orange and Green and focus instead on the even longer path of shared folkways. Fitzgerald looked way back, and was among those who found a Celtic continuum starting somewhere in southwestern Asia and expanding outward everywhere. In the editor's introduction it is even noted that Fitzgerald was much taken with the notion that the words *Erin* and *Iran* were at root the same thing, making Omar the Persian into a Celt. This ethnic romanticism, especially the rebellious dissatisfaction with things properly English and Victorian, is there in Fitzgerald, and it was welcomed by a boy proud of his Scots ancestors but skeptical about their American Presbyterianism: and here it was, proof in verse that over a longer stretch there was a wild pagan Scot soul, spiritual and in tune with God all right, but not religious in the sense of pietistic service to the orthodox preachments of some priestly caste. Indeed, the very Tennyson whom his mother had recited to him at her breast since Greene's infancy says in an epilogue "To E. Fitzgerald": "[T]hat large infidel / Your Omar" in "your Golden Eastern lay" . . . "A planet equal to the sun / Which cast it" so that "on me, half-asleep, came back / That wholesome heat the blood had lost."[19]

And the welcomed invigoration not only set Tennyson "climbing icy capes / and glories" warmed by the wine of the translation "wrought / To mould the dream," it set Greene climbing as well. Omar was many things, according to the scholars and the cultists, and all of those things were crucial to Greene. Along with his poetry writing, Omar was an astronomer, a mathematician, and a respected scholar with the privileges of the court of the vizier. But even better for the believing tale bearer, Omar had passed through a period of financial hardship during which, according to his self-woven myth, he made tents and thus took the poetical surname (that is, his *Takhallus*) *Khayyám* to signify that craft as his trade. When a former classmate became a vizier, and by tradition owed a portion of his fortune to old friends, Omar came to him, but only to claim a modest pension and the time and space for studies and writing. Fitzgerald's introduction notes that Omar the Tentmaker "stitched the tents of science" (again, thread) well enough to make a calendar more accurate than the contemporaneous Western one, to develop theories in algebra, and to rewrite the astronomer's tables. But what drew Fitzgerald to him, and likely the fatalist Greene, is Omar's epitaph for himself:

> The shears of Fate have cut the tent rope of his Life,
> And the broker of Hope has sold him for nothing![20]

Finally, and most aptly, Fitzgerald insists in his biographical sketch that Omar was not a Sufi religionist, but like himself a heretic; and he says that all the verses about drinking are neither metaphors describing the wine of religion nor the self-indulgence of the hedonist dipsomaniac. No, Fitzgerald's Omar drinks the wine of life, foreswearing the mere physical grape for the "long-arm'd vines with grape of Eschol hugeness" found in reading and writing verses. While young Greene was not about to abandon the physical grape, he also drank deeply of the metaphysical wine of life, doing so away from the professors and the students, preferably alone or in the company of one or two other Celtic souls.[21]

In such company, another Celtic soul whose verses they visited often was John Masefield, then a wildly popular poet, albeit not one honored with a cult. Masefield, nominally a New Yorker, had spent his youth wandering, including long seasons at sea and years of labor and relaxation in London. Like Greene, he largely educated himself as a teenager by reading Tennyson, Sir Walter Scott, and Henry Wadsworth Longfellow, from those deriving a passion for the grand theme unfolded through the long story in verse. Rather late in this self-guided education, after he had already written much imitative poetry, Masefield discovered Geoffrey Chaucer, and suddenly he found a way to tell simply and directly stories of great length and expansive theme, but with extensive quotation from commoners speaking their own unique languages.

That a woman's slow and hobbling descent from joy and serenity could be told in her words, and those words still achieve grandness of style, Masefield demonstrated in "The Widow in the Bye Street," a work read with its own ironic tribute to Chaucer. That sailors and day laborers and peasant farmers would have their turn to tell their stories he showed in sonnets often published in popular magazines. And that a painter could subject himself to the slings and arrows of outrageous class tensions by going to sea he showed in the lengthy "The Dauber." For today's reader Masefield's work may seem too much of a period long gone away, especially since the turmoils and terrors of his characters seem so overwhelmed by, in fact almost trivialized by, the vastness of subsequent world war and totalitarian horrors.[22]

In fact, Masefield himself could see some of this coming, and he wrote, in his preface to a period collection of poems available to Greene, that he looked ahead to the end of "the mess of the war," when the world, especially the English world, "is at some sort of peace" and "there may be leisure and feeling for verse-making." Masefield went on to suggest, however, that these fondest of his hopes were only hopes. The postwar future that he dreaded but also expected was that, in Robert Graves's phrase, most writers and readers would say "goodbye to all that" and never return to a poetry elegantly unassailed by deep ambiguity. These regrets the poet stated poignantly in this very preface, written at the midpoint of World War I. Yet, for Greene in 1916, the relevant thing about Masefield was not at all the allegedly simplistic themes or tones in these works. No, it was the subject, the varieties of folk, and specifically the sharply limned characterizations of those disparate peoples that Greene admired. Masefield would move gradually from sonnets to ballads to epics and then plays with organic verses in controlling themes; and this was the course whose order of march Greene would follow, at least partly on purpose. Whatever else, in Greene's copybooks and in his obviously imitative verses written between 1916 and 1920, it is Masefield who is the model. And even when Greene's own wartime nightmares and his own eastern Carolina fatalism moved him into darker themes and more ironic treatments of those themes, there are still traces of Masefield everywhere. Too, when Greene in the final third of his long career adopted brighter themes and lighter treatments for commercial audiences, the trace of Masefield expands:

> A spring comes bubbling up there, cold as glass,
> It bubbles down, crusting the leaves with lime,
> Bubbling the self-same song that it has sung through time.[23]

Self-same songs. Sung through time. Both are phrases that Greene appropriated in his diary writing and in his letter writing, and he aptly lived what he read and wrote, for he always read and wrote with a clear sense of drawing on traditional folk sources immanent in his being. Given his passion for the sandhills place, however, there was a sort of missing link, or perhaps a misplaced connection, between the ages-old Celtic music and his contemporaneous North Carolina literature. After all, his *self-same* proclamation was to be a scholar of North Carolina literature as well as a writer who *sang* North Carolina literature. It was not absolutely essential that he locate a previous eastern Carolina Orpheus who sang for these spirits, but if he could find such a person, that would certainly legitimate his own efforts in unequivocal fashion.

Back home, he had located, in a ruined antebellum mansion of a certain Dr. Marshall, a personal library of nineteenth-century writers from Harnett and Cumberland and contiguous counties. And the songs and folklore he had collected and shared with students and teachers back home were just right, that is, they were Scottish and Irish in spirit and Carolinian in enunciation: many Celtic voices, but one soul with roots in the sandhills. Too, at UNC, he had learned of Carolina's black Orpheus. This was George Moses Horton, an antebellum slave who provided verses for the college boys in their assignments. Although most times the honorable planters' sons relied on Horton to help them meet course deadlines or to impress their girlfriends, there was at least some local appreciation for his accomplishments, and a university president had helped him to publish his verses. During the Civil War, Horton had gone off to fight for his freedom in a Union battalion. Greene loved the story of this creative slave who liberated himself from illiteracy and later from slavery itself; but even George Moses Horton was not quite the missing link in the usable history Greene was making for himself. Unfortunately for these purposes, Horton was from the central piedmont and not from the sandhills. Greene had to search a little longer to find his own local poet hero.

When he found the truly regional poet of the sandhills, it turned out to be someone whose work had already been introduced: John Charles McNeill. Greene's hometown English instructor, Hubbard Fulton Page, had read aloud—indeed *performed* with gusto—lines by that poet from Scotland County, just south of the Greenes' Harnett. Now, however, McNeill grew in importance for Greene while he studied at Carolina. Soon Greene found himself writing at least one poem in tribute to his "Sandhills bard." McNeill had died young, in 1907, once again that romantic evanescence, that Masefield *bubbling;* and the rumor was that McNeill died young from too much drinking and smoking and more vaguely associated "hard living"—that too a legendary and fabler's notion of the romantic poets' traits. Most important, however, was McNeill's close attention to the detail in the sandhills people. Where poets of other Carolina regions depicted the physical spectacles, the coast facing the mighty ocean, the Blue Ridge of the powerful mountains, McNeill painted the more muted colors of his land between the littoral and the mountain spine. He painted the land and rivers with care: "[E]ach gnarly bole . . . each tuft of flags and rushes . . . [d]own on the Lumbee river."[24] Of the upper valley's "Autumn":

> Oh, the smell of the fennel is the autumn's own breath,
>   And the sumac is dyed in her blood;
> The char of the locust is what her voice saith,
>   And the cricket is one with her mood.
> Soft are her arms as soft-seeded grass,
>   The bluebells at dawn are her eyes,
> And slow as slow winds are her feet as they pass
>   Her bees and her butterflies.

And for the old McDuffie path to McNeill's boyhood school, a path that reminded Greene of his own trips to the Pleasant Union school of Vassar Matthews, the predecessor poet had written "Old Spring Hill":

> But, oh, the vines of muscadine
>   That cluster in those woods!
> Those ripe persimmons, hanging high,
>   Loose in their browning hoods;
> Those tough dward-apples, full of seed,
>   Are ready now to eat.
> And those of prickly-ear, though dead,
>   Are quite alert for feet.

But he painted the landscape purely as an understated backdrop, for it was the people themselves, "Croatans," blacks, mill hands, farmers, on whom he focused in his foreground:

> Chris'mas is yur off now:
>   Plant an' plough an' gether.
> Peg the traces, bolt the plough,
>   Ile the hamestring leather.

Chris'mas ain't so turble strong.
   It gits by too soon.
All that whole week ain't as long
   As one day in June.
Workin', wishin' week by week,
   Countin' days, and then
Pop yore crackers, eat yore cake
   An' gear yore mule again. [25]

A sandhills boy on a break from farm work. That was the kind of image Greene needed as he reconstructed and reinterpreted the past of the Greenes before him—and his very own ploughboy past. There was a beauty there in the place and in the people of that place, and now he had a firm handhold on the fact that at least one of those sandhills people recognized that beauty and recorded it true enough.

Too, McNeill protested with bitter sarcasm the race baiting of these days, even including a sharp cry of pain at North Carolina's disfranchisement of African Americans in 1898. He tried to develop an ear for "Black voices" and for Croatan (Lumbee) "Indian voices," and he labored, with some success, to capture those voices as they sang at their work and at their play and at their worship. It is obvious that Greene cultivated in his copybooks Masefield's technique of taking the voice of a peasant or a working-class laborer; yet no less obvious is the way that Greene inherited much more directly the eastern countryman's particularization of the region's ethnic voices.

With the studied use of McNeill and the appropriation of his concerns, Paul could fit in the link for this chain that bound him to the Celtic past. He had the general Celtic spirit from Masefield and from Fitzgerald's Omar Khayyám, he had the specific sandhills spirits from McNeill, and thus he had his subjects for study. Now these fit subjects, appropriately ingathered, gave him as well *a way to write,* so that he too could contribute to North Carolina literature. Moreover, UNC gave him resources of time and books and good listeners, so that subjects and author and audience in combination could produce their unique literature. The two literary societies together published the UNC *Magazine,* and this ardent scribbler joined in that enterprise by the winter quarter of 1917. He became one of four associate editors and took both this title and the work that went with it very seriously. Proudly, he wrote home to Mary on the stationery with its embossed heading and the little column of names that contained his own. Professors Greenlaw and Hibbard noticed him, and he won the freshman medal for his performance on the first-year examinations in English. Although poetry was his muse in those days, he did experiment with playwriting. This was before the arrival of Frederick Koch, and there were before "Proff Koch" no special traditions of drama or comedy on the Hill, but he recorded in a letter that he entered a campus playwriting contest and won it, though it is unclear what his play concerned, and it evidently was not performed, other than in a "read through" by fellow student dramatists.[26]

The earliest surviving play among his papers concerns a comedy about the gods of Olympus, but this is only a fragment and its humor is labored. Evidently, he had yet to take his poet's ear for real speech and his anthropologist's eye for significant detail and apply these senses to plays about his own people. Too, the lines of verse from this period show few of the talents for description which his diaries and his correspondence of the era already show. Instead, he tried to be an abstract Omar Khayyám, writing in a universal way about loneliness, honor, love, loss, and friendships as qualities that existed almost anywhere in a pure state suspended in ideas. Like McNeill's ploughboy, he had at least "a yur to go," but like his own farmer personae, the work itself made him feel "sorter good."

Evidently Carolina was everything that Greene had hoped for, and for his part, the grades and the medal and the recognition that he earned legitimated his own struggles to matriculate there. However, neither his sash filled with merit badges nor the *socdolager* qualities of the university could forestall consciousness of World War I. After all, his very exemplar Masefield, in the preface to his latest collection of poems, had noted the way that the Great War had altered and sometimes stopped his communication with his audience. It is hard to know Greene's opinion about the war before April 1917; he did not mention it in his diaries or correspondence. As a general rule, the boys in Chapel Hill were predisposed to cheer on the British, with somewhat less enthusiasm for the French and a real dislike for the Prussians. These things were complex, however, because the conservative intellectual tendencies on most southern campuses, especially Chapel Hill, were markedly German: Hegel was invoked often, especially by Horace Williams, to explain the grand sweep of orderly progress, namely, Jim Crow segregation; and much of the growing professionalization, particularly history and chemistry, was derived from German universities, with Berlin the preferred campus.[27] A Carolina student, coming from a region of ancestor worship into a university center of devotion to the European fathers, could be little other than ambivalent about the start of a war between these cultural forebears, the British and the Germans. For all that, however, Greene's reading and his letter writing between 1914 and April 1917 are not much concerned with things German or things English.[28]

Of course, the frightening new German weapons such as the U-boat and nerve gas won sympathy for the Allies; and when U-boats began attacking civilian ships carrying American goods and passengers, still more American people turned against the Central Powers. Too, there was clumsy German diplomacy, as seen in the exposure of Ambassador Zimmermann's message urging

Mexico to attack the United States. And there was very clever British propaganda, alongside the never-neutral pronouncements of the Woodrow Wilson presidential administration, many of whose members were determined that the United States join the allies in this conflict. Finally, scholars have often noted that many southerners, ambivalent about their heritage of Confederate rebelliousness, were anxious to demonstrate their patriotism through military service: these urges were seen in the Spanish-American War, but even more so in World War I.[29]

There certainly were those on the faculty and in the university community who were more than ready for war. One was Joseph Hyde Pratt, a professor of geology whom Greene came to admire. Pratt, who was born in Hartford and thus was literally a Connecticut Yankee in this southern Camelot, had earned the Ph.D. at Yale University, with some additional training at Harvard University; he came into these courts with praises that spoke good of his name, as the liturgist puts it. On the Hill since 1898, Pratt had not rested content with his academic pedigree but instead had thrown himself into scholarly and reformist activities that made him at once a worthy successor to the original great Carolina geologist, Elisha P. Mitchell, and a fit precursor to the scholar activists who would distinguish themselves in the next decades under the administration of Harry Woodburn Chase and Frank Porter Graham.[30]

Pratt was North Carolina state geologist, and as such he campaigned to manage the forest lands with conservation and the environment as much in mind as timber profits. He sponsored soil and water conservation as self-consciously as his hero Theodore Roosevelt and the progressive reformist Amos Pinchot, with whom he served on a number of national conservation commissions. To these ends, he helped found the Southern Forestry Conference and the North Carolina Drainage Association. He was also secretary of the Good Roads Association that, in Progressive Party fashion, intended to improve the South by industrializing—and the first step in this goal was reckoned to be modernizing transportation. Finally, in a foretaste of the so-styled Regionalist reformists to be led by Howard Washington Odum in the next decade, he collected data from the most rural state in the nation with an eye toward structural reform; to do so, he founded and directed the North Carolina Geological and Economic Survey.[31]

By the winter of 1917, this Wilsonian reformist had joined a National Guard unit, the 105th Regiment, which was composed of guardsmen in the two Carolinas and Tennessee and was attached to the 30th Infantry Division, "the true and tried." The 105th was a unit of engineers, actually sappers who had to dismantle enemy mines and set new ones as well as rebuild damaged roads and build pontoon and other bridges for assaults across rivers and other difficult terrain. Pratt was given command of the regiment, as commissioned major, and he enthusiastically urged anyone who would listen to join up in the cause of war preparedness. When war was declared, Pratt at once founded the State Council of Defense and, among other things, organized the War Preparedness Parade for 5 June 1917 in Chapel Hill, to be followed by a registration day when students and others could sign up to be enlisted at a later date.[32]

Whatever Greene thought about the war before April, there is no question what he wrote and said about it from the second day of that month, when President Wilson appeared before Congress to ask that this war be fought to end all wars and to make the world safe for democracy. Greene was stirred by accounts of Wilson's call to arms. More, a campus address, probably by Professor Pratt sometime in the same week, produced an even greater response, one that subsequent raconteuring has developed into melodrama: Greene told people often that he heard the speech and marched posthaste from the site of the rally to a recruiting station to enlist. Perhaps he did march over to get information, but the record is quite clear that Pratt's registration day, itself only a preliminary step to enlistment, did not come until much later in June. More to the point, it is also quite clear that Greene deliberated with considerable care and pain for more than a hundred days before enlisting in the dead of summer.[33]

Papa Greene was most displeased, especially when Hugh Greene also signed up. Not only did Papa fear for his boys' lives in this strange and faraway fight, but he also needed their strong backs and quick hands in his cotton and tobacco fields. Only John Greene's promise to remain, no matter what, assuaged Papa in his manifold agony, and that promise only in part ameliorated the patriarch's sense of impending disaster.[34]

These things, all of them, were much with Paul Greene, but the demand for sacrifice to the ideal was most with him. After all, John Charles McNeill had long ago reduced the tangle of issues in any war to a Celtic duty:

> Sae the deil wan the fights, an' wrang hauds the ground,
>   But God an' mysel' winna bide it.
> I hae strength in my airm yet for many a round
>   An' purpose in plenty tae guide it.[35]

3 : THE GREAT WAR

1917–1919

By July of 1917, Professor Pratt was Major Pratt in command of the 105th Engineers Regiment of the American Expeditionary Forces, and one of his recruited troops was his former student Paul Greene. In August this unit was officially federalized as part of the 30th Infantry Division under the overall command of Major General John F. Morrison. Many of the troops in Major Pratt's regiment were Carolina students, and thus at least some of the soldiers with whom Greene would serve shared his college experiences. Moreover, since the 30th Division had been formed in the Carolinas and Tennessee and was itself nicknamed "Old Hickory" in honor of Andrew Jackson, Greene's encampments generally included a king's portion of troopers from this region. Indeed, throughout the period 1917–19, whether stateside, in France, or in Belgium, he was able to keep in touch with the "Harnett Boys," including those in the 103d Infantry with whom brother Hugh Greene encamped, messed, marched, entrenched, and—in the final and fateful *push* of 1918—charged.[1]

In later years Greene often confused friends and associates about his wartime experiences. Generally, he did not talk about the trenches, although he was often pressed to do so by some of his closest associates. Indeed, one of his best friends, Barrett Harper Clark, remarked that for a long time he thought Greene occupied a desk job, pushing papers far from the howl of the carnage. Even those who knew that he had fought on the front lines were generally given to think that he served as a private or perhaps as a sergeant. Actually, he was not only *in* the heaviest of the fighting, but he also *led* troops into action, once even pointing his loaded pistol at the head of a soldier who was afraid to charge. He was promoted through the ranks of noncommissioned officers, he was rushed through combat-zone officers' training, and he was commissioned second lieutenant for his efforts. Nightmares shared with family members, a carefully tended diary, workbooks of poetry, correspondence, and notes, all carefully preserved by Greene himself, lay out the story of a young southern poet who would one day collaborate on the avant-garde antiwar musical tragicomedy *Johnny Johnson* and still later would write a paean to a Moravian mission of peace to Ohio's Indians with his symphonic drama *Trumpet in the Land*. Yet the same sources also show a man who, despite profound and even painful reservations, came to support the effort in both World War I and World War II; and the same sources finally reveal the man who would write immensely popular drama affirming the wartime missions of people and plans as diverse as Ohio's territorial settlers, George Washington, and Robert Edward Lee.[2]

The complexities, especially the contradictions, in this man were always most apparent when he confronted issues of war, and this after all was *his* war. He embraced it because he believed it would end all war, and he served more particularly because he believed in Woodrow Wilson and the highly personalized cause of the League of Nations. Long after it became obvious that this war would not end war, Greene continued to support both the effort in World War I and the League of Nations, as he came to support their respective successors, World War II and the United Nations. He did protest the Vietnam War in the late 1960s and early 1970s, but this protest was more in the nature of selective antiwar activity waged against a particular war. The Vietnam War protester even in the late 1960s was no pacifist, and the horrors of his own war sharpened his perceptions of pain and deepened a sense of the tragedy rather than sharpening his thought processes about war itself.

The overwhelming impact of World War I on Greene was social, and specifically racial. What emerges from his wartime experiences is the thing that distinguished this Chapel Hill liberal from other liberals, that is, the radical announcement that racial segregation is no virtue and racial integration no vice. Through the war years he completed a very long march, not to Tipperary, but to the realization that racial miscegenation is not evil, is indeed naturally occurring in human societies. These years in the army are even more prismatic than all the rest of his long career as idealist/observer, and Greene's notebooks and letters home and his diary entries and his poetry refract the most tender hopes and the coarsest dreads about his fellows, those American farm boys and small-town clerks whom he later named *Johnny Johnson*. Too, those same sources also refract hopes and dreads fully as tender and as coarse about himself.

Above all, the war "across the pond" compelled Greene to face the dense and forbidding tangle of racism, poverty, and sexuality that he thought he was leaving back in Carolina. He found instead that he brought the thoughts and memories with him in his head; indeed, the very perpetrators themselves— Lloyd Johnson, Rass Matthews, and yes, Hugh Greene and Paul Greene— came along with him in full combat gear in the leaking, stinking ocean transport *Talthybius*.

Lloyd Johnson was from a farm near the Greenes' back in Harnett County, and Greene was initially pleased to go off to service in his company. The two rode the train together in July 1917 to a transshipment and induction station in Goldsboro, a tobacco- and cotton-market center in their own eastern Carolina. The Johnson family had cried and cried as the two boys boarded the train, and Greene had finally promised the Johnsons that he would help take care of their son. Greene did comfort his homesick neighbor during the train trip. Later, however, roles were reversed, and Johnson became the comforter to Greene, who did not complain of homesickness, but who did bewail the "kind of living" of his other new comrades, "whose ceaseless vulgarity and profanity are hateful in the greatest degree." In that transshipment station where there were yet no uniforms and no real assignment, many of the bored young men surely were "vulgar" and "coarse," and Greene was grateful to have the companionship of a decent farm boy like Lloyd Johnson.[3]

Johnson's friendship became even more important in August, after the engineer trainees were transported to Camp Greene in Charlotte. This brand-new campsite, named for the Revolutionary War hero Nathaniel Greene, was laid out on the perimeter of the two Carolinas' most self-consciously progressive city, and both boys were delighted with the move. Among other things, they and their "brutish" comrades were now actually being trained, and there was less time—and less energy—for mischief. However, along with the change of scene came a new directive from Captain Clarence E. Boesch, "a full-blooded German" who ordered all soldiers to keep only "the necessaries." For Paul Greene this command entailed shipping home most of his books. "Nevertheless," he "succeeded in keeping three French books, 'The Rubaiyat of Omar Khayyam,' 'The Iliad,' and the plays of Sophocles & Aeschylus hidden in the roll of the tent edge." Although his diary does not record it, he also hung onto *Woolley's,* a little stylebook and guide to usage and grammar; this volume he came to describe as his "vade mecum," his little friend who provided a way of getting through it all. With literary and philosophical diversions thus reduced, Greene appreciated all the more Johnson's companionship, honest albeit unintellectual, on walking tours through the nearby Queen City, which impressed both eastern country boys with its obviously dynamic economy leavened by the manners of traditional civility.[4]

On 15 August, however, Charlotte and the trainees combined to demonstrate that piedmont traditions included incivilities and that American army practices included southern offenses already quite well known to any eastern Carolinian. His diary notes: "At dinner several of the fellows caught a 17-year-old negro boy and tossed him up in a blanket. During the performance one fellow dropped his corner of the blanket. Consequently the colored lad fell to the ground and severely sprained his back. Shame on such outrage." In fact, this was not the first such racist act taken against a young African American by the Camp Greene troops. But this particular outrage was different in kind from earlier ones in a special way: "I noticed that Johnson was into the game." Now Greene was effectively alone. He could not trust his hometown friend on the race issue, and Lloyd Johnson became in the diary, coldly, "Johnson," and later his name disappeared from the ledger's descriptions of intimate revelations.

Captain Boesch, the German-born leader, "brawny and lithe," who had ordered the removal of books now emerged as genuinely "more right than hard" on this vital question. "The Captain has ordered a stop to all such actions." And in his new isolation Greene concluded his account of these episodes with the unconvinced and unconvincing note: "Perhaps the negro boys will enjoy more peace hereafter."[5]

Although Greene was completely opposed to the racial violence in which Lloyd Johnson and other troops indulged, he himself still condescended to the black people in his Carolinas. For instance, another hometown friend, Rass Matthews, often performed for the Harnett Boys from the 30th Infantry who assembled during spare time for singing, dancing, and "bulling." Rass Matthews was a real comedian in all fields, but his forte was mimicry, and especially mimicry of black people. Paul Greene laughed as hard as the other regular fellows at Matthews's imitations of black farmers, preachers, and teachers. Some of the same boys would then go into the black communities near the Camp Greene base and do violence to young African Americans. Throughout his stateside training Greene could laugh and laugh with Rass Matthews "doing" a black minister; but then he would decry bitterly Lloyd Johnson's brutalizing of black victims, none of which stopped just because of Captain Boesch's orders. Racism has always strung itself down a very long continuum, and self-knowledge of sin does not come all at once; Paul Greene simply had more lessons to learn. These lessons would sink in effectively only after he actually saw the great courage of the African American—and the African—troops fighting in Flanders.[6]

A sensitive poet amidst a rough group, Greene could have played the role of the supremely suffering aesthete, the pearl cast before swine; but he was no such egoist. Instead, he scolded himself in his diary. He lectured himself that there was bound to be some good in every single one of these soldiers, and he gave himself the command, "Look for it!"[7]

Determined to find the good in each man, he soon found it, and for their part they found the good qualities in him. Although he refused to join the priapic wrestling matches and the hateful bragging rituals about sexual exploits, Greene could still win respect from all the troops with his skill at sports. The big country kid wowed them with his either-handed delivery in baseball; and he caught everyone's admiring attention in football with his solid play on the line, including a memorable divisional-championship performance in which he kept at it despite a broken and bleeding nose.[8]

By October, when the engineers had been transferred yet again—this time to Camp Sevier in Paris, South Carolina, in the hills outside Greenville—Greene was earning respect not only from fellow troops but also from Colonel Pratt and Captain Boesch and from his own supervisor, Lieutenant Guy Winthrop.

Autumn 1917 in South Carolina's piedmont turned out to be characteristically wet and uncharacteristically cold, and meningitis and other infectious diseases debilitated the engineers' crowded campsite; but Greene showed great stamina and a cheerful disposition that inspired others. The officers promoted him and began training him to become a noncommissioned officer so that he could help lead the engineers in the deadly "sapper" exercises: finding land mines, digging up explosives, and cleaning up the damage done by the enemy, but also setting and resetting explosives to be deployed against the enemy. This work, whether done for practice in Carolina or "for real" in Flanders, was generally done at night and underground and was invariably dangerous, with heavy casualties even in stateside training. The football team captain became squad leader and sergeant in charge of sapping between the trenches in no-man's land.[9]

There were privileges that came with his new rank and station. In camp and later on oceangoing transport and still later on the battlefield, this sergeant usually slept by himself in his own chambers, and he was given time and space to read and to write in solitude. He also obtained at least his share of "liberty," and he used his passes to go into the town of Greenville, sometimes to the Young Men's Christian Association if he wanted fellowship, other times to an ill-tended but restful park in the center of town if he wanted to reflect alone.[10]

Soon, however, he began using his passes to visit his cousin Beatrice Byrd at the Women's College of Furman University. Allowed on campus to visit Beatrice Byrd, he was not really visiting her at all but her roommate, Mabel Byrd. This Byrd, a still more distant or "kissing cousin," he described as a blonde beauty with "large, dreamy eyes." He also described her as very wealthy and, in the scheme of things in his region, a good "catch" for him to make a good marriage, as had his father, grandfather, and great-grandfather before him. Despite diligent campus chaperones, things became serious enough for her parents to come meet this engineer noncom. The Byrds too followed time-worn paths, the father open after he happily sized up Paul Greene but the mother distrustful and wary. How that parental difference of perspective and judgment might play out over time became a fascinating but entirely moot question, for Greene eventually backed away from Mabel Byrd. He was unsure that he loved her as much as she loved him, he was worried that he might be using her, and he began to distrust himself and his motives. He resolved his doubts by staying away from the Women's College, declaring the romance over because it was dangerously unfair to her, with himself unfitted to be her lover.[11]

A brief and mild winter was followed by a wet spring, and then in May the engineers at last left for the front lines of the Great War, arriving in France in June. For the next thirteen months Greene was with the French, serving either in French-speaking Flanders or in Gaul itself. In his way he took the French as his own, especially the peasants of the low country, whom he regarded much as he did the peasants of his own eastern Carolina. He was permitted to live with French families in the intervals between active military campaigns. He adapted a kind of Gallic peasant syndicalism, blending it with his own Carolina populism; and he was vigorous in his denunciations of unrestrained capitalism, of unregulated industry, of too rapidly growing cities.[12]

Greene's diary notes from Flanders and Belgium reveal what the historians of the Great War have told us; unlike those historians, however, he was on the front lines, and indeed as a sapper with Company B of the 105th he was often *underneath* the front lines. The battle strategy of the generals echoed the injunction of Napoleon's aide and chronicler Baron Antoine Henri Jomini: aggressively apply offensive force and offensive mass at the weak point in the enemy's defensive line. The Germans called such an execution a *putsch,* and in 1915 a concerted advance had brought Central Powers forces within an ar-tillerist's quadrant reading of Paris itself. On that occasion the Allies had stiff-ened, and the primarily German troops, having suffered frightful losses dur-ing the putsch, were compelled to fall back to an original entrenched position hundreds of miles east. Yet the memory of that putsch lived on, the Central Powers dreaming of another dramatic putsch into France, the Allied Powers for their part dreaming of their own push into Germany—force and mass at the weak point in the enemy's line. Meantime, for most of the war, both sides were dug in, facing each other across no-man's land in parallel trenches that ran longitudinally for hundreds of miles between France and Germany—and dead through Belgium.[13]

Nevertheless, these trenches themselves, plus a number of other twentieth-century techniques and inventions, changed the rules of warfare by shifting the advantage from quick-striking offense to entrenched defense. Baron Jo-mini's words applied well enough at Tilsit or Mainz, but they fit badly at Ypres, Proven, and Bellicourt, all places where Greene and his company would serve. Troops attempting bold charges were cut down quickly by rifles that shot far-ther and more accurately than the ones that Baron Jomini had chronicled 112 years earlier. Too, machine guns could set a moving wall of lead into the very air through which troops charged. Quick feints and other maneuvers of in-fantry movements could now be picked up by observers in balloons or in air-planes, eliminating the chance of surprise or deception. And those airplanes could drop bombs on the forward routes for the troops attempting a charge— or indeed they could drop bombs on the troops themselves. Most deadly of all, mustard gas and nerve gas and other chemical weapons could be sprayed against the charging troops, and these weapons would leave a man to suffer an especially slow, body-imploding death whose physical regression ironically mocked the very idea of a hard charge.

So the advantage was to the defense, and troops dug themselves in quite deeply and appointed their trenches quite fully, complete with kitchens and desks and beds. As Paul Fussell has pointed out, "[T]here were 'national styles' in trenches as in other things. The French trenches were nasty, cynical, efficient, and temporary. Kipling remembered the smell of delicious cooking emanating from some in Alsace. The English were amateur, vague, ad hoc, and temporary. The Germans were efficient, clean, pedantic, and permanent. Their occupants proposed to stay where they were."[14]

These trenches were generally laid out in rows of three, with a forward trench facing the enemy's forward trench and with two trenches behind filled with reinforcement troops. Although the trenches were far easier to defend than to attack, Jomini's injunction still held sway, and at periodic intervals commanders would give the order to the forward troops: *Up, and over!* Then the troops would climb out of their entrenchment and run across no-man's land toward the enemy's forward trenches. Most times, such advancing troops were cut down as quickly and in as large numbers as Caligula's heads of wheat had been when the crazed emperor once ordered his legions to destroy some tares in a field and then recorded the "body count" of "casualties." But unlike Caligula's casualties, these body counts were all too real. After their bloody charge, the survivors in these twentieth-century legions retreated to their own trenches, and there followed a long spell of shifting troops between trenches, with survivors going to the reserve trenches in back and replacements coming to the forward trench. These charges were not so much bloody as actually suicidal, and one of the mysteries that historians cannot explain is why troops on both sides continued to obey the order, *Up, and over!* It was evidently during that September in Belgium that Greene himself used his gun to force a frightened soldier to go up and over; but most times most of the troops obeyed readily enough without such extreme threats. The partial, if unsatisfactory, answer is that it had almost worked for the Germans in 1915, and everyone was convinced that he could make it work for his side sometime in 1918.[15]

American commander John J. Pershing, ominously nicknamed Black Jack, was told by his French and British superiors that the Central Powers would likely send an enormous putsch against the American forward trenches sometime early in the fall of 1918. He was also told that it made sense to launch an Allied push, featuring the newly arrived American troops, against the heretofore impregnable Hindenburg line, which the Germans had stretched down Belgium. The gamble was thus laid out for Black Jack: *charge or be charged*. And, whichever wild charge took place first, it would be American troops, many of them African Americans in segregated trenches, who would bear the assault—or even more deadly, who would be ordered up and over and into no-man's land.

The geology professor was now Colonel Pratt, and he understood the strategy even if he did not then understand the bloodiest implications of it all. He knew why Americans were inside the most dangerous trenches: it did not take much experience to be there as a sacrificial "shock trooper," and in fact the less a man actually knew about that designedly morbid role, the better. If there were any survivors in the Allied push, the combat-tested Brits and Frogs and Aussies could come in afterward to do the tasks requiring experience and high skills, those things noted in the geologist's records as "exploitation of advantage." [16] Colonel Pratt's regiment arrived in Flanders in late June and picked its way through the Ypres salient to arrive at the ruined town. Greene noted the almost biblical "abomination of desolation" of Cloth Hall, once a monument to Flemish textile artistry. Equally desolate were the remains of the Ypres Asylum, only recently a world model for humane treatment of the mentally disturbed. From Ypres, it was on to the appointed trenches of Belgium, with a September destiny to hit the Hindenburg line by crossing the La Selle River at Bellicourt, a once-pleasant town whose battle scenes would ever after associate its literally pretty name with images of carnage. Since Pratt had his own marching orders from Black Jack Pershing, the colonel understood the significance of his sapper troops, who would have to slip out after midnight to defuse westward-facing enemy mines and explosives and to lay advance tape and then string eastward-facing mines. When daylight came, if the push worked, the engineers would have to shift emotional gears and become builders instead of destroyers, for they would have to make a passageway across the La Selle River for several thousand infantry troops, including the 119th, in which Hugh Greene now served. [17]

So heavy were the casualties for the Americans in this deadly season that Pratt lost many of his officers and sergeants, and he had to brevet new leaders to take positions in place of those who had, as the boys sang, "gone west, gone home." On 31 July, he had breveted Greene sergeant major, and he had also marked this young but suddenly very senior noncom for officer candidate training, to be administered very soon, if need be in the rear trenches during the fall offensive. [18]

On 15 September the brevet sergeant major received his orders for the Bellicourt assault and was finally given a view of the larger strategy. The plan made him nervous: young American artillerists were "to bombard the enemy's positions for several hours"; then, "with a smokescreen on their flank," the 119th Infantry and the 120th Infantry were to climb out of the trenches and "go over the top" to break the Hindenburg line. Only after the two American infantry battalions had swarmed the German trenches were the much more experienced Australian infantry forces to come in and "exploit" the results to "follow up" the first wave; and only after all this would the veteran multinational Allied cavalry enter the campaign. Greene's job would be the same no matter what the order of attack, for he had to drive the powerful but unarmored British motor lorry filled with communications materiel into the immediate aftermath of the battle; then he would supervise rebuilding and resetting on the new front line, whether that new boundary was pushed deep into former German positions or dropped back far behind old Allied "back-up" trenches. He queried his diary rhetorically if it would not make more sense to let the veterans attack first and the "raw" and "green" Americans "exploit" and "follow up." But even as he wrote this, he must have remembered that the exigencies of this war demanded that such bold gambles be assayed with the most expendable troops in the first wave. That day, in those terms, the most expendable troops certainly included the largely untested Carolinians in the 119th.[19]

Given a moment to see his brother Hugh, the brevet sergeant major wished him well, but with "many a misgiving," for "I may never see him again." After their visit, Greene began his own dangerous work of stringing communications lines and removing explosives. As he went about these tasks, he could only "wonder how my brother will go over the top" of the long-established Allied trenches, much more how he would enter the notorious Hindenburg line. Hugh Greene's saucy demurral—"cheero, he was no better to be knocked off than anyone else"—stayed with the sapper, especially because Greene was daily accumulating at regimental headquarters statistics that showed exactly how true were the Harnett infantryman's words. Unlike the infantrymen, Greene knew that, behind the Hindenburg line, tiny Bellicourt itself was "a dangerous place because of subterranean passages and tunnels under the town." The Buies Creek family could easily lose two sons in this action, and in any case, "a real inferno it may prove to be."[20]

As the soldiers often remarked during World War I, the onset of the fighting was actually a relief, for the tasks of killing and of trying not to be killed are actually less straining than the emotions of getting ready to kill and getting ready to avoid being killed. Bellicourt proved this again for Greene. Not able to sleep because of the multiple anxieties of it all, Greene found that by 9:00 A.M. on 29 September he could pause to record, almost placidly, in his diary that the village was already outflanked and the Hindenburg line "smashed." As feared, Germans in machine-gun nests hidden away in tunnels killed many of the American infantrymen; but "we soon cleared them out."[21]

There were heavy casualties for the 105th, ten engineers killed and ninety-eight wounded. As for the infantry supported by the 105th, all the officers of the 120th and most officers attached to the 119th were killed. Some of the fatality statistics represented losses that affected him deeply, including a Lieutenant Fields whom Greene had grown to admire. The diarist listed friends "who sleep in France forever," and he marked Fields's name there with a note of special sadness. But Hugh Greene at last had come through it alive, and so had most of the Harnett Boys. With more astonishment than bravura, the grateful noncom wrote: "Think of it! Boys who were plowing the fields of Carolina a year ago breaking thro that terrible line."[22]

The courage and the steadiness under fire of one particular ploughboy engineer had again caught the eye of his superiors, and Pratt sent Greene off to officer candidate school, effective 2 October. This program of accelerated promotion through a short but intensive training session near the battle lines reflected the fact that the fall offensives were rapidly depleting the corps of field-grade officers in the American units. In these sessions, he made friends with two Texas officer-candidates, Herbert L. Gallegly of San Antonio and M. G. Cheney of Fort Worth. Each was bright and spirited and a good companion during the long, slow lorry and train rides between training sites. Both men were students in the most radical sense of the word, wide open to new experiences and anxious to see more of the world beyond Texas. Gallegly turned out to be a fine artist who entertained, and sometimes amazed, his two friends with his charcoal sketches, quickly but expertly brought off. He made one of Greene, and that surviving profile shows a particularly intense idealist.[23]

The training itself was no less intense—and considerably risky. Many became very ill from the gas-warfare drills, and one was killed by an errant explosive during other exercises. The candidates' schedules were full, and, when not drilling, exercising, studying, or testing, they were set in competition against one another in track and field events. As usual, Greene's big and powerful body responded well to such an environment, and he was grateful that the exercises so exhausted other men that they had less inclination—and certainly very little spare time—to drink and fight.[24]

During a break in his officer training, Greene visited a small village that was in the valley of the Marne and at least temporarily safe from the mad charges and the artillery shellings of the front. Completely in love with the French peasantry, he recorded his admiration for their courage and their steadiness, and he likened them to his own favored folk of the eastern Carolina countryside. But he also recorded surprise when he saw French peasant girls, good girls from good homes, walking arm in arm and obviously in love with African American troops. Nor was this casual sex, for Greene reported, "many of the negroes are marrying French girls." Indeed, these good French girls in the beloved country were treating the sable troops as "the real Americans," as "true Americans."[25]

There was a well-understood coda in North Carolina's racism in that era of damnable Jim Crow: *miscegenation* was defined as an embarrassment, and it happened when a white man slept with a black woman for sport but produced a child. No such casual attitude was attached to a black man sleeping with a white woman; that act was always defined as rape. The latter kind of racial mixing was supposed to be the southern boy's ultimate nightmare. It was supposed to be what lynching was all about. Yet these French peasant women were clearly not being raped, and Greene did not consider them any less virtuous than Carolina's white women. After some initial shock, he recorded again that the French peasantry accepted his African American comrades in arms as "real" and "true" Americans. And so they became in his mind as well by the time he left France. When he returned home to announce this new attitude, he would shock even those who styled themselves liberal in that day, and when he announces in several wartime poems that black men are his equal in all respects, it can still shock a reader today, accustomed as we are to the letters and diary entries of everybody else in 1918. The black soldiers with whom he served changed his opinions about black people's character and changed the ways he talked, but the French peasant women changed the way that he lived his life. [26]

The regiment he would rejoin as an officer was marching steadily through battles as the Hindenburg line was reduced to a dreaded memory, and Greene kept a list of their engagements as October waned (and as the time remaining for manageable offensive campaigns shrank): Brancourt, 9 October; Premont, 10 October; the actual crossing of the La Selle River, 17 October; Vaux, Andigny, 18 October; Mazingheim, 19–20 October. [27]

Then on 11 November came news of armistice. As soon as he learned of the agreement, Greene opened his diary and wrote in large letters P-E-A-C-E! He then repeated the line, that way, in all capital letters and with an exclamation point. Then he wrote it exactly that way one more time. That it was the eleventh hour of the eleventh month appealed to his Celtic soul, as he noted elsewhere in his diary and repeated often. [28]

It was some time before this proclaimed armistice could be confirmed as an authentic peace, and for the next several weeks Greene and his friends Cheney and Gallegly continued their dangerous training with explosives. In that time there were several frightful incidents, including one in which an officer candidate lost both his hands when his explosive device was detonated prematurely. During this tense and uncertain period, Greene was breveted second lieutenant on 2 December, and he was served a Christmas meal by Colonel Pratt and other field officers following a tradition in which the old officers serve the new officers even if the formal commission papers are slow to arrive. During that same Christmas season of 1918, Colonel Pratt organized Greene and the other officers in his charge to provide Christmas meals and Christmas gifts for the children in the heavily shelled village of Langres, near their training headquarters. [29]

Colonel Pratt also told Greene about the chance to work in Paris as a clerk with a Monday-to-Friday schedule that included long breaks for lunch and an early-afternoon dismissal that left plenty of time to visit museums. This was the clerk job that some of Greene's friends heard about, and he held it from late December 1918 until his official discharge on 21 June 1919. It was during this period that Greene wrote poems with special fervor, including revisions of many that he had written in the trenches while the ground shook under his feet, as he recorded in the flyleaf of one of his copybooks. Still a latter-day populist with sympathies for the French peasants, Greene is in these poems very much the ideologue, railing against the war profiteers and the self-satisfied bourgeoisie of Paris who benefited from the sacrifices made by peasants wounded in the front lines and since forgotten in the cities.[30]

He also worked and reworked "Negro Poems," which were dialogues in dialect that he had begun as a stateside civilian. In this wartime period and in his Parisian clerkship, he dramatically changed these poems from objective humor to a subjective sense of black bravery and sacrifice. Besides changing the voice and the point of view in his "Negro Poems," he also changed his own voice in his diary, declaring a mission to fight racial injustice back in the United States. It was not Chapel Hill or the university that liberalized him on the race issue, but rather the segregated African American, African, and Asian troops that he saw on the frontlines. Indeed, by the bleak midwinter of 1919 he was taking a stand on integration and miscegenation utterly different from other southern reformists; and he had gotten it from black people themselves—and the French peasantry's approval of those sable troops.[31]

Working long hours to perfect his different poems, Greene was also working extra hours to study French language, history, and art. However, he was no less conscientious about being an efficient clerk, albeit in an office beset with petty larcenies and grand inefficiencies. Plainly, he tried to do too much. He developed severe eyestrain, headaches, and above all digestive problems; and he also recorded chilling nightmares, many of which were essentially replays of his actual combat experiences. He sought release from these enormous pressures through hard drinking and other "foolish fallings down." These latter appeared to involve casual sex with "pretty hotel maids" and the "prodigals of Paris," as he noted them in his diary. He was also careful to state on more than one occasion that a gentleman cannot tell everything that he does.[32]

There was in those winter days at least one intimate relationship, with Ellen Cummings of Nebraska, whom he apparently met at a YMCA event. She was his love for some time, but he tired of her, and their breakup brought a great deal of awkwardness, since the two subsequently kept running into each other at the YMCA or in the clerical offices of the army. Greene regretted the affair and began to resent her, complaining in his diary—and later in a novel concerning these episodes—about "Miss C—with her everlasting pale face." Far more serious was an affair that began in late May with Renée Boiscelleur, a Parisian office worker and the sole support of her invalid mother. These two fell immediately and deeply in love, and Greene declared then and repeated later that they were "married in fact if not in law."[33]

With Renée Boiscelleur he found not only a sympathetic ear for his poetry but also an intelligent student of art who could teach him much about French aesthetics. Too, she was a woman who could show him the remarkable abuse that she and others suffered in a society where men held all the power and the wealth. Of course, their affair was not limited to intellectual and political discussions, and their passion for each other—expressed openly on the lawns of the Bois de Boulogne—often caught the scornful notice of the Parisian middle class, who presumed that the two were products of the new postbellum sexual morality. In fact, however, the couple was far too *traditional* to marry and make it all legal: Boiscelleur had to stay in Paris to take care of her mother, and Greene had to leave Paris in order to meet his duties back in Carolina. While the parting with Ellen Cummings brought some awkwardness, the parting with Renée Boiscelleur would thus extract considerable pain—and plenty of awkwardness in the future.

Honorably discharged on 21 June, Paul Greene was reunited with his brother Hugh, also discharged the same week, and the two made a remarkable trip in early July back to the battlefields of the previous fall to locate, mark, and pray at the grave of Rass Matthews, the erstwhile comedian slain at Mazingheim in the final triumphant offensive. The engineer sketched the graveyard with care and mapped the plot's location. Then he paid a peasant farmer to look after the grave and tend it with flowers on special days.[34]

It was time to return to Paris and to let the army take charge of their separate transshipments, Hugh Greene to leave with the noncommissioned infantrymen and Paul Greene with the commissioned engineers. Army regulations stipulated that the noncom Greene could carry 75 pounds of baggage with him to the United States, but Paul Greene the lieutenant could carry 150 pounds of baggage. The diary notes of that and of subsequent years show that the officer Greene also carried away at least twice as much metaphorical baggage from that conflict as did his own deeply conflicted infantryman brother.[35]

By 9 July, Paul Greene was in Brest, with his ship weighing anchor. He wrote tearfully in his diary that he must say goodbye to all the dreams and the nightmares that France represented for him. During a moonlit evening he sat on the deck with the sage captain and let the memories take over while thinking about it all—and not least about Renée Boiscelleur. But the tasks back home would be too overwhelming to permit very much reminiscing about anything in France.[36]

On 11 July he recorded the hometown reality of Carolina and America, on his ship in the North Atlantic:

A Y.M.C.A. lady was playing the piano for all the hundreds of Gobs and Doughboys to sing. Of course the negroes were enjoying every minute of it as rows of white teeth against a dark background testified but few of them sang. They left all that pleasure to the white soldiers and sailors. And as I looked down on them from a deck I seemed to see the negro in his forlorn condition. Here were hundreds of black soldiers who came to do their bit, soldiers every one of them. But, in all the enjoyment they did not forget, could not forget, that they were black. And, therefore they let their white brothers sing and shout and be happy while they stood silent. And again it is shown by the isolated condition of the negro officers. There are several aboard. They always walk together, a people of another race. Is it right? O Lord![37]

1919–1921

Greene found the Carolina campus to be an exciting place on his return in the fall of 1919. He was most excited by the dramatic red-haired Yankee Elizabeth Lay. Lib Lay, one of the few women students on the campus, captured his attention so thoroughly that she virtually defined his second student career at Carolina. This she achieved despite the fact that many talented new people, really a new generation of scholars and activists, were themselves redefining the Hill. Although Greene met the new cast of professorial characters before he came to know Elizabeth Lay very well, she so overwhelmed all his senses, not least his artistic plans, that he came to understand these new leaders, and even some of the old ones, largely on her terms. We too should meet the new cast before we meet Lib Lay, because that is how the story unfolded itself, but remember that from now on, this is largely her show. It is no less hers when Renée Boiscelleur calls from stageside most poignantly. Even and especially Renée Boiscelleur will be redefined Lib Lay's way, but those processes will be slow, fitful, and not without pain all around.

The wonderful prewar figures Williams, Henderson, Chase, Greenlaw, and Coker remained, but they were joined now by some even more remarkable characters. Most prominent was Frederick Henry Koch, just blown in from the Badlands of North Dakota. This "Proff" Koch, the new drama teacher, was a presence, and a presence felt so fully and so quickly on the campus after his arrival in academic year 1918–19 that he merits some special consideration in this story.

Dramatic and comic by personal choice as well as by profession, Proff Koch affected a big hat and a bigger stride, and biggest of all a voice with which he often yelled out, *Tell it, express it, write what you yourself know! Write about the folk you know,* he would insist; *and even better, write about the folk you are! Whatever* (and here he was most tellingly effective), he would say, *never, never try to write about places you've never been or things you've never done.* The man's magnetism is harder to understand decades later, when no campus personality would be permitted so much intellectual and emotional freedom: students, despite the lack of prestige and money in the acting profession in the South, rushed to his classes, and, perhaps most important, students in large numbers and with great enthusiasm attended and really listened to the theatrical productions. And for their part, administrators at Carolina supported Koch despite the relatively high costs of production and the slowly accreting, and even then slight, material return on the institutional investment. Koch, then, was not only hardworking and talented, but he had luck as well as pluck.[1]

Koch's ancestry, birth, and upbringing in combination provided him the deeply ingrained sense of place that he emphasized in his teaching and directing. That is, on both sides of the ancestral lines there were people powerfully identified by sharply etched regional contours; and the very contrasts in those identifying and signifying contours lent a profound sense of the culture of the folk. His mother, née Rebecca Cornelia Julian, was the daughter of a wealthy Mississippi planter and granddaughter of a member of that most exotic of southern species, the French Huguenots. His father, August William Koch, was a second-generation German American insurance broker in Peoria, Illinois, who publicly decried the arts but privately labored at painting and sketching.

These parents arranged a good education for young Koch, concluding with postbaccalaureate studies at the Emerson School of Oratory in Boston, where he graduated in 1903. The next step for him seemed a bit improbable, not acting at all and in an utterly different place, for he became an all-purpose humanities teacher in Grand Forks, at the University of North Dakota. But in another, grander sense, this assignment only deepened the already acute awareness of place and its effect on character by adding a sense of the Cyclone Belt of the Red River Valley and of the frontier to a wide-awake young man fresh from oratorical training in Puritan Boston, infancy in the hills of the Kentucky border country, and an upbringing in Peoria superintended by parents with their own unique senses of geography, time, ethnicity, and character. He drank it in thirstily, all of it, and paused occasionally to swallow: *Really!* he shouted at friends, *It has been going with a* wow![2]

And much of the wow he still found in the father-forbidden theater, for, despite a heavy teaching load in the humanities, Koch became more and more involved on a voluntary basis with the University of North Dakota Theater. After a couple years, he abandoned other teaching at the university and went off to Harvard to study drama under George Pierce Baker, with the understanding that he would return to direct the UND Theater. He was in Cambridge only about a year, taking a master's degree in 1909, but he was profoundly influenced by Baker. For one thing, Baker eloquently upheld the goal of an American, rather than a derivative, theater; and this affirmed in a coherent and highly articulated form of argument Koch's already existing impulses to do something different by "giv[ing] us a drama of our own expressions, the measure of our own rhythms, acceptable because of their closeness to us."[3] Too, Baker was the quintessence of the technical professional, and this "pro" gave Koch his first real apprehension of fitting dialogue to the available action and to the given audience, as well as showing the right way to build and move a set and the best ways to sell a production. But most of all Baker did what Harvard men have always done best, that is, he put Koch into the network of the profession, in this case the network being primarily his own former students now producing, directing, and acting, and his friends in the little group of New York critics and agents who assessed the many, many contending productions to cull the very, very few dramas and comedies that the public would then "freely" judge.

Returning to Grand Forks in 1910, Koch organized a hardy little group of like-minded UND faculty members and students who specialized in one-act plays concerning the regions of the Dakotas. By 1912 he was calling his troupe Dakota Playmakers; and the Playmakers themselves wrote one-act plays drama-tizing the disputes and the lovemaking, the fun and the tragedy of their state. They traveled to each corner of the nation's most rural state, building their own sets on the fly and promoting themselves as hard as any patent-medicine sales agent or visiting hot-gospeler.

Each place they appeared witnessed a revolution: the people of the cities in the valley who thought they knew something about theater were surprised to find that drama and comedy included the stories of their distant neighbors in the Coteau or the Badlands; and the inhabitants of the villages beyond the lowlands were even more surprised, seeing their own family lives captured in such an unfamiliar form of art. Ever the student, Proff put in time studying and really listening, especially to the Native Americans and their rituals and myths. The most famous of his UND student playwrights was Maxwell Ander-son, a Pennsylvanian come to study with Proff, who received his baccalaureate degree in 1911 after performing in and writing for a number of frontier, prairie farm, Badland, Native American, and other Dakotas-theme productions. By 1923 this Koch student had made his way onto Broadway, with *White Desert* and (with Lawrence Stallings) *What Price Glory?* After these and other com-mercial successes, he would earn the Pulitzer Prize in 1933 for *Both Your Houses*.

Even before his student Anderson gained critical and popular notice, Proff had been smelled out and treed by that superb bird dog Edwin Almiron Green-law, who moved easily in Baker's and other such networks and who wanted a uniquely Carolina folk-regional theater at the University of North Carolina. Greenlaw was himself committed both to the study of and the nurturing of regional literature and soon would found "The Literary Lantern," a syndicated newspaper column, still published, which has sought to inform Carolinians about regional authors and publications. Koch pleased Greenlaw when the Dakota Playmaker said that regional theater must stress "folk subject mat-ter: . . . the legends, superstitions, customs, environmental differences, and the vernacular of the common people."[4]

In the fall quarter of 1918 the newly arrived Koch formed the Carolina Play-makers, using as a model his own UND team, which could write, direct, pro-duce, publicize, and act all on their own. He found talented writers, including Elizabeth Lay, Legette Blythe, and Thomas Wolfe, then a six-foot-six troubled soul from the Great Smoky Mountains who, despite his popularity, brooded often over his self-perceived lack of acceptance. Putting these and other stu-dents to work creating Carolina folk plays, Proff persuaded the high school in town to let him build a stage in its auditorium for Playmaker productions. Then he persuaded the pharmacist-owner of Eubanks Drugstore in town to sell tickets to performances, and his folk drama was in business. Before he had really trained a group of playwrights or actors, Proff put them on the road in the counties of the neighboring central piedmont, building a following for his works. To him, creating a "native audience" appreciative of folk plays was fully as important as actually writing new plays, and in some ways it was of more immediate concern. Although he received logistical support from the university extension service, he and a handful of inexperienced undergraduates were the production staff and the cast as well as the technical designers, stage crew, and publicists. As for gaining membership in the Playmakers, Proff was succinct: "Anyone who did anything toward the making of a play was counted a Playmaker."

One whom he counted as a very special Playmaker among student dramatists of that yeasty academic year of 1918–19 was Elizabeth Lay, whom Proff Koch judged to be the class of the class. Her original play, *When Witches Ride,* which dealt with a folk tale and the languages and practices that produced such lore in Northampton County, where she had taught school, earned his prize as the best of the year, and he featured it as the major Playmakers pro-duction at the high school "campus center." Koch also took Elizabeth Lay's play on tour around the Old North State. It was noted of Koch that he had a lot of William Butler Yeats in him, that is, the contemporaneous Yeats, the poet of self-styled "racial pride" who avidly collected vernacular Irish fairy tales and sayings and wove those into his verse and scripts. Koch, not writing much himself, pushed Lay and others toward a Carolina folk version of a Celtic Re-vival, and *When Witches Ride* reflects his preaching that students "dip their pens in problems, characters, passions, nearest home." Like her teacher, Lay, exactly because she had traveled from New England to the central piedmont and thence to the northeastern Carolina coastal plain, was especially "awake"— a Proff Koch word—to the voices around her.[5]

Her play was set in the remote backcountry of that northeastern coastal plain in a cotton-and-peanuts subregion beyond the settled towns of the coastline but also east of the relatively populated southern valley of the Roanoke River. This one-acter was a hybrid produced by the canny scholar who employed the techniques of the modern folklorist and the poet. Perhaps she was a bit less self-consciously intellectual and a bit less systematic than her more famed contemporaries the Regionalist sociologists, but she too was developing nothing less than an emotional identity with the "human geography" of a southern place. From the onetime Carolina folklorist and later University of Chicago scholar Tom Peete Cross, Elizabeth found an accurate transcription of the Northampton tradition that a witch, Phoebe, a consort of the devil, traveled the roads with her fated toad, Gibbie, on her way riding on the heads of horses and sometimes the heads of people by hooking her feet into equine manes or human hair. When Gibbie made his final exit hop, that move would signal the time for Phoebe's final descent into hell; but it was also known that the witch might transfer her destiny to someone else, in which case Gibbie's last hop would damn a substitute to hell. Mastering that tale as a folklorist, Elizabeth in her playwright identity then built a dramatic world around a liquor-jug scene in a Northampton country store. She set a hard-drinking locomotive engineer, Jake, as a foil to the powers of the folk traditions of Phoebe the witch. It was, then, the man of iron and steam and rationalism against the *longue durée* of Phoebe. The conflict as portrayed was believably tense, the toad did his work, and folk ways overwhelmed the laws of industrial man. It was the mutually wide-eyed confrontation between Phoebe and Jake during the witch's first appearance at the store that the pioneering artist Mary Bayard Wooten photographed and distributed from that first Carolina Playmaker season.[6]

Greene fell in with this company almost at once, although his prewar admiration for philosophy—and the prewar attraction to the philosophy professor Horace Williams—had by no means abated. The campus was crowded with veterans like Greene returning from interrupted courses of study, and it was further crowded by veterans who had not earlier considered a college education. Briefly there was prosperity in Carolina, with piedmont textile mills providing uniforms and sheets and other materiel of war and with eastern farmers providing cotton and tobacco for the rapidly expanding domestic markets, and this end-of-war prosperity encouraged many families to send their boys off to college, in many cases the first generation of a family to matriculate. This wartime rise in demand for textiles and farm produce was short-lived, to be followed by a short but sharp business downturn in textiles and an extended agricultural recession that would be especially chronic in the Greene family's Harnett. Some of the young men newly arrived on the Hill already understood how quickly their family's recently amassed fortune would disappear, but most would have to be painfully disabused of such illusions about perpetual wealth. In either case, however, there was a mood of busting loose, of celebrating the freedom from the restraints of military life and the constraints of wartime civilian life: for many of those whose money was running out quickly, *Eat now and drink now and be merry now, for tomorrow* . . . As for those who could see no vanishing point for their wealth, why not pleasure forever? To the intellectual exuberance of the scholars at the war's end thus was added the dionysiac exuberance of those for whom scholarship was a very irrelevant abstraction. So it was that excitement of many kinds enveloped Greene as he went back to study philosophy and as he started his new instruction in drama.

The big farm boy with all the dark curly hair attracted plenty of notice, partly because he spent extra money on a new suit and some dress shirts and was self-consciously neat and well turned out, whereas many of the college boys were equally but oppositely self-conscious in their very casual, even sloppy, dress. Somehow he had saved the princely sum of one thousand dollars from his clerical work in Paris, and he spent the money judiciously on his education and on his appearance.[7]

He attracted the attention of student-playwright Elizabeth Lay almost at once that fall quarter; and she, for her part, with her sharp-edged good looks and Playmaker name from that first Koch season, drew his eyes her way. The initial two-way attraction did not last, however, and soon it was a case of Paul Greene in hot but seemingly futile pursuit of Lib Lay, the bright-as-a-penny and pretty-as-a-penny who had plenty of would-be suitors, most of whom she kept at a distance. While in later years the couple would speak of this fall quarter as a time of mutual courtship, she initially gave little time to the smitten man, who complained to his sister/mother Mary Greene that Elizabeth Lay virtually ignored him. And, in his letters home and in talks with his sisters, Greene characterized his love life as erratic, sometimes even stormy. However, Mary Greene the confidante noted that the one-way nature of this love affair was producing its own unique sweetness for her brother the pursuer.[8]

Actually, the courtship involved a series of poses consciously struck and held by two lovers who were also playwrights, poets, songwriters, and actors. It may not be possible to apprehend what "really" happened, for capturing that knowledge would involve getting inside two different imaginations, both of which are gone now—and both of which were in fact long gone by summer 1921, after which time they joined in a mutual love that flourished until his death separated them in 1981. Mary Greene delighted in the role of family historian who could set the record straight, and it was fine with her that the outside, larger audience consume the script that described instant, and mutual, love. However, for the family—that is, the inside audience—Mary Greene read off a script that described a difficult first year: Paul Greene, ignored, sometimes even rebuffed, nevertheless always in the chase; Elizabeth Lay, tentative, sometimes even hostile, always on the run. And Mary Greene was not above throwing that script in Elizabeth Lay Green's face in later decades, especially the 1930s and 1940s, as one sort of reproof if her sister-in-law paid attention to rumors of the playwright's Hollywood, Broadway, or writers' retreat girlfriends.[9]

But there was still another level of interior dialogue, and there, in Greene's 1920 letters to Lib Lay, it is clear that he was afraid of such emotional commitments, that he was self-consciously cynical about love, and that he was using his readings in philosophy and his playwright techniques to develop his own melodrama in which he kept his lover at some distance, turning down invitations to visit with her family in the newly assigned rectory in Beaufort on the Bogue Sound. Some of his reasoning was sophistical, practically daring Lib Lay to prove by a priori logic that he was capable of love, and some of it was shamefully posed, the worldly, dark, daemon force, almost a reluctant spider warning off a victim from his web. He understood enough about romantic traditions in literature, and he was himself enough a part of such traditions, to know how compelling such a pose would be to a rebellious, bright, idealistic young woman who was not afraid of anything. Another, related, stance he maintained was that he, the schoolteacher, farm boy, and combat veteran, knew about work, real work ("nigger work" he called it, in a phrase that he had not invented), and knew it in a way that she, the pampered child of the New England cleric, could not. The latter pose was patently unfair, for the Lays lived a very modest life, and their children knew plenty about hard work and sacrifice. Elizabeth Lay, after all, was herself a former schoolteacher in the countryside, and she suffered compound liabilities on the Hill: a New Englander and a woman and an "irrelevant artist" on a campus and in a community dedicated to training southern boys for leadership in "important" things in life. It appears that the couple never revealed to Mary Greene this aspect of the early courtship that proceeded on its way through some rituals that were extremely complex, ambivalent, and marked by mixed signals.[10]

Through this painful dialogue, Greene and Lay began to learn of each other's families and communities. Lib Lay could tell stories and recall truths as fascinating as, though certainly different from, Paul Greene's. Her father, the Reverend George Atkinson Lay, was rector at Saint Mary's Episcopal Church in Raleigh, which included a residential college for women. The rector was headmaster for the preparatory school there as well as pastor for the congregation, and he had some duties in the college. He was a busy man about Raleigh, but this was very recent, for the Reverend Lay had been in Carolina with his family for only a few years, during which time Lib Lay and her sister, Ellen—Ellie to Paul—finished the preparatory school at Saint Mary's and then entered the state's university system. Her mother, Anna Booth Balche Lay, was also from the Granite State of New Hampshire, and her people were seafarers; her family album is peopled with marvelous captains and characters of the Yankee trading coast, figures both merchant marine and naval. They were, all of them, "Yan Cheese" nor'easters, and the Lays and the Balches could follow their family stories as deep back into the colonial New England past, as could the Greenes and Byrds for colonial Carolina.

In the eighteenth century, the Lays had lived with a few hundred other people in Old Lyme, on the eastern bank of the upper valley of the Connecticut River. Leaving the valley town, the Lays then moved up into the White Mountains and established the hamlet of Laysville, which sat at an altitude of several thousand feet above sea level. This was dairy country; it was rural and isolated, English to the core and marked by the Puritan rectitude, common sense, thrift, and the passion for dispassionate logic limned so memorably of Albion's seed by David Hackett Fischer. The Lays exhibited all of these traits, tempered a bit by the Episcopalian's sense of relative tolerance vouchsafed by family wealth and comfort. In the nineteenth century George Lay studied at an Episcopal seminary and earned his doctorate in divinity, shortly thereafter becoming rector at Saint Paul's Preparatory Academy in Concord, the state's capital, fifty miles southeast of the Laysville ancestral hamlet. It was, however, a long, slow, and hard fifty miles in those days, since Concord was all the way on the other side of the White Mountains and lay alongside the banks of the Merrimack River. This too was dairy country in foothills of six- or seven-hundred-foot elevation, but to the rector it was virtually low country after the White Mountains. Elizabeth Lay was born there in Concord. From dairy farmers to shrewd merchants to sea captains, these New Hampshire family members and friends beguiled the young girls Lib and Ellie Lay with wonderful stories told with wit and vigor in crisp language with no waste motion, almost the opposite of the elaborately spun and extremely wordy southern stories she was hearing in Raleigh and Chapel Hill.[11]

As girls Lib and Ellie Lay reveled in the outdoors, boating and skating and hiking, and the colder and the more snow and ice the better. By contrast, Carolina, with its occasional light snow and relatively low elevation and its long, long summer, was unhappy territory for Lib Lay, who studied hard, wrote songs, wrote plays, and otherwise used her mind actively as an antidote to the sorrow and regret that came when she gave herself over to the green memory of the backward look to her native land. The Lays kept some photographs that showed the old place: Saint Paul's Church and School, set against a lake hedged by a deep hardwood forest, with the White Mountains along the horizon on the west just past Concord's own rolling hills. Also: the girls tricked out for boat races with bows and banners; and again the girls, fixed up like ladies but obviously unreconstructed tomboys frozen by a camera in the middle of playing ball or lobbing rocks at each other. And: glorious naval officers with pipes stuck into their ruddy faces, and everything, their caps, epaulets, even their wide-browed faces overrun by beards as tangled and as dense as seaweed. Finally: the Reverend Lay himself, strong-jawed and with a penetrating gaze ameliorated by a bemused and forgiving twinkle. Paul Greene was instantly sympathetic with one aspect of Lib Lay's personality, that is, her melancholic wish to go back to her real home: then and later he told his diary and his correspondents that he understood her homesickness, what with these carefully preserved childhood memories of Saint Paul's set against the forested hills, of the ice-skating on the frozen pond, of songs and hikes and games, and above all the patriarch of the church and family, the Reverend Dr. Lay and his wife, Anna Lay, the equally strong matriarch of family and neighborhood. [12]

This love, then, involved some very complex games played on both sides, for not only were these two possessed of strong wills and compelling dreams, but they also bore sad memories of what was and what never was. Occasionally, the whole thing got out of hand, and Elizabeth Lay would put her foot down and demand that the brilliant, suffering soul talk and act straight. So called down, Greene would thank her for her candor and frankness, even if it be a brutal and hard honesty, and he would confess his appreciation for the oceanic size and force of an honest friendship. He could even laugh at the way Lib Lay dismantled his elaborate constructions and popped the big, but obviously airy, bubbles of his ego's conceits. Of course, foolishness is not necessarily insincerity, and even sophistical logic may be more honest than it appears; Greene was in the grip of a compelling love he could not understand, much less control, and he was in postwar fashion digging himself emotional trenches to defend himself. There is a profound honesty in his oft-repeated statement that he was unready for love in 1919 and the first half of 1920. In any case, by the summer of 1920, back at home chopping and hoeing cotton and also keeping the books for the county auditor, he had abandoned all stratagems, and he confessed that he loved Elizabeth Lay. He used that word *love* after consciously avoiding it earlier, but now he told Lib Lay all about Renée Boiscelleur, even revealing that he still exchanged love letters with her. He spoke candidly—in fact bluntly and rather insensitively—about his continuing passion for Boiscelleur. Elizabeth Lay, he was coming to see, was one tough, tough cookie who could take it, endure anything except that solipsistic and elusive faux philosophy he had tried to use on her earlier. He even told Elizabeth Lay that, in the moral *weltanschauung* of young lovers, Paul Greene and Renée Boiscelleur had been a married couple, and that she could in 1920 go down to the Seine and look in the waters and not only remember but still *be* in love, as he could go down to the Cape Fear River right then and not only remember but still *be* in love. He told Lib Lay that in 1919 he and Boiscelleur had been married in their own eyes and in God's eyes, and he swore to this claim in the name of the *God that is,* using that ancient phrase in this confessional invocation. [13]

Much as he loved Elizabeth Lay, there was a permanent place in his heart's memory for Renée Boiscelleur, and not even Elizabeth Lay could obliterate that place. On the other hand, he repeated the statement of facts: memories make people wiser, and Renée Boiscelleur could not leave France and Paul Greene could not stay there. He and Elizabeth Lay, then, could be a couple, could marry, and could have a life together if she left this corner of his heart alone: I love you much as I *kin,* he told her, quoting the vernacular of the Croatan (later Lumbee) Indians of Harnett. And then he laid it all open and showed her the Trojan horse, if she would but drag it in and thus finish this long siege. Please, he begged, do something to make me trust you enough so that I can confess everything, and share everything. Of course in time she did do many such *somethings,* and he did bare his soul, in the processes of which he also gave her his soul, she gave him hers, and the two gained back in this giving much more than either gave away. Thus, eliminating all that we cannot know from the fall of 1919 to the midsummer of 1921, we find that the public story is correct, if we specify summer 1921 and then speak of a powerful, two-way attraction.

While he and Elizabeth were just beginning their slow and tortured dance of courtship, he was attracting another kind and degree of notice from some of the professors. The school was still compact enough for the teachers to know the students, and some of the faculty had admired Greene before he went off to war. Now, however, the professors saw a fetching new combination: a young man with all the idealism, energy, and enthusiasm of the classically defined *sophomore* ("the wise fool"), but also a young man who had survived the war, who spoke and read French, who had learned lessons in the Parisian streets, and who had kept the books balanced in the countinghouse. One result was a funny little rivalry between professors in two of the departments on campus. Horace Williams considered that he had a prior and overriding claim staked on Greene anyway, for everyone knew that the boy had spoken of studying philosophy as early as fall quarter 1917. But members of the English department knew of his verse scribbling and, as noted, were publishing some of his poetry in the newly established UNC *Magazine* for student writers. One of the English professors, probably Addison Hibbard but possibly Greenlaw himself, approached Greene, urging him to declare a major in English. In today's era of student consumerism, such aggressive and straightforward recruitment is virtually the norm, but in that long-ago era, professors—especially the senior scholars of the regnant humanities—resided on Olympus and were approached on one's knees through intermediary secretaries and very young and untenured instructors, and even these intermediaries were delphic in their utterances about the rules for communicating with the gods. But the English professor's bold humbling of himself was not enough: Williams the legend had already walked on earth, spoken to Greene, and had even promised a scholarship prize worth fifteen hundred dollars for him (an amount comparable to the net sum of the Greene family cotton and tobacco sales in this season and an amount half again greater than his savings from his overseas pay). Greene, dumbfounded, had accepted immediately; he would have likely declared this major with no prompting anyway. When he later found himself courted by yet another department, he was no less surprised, but he politely and promptly declined. Six decades later he recalled the English professor's reaction: "I'll never forget his anger. [The professor shouted,] 'That man Williams! You know, Green[e], some of these days I'm gonna grab a chair and bust it over his head.'"[14]

In between the heady moment of youth being recruited and the fey season of the old man's recollections, Greene would learn of good reasons for defending oneself, with chair or otherwise, against the legendary Williams. But for the nonce the little world of the Hill spread its treasures before him. Here were bright young student-writers to talk with and to walk with—not only Lib Lay, but Jonathan Worth Daniels, Legette Blythe, and Thomas Wolfe. Here were sources of encouragement and inspiration. Here finally were the friends he had sought a year—and a world war—ago: people to hold his hand and to recite with him the words of the prophet Omar Khayyám. The bright new instructor-writers Hibbard, Greenlaw, and Koch, albeit a little more distant than the students, could engage him critically in a career, coaching him in the techniques of the craft. At a greater distance still, there were the wisdom and the knowledge emerging in the lectures of the polymath Henderson; and of course there was the teacher Horace Williams.

And the man so grateful to return to the peacetime university would actively gather up and use the treasure: unlike the biblical servant, in a parable known well to him, Greene would not be one to bury his talents somewhere. He would use, and increase, the talents willed him by the father-professors. For several academic quarters, he published one poem per issue in the UNC *Magazine*. He also busied himself with essays about philosophy and philosophers in workbooks and copybooks; a later era would describe such labors usefully as "writing to know" philosophy. He was consciously sitting at the feet of Horace Williams, and he was already an understudy, an apprentice professor. He wandered the muddy streets of the little campus and the little town, staring and listening. He pursued and ran away from and then loved Elizabeth Lay. He drank with and played cards with and talked with new friends, the aspiring writers Legette Blythe and Thomas Wolfe and Jonathan Worth Daniels.

And he tried to write plays, evidently the first one being a description of the Greek gods, an understandable choice given his approach to the faculty; but it seemed fitting that he was unable to finish that project. He strained to give each of the gods a sense of humor and other believable passions, but finally the writing ground to a halt, and for exactly the cause suggested by Proff Koch: the Olympians were beyond Greene's creative imagining, not because they were supernatural, but because the cultural conception, the notion of their supernatural qualities, came from a time and a place unfathomable and unknowable for Greene. He had been trying to write about what he did not know.[15] Instead, he joined the Playmakers and thus rejoined the tasks he had announced to his teacher Hibbard Page at the Reverend Campbell's academy in Buies Creek: he would make a serious study of North Carolina literature, and he would write North Carolina literature.

The hot, quick little contest between the professors, like most things in the academy, today seems trivial and comic; in another day, for a time, it exercised the passions and energies of good men who finally came to realize that they had better things to do. Greene did not then, and could not then, follow much of the story: he certainly had not known of reasons why good men would want to break chairs over the head of Professor Williams. In fact, if he noticed at all that Williams caused controversies, he, like most of the adoring Carolina students, probably assumed that Williams's opponents were knaves and fools. Anyway, that dispute, or at least that phase of that dispute, was over and done with quickly, and Greene could get down again to college work, the errand delayed by poverty and family responsibilities and then interrupted by war. In a way, the delays, problematic and even life-threatening as they were, were good for him, because Carolina in the 1920s was a much better school than it had ever been before. And, in terms of using its resources fully and fairly to serve a worthwhile vision of a public education, it was much better in the 1920s than it ever would be afterward. The little groups of serious writers and serious reformists in the student body would be meaningfully challenged by the little groups of scholars and artists and teachers in the faculty and in the outlying neighborhoods, which included good people at Duke University in Durham, State College in Raleigh, the black Shaw University in Raleigh, and some hardy-souled consciences otherwise without academic portfolio who seemed to be in all of those places at the same time.

It was also likely a good result that Williams so aggressively recruited Greene. The philosophy professor had done so for supererogatory rather than for academic reasons, and he intended nothing less than that he start Greene down the right path to reform the teaching of philosophy among southerners. By virtually force-marching the returning veteran into his program, Williams ensured that the student would remain under his own personal influence at the same time that Greene was coming under the no less emotionally charged and deeply affecting influence of Proff Koch. The imprint each man left cannot be gainsaid, despite the fact, and in a way *because* of the fact, that each man had fundamental defects, which also cannot be gainsaid. Although Williams and Koch dominated and even personified the disciplines of philosophy and playwriting on the campus, their greatest impact on Greene was personal rather than professional. Either of the two, with his straight back and stiff neck, could clear out a faculty meeting or a conference session by taking a moral stand on an issue that reasonable men and women judged minor and irrelevant. In their different ways, each could be not only cantankerous but also self-righteous and arrogantly tone-deaf in hearing evil where there might be only the vexing complexities of human existence. Moreover, though Greene would not realize this until a decade later, neither Williams nor Koch was a real craftsman; in fact, each was rather sloppy in the practice of his professed discipline. Nor was either particularly well informed, even in the secondary literature of his field. Instead, they inspired Greene to inform himself. Most important, for all their manifest flaws, not least self-serving hypocrisy, Koch and Williams were men who insisted that a scholar and an artist had a profound moral responsibility to serve the broader community; and it was the sense of immediate involvement in a struggle between right and wrong that most significantly marked their effects on Greene's character.

Yet their defects as scholars could be frustrating and even defeating, not less so because of Greene's great admiration for the two rivals. One evening at Proff Koch's, probably in fall 1920, Greene fell into a serious disagreement with the king Playmaker as Koch showed off before a group of student Playmakers about the grand plans he dreamed for the academic year 1920–21, just begun. To Greene, Koch seemed not to comprehend that the plans were self-contradicting, vague, and aesthetically compromised. Greene told Proff in front of the other students that the plans were timid and indefinite. We don't know how harsh was his language—probably not as harsh as Greene remembered it—but the student thought himself rude and blokeish, and he regretted saying anything of the kind. And later, at the end of the same academic year, Greene returned from a long talk with Horace Williams feeling equally discouraged: Williams again insisted that students and everyone else needed a "new view of religion," but Greene could find little that was spiritually satisfying in the old Hegelian idealism. The student philosopher, like the student playwright, had things to say that he could not get across to his inspirators, and he fretted that he was most incoherent when he had most that he needed to say. Greene brooded over these failures, blaming himself in large part but also sensing that part of the problem was Koch and Williams themselves, that is, students needed other instructors, who were craftspeople competent to teach techniques. Most of all, they needed listeners willing to really listen, with ears tuned more finely than Koch's or Williams's for the nuances of meaning, the traces of the unrealized, but for that no less vital, understanding in a troubled student's words.[16]

Fortunately, there were on the Hill other professors who were craftspeople, and it was these who showed Greene the rigors of his two, really three, disciplines, these who showed him the fine points of writing, of reasoning, of doing research, of observing, of presenting, and of figuring out an audience. These things, so obviously important to a playwright, a philosophy teacher, and a folklore collector, were not in the experience or expertise of Koch or Williams. Instead, men of less personal magnetism would with more detachment show him these ropes. In particular, the Department of English, though not even bridesmaid to a Carolina Playmaker whose troth was plighted to the Department of Philosophy, provided help and counsel in the persons of Greenlaw, Hibbard, Norman Foerster, and Howard Mumford Jones. One sad but unavoidable fact is that each of these four eventually left Chapel Hill, partly because of low pay, partly because of the region's anti-intellectualism, but also because there were not on the campus enough like-minded scholars skilled and dedicated to their crafts. Had Greene come to study a little sooner or a little later than he did, he would have missed these men and their coaching: he would have absorbed the energies of commitment to a mission, but he, like Williams and Koch, might have been sloppy and clumsy and fumbling in his efforts to use those enormous energies.

Hibbard and Greenlaw, men of wisdom and vision, had the knack for administering, for eliminating waste motion in pursuit of a worthy end. Where Hibbard was the most patient of carpenters, Greenlaw was a bold architect, though neither wore blinders and Greenlaw knew how to make little things work just as Hibbard could spin out grand designs. But in Chapel Hill, Hibbard built things within the plans conjured by Greenlaw. This kind of coordinated effort was crucial, for Carolina in those days was woefully short of operating capital for taking educational risks, and many professors had, in that southern way, accepted and even become comfortable with a college system that, like the delta region described by the Mississippi poet William Alexander Percy, had "gone to seed."[17] In particular, both men helped Greene in this crucial phase of his second undergraduate career. As much as Greene had chafed under his clerk's training in postbellum Paris, these very bookkeeping and filing skills could come in handy for him in a number of academic tasks, as Hibbard and Greenlaw showed him. Hibbard encouraged Greene to write for the UNC *Magazine* and later would help Greene in the creation, really the salvific recreation, of the regional journal *The Reviewer.* Greenlaw *was* the modern-day English department at UNC and would infuse its members with a broad sense of professional responsibility: he was showing by personal example that the good teacher could still be a good scholar, and that good teachers and good scholars could be genuinely collegial in the academy. And, just as he had tracked down Koch, Greenlaw found other talented people, and the university benefited from those finds, even if only for the relatively brief period that constituted Greenlaw's own tenure at Carolina.

Two of his best finds were Foerster and Jones, and both of these, given their heads by Greenlaw and encouraged in little things by Hibbard, developed superb careers in literary criticism, despite the fact that neither of them really liked Chapel Hill. For Greene in this particular instant, Foerster was a leavening agent. The Victorian standards for taking the aesthetic and moral measures of literature had been weakened even before the world war and were now all but wrecked. But what would emerge to replace the Victorians? Sometimes too many values, at other times none at all; but there was at least Foerster, who, as Greene remembered it, stood up for standards of excellence in the midst of self-conscious modernism that challenged the legitimacy of the Western canon of art and its aesthetic values. If we accept the simple definition that modernism involves a focus on the individual psyche, an assumption that conflict is good in the long run because it forces clarification of values, and that disorder, even chaos, is everywhere, then Paul Greene by 1920 was certainly a part of that camp. Foerster, by contrast, was not. In fact, the professor swam with a steady stroke in the main current of liberalism and rationalism that, good or not, always runs somewhere in the stream of national consciousness. It was exactly this force of traditionalism against which Greene's innovative, and rebellious, soul strained. But there was a point of agreement and even bonded brotherhood, for Foerster was an utterly unreconstructed humanist who rejected the claims of science "to be the final interpreter for the king." Foerster said, to Greene's enthusiastic affirmation, that "the individual . . . at bottom is not a scientist," but instead there was a philosopher, an ethicist, perhaps also a poet "back of the man of acids and tests." And Greene came to see that genuine innovation develops when it is provided a bedrock of genuine tradition, that the worth of the new is more apparent when the old receives its due honor. Foerster was a worthy liberal-rationalist, "thorough, brilliant, and at all times sympathetic"; and he gave Greene the experience of sharp critical analysis of art, something unavailable elsewhere in town to anything like that remarkable degree.[18]

Howard Mumford Jones had a much less direct influence on Greene the student, but his presence and his example worked effects that, albeit less obvious, were still vital. Not so much concerned with establishing a usable canon to measure contemporary literature, Jones instead set about the task of developing a meaningful historical context for studying American literature from the colonial day to the epoch of the Civil War. He defined this context broadly to include a Western literature more catholic and continental than the rather narrowly Anglican and Puritan brand taught, or really preached, by most scholars of the day. The result in the classroom may often have been a bewildering pastiche, but the result in his publications was a deep and rich texture and an intricate embroidery that showed how American literature was at once genuinely distinct—"O strange new world!"—and yet still derivative of long-running cultural developments bigger and older than the republic and even bigger and older than the English forebears of the republic.[19] In a way dear to Greene, Jones gave the historians he met a new way to use the old literature, and he gave his fellow literature professors a new way to use history; and the result was a discourse considerably more elevated, and certainly more interesting, than the old segregated discussions. Although Jones, as noted, did not teach Greene, his being in the community encouraged the serious pursuit of interdisciplinary studies of high culture and raised the expectations of what a Carolina professor could and should do as a scholar. Paul Greene could see this example and then apply it to his own interdisciplinary studies of folk culture, and he continued to benefit from the experiences of the example even after Jones, like the others, had left the Hill.

Certainly these were disparate personalities who, each in his own way, changed Greene, each adding something to his fund of knowledge and to his bag of tricks for using that knowledge. However, it was not from any of these that Greene derived his most noted trait, that is to say, his almost unerring knack for making the most effective stand possible without ever really breaking out of the "sacred circle" of the regional community. Somehow, despite his direct confrontation of class structure, caste prerogative, racial etiquette, and gender proscriptions, his basic southernness, more pointedly his specifically North Carolina characteristics, were never doubted; nor did he ever really suffer the slings and arrows aimed at the reprobate (or in regional language, the *scalawag* who had backslid from right thinking). Though he would sometimes become very uneasy and though there was plenty of tension, including the possibility of physical violence, Greene's disputes would always be family disputes, and no one would ever consider reading him out of the family, though plenty contemplated, after ancient fashion, thrashing him within the context of gothic-family "unpleasantnesses." This quality, of charmed and charming rebelliousness, was partly in the grain of his character, but it was also a canny quiddity, something learned by observing the man who provided the atmosphere for all the different kinds of people reaching for greatness at Carolina and in Chapel Hill during the 1920s. This was Harry Woodburn Chase, president from 1919 to 1930.

In the long decades since Paul Greene first matriculated at the state university, it is Frank Porter Graham's name that has become synonymous with Chapel Hill liberalism. Actually, however, Chase created much of the reformist and liberal atmosphere in this environment in the decade before Frank Graham, whom he tutored in these matters, succeeded him. Recall that, before 1918, Edward Kidder Graham had begun to inspire substantive reform in the curriculum and had encouraged and supported a talented and energetic, if small, group of academics on campus. Unfortunately, while Paul served in the army, the young UNC president's career ended with all the abruptness of a wartime casualty. In this case, it was not an artillery shell but an epidemic of influenza that landed suddenly in the small community in the central piedmont in the fall of 1918, taking in its strike Graham before he could realize much at all of the fine plans limned out in his famed black notebook. Graham had gotten far enough in his plans to hire and to empower Harry Chase in his academy. With the sudden passing from the scene of his benefactor and mentor, Chase emerged as the best hope and most logical choice to continue the reform movement.

Born in Groveland, Massachusetts, Chase came to Carolina by way of New England and left by way of New York, but for eleven building-years he fitted himself fully into southern place on the Hill, especially by mastering the southern art of communication and leadership by indirection. What he had picked up and used so successfully was southern "manners," as John Shelton Reed defines those "styles": "All social types, of course, are embodied in 'manners,' styles, of some sort. But the Southern lady and gentleman are defined in large part by their good manners, in the conventional 'yes, ma'am' sense. . . . Southerners understand that this sort of behavior means only that those who display it have had proper raising, or have made up for the lack of it. It says very little about their character or their attitudes toward the people they are interacting with. But non-Southerners often misunderstand." Chase understood, and he knew enough to make himself understood, and when need be, misunderstood to his benefit.[20]

No less demanding a dissident than Wilbur J. Cash was convinced that it was Chase who established UNC as the South's leading center for academic dissidence and scholarly dissent in this era between the two world wars. And Cash in his bittersweet plaint against southern conforming specifically excepted Chapel Hill, as he specifically credited its Yankee president for making possible this exceptionalism. Actually, Chase was much more, but also less, than Cash thought: not by any means forthright, and much more *not* plain-speaking, Chase permitted academic inquiry by telling the conservative trustees one thing, the reformist scholars another. He believed, and said often, that the function of universities is to negotiate among themselves, and his negotiations were always to keep the trustees talking and not thinking and the faculty thinking and not talking. Above all, his negotiations were to keep the talking trustees and the thinking faculty away from each other, to keep them unclear, even misinformed, about the others' thoughts and words.[21]

This shrewd craftsman had been educated at Dartmouth College and then had entered graduate research studies at Clark University under G. Stanley Hall, an educational psychologist who had helped to translate, and also to teach in popular vein, the clinical studies of Sigmund Freud. Chase studied and worked at Clark University until 1910, when he came to Chapel Hill to teach education and psychology in an era when those two things could be comfortably and reasonably housed in one department. Serving as dean of arts and sciences, he was heir apparent to an eventual presidency, but he was elevated way ahead of schedule in 1919 as a result of Edward Kidder Graham's sudden death. At once Chase hired young Howard Washington Odum away from Emory University and helped the sociologist to establish the most distinctive center at

Chapel Hill, the Institute for Research in the Social Sciences, in the process accepting Odum's plan that IRSS would be "a great social training school for the South," brave enough to do that which Emory University, Duke University, the University of Virginia, Vanderbilt University would be unwilling to do, and capable of doing that which other southern schools would lack the resources to do.[22]

Odum was immediately and often in hot water because his IRSS fellows of both genders began to ask embarrassing questions, and to provide even more embarrassing answers, about textiles, cigarette manufacturing, general labor conditions, plantation economics, racial violence, railroad rate setting, utility services, and the public school systems damaged by intrusion from religious fundamentalists. Chase, to put it straight, lied to the trustees in telling them that the IRSS was self-funding and in telling them that the institute would not ask any more embarrassing questions. However, he pointedly ordered Odum and the rest of the university faculty not to advocate "particular forms of taxation, or the organization of labor, of social equality between the races, of a socialistic regime." On the other hand, Chase worked cleverly and effectively to help find Rockefeller, Spelman, and other foundation money to support IRSS; and he worked with Odum to make IRSS a real scholar's center, one able to investigate controversial things, albeit one unable to broadcast policy pronouncements in the classroom or in its journal, *Social Forces*. Lesser administrators with narrower vision, including better and more honest people, would have lost the IRSS and much more by handling the trustees and the professors in some other manner, no matter how nobly done.[23]

In like manner, Chase encouraged the talented English professors. Recognizing the organizational talent in Greenlaw and Hibbard, Chase gave them their heads and let them build a superb department. So too did Chase permit room to dream and to build for Louis Round Wilson, who was told to shape up the library and to find someone (it turned out to be the pioneer William Terry Couch) to direct the struggling University of North Carolina Press. As Odum recalled it, Chase was a genius at "seem[ing] to be loafing along easily but when the test came he always delivered over and above requirements." Too, Odum marked Chase's "maximum delegation of authority" to bright and energetic scholars—a tactic that also gave him the presidential "deniability" of responsibility if trustees, alumni, or politicians became angered over something.[24]

If Koch and Williams each in his way had inspired Greene to educate himself by asking tough questions, and asking those questions anywhere and at all times, then the two had also encouraged him in a tendency already existing, but previously acknowledged only as a quirk, even a flaw. That tendency was to make all of life into art, to shape the stuff of the quotidian and the extraordinary into the contours of a song, a play, a novel, a poem. In the breaks between academic quarters when he went home to Lillington, the Chapel Hill professors went with him, *spiritus mundi,* and so too did Elizabeth Lay. This was the romantic's identification of himself with all of life, especially nature and the organic growing-together of all things, not least things imagined and things remembered. To him in that day, no deep thought and certainly no deep impulse was ever false, and thus not evil at its source; but it also involved the acknowledging that the imagined and the remembered were very real, were always there, or better always here, and could break in on one in his daily rounds. And sometimes that could surely be harmful. Greene, "making love" in the high Victorian way to Elizabeth Lay, might feel compelled to blurt out that he was at that moment thinking of Renée Boiscelleur; or again, lunching with Proff Koch, to declare that the mentor dramatist lacked both focus and courage. Or Greene might feel the need to show his political colors despite the hopelessness of the odds or the pointlessness of the struggle, for that too would be romantic.

These forms of out-of-classroom learning by questioning, by talking, even by putting his foot in his mouth, Greene conducted arduously during the Christmas break, spring break, and the long summer months between academic quarter sessions on the Hill. Away from the Hill, he still mingled the playwriting, the Socratic questioning, the songwriting, and the small-town folklore-sleuthing with farming, tax auditing, playing baseball (sometimes for pay). And loving Lib Lay, though most of those times he was not physically with her. The unremitting financial pressures of the Harnett family farm pushed the lovers apart and left them only occasional moments together.

Piquant was the fact of those few opportunities, for by 1921 Greene was a welcome guest in Beaufort, where the Reverend George Lay had taken a church and thus moved his family. Lib Lay, the top Playmaker of one season, was now out of season: holder of a degree, she was yet daughter of an Episcopal rector far from Chapel Hill, and now she too lived in Beaufort and tried to keep her playwriting skills sharp and her spirits high. In that new setting the visitor Greene quickly became friends with, and in fact enthusiastic pen pals with, Lib Lay's sister, Ellie; and he became as quickly the doted-upon extra child of their mother, Anna Balche Lay. Although the Reverend Lay, the wise and sardonic minister-father, remained skeptical about so much energy and so much idealism, he too was amused. In his own way the rector was quite charmed by Greene. Beaufort is a pretty, old town, not truly a seaport, but with clean and usually calm beaches formed by the Beaufort Sound and the Bogue Sound. No one here was a flapper, but Elizabeth and Ellen Lay were rebellious and adventurous and certainly sensuous in their own ways, and they loved to go for midnight and early morning swims in the sound, something officially frowned upon by the paterfamilias but tacitly put up with. They giggled and gossiped about boys and girls and neighbors, and then they talked seriously and knowingly about politics, theater, art, the economy. More and more they spoke of Paul Greene, sharing his long letters and writing him letters together and playing with the big kid in the dark, salty waters. But, despite her conscious and stylized flirtation, Ellie Lay was no rival for Greene's hand, and she knew when to "get lost" so that the lovers could have time together. These Beaufort days relaxed the man and the woman playwright who could for a few moments forget professors and critics and fellow students and the tight finances of a preacher's family and of a farmer's family; but they were a man and a woman in love, and there was a sexual tension, not of course unpleasurable, but still a tension, in their brief holidays there.

And the time was never long, even by the standards of outsiders who were not painfully in love; Greene had to work for money during school vacations, and thus visits with the Lay family had to be budgeted in with other uses of time and money. To Greene, who wrote long letters daily and made notes in his diary for long weeks about an upcoming weekend and who received equally long letters from the Beaufort girls about such anticipated visits, the moments there became quicksilver that could be captured only by writing and talking and imagining until the daydreamed, the actual, and the remembered experiences were hopelessly intermingled, the old town and the sound and the young redhead and her family and friends existing always with him, wherever he was. This was a moral as well as an emotional component of his artistry, Lib Lay's artistry, their love, and their friendship. The pained daydreaming and the pampering, indulgent letters and the grand and the tiny plans, all these things moved somewhere in his consciousness when he was away from Lib, and especially so when he was in Lillington away from her, a double separating and an exponential distancing since such moments, especially the summers, pulled Greene away from and back from other intellectuals at the university as well as removing Elizabeth Lay from him.

In Lillington, especially in those summers, Greene worried, even agonized about these folk he loved, the blacks, the poor white farmers, landowning whites, mill workers, the new managers of the new industrial order, the wandering Croatan. Sometimes he discussed things, sometimes (though this was more likely in Chapel Hill) he acted to interpose, sometimes he consciously and deliberately retreated, but always he observed; and when he observed, he was the playwright shaping what he saw, and what he did and thought about doing, into a script. These were never simple processes, and Greene was acutely sensitive about his own role, for he was after all director/actor in these productions. Respected, indeed honored, because of his war record, appreciated for his farming prowess—the champion cotton picker and the proponent of tobacco planting as alternative to the one-crop system—Greene was all but lionized because of his athletic skills, since he could pitch with either hand and he could play several positions in the field, and most of all, he was strong enough to play well in long games after a long day's work and a long trip to a game site in another town. There was too a tolerance, and even an encouraging, of his artistic side, for many in Harnett County were proud to have a citizen who could write songs and plays and who could teach philosophy; and country towns in the East never were as anti-intellectual, much more as sterile, as knowing cosmopolites often presume. But for all that, Greene was a threat to this community, the one-time Sunday school teacher who now doubted organized religion and who even described God in eccentric and idiosyncratic terms. Too, his probing questions, no matter how adroitly slipped in, nettled. Life was tough in the 1920s in Harnett, and men and women struggled to hang onto their little bit; here was an attractive, energetic local boy asking about radical changes that might help everybody, but it also might further reduce *my little bit.*

Greene came to understand the singularity and the loneliness of the true radical during a scene whose script got away from him "down to the courthouse." "Hanging out" at the courthouse was a venerable pastime in small towns; there were comedies high and low and more than a tithe of tragedies to witness for, and the trial lawyers and even some of the judges played enthusiastically to the audiences in the courtroom, of which they were fully aware. Between sessions "the boys" of all ages would slouch against the walls in the anteroom or perhaps in the balcony or on the steps outdoors; women, of course, stayed well clear of such knots of men talking the mysteries of baseball, politics, "bidness," Yankees, automobiles, and terrible ice storms. Greene too would be there, and though not prone to slouch, he fit into his own niche with the "crowd of loafers," most of whom genuinely liked him. One summer day in 1921, Greene grew silver-tongued as he amazed all comers with a long and deeply felt sermonette.[25]

But tolerance and even encouragement of a native white son (who was also star pitcher, combat hero, best cotton picker) was not the same as genuine tolerance for all Harnett's creatures, great and small, since the small were seldom deemed wise and wonderful. Pausing in his performance, Greene noticed across the street in the upstairs room of the county jailhouse a pair of female hands gripping the bars of the cell window. Sensing the crowd was with him, *simpatico,* Greene asked rhetorically about this woman and repeated their answer that she was an old slut imprisoned because of her extramarital sexual relations with a man. He then tried to shock them into a statement of political reformism. Why should she be in prison? he asked rhetorically. Perhaps, he suggested, the couple were in love. It was, however, Greene who would be stunned, for the men in the crowd callously dismissed her as an old hussy who stayed in trouble of her own making. He lost this argument utterly and retreated home. In a letter he desperately cried to Elizabeth Lay that the tangle of such injustices was driving him crazy. He begged her to help him see through the confusion. He had to cry to her, for Horace Williams would only say, "Take a new view of religion," and Proff Koch could only talk about building a real theater at Carolina. [26]

The professors, after all, had promised only to raise in him the questioning spirit and to help form the habit of asking hard questions. The rest after that was up to him—and to her.

1921–1922

As Greene concluded his undergraduate studies, he had to resolve the situation back home on the Harnett County farm. Papa Greene, still the overbearing patriarch, was weakening in everything except his resolve that the large and sprawling family devote itself to his cotton, tobacco, and timber lands. Stepbrother John Greene had run things during the Great War, but now Hugh Greene was ready to manage the farms. Hugh and John Greene got in each other's way, and Papa got in the way of both. Worse, Papa Greene seemed to think that Paul would take over the management, at the very least the bookkeeping that so befuddled everyone else but came easily to the onetime army clerk.

Paul Greene made it clear that he was leaving the farm for another career, but he did keep the books, give advice and consent, lend money, and above all talk to the tax authorities on behalf of the struggling operations. It was an awkward arrangement, but his long-distance help was needed—and indeed he needed the revenues from the crops, plus his share of the equity in the lands.

The women's side of this subdivided, multilayered, and conflicted family was no more pleasant or workable than the men's side. Mary Greene functioned still as sister/mother, and she did the most to impose some order on the essential disorder, but all of it was a great trial. Paul's stepsister Allie Greene soon married a nearby farmer and moved away, but she was resented from time to time both for her going away and for her occasional coming back. Gladys Greene married and left, but on the one hand her leave-taking angered Papa because she was independent, and on the other hand it angered Paul Greene because her new life included no possibility of a musical or other artistic career. Erma and Caro Mae Greene, the sisters closest to Paul Greene in aptitude and in attitude, struggled bitterly with Papa in order to leave the farm and pursue artistic careers in faraway big cities on the order of New York and Berlin and Paris. Yet having won that fight, the two subsequently quarreled often with their adoring brother Paul, who had his own ideas about the best directions for their artistic careers.[1]

By 1921 Greene had finally established the right to a career away from the farm, that is, under the condition that he continue to help out with the finances and the legal problems. By that year he had the baccalaureate degree in hand, and if he wanted it, there were opportunities for graduate work in his chosen discipline. But in which path? He wrote poetry every day in those early years of the 1920s, and he styled himself a poet; yet he also wrote plays every day, and he was proud to be a Carolina Playmaker. And he read philosophy systematically, often talking about following the lead of Horace Williams. At the same time, he vigorously collected folk songs and folk sayings, and he considered himself at the least an amateur folklorist.

Both Proff Koch and Horace Williams urged him to seek graduate training elsewhere, with the idea that he would eventually return to the Hill to teach, write, and work. As generally happened in disputes over academic turf in those days, it was Williams who prevailed, enrolling Greene in special graduate readings courses in Chapel Hill for the fall quarter of 1921. His idea was to find money for Greene to study at another graduate center and then to have him return to run the Carolina philosophy department. These 1921 readings were partly to prepare for the next academic challenge and partly to buy a little time to find money to cover the long-term plan.

The philosopher certainly had grand plans for the long haul, envisioning a modern department of philosophy "at the South" with his star graduate Greene the centerpiece of those plans. Greene could then carry out the mission to improve the study and teaching of philosophy not only at Carolina but throughout the states of the former Confederacy. The venerable one could explain the existing poor quality of southern professional philosophy his own Hegelian way: "We've had no philosophical books written in the South, because our life has been so smooth." He was obviously not talking about race relations or labor relations, but about the dialectic of contrasting ideas. Williams preached to all students, but especially to Greene: "Hegelize yourself. That is, find the truth in the opposite side, see the reality in the other individual's side. . . . Hegelize your problems. See the unity between the two, or three differences. . . . absorb the moment of negation." All of which dialectical "progressing" toward "more reality, more of God," "more of spirit" would come through "collisions of ideas" and "moving up through spheres" by processes of rigorous philosophical inquiry, and preferably at a graduate center with other and more advanced instructors, for Williams, despite his very large ego, rightly sensed his own weaknesses and inappropriateness for such intensive specialized training.[2]

For his part, Proff Koch thought that Greene could study and teach playwriting and then teach and practice it for the Playmakers while also studying and teaching and practicing philosophy. Both Koch and Williams understood *practicing philosophy* to include significant scholarly publication on the professional and indeed on the technical levels of the discipline. In later decades there would be some sad confusion about all of these ambitious plans and what finally became of them. In the chaos of disagreement about what Greene would do in 1928 and 1929, Williams would descend from legendary status, and the onetime student would become contemptuous of his onetime hero, while Frank Porter Graham as dean would gain accolades for defending the playwright genius against the machinations of a tired old egomaniac once beloved by the student body.[3]

Picking through the records, however, one finds that it is Horace Williams who was true all along and Paul Greene who went into things ambivalently and then tried to change the rules. The academy was changing rapidly, and specialization in a subfield of one discipline would be the expected model: the same person styled renaissance humanist in one era would in the next era be called dilettante. Williams, to his credit, saw these things coming, and very early and often thereafter he warned Greene that there was no place in the modern university for a man without an earned doctorate and a clearly articulated specialization in a discipline. That Williams was himself a classic generalist is here irrelevant: he was closing a career and giving advice to a favored student who was beginning a career in new and utterly different circumstances.[4]

Nor could Greene himself claim to have missed Williams's warnings. During the winter interim of 1922, Williams came to Greene with news that Sarah Graham Kenan, widow of an oil millionaire who had diversified and broadened (with riotous success) his interests, was on her way to becoming the major benefactor of the University of North Carolina in this period between the two world wars. To the point, for this winter's day early in 1922, Kenan had provided enough money to start a graduate fellowship in philosophy at Carolina. Williams wanted to take the first year's interest earnings from the bequest and use it as a stipend for Greene to study logic, with a view to preparing his student for a career in philosophy. Accepting the stipend, $500 for the period January to May, would commit Greene to a focused graduate program, the bulk of which would be conducted somewhere else, with moral commitments to return to the Hill as instructor in philosophy. Here at last was the real job Greene had searched for, one that could wean him for good and all from dependence on the Buies Creek farm. Beginning in the fall, it would pay him $1,500 per annum, and Sarah Graham Kenan had agreed that Greene could receive an installment of $750 as early as 1 July in order to travel to England. However, such a plan would entail abandoning his broad-gauged reading in ideas in favor of a more concentrated and more specialized drilling in logic and in contemporary scholarly literature.[5]

As Greene studied his account books and the proposal with his clerk's eye sharpened by a cotton farmer's poverty, he realized that this Kenan fund would be best applied to a graduate program at Cornell University. He decided to use the stipend to enroll in the Ivy League school in Ithaca, New York, earn the A.M. degree in philosophy, and return to teach that discipline in Carolina's department in the academic year 1923–24. Whatever path he chose, he would travel it with Lib Lay, whom he arranged to marry in the summer of 1922. Each could earn money and save during the winter of 1921–22 and the spring of 1922; and once they were actually married, Lib's salary would have to carry them during any graduate studies. Perhaps, perhaps, he could use a stipend again, after teaching several years, to earn the doctorate from England's venerable Oxford University, where Lib wanted him to go. In the meantime, the young couple would move to Ithaca in September. World travel could wait. Work outside the home, and bringing up babies inside the home, were to be Lib Lay's marching orders for the years 1922 and 1923.[6]

Although Lib Lay would be disappointed and her father would need to be reassured about prospects of future travel, Williams was well pleased by this decision, which affirmed his advice. There followed a happy, hectic period of planning: planning for a move, planning how to wrap up the last graduate readings with Williams at Carolina, planning for the start of graduate readings at Cornell, planning for a job in Ithaca for Lib Green.

And always there was the writing. More and more Greene was turning to African American subjects for dramatic treatment, now comic, now tragic. In particular, he looked hard at the tangle of his own emotions about the black versions of Jude the Obscure (Greene's favorite Thomas Hardy character, a plain and poor countryman who sought a university education at Oxford); close at home on his own eastern heath there were "freedmen" of both genders who demanded their own kind of freedom, which included a real education instead of the proffered Jim Crow brand of miseducation.

Throughout the winter and spring of 1921–22 Greene talked extensively with Lib Lay. When they were away from each other, he wrote her lengthy confessional letters. He made a few emotionally charged trips to Buies Creek to see the skeptical Papa and John and Hugh Greene—and the adoring sisters. He made at least one journey to Ocracoke Island, to the site of Sir Walter Raleigh's Lost Colony, whose sixteenth-century rise and disappearance continued to compel his imaginative attentions. All emotional circuits were obviously loaded to capacity, and some likely overburdened, as he figuratively traveled in his studies, his thoughts, and his letters, and as he literally traveled on the "awful little train," sleek new trains, borrowed automobiles, ferries and barges, and other vehicles.

Paul Greene and Lib Lay set their date for 6 July 1922. In June, on the verge of this most hope-filled marriage, Greene again went to the medical center at Johns Hopkins University, in this case for a nose operation to unblock a breathing passage, damages perhaps from that kick in the face during the army football championship game back in the Camp Sevier training post. This return to the scene of a youthful shoulder operation brought its own tangle of good and bad memories and hopes and misapprehensions. But this nose operation did not work; he developed severe headaches and dizziness, and he had to seek more treatment, this time from Dr. McPherson in Durham, who operated on him again in June, only weeks before the scheduled wedding. Coming to consciousness in Dr. McPherson's office, he lay there woozy and scared, wondering if he would ever recover. Dr. McPherson declared that he had never seen a fellow in such a predicament and so would not release him, instead making him register at the local Hotel Malbourne and from there come in daily for a checkup and more therapy. Getting dressed three times a day for therapy that seemed to do no good, he despaired; and he even recorded in his diary, in decidedly un-Victorian fashion, doubts about his ability to perform sexually in this period. He used the virtually verboten term *physical nature* to refer to Elizabeth Lay's own needs, and he asked plaintively, What will marriage be like so soon after this operation? In the trough of this despair, he pronounced himself a defeated trooper. By 1 July he was dismissed, but with fewer than five days remaining before the ceremonies, he did not feel any better. As he rode back in the family's old Ford with his brother Hugh at the wheel, Paul Greene was sad and abstracted.[7] Then there was the wedding, with Hugh Greene evidently surprised but delighted to be the best man and with Caro Mae and Erma Greene hardly surprised but no less delighted to be bridesmaids. The ceremony uniting the New England seafaring Episcopal Lay family with the eastern Scots evangelical—and decidedly landlocked—Greene family went off well. The sects and geographical sections represented different traditions of course, but John Calvin's disciples had predestined this course for believers in each family. The union of differences was formalized in emphatic fashion by the officiant, none other than the Reverend Lay himself. In any case, a hundred years of travel had taught the Lays the tolerance learned by Paul and Hugh Greene in one year of the Great War. Among other things, Lib Lay stopped the confusion of name spelling, decreeing that her new family name—and her man's new name for his old family—would be Green, as spelled without the final *e* by the typesetters at Edwards and Broughton printshop and press in Raleigh.[8] The Harnett family, always pretty casual about such things, acquiesced readily to her pronouncement, and Bettie Greene's chosen Paul now had a new surname.

Yet Paul Green remained relatively weak and absolutely anxious. He did recuperate from the respiratory maladies and their difficult surgical treatments sufficiently for the two to enjoy a honeymoon period fit for a young and healthy couple. However, he would not regain his full strength and health until the end of the summer.[9]

That harried summer at last over, Paul and Lib Green went to Ithaca. They made a home at a place on 416 Eddy Street, very near the campus. And because Cornell University was not only a fine private liberal arts school, but also a historic center for farmer education through extension services, Lib Green found work with the university's Department of Rural Social Organization. Her communications skills, her excellent academic record, and her tough, bright presentation on an interview obtained the job for her. Nevertheless, the long hours of travel on roads as removed and as bumpy as those of the Carolina backcountry, but iced over, required still other qualities: patience, quiet courage, a sense of humor, considerable physical stamina. These she demonstrated in abundance, giving the lie to her lover's cruel taunt of the courtship days that he, not she, was the one accustomed to demanding physical labor. The woman never broke under these strains, seldom even complained. And all of it would be valued preparation for trials equally wearing on other trips in other years. Often the graduate student, the cotton farmer, and the combat veteran sat and mused over his favorite late-night snack, bananas and powdered milk, in the drafty old Eddy Street house while Lib Green, the redhead accused of being a spoiled lady, drove through snowstorms to teach farmers and rural educators in far-removed upstate New York communities. Then it was he who was self-styled, pitiable, and a piece of a man; she was by contrast the brave and unbending one. These facts, emotions, and relationships were in the foreground as the playwright sat in that Eddy Street structure and sketched out the plots and worked on the dialogues for the themes of his black plays.[10]

Yet he did not wallow in these ironies long; instead, being appreciative of his wife's sacrifices, he used the late-night hours for creative efforts after accomplishing his graduate readings. He forged ahead on a number of projects, and looking back at his records, one wonders that he did not confuse himself, as one wonders that he did not burn himself out. There were "Negro Songs," his poems that attempted to speak in the voice of an African American veteran of the wartime trenches. This veteran was originally called Uncle Sandy, but late became Uncle Joe, and later still Comrade Joe and finally Joe. But there were also at least a dozen plays, including early versions of his best play, *In Abraham's Bosom,* and of his most commercially successful play, *Lost Colony.*

As he worked away at broader themes concerning black people in eastern Carolina, Green began to focus on men not entirely unlike himself and somewhat like his favorite Hardy character, Jude the Obscure; but these black people, existing in the day of damnable Jim Crow, had to proceed differently than did Jude or other disadvantaged whites: the sable farm boys who seek to educate themselves decide that they must also educate the rest of their people and thereby bring an entire caste up in the economic world—and only political action will let that happen.

There in Ithaca he began to transmogrify the character Sam Tucker, a light-skinned mulatto and "wrong sheet" offspring of the landed white gentry, into such a tragic figure who worked in his own Hegelian conflicts to save himself

and his people. Sam Tucker gradually became Abraham, or the even more bib-
lically charged Abram. And his surname became the more propitiously eastern
Scots McCrannie. The masterpiece *In Abraham's Bosom* began to emerge from
shorter versions with other titles and other themes. That issue of miscegenation, central to the life and trials of so many characters, Green found in the
question of the fate of the Lost Colonists, for the Croatan/Lumbees of his
region were clearly part black, and they claimed to be descendants of the old
colonists. Miscegenation, of course, involved not only racial and ethnic and
cultural issues but also sexuality, and Green wrote about the sexual energies
and the sexual misadventures of characters of all classes and all groups.

And when the morning came, there were the classes, the seminar papers, and the library reading room. Here in Ithaca, as in Chapel Hill, Hegelian
idealism still held sway, even though the pragmatism of William James was
gaining ascendancy in the other national centers for philosophical studies. This
may seem surprising, for Cornell's graduate program, the Sage School of Philosophy, was otherwise much more in tune with contemporaneous intellectual
developments than was Chapel Hill, and liberal reformists in the twentieth
century were attracted to the pragmatic James, much more so than to any
other philosopher. Nevertheless, this liberal reformist delved yet more deeply
into Hegelian idealism as taught him by the superb practitioners Frank Thilly,
James Edwin Creighton, and Ernest Albee. Unlike Williams, these three were
serious scholars and close students of the techniques of reason and logic, and
they drilled Green hard in the textual analysis of Hegelian syllogisms.[11]
In addition, the Sage School trio was fascinated with the contemporaneous
thinker Benedetto Croce, and their graduate student also became enamored of
the Italian idealist who declared that the study of history itself was the study
of liberty. Creighton, Albee, and Thilly assigned readings by Croce and about
Croce, and the interpretation in their lecture notes is that the antifascist idealist
was a kind of flawed Hegelian—nowhere near the master but at least reflecting
some of Hegel's better qualities in an era otherwise given over to extremely
misguided pragmatists—interested only in ideas once put into action—and
positivists—interested only in an abstracted and uninvolved and disengaged
description of ideas with no responsibility for ethical judgment. Ever the serious note taker and task assigner, Green wrote to himself in his notebook that
he must work hard to understand Croce's criticisms of Hegel, since his Cornell professors did not understand that criticism. Yet, when his studies were
finished and when he went out to teach, he remained as much a true Hegelian
as Horace Williams or the men of Ithaca.[12]
Although his notes are thorough and accurate, it seems that Green was not
fully engaged with his distinguished professors at Cornell. For instance, in all
of his many notebooks on Horace Williams, he had patiently written down the

instructor's words, even if something were repeated many, many times. The only "doodles" or other scribblings seem to be from Williams's own notes, usually Hegelian spirals upward and onward to the ultimate expansive Truth and Spirit. On the other hand, with Creighton, Thilly, and Albee, Green often fell to illustrating things that seem to have nothing to do with what they were teaching. On one set of notes he drew a very detailed cathedral, less a "doodle" than a drawing for a play set, and on another he drew a log cabin, again less an idle scribble than a sketch for a set in a dramatic production. The all-night work on drama echoed in his note taking, and one reading these notes later gets the sense that the student would much rather work on his dramatic productions than study this philosophy. The point seems worth pressing because Green's preparatory notes as a professor of philosophy are similarly illustrated, suggesting that the professor would much rather have been writing and directing a play than teaching the class. In his playwriting Green liked to use portents, especially hoot owls, to signal trouble on the way. In this sense, then, those set designs and doodles in his philosophy notebooks seem to be hoot-owl portents about his own career in Carolina's philosophy department.[13]

Curiously, for a man who often agonized himself and his wife and his family and his friends over decisions and then recorded these debates and discussions fully in his diary and in his correspondence, Green decided to leave Cornell without completing the degree, and he did so with virtually no notice in the diary or in his correspondence. He took with him the reassurances of three Ivy League philosophers that Hegel was not only important but was even "gradually taking over the world"—and that a special *geist* worthy of serious study flowed through the spirit of the folk themselves.

What he was not taking back was the A.M. degree, nor any serious plan to attain it, despite Horace Williams's redundant warnings that the modern university would start by demanding the master's and end by demanding the doctorate. More to the point, Green had certainly seen at close hand Williams's own model of the modern professional philosopher in Frank Thilly, and he clearly had no intentions of developing himself into the kind of scholar who could publish in *Philosophical Review,* or even attend conference sessions of the American Philosophical Association.

While Green was away in Ithaca in academic year 1922–23, Horace Williams hired Katherine Elizabeth Gilbert to teach philosophy courses on the Hill. Green learned of her hiring while he was at Cornell, he approved of hiring her, and he became good friends with her. She was in fact much closer than Green to Williams's model philosophy professor—a committed scholar active in the American Philosophical Association, effective in the classroom, and successfully publishing in *Philosophical Review* and other journals in the discipline.[14]

However, for the period 1923–28, Paul Green clearly remained Williams's chosen one, his brightest hope for a "real" philosophy department. Williams presumed that Green's graduate degree would be accomplished in due course, that Green would publish and would advance, perhaps with the assistance of Kenan funds, or perhaps with a prestigious grant from outside the university, such as a Guggenheim Fellowship.

Indeed, when students matriculated for fall 1923 studies, it was Green and not Gilbert who was available to them—along with the redoubtable Horace Williams. For her part, Gilbert would remain in the area, would teach at both Carolina and Duke, and would be a big part of the small circle of liberal reformists that Paul worked with during the next three decades. She would be better paid at Duke than on the Hill, but that difference in salary was only part of the issue. She knew that for Williams she would never be more than a role player, while at Duke she would get the real chance to perform as a philosopher. Thus, Williams proudly greeted Paul and Lib Green on their return, and he approved Green's proposal for a new course, Philosophy 16, "The Philosophy of Literature."[15]

Philosophy 16 concerned itself with the "moral purpose of art," and its instructor selected literary "representations from the ideal side." The focus was on Thomas Hardy and "the problem of fate and purpose and human endeavor," as seen in his poetry and in his novels *Tess of the D'Urbervilles* and *Jude the Obscure*. Additionally, Green offered philosophical readings of Balzac, Ibsen, Dostoevski, and Anatole France. He concluded with "recent" criticism, offering "standards of judgment in literature"; these critics included among others Henry Louis Mencken, George Jean Nathan, Upton Sinclair, Carl Van Doren, John Erskine, Hippolyte Taine, Flaubert, and Carolina's own Norman Foerster.[16]

Green also promised some recent American examples of such literature; indeed, his own ongoing works often served as counterpoint examples even for the European selections. Students probably enjoyed this aspect of things very much, for it engaged them in the processes of the creation of art. But it must also be noted that the professor's preparatory notes for his lectures are often marked by the playwright's plans for the next drama—not to share with the class, but just to plan for the next drama in the oddments of time and space otherwise given over to class preparation. As a graduate student he had only partially engaged himself with preparation for class; now, as a professor, he was no more engaged in it. On more than one occasion the playwright's needs took precedence over the professor's duties. Such notations show up as well in his preparatory notes for his more traditional courses, befitting one who was not actually pursuing simultaneous vocations but was instead going to subsidize a playwright's career with a professorial salary in another field.[17]

Whatever Philosophy 16 or his other courses did for students of philosophy, students of the reform aesthetic were certainly served, and served passionately. "The best literature as art is the imaginative expression of significant human experiences in character, impression, mood, plot, or fable." More to the point, he told them that "literature if great will always deal with the philosophical and paradoxical notions of human experience. . . . By philosophical and paradoxical notions of human experience I mean as exemplified in such matters as evil, good, individual impetus and urge against institutional conservatism; honor, love, will against intelligence, etc., all growing out of and related to human beings, either depicted or suggested." Then he stated unequivocally that "tragedy is the highest kind of literature." He intended to write the highest kind of literature.[18]

The tragedy he intended to stage involved the denizens, a word actually used in the Carolinas to describe the people of color, those at least partly African American and at least partly Native American in the regions of the sandhills and of the eastern littoral. Again he was true to Proff Koch's Playmaker maxim, *Come alive in your own soil!* There was no way around it: in Harnett the sandhills soil was white, the bottomland loam was black, much of the labor was black, much of the labor was white, but even more of the labor was shades of brown and red. The authentic folk dramatist could come alive in such soil and with such characters only by telling the stories of the denizens of all colors. Often too, an accurate telling of the stories would have to record the clashing of the denizens. Many people were poor, many people were in debt, there was anger, things were unsettled, and there was blood on the Carolina moon.[19]

Much as he had back in Buies Creek and then in Ithaca, Green wrote and rewrote, especially through the device of his shadow diary character Harvey Easom, who lived in the imaginary and the real Little Bethel of Harnett County. Paul Green developed his plays that would be staged in the late 1920s out of three sources: real-life observations recorded in his diary, shadow diary revisions of the real, and purely imaginative writing experiences. From 1912 and continuing throughout his long life, Green learned from Harnett people by talking with them—and above all by listening to them. Especially significant was the garrulous yarn spinner Dan Hugh McLean, known through the region as the War Horse of the Cape Fear; from him Green took copious notes and thus absorbed not only specific facts but also rich insights. Sometimes the playwright wrote of events that he could remember in precise detail. Other times, the playwright wrote of people inspired by real Harnett characters described for him by McLean and others; and these "people" are engaged in events that never happened as such, but their "fictional" actions are the logical extensions of the chain of occurrences set in motion by actions true to the character of the "real" people who inspired Harvey Easom's "creations." As historian C. Vann Woodward put it when looking back at the literary work of his own friends and contemporaries in this era—Robert Penn Warren and Paul Green, whom he knew well, and Donald Davidson and Allen Tate and William Faulkner, whom he knew only causally—such work is not the "historical novel," that is, such work is not the fictional treatment of real characters. Instead, it is filled with "historical consciousness," that is, "literature conscious of the past in the present" and literature true to place and to time.[20]

A tone emerges from these early works, and the tone comes through Harvey Easom from his Little Bethel. There is fatalism, and an accompanying dark humor. There is a sense of tight-knitting in the fabric of the community, but that tight-knitting includes some oddly colored threads that are woven into some strange patterns. There is a compassion for the sinner who will remain thus a part of the "sacred circle"[21] despite his transgressions; but there is also some deep cruelty to those who are described as "queer" (in that earlier era a term denoting any eccentricity without specific connotations about sexuality or sexual preferences). There is a frankness about sexuality and its related sensualities that does not fit the bourgeois moralism usually associated with the late Victorians; but of course no one in that place is really bourgeois. On the other hand, sexuality, while fully acknowledged, is usually punished (often by its own logical consequences), thereby reaffirming some traditional Calvinist attitudes about the virtues of sexual restraint and the vices of sexual freedom. The final tone, given by those Green walked with and talked with, is a sense of dark comedy with as many tears as laughs, and a hard-won understanding declared by the ancient Hebrew as recorded in Ecclesiastes: "For in much wisdom is much grief; and he that increaseth knowledge increaseth sorrow."[22]

Whether all southern writers of this era can be so described is not the issue here: this specific poet and playwright, Paul Green, wrote what *he was* and what his fellow Harnett countrymen were. The crucial distinction between Green and his relatives and his friends is in his conscious abstracting: he began to make a literature out of what he saw and heard and felt. And this deliberate choice immediately sucked him into another enveloping irony: authors were told, especially in the classical tradition then regnant, to be detached, to step back in order to observe, to rise above the villages, and, in William Butler Yeats's fine phrase, to "cast a cold eye on life, on death."[23]

In trying to do these things, Green turned loose his powerful imagination, but he found that he was then only that much more deeply *in* his creation, which was not his creation at all, but the Harnett where he grew up. In trying to step back, he had instead stepped more deeply inside; in seeking to abstract, he had made things as concrete and as particular as any remembered "reality." Like the Croatans who wandered through, Green believed what he saw and saw what he believed, and he, like they, sometimes believed things that professional social scientists did not and do not and cannot credit; and he, like them, definitely saw and believed things that the fervent urban boosters of the self-styled New South refused to believe or even to acknowledge seeing. In trying to be objective, to take notes and to document and to put distance between himself and what he observed, Green actually became more subjective, more deeply involved. His art would become just as entangled in his political agenda as his memories and on-site observations would become entangled with his imaginings. Able neither to leave nor to stay, Green would do both at once, taking Harnett with him wherever he went, even as he kept the outside world of the artist firmly in his head while hoeing, plowing, pulling fodder, seeding tobacco, or hauling kindling. For some, this subjectivity and deep involvement of art with agenda is a weakness in any artist and especially in Green. Surely these things troubled Green about himself; and he was in all cases, as we have begun to note, a deeply troubled man. But this entangling of the remembered with the imagined was his personal strength; it was what lent his plays their verisimilitude of detail and their undeniable moral power and their sense of profound energy. Unknown youth or éminence grise, this man cared.

1923–1925

Paul and Lib Green set up housekeeping on Greenwood Road in Chapel Hill. Close by the university, the road led into the campus proper, and it was aptly named, for it was shaded by tall, evergreen pine trees and even by some of the robust piedmont hardwoods that Green had seldom seen back in the upper valley of the Cape Fear River. Lib Green in particular had a challenging role to play on Greenwood Road, and she not only played it, but brought it off with élan. No longer able to do much creative writing for herself, this most talented of Proff Koch's first class of Carolina Playmakers consciously made her own career secondary to her husband's. She wrote words for music in plays, she helped with "concepts," she edited story lines, she checked facts, and she helped with research. He was careful to credit her specific contributions on title pages, but she was really more than an occasionally credited coauthor or collaborator. She was coconspirator in everything that he wrote and every political stance that he took from 1923 onward.

Too, she became a New South hostess extraordinaire, a striking irony given her Yankee background and upbringing and her disdain for cooking, cleaning, and the other oddments of housekeeping. Moreover, the Greens were young and enjoyed few financial resources other than the assistant professor's salary and a share of farm income from the Green family's lands in Harnett County. Still and all, Lib Green organized social gatherings at their home for writers and other artists and for reformists and political activists. By the middle of the 1920s, the household had become the required place to visit for artists and reformists, literati, and hangers-on who were coming through the central piedmont. A series of maids and cooks tended house while Lib Green coordinated activities and events. Often she gave parties, but even more often people just "dropped by." Most often, Paul Green brought somebody by the house, generally unannounced.[1]

These tasks never seemed to weary Lib Green, and it is a remarkable story. Part of her success is that she obviously enjoyed all the company; visitors quickly saw that the woman with the brilliant eyes and the brilliant red hair was endowed equally with a brilliant mind. This child of seafarers and settlers had been denied her European trip in 1922, and she missed her travels, but at least she could talk with these travelers who came through. Certainly the visitors hailed from interesting places. Yet her accomplishments remain extraordinary, whatever pleasures they gave her. There was Paul Eliot Green Jr. (born 14 January 1924) to bring up, and by summer of 1925 she would be pregnant with their second child (Nancy Byrd Green, born 25 February 1926), but somehow she could entertain the many guests without in any way ignoring the needs of the children. In addition, her husband would have to travel extensively in pursuit of his playwriting career, and thus often Lib Green would be alone with the babies for long weeks at a time.

During those years on Greenwood, she would somehow juggle the roles of wife, mother, hostess, editor, and coauthor. But with a particularly strange twist of plot, Paul Green, the onetime army clerk, county auditor's assistant, and organization bookkeeper, could not find the time to keep properly the books for his family's strapped and very complicated finances. Lib Green stepped into the unexpected and inexplicable breach and balanced the books adroitly. After all, there was a farm operation, there was an academic's salary, there was an editor's compensation, and there were royalties. Generally, these disparate sources, even taken all together, were barely equal to the many expenses, but she kept the books for all of these activities. And her husband wrote in his diary about *his* attempt to ride two horses!

Thus supported by his wife at home and by professors at his university, Paul Green was all set to join the literary movement in the region. It would be named the southern literary renaissance by a friend of his, Frances Newman, whom he sponsored in a "small magazine" that he ran. (An interesting aspect of his role in the period is his help and publicity given other writers.) In particular, he used his own small magazine to issue a call for a new literature that concerned itself with "The Real South."[2]

Green deplored the sentimental, even soggy, qualities of most of the available literature about North Carolina and the rest of the South. What he wanted, he said often, was not a literature about the self-conscious Old South with a romance of the stone of the Lost Cause, nor a literature of the self-proclaimed New South of industrial entrepreneurs who refused to look at the injustices of racism, sexism, abuse of labor, and destruction of the environment. His plain statement was starkly political: art must deal with injustice, and both the injustice and the "rightest" kind of literature constitute the Real South.

For him, literature about the Real South must focus on the denizens of the deep woods of eastern Carolina as the subjects of both art and politics. Such a focus sharpened the view of race and color and caste. Blackness. Whiteness. Brownness. High Yellow. Passing. The mixing of these peoples. They were the denizens, and they were still around. They wouldn't be denizens if they disappeared. Most lived as before, but among them were some restless people who would not sit and smile through it all any longer. These attracted Green's attention. They wanted things. Perhaps there had always been that wanting, but now he could not ignore it—or them. "Freedmen" of both genders complained about damnable Jim Crow, and they reached for that good life that seemed so close for all southerners at the very end of the Great War. Sometimes their aspirations seemed so funny, because so clumsily incongruous, that he had to laugh wearily, with the comedian's germane hopelessness, at the distance between a character's ideals and his or her real life. From such stuff came *The No 'Count Boy* and *The Old Man of Edenton,* one-act dark comedies that drew on the Harvey Easom account. Other times, the undeniable sense of the injustice in southern Jim Crow was so with him that Green could only treat it as a tragedy "clear to the b-b-b-bone," as the piedmont blues singers put it. In that tragic form were *Sam Tucker* and *White Dresses* and eventually *In Abraham's Bosom;* and these were also drawn down from Harvey Easom's diary and collection of poems. As noted, rudimentary versions of these early works show up in his various notes as early as 1920; and throughout these first years of his appointment as philosophy professor, Green rewrote and rewrote these plays. In many ways, they are the very best things that he ever did.[3]

In all of these works, Green was concerned with people who lived in spiritual no-man's land: reluctant to enter the trenches dug for either black or white people, the denizens charged across dangerous territory, usually without making it into enemy land; and if they did make it, they found themselves again trapped in trenches new to them but actually dug long ago. To laugh or to cry while looking at such subjects was not much of an accomplishment for a competent playwright. But to laugh in genuine sympathy *with* such subjects was almost impossible for a white southerner whose daddy owned land and was lord of tenants. Nevertheless this survivor of the wartime trenches did so, and in a way that made Hungarian playwright Andar Garvay compare him to Molière.[4]

Whether tragic or comic in form, each play in this era is fatalistic, with a sad, even chalky, undertaste. Like Harvey Easom and Paul Green, one cares for all these people; but like the creature creator and the creator creature, we readers cannot do much for them except to open our eyes to the fact that they are sentient human beings: cut them, and they bleed; break their hearts, and they cry. Even and especially so simple and so decent a thing as to grant that a mulatto woman or a Croatan (Lumbee) man had feelings about their failures, even this, for most white Carolinians in 1922, was "yar to seek"; and Green strained at the task of making his readers see and hear and feel.

His subjects were farmers, preachers, teachers, and outlaws, and in every case these eastern Carolinians struggle to make moral sense of their lives in the midst of economic changes. The ethnography of the upper valley's rural peoples—Scots, African Americans, Croatans—fascinated the playwright, and their marginalism and their multiculturalism gave him a counterpoint to national assumptions about the "fit subjects of art," namely, the prospering white bourgeoisie beset with emotional instead of economic burdens. In these plays black peasants are deeply spiritualistic, but they seek the white world's material treasures; and in that futile seeking they grow dissatisfied with their traditional God. White peasants of the same countryside are lured by the same material treasures, and they also strain against the trammels imposed by their traditional God. Neither group of peasants can escape the judgment of the traditional God, and neither group can win the pearl of great price in the ungodly world of progress, machinery, technology, and materialism. Yet neither black nor white peasant can offer up an Augustinian or any other confession and thereby return to the bosom of Abraham, even if only to be properly punished. After all, they have left the old tribe for good reasons, but they cannot get into the new tribe, for they are excluded by law and by custom. All that they can do is wander. Mulattos, who are black and white, and Croatans, who are Indian and black and white, are particularly victimized by the crossfire coming from plural, antagonistic regional histories and by the tragedies wrought by genetics.[5]

The subject was miscegenation, the cultural, really political, expressions of the physical mixing among African Americans, Scots, Irish, English Americans, and various Indians. Croatans, the ultimate marginalists, embodied all of these groups, and yet lived apart as a separate entity. They had their own schools, recognized as such by state and local laws, and they had their own churches and music and food and stories; and in both legal and practical terms they occupied a position lower than that of whites but higher than that of blacks. They were seldom recognized as Indians by professional anthropologists, and of course the dominant Native American group of North Carolina, the Cherokees, insisted that Croatans were not Indians. Yet there they were, copper-skinned, nappy-haired, high-cheekboned, often blue-eyed, and with broad foreheads and even broader country-Carolina accents. Living all over the valley of the Cape Fear, they were clustered in the upper valley, with an especially concentrated population in Robeson County, south of Harnett. They stubbornly declined to disappear by blending in with white people or with black people. Above all, they were the obvious and undeniable fact of sexual and cultural mixing, the indisputable proof that black folk and white folk and red folk were attracted to one another.

Although Robeson County was heavily Croatan and thus something of a cultural rallying point for them, the huge county often called the state inside the state was still dominated economically by Presbyterian Scot landowners, especially the McLean family, which would produce a North Carolina governor. If the Croatans did not have a fully recognized place in society and if they did not have a fully recognized place in the Robeson geography, they did have a hero, Henry Berry Lowrie, appropriately also a marginal figure. And this man became subject of Paul Green's first successful student play for the Carolina Playmakers.

This play, called *The Last of the Lowries,* he would revise and publish in 1925 in the collection *The Lord's Will.* To write it, he took Robeson folk history, the tale of Robin Hood, something of John Millington Synge's *Riders to the Sea,* and Harvey Easom's observation that Croatans were compelled to wander much as were the biblical Aramaians. During Reconstruction in the first half of the 1870s, there was a Lowrie gang of Croatans in the swampy region of the huge cotton and tobacco county, and these family members fought for "colored rights" in a sort of *Back at you, whitey!* politicized violence that was a mirror to the negrophobic and Indian-targeted abuse by the Ku Klux Klan, Red Shirts, and other organized terrorist groups whose goal was to keep blacks and Croatans from voting, seeking office, or even making much of a living. The Lowries sometimes defended people of color against white attacks, and they were said to give money and other support on occasion to the poor farmers among the minority ethnic groups (who actually were the majority numerically in Robeson County). The Lowries generally harassed conservative white authorities with quick-strike guerrilla tactics, just as the Carolina Klan harassed Reconstruction authorities with such tactics. The historical figure who was actually "last of the Lowries" was Steve Lowrie, according to the notes of local historian Mary C. Norment; but Henry Berry Lowrie was the most famous of the swamp-riding gang, and Green simplified and dramatized this history by combining and compacting the dominant leader's career and character with that of the very last gang member.[6]

As to development of theme, the insightful drama student Grant Herbstruth points out that Synge's theme of mortal helplessness in the face of natural forces is echoed but redirected: where Synge's riders are killed by drowning in the irresistible sea, Green's riders are killed by the human and the political, by the irresistible white authorities.[7] The populists of the 1890s ride offstage, left, with the author here, albeit a little too soon for the actual Lowries and a little too late for Paul Green; but at just the right time, and in just the right tone, for Harvey Easom.

Although his plays about Lumbees and other denizens of the eastern woodlands were intriguing in their own right, it is Harvey Easom's "Negro dialect" notes and "Negro songs" and Paul Green's "Negro plays" that most compel attention, especially as those sources are revealed in *The No 'Count Boy* and *In Abraham's Bosom,* each of which won major critical recognition and which together established Paul as an integral part of the southern literary renaissance in its earliest moments. Yet again it is miscegenation that draws in and then fixes the attention of the boy observer and the young playwright. That yearning toward each other, that integrationist impulse that is expressed sexually, gives the lie at once to Jim Crow for white supremacists and to black separatism for those African Americans who insist on separate spheres.

One reason that Green could write so affectingly about the issue is that it tore at him: he was in this era by no means at peace with "the race question," and was himself a morass of contradictions about blacks. There is a rawness and an edge to each of these plays, and he is here more than anywhere else the insider/outsider: he could reach into his own personhood to feel and to express the desire of the country farmer to teach and to write and thus to have the city boys sit up and take notice; but he could reach into those same personal emotions to feel and to express the refusal of white people to accept such strivings among the black denizens, and he could go to the same place to feel and to express the on-again, off-again, pat-on-the-back-that-just-might-hold-you-back white emotions when a light-skinned mulatto grabbed for Harvey's dream, even and especially because the grasp was in that case so likely to be within reach—except that eventually all such aspirations would be blocked by racist intervention.

In his comedy *The No 'Count Boy,* the first of his prize plays, Green uses the unlikely device of comedy to examine "Negro degradation" in a harsh environment. Pheelie is an adolescent farm girl with dreams, those dreams recently intensified by focus on some dime-store romance stories. She dreams in particular of travel, especially travel far away from the unremitting demands of a tenant farm. It is Sunday, and "her beau Enos" has come to take her for an early ride before morning church services. Although her attachment to Enos is tenuous at best, he pulls her toward him in at least a figurative sense by describing in concrete detail the particularities of the farmhouse that he plans for their married days. These images are broken by the sudden appearance of an enticing wanderer, a "no 'count boy" who is too physically slight and too mentally unfocused to do farm chores. He plays a mouth organ, and he offers to earn a meal by entertaining with his music and with his tales of wide-flung travels.

Enos is annoyed, vaguely threatened, and anxiously on his guard against this potential rival. Pheelie is at once charmed, and she confirms Enos's worst dreads when she makes plans to "hit the road" alongside this creative fellow. But before anything can develop, an old African American woman—she could be Granny Boling, or she could be Pheelie herself in old age—comes on the scene to capture her errant son. Dragging him by his ear, she hauls him back to the farm, revealing in the processes by body language and attitude that this young man has never traveled very far after all. The "no 'count boy" cries for Pheelie, and she cries for herself, brought as she is to the reality of Enos and the old woman and an inescapable fate that she will live into her own old age on a farm with her practical, even antiromantic, beau.[8]

The No 'Count Boy is funny, especially if the wanderer's mother plays her role with a convincing pastiche of the practical mom and the petty tyrant. Yet, as in the best of Green's early work, the laughter leaves an aftertaste of hopelessness and pointlessness, the more so as playwright, director, and actors force an audience to realize that black girls have dreams, as do all girls. That the dream itself is not only futile but of no intrinsic value is the sad twist of the comic resolution. There is no brooding physical presence of a man tyrant here: Enos could "get ugly" and rearrange a body frame if cornered, but he is here restrained, even though anxious. The iron law of the African American's permanent station on a tenant farm will enforce the status quo soon enough, without Enos's having to whip his girl or her suitor. This good and decent practical fellow, himself a victim of the political economy, and the hard-working old woman have each made their separate peace with the way southern country things are. As Wystan Hugh Auden says in another context, there is no satire here, for satire is "angry and optimistic"; rather, there is the comedian's celebration of the low humor in the midst of high expectations, a celebration that also accepts pessimistically the incurable nature of the state of being.[9]

Played another way, the "Negro plight" angers and inspires rebellion, even revolution. In this key, however, the play makes the audience laugh, not mockingly at Pheelie's condition, but emphatically *with* her, for we are all doomed to go nowhere exciting and to do nothing entertaining. Much of the time, Green was in this wry, comic, fey mood, and he refined the comedy until it became a very useful little device for African American comedic talents. He could take it far from its eastern Carolina origins and still make it work, especially because the roles allowed African American actors to move beyond stereotypes of stale conventions. Instead, Green let them produce a comedy with nuance and resonance rather than slapstick. It was performed well by actors from Chicago's Studio Players and in the Dallas Little Theater. In fact, the Dallas group eventually entered competitions and won the Belasco Cup in May 1925 for their performance at the Wallack Theater.

Yet, pessimistic, even clinically depressed, as he sometimes was about some things down home, Green also had another side, the unaccepting, angry, protesting, radical side; and that side of him he expressed in the evolving Sam Tucker/Abraham McCrannie tragedy of black male aspirations.

Green took all these elements of the shadow diary, elements of these plays reviewed, elements of the playwright Synge and Proff Koch and the poets Masefield, Fitzgerald, and McNeill, and he produced a compound, which he called *Sam Tucker*. He published it in Boston's *Poet Lore* of 1923. He would revise *Sam Tucker,* change the name of his mulatto protagonist to Abraham McCrannie, and produce *Your Fiery Furnace* later the same year, publishing that version in his collection *The Lonesome Road*. Over the next two years, he would refine and distill elements of these plays until he had *In Abraham's Bosom*.

He features a black woman who dreams of the good life for her favored son, but now he is writing tragedy. The Tucker materfamilias, called Muh Tuck, has been alternately raped and pampered by the white landowner, Mr. Tucker. In the Old South pattern Mr. Tucker is the head of the Abramic household, that is, he and his land dominate an extended white family that includes the conjugal unit and many cousins, but he also dominates an extended "shadow family" of the black Tuckers, and he is both literal father to Muh Tuck's Sam and figurative father to her own community of people. As Bertram Wyatt-Brown and Orville Vernon Burton show about such Abramic fathers of the Old South, Mr. Tucker demands personal loyalty and uses control of the land, and control of the unfree labor that works the land, to enforce his wishes. Honor is demanded by Mr. Tucker, and those in both extended families who give him what he wants enjoy the refracted honor of the contented paterfamilias. Thus, Muh Tuck once, and occasionally later, enjoys favors from her raper/lover and part-time protector. Thus, Sam Tucker, son of Mr. Tucker, is taught to read and to write and is encouraged to make something of himself. On the other hand, shame is the weapon of enforcement, the punishment laid on those who cross or get ugly with or otherwise offend the Abramic paterfamilias, and Muh Tuck is often reminded that she played the whore and does not deserve a legally sanctioned husband in her family, that she is, finally, only a shadow bedroom among many mansions. Too, Sam is reminded, usually wordlessly, that he is not only "wrong side of the sheets" in the marital bed, but is also half black, and thus, in the eyes of this prejudiced world, he is no more than half a man. Withal, as Wyatt-Brown demonstrates redundantly, the whole Abramic household in its "primitive" and "tribal" system of traditional honor is also one of violence, for a man's greatest shame is to be bested in a fight, a woman's greatest shame is to be "taken" or "cut" in a primal rape. [10] All of the Old South patterns are here, and in the early twentieth century a postbellum harshness was added, as industrialization and urbanization came near the scene and as the white fathers brooded over losing the Civil War. It is these historic themes that produce the Tucker blood on the play's Carolina moon.

Wiley Boy, the playboy from Granny Boling, reappears, cast now as the child of Sam and his wife, Mallie. Sam is a cropper and a schoolteacher whose household wall sign proclaims, "We are rising." His current project is to found the Cape Fear Training School for Negroes; but he has grander dreams of integrating schools and workplaces. This son Wiley, on his birth, was "dedicated" by the crusading father Sam "to the cause of the Negro," but, as Wiley Boy has matured, he has "dedicated" himself only to sporting sex. Green notes that the son is "pitifully incapable of fulfilling the character envisioned by his father." Eventually, Sam disowns Wiley Boy, banishing him from the house despite the protests of grandmother Muh Tuck and mother Mallie Tucker. The play's action starts when Sam goes off to a planning session for his training school; after he leaves for the meeting, Wiley Boy slips in and enjoys a reunion with Muh Tuck, the two singing old playful songs as Muh is led to confess with both pride and shame: "You 'herited my spo'ting blood!" Right after that revelation, Mallie returns from her work as maid and cook for a local white family. Although pleased to see her son Wiley, Mallie is drawn up short by the call of one of Paul Green's hoot owls sounding his portentous note deep in the dismal swamp beyond the house.[11]

Sam returns early from his meeting, bruised from two encounters with white people. A gang of racist toughs, perhaps tipped off by Wiley Boy, had interrupted Sam's speech and beat him up, ending the rally for Cape Fear Training School. Leaving the scene of that shaming assault, Sam has met his half brother, the white son of Mr. Tucker and the one from the "right side of the bed sheets." This Mr. Tucker, now himself the lord of labor and land and cotton for this Abramic family, stopped Sam to talk about this year's crop, doing so in an abusive and chiding way. Sam, never one to hold his temper and long jealous of his half brother, answered the verbal assault with physical blows and killed him. He now returns home, intent on saving Mallie and Muh Tuck.

In his own house he begs his people to escape the lynch mob that he knows is already on its way. Muh Tuck and Wiley Boy of the sporting life do indeed run to safety, but Mallie remains at Sam's side. As the gang rides up, Sam steps into the doorway to provide a target, and the expected shooting resolves the conflict between white and black and ends the story. What fascinated Green here was the way that the black-white conflict is as much internal and individual and psychological within Sam himself as it is external and collective and political. Sam struggles against more than external racism and damnable Jim Crow: he struggles against the whiteness in himself. The playwright/poet wrote for the Boston magazine: "One senses by the wide nostrils and sensuous lips that the journey to greatness would be through a mighty struggle with self. It would be guessed that reason and feeling are at continuous war within him and that when passion is in possession he is dangerous. With a kindly environment, perhaps the reasonableness of his nature would have led him to accomplishments and peace."[12]

Perhaps. But the playwright's fatalism is never environmental or behaviorist, and he once again insists in revealing a tragic flaw "clear to the b-b-bone" in the protagonist. He says also that Sam Tucker's "tragedy is not altogether the tragedy of the Negro in a white man's world; his failure ultimately lies within himself, attributable to his shortcomings as a human being. If Sam had not been a Negro the chances are that he would still have had to face the same obstacles that would bring about his tragic failure."[13] None of that hopelessness in the human condition draws the sting away from the racism, poverty, and violence in Mr. Tucker's families. The will to resist, hopeless or otherwise, outlives everything else, as this dialogue reveals:

> *Muh Tuck:* God made de white to allus be beddern de black.
> *Sam Tucker:* It's the man that lasts. [14]

If the man lasts, then his message lasts. But Green wanted no less that this play last. And to last, it must be rewritten. Thus, he revised and revised, tightening thematic focus and clarifying elements of the plot to make an effective one-act melodrama that still offered believable, and recognizable, human emotions. Above all, he wanted to make the audience see a man's tragedy, with a man in a double bind, strapped by overweaning personal ambition and by the racism of the region. And he wanted all characters to be sympathetic, for all in the family are to some extent victims, not only of racism but also of the black paterfamilias's impatient and uncompromising drive toward unreachable goals. A deceptively simple renaming changed things overwhelmingly. In renaming Sam Tucker Abraham, Green in a stroke restored the region's biblical language and its familial structure, for it was the Abramic household that produced the miscegenation/segregation, the hot/cold paternalism, the man-centered identities; and the Abramic household was thus the focal point for questions about power, authority, and justice—and the answer to the resolution of the conflict. As a fillip to better comprehension of his themes, he gave Abraham the Scottish surname *McCrannie,* and thereby vouchsafed at once the Celtic and the Presbyterian, the unrestrained and the penny-pinching, the dreamy and the canny that was in the people throughout the upper valley of the Cape Fear River, regardless of their skin color.

Two more renamings help: Abraham's wife becomes Goldie, a name that suggests both her mulatto (or, in southern race-talk, "high yellow") status and her allure because of rare, somewhat elusive, perhaps overly precious qualities; and the son Wiley Boy, still a spo'tin' man, becomes Douglass, a heroic clan name such as a romantic Scot and a romantic racial reformist would lay on his son. As for plot and theme, Douglass's actions are easy to decipher: "[F]rom the moment of [his] entrance we know for sure that he has tipped off the gang as to Abraham's meeting." [15] On the other hand, Douglass's hard task, to be the mantle bearer of racial uplift and the restorer of family prerogative, is more obviously overwhelming than the vaguer tasks ascribed Wiley Boy. Too, the precipitant of Douglass's revengeful betrayal is more charitably drawn: he did not go to the authorities, but rather was sought out by them because a white man thought that Douglass may have recognized and could identify *him.* Finally, Douglass has a more fully developed sense of moral responsibility for consequences than did Wiley Boy. He sees what his revenge has done, he owns his crimes, and he breaks down and begs his father's forgiveness.

Another small, but valuable, change explains something about the Cape Fear River upper-valley history and mythos as those things were left probed but unproven in *Prayer Meeting*, where this family is first encountered. We learn the fate of Angie, another doomed rebel who was done in by the deadly admixture of spo'tin' life and political ambitions; Angie, as he was being led away by the sheriff, had turned on the officer and attacked him with a knife, and for this action he was lynched. The trace of this previous tale reminds the audience of family and regional histories, and it also portends Abraham's fate in this script.

As for Abraham, his actions and the consequences for them are very much his own. It is his speech in protest of Angie's lynching that has brought the white furies down on him. Furthermore, Green here focuses the melodrama by spelling out the simultaneous resolution of conflict, enduring theme, and conclusion of plot. When Abraham realizes that the lynch mob is on his land, he opens the door, calls for freedom for his people, and is shot dead in mid-sentence. Robert Burns could say, "This was a man, . . . and a man for a' that and a' that and a' that." The contemporary social scientist could say, This was an agent, autonomous and assertive, no passive victim, but an agent, for a' that and a' that.

Late in 1924 Paul and Lib Green agreed to take on still another project, the editorship of *The Reviewer*, a fine magazine that had been started in Richmond in 1921 and immediately cut an impressive figure. Right from the start of their editorship, the Greens faced financial and personnel matters with *The Reviewer* that were decidedly discordant, but these discordant notes were played far beneath the surface harmony of the magazine in 1924 and 1925. It was after all a writer's magazine in the flush days of the self-announced southern literary renaissance, and it was avowedly avant-garde and even reckless. There was excitement, and Green increased the excitement in his personal appearances at different venues where poets gathered in North Carolina and with his editorial "plain statement" calling for a new literature of a Real South.[16]

Art is about truth, says the impassioned editor, and thus plain speaking, especially in verse, is the stuff of beautiful writing. Green's aesthetic, then, is a moral one, and it was always communal rather than individual. He demanded of a regional art that it treat honestly of real people, adopting the idiom of their lives rather than the psychic agenda of the artist. Such art he had learned about from Proff Koch: It must be fundamentally useful and practical, but it could be so only where real people were the moral subjects telling their own stories their way instead of fancified objects having their stories told for them. The artist is thus a special amanuensis whose two greatest talents are keen observation and clear translation between the subjects and the audience. All of this suggests that a moral teaching occurs in art, and such didacticism Green readily accepted, albeit with an emphasis peculiar to Proff Koch: everybody taught and everybody learned in this artistic process, but it was the privileged middle class who sat in the audience who had the most to learn and the peasant subjects who had the most to teach.[17]

This plain statement signaled an important editorial departure from the norm. Well-known writers were surprised to have their solicited verse returned with critical remarks and sometimes even marked "unavailable." Some, such as Du Bose Heyward, Josephine Pinckney, and Archibald Rutledge, became enthusiasts of *The Reviewer* and of its energetic editor. Others, likely the majority, simply noted the fact that they could make a lot more money for a lot less work and still receive wider notice by sending their verse elsewhere. It was thus always the struggling aspirants who were most devoted to *The Reviewer,* and they provided at once the bulk of the submissions and the majority of the paying subscribers. Since even the obviously talented Allen Tate, Donald Davidson, Julia Peterkin, and Frances Newman were then still struggling to establish and to hold an audience, *The Reviewer*'s importance is underscored. This was especially so because *The Fugitive,* a magazine once produced in Nashville by a group of talented writers and thinkers associated with Vanderbilt University, had ceased publication and there were very few other regional outlets available to southern writers in 1925 when national publications remained skeptical about the movement.[18]

Certainly the Greens took chances and accepted the consequences of the risks. They threw the pages open to literary and graphics offerings from feminists, from advocates of civil rights for blacks, and from socialists and laborites. More pointedly, Paul Green aggressively pursued and then showcased opinion pieces by the same kinds of dissidents. Although he was learning as much as he was teaching, and he was growing as much as he was inspiring, Green in working with this project was moving himself and others farther and farther leftward, especially on the issues of racial and sexual roles. Carefully highlighted pieces by the African American Benjamin Brawley concerning racial violence and major feminist statements by Frances Newman and Sara Haardt drive home the point that *The Reviewer* under Paul Green's editorship, and specifically because of Paul Green's editorship, was lending a decidedly radical cast to the cultural awakening in the region.[19]

Of course, *The Reviewer* pages were also deliberately wide open to other perspectives as well, including the nonfeminist male artists Archibald Rutledge and Donald Davidson. Thus, quite a lot was going on in the editorial offices, both in the professor's cubbyhole on campus and at the rambling home where Paul and Lib Green did much of their critical analysis and blue-pencil work. Yet, even as *The Reviewer* reached a peak in its quality, the playwright was becoming very restive. He longed to specialize in teaching what he knew best, but he also longed to write all the time.

In spite of the many conflicting demands on his time, Green's writing was going well. He had placed just enough stories and one-act plays in just enough regional publications, and *The Reviewer* itself was just well enough known among writers, that the influential critics and writers H. L. Mencken, Louis Untermeyer, Carl Van Vechten, Du Bose Heyward, James Branch Cabell, Emily Clark, and Proff Koch could persuade other writers and critics to look closely at this emerging writer and thinker Paul Green (and they were looking at the fine work of Elizabeth Green, the editor and consultant, too, but did not know it). In fact, it was this spring of 1925 that New York theater critics awarded Green's *No 'Count Boy* the Belasco Cup for new drama; and in that same season the publishing house Henry Holt had arranged to print a collection of his "negro dialect stories."

Not surprisingly, then, Green came to the attention of Barrett Harper Clark, the quick-witted and energetic critic, essayist, and literary agent for Samuel French, a publishing house that enjoyed virtual monopoly over the production rights of plays. This savvy professional agent would develop a long and deep friendship and partnership with Paul and Lib Green, and his first and wisest advice rendered early in 1925 was that the playwright focus his talents on playwriting rather than on teaching and editing. Clark pointed to his own recent success with Eugene O'Neill, with whom he often compared Paul Green; and the agent could effectively and believably describe the working lives of professional playwrights and other writers, always making the point that the best writers lived by their pens rather than trying to do many other tasks.[20]

Others, at all levels, including many writers who desperately needed the forum provided by *The Reviewer,* gave Paul and Lib Green related advice: even if the magazine had to die, the couple needed to tend other fields. Emily Clark, a fine stylist in her own right who had originally run the little magazine in Richmond, reminded them that even her own wealthy husband had given up on the project as hopelessly expensive, as had such patrons of regional literature as James Branch Cabell. In any case, marketplace realities and university budgets were also heavy players in the decision about continuing *The Reviewer.* In his enthusiasm Paul Green had actually guaranteed to cover two-year deficits up to a sum of two thousand dollars, a hefty sum for an assistant professor with two children and investments in a farm in the east. At some point officials in the university quietly dropped all claims on the frantic editor, even though the scraps of financial records and the correspondence that remain both make it obvious that *The Reviewer* was running up deficits exceeding two thousand dollars.[21]

At first, Paul and Lib Green resisted the advice to focus their activities more finely on playwriting, for each recognized the "bully pulpit" afforded them by the little magazine. Nevertheless, there remained another kind of question: Where, finally, was the time and the space to do all of these many things? Each project was worthy, but taken altogether, the heroic assaults were draining creative juices and lessening the power of Paul Green's playwriting and Lib Green's songwriting and blue-pencil work on her husband's plays. The play's the thing, Shakespeare says and Proff Koch repeats. By leaving *The Reviewer,* Paul and Lib Green became professional writers without fully abandoning political activities or other concerns, such as folklore and local history.

Even so, *The Reviewer* did not quite die in the sense used here, for Paul and Lib Green transferred the editorship to their friends Jay Broadus Hubbell and William Stanley Hoole at Southern Methodist University in Dallas. With some changes, Hubbell combined much of the spirit, most of the authors, and almost all of the accepted but as yet unpublished manuscripts into *The Southwest Review,* still another important small magazine whose own brief career again underscores the fact that artistic renaissance activities occurred in every region, not just Nashville, not just Oxford, Mississippi, not just Richmond or Chapel Hill. Hubbell's magazine would often serve as a forum for Paul Green to write creative pieces, and it was very much a supporter of his poems and plays.[22]

It was time, and even past time, for *The Reviewer* to leave the university and the Greenwood Road scenes, and thus also time for the playwright in his own career to start a new act with new scenes. Yet, for all that, after 1925 the Green careers, like much of the broader cultural renaissance in their region, would be more effective—but never again quite so interesting as in those hectic days of running their little magazine.

Paul Green on the campus of the University of North Carolina, Chapel Hill, in autumn quarter of 1919. Having saved the then princely sum of one thousand dollars, the veteran of World War I bought relatively expensive clothes and so cut a figure very different from his more casually dressed and younger classmates. Courtesy of the North Carolina Collection, University of North Carolina Library at Chapel Hill.

Horace Williams, circa 1919, the legend among UNC professors in the era of World War I. Memorialized as character Ovid Pierce by Thomas Wolfe, Williams was an early benefactor of Green but later turned on him in 1929 when the playwright abandoned the study of philosophy for full-time commitments to drama. Sketch by Mary deB. Graves. Courtesy of the North Carolina Collection, University of North Carolina Library at Chapel Hill.

Elizabeth Lay (Green), 1919. The most prominent of the original Carolina Playmakers, Lib was bright and pretty as a penny. Courtesy of the Paul Green Foundation and the Paul Green Papers, Southern Historical Collection, Library of the University of North Carolina at Chapel Hill.

Action from the Pulitzer Prize-winning play *In Abraham's Bosom* (1927). At the time of the award, Green was the most prominent Broadway playwright providing serious roles for African American actors. This shot is from a 1984 production at the Café Theatre in the Allens Lane Art Center, Mt. Airy, Pennsylvania. Courtesy of the Paul Green Foundation and the Paul Green Papers, Southern Historical Collection, Library of the University of North Carolina at Chapel Hill.

New York Times line drawing, 15 May 1927, on the occasion of his receipt of the Pulitzer Price for *In Abraham's Bosom,* then "in revival" by Provincetown Players at the Provincetown. Sketch by unknown artist, identified only as Marcus. Courtesy of the North Carolina Collection, University of North Carolina Library at Chapel Hill.

Action from the Café Theatre's 1984 production of *In Abraham's Bosom*. Abraham, the illegitimate son of the patriarch, is beaten by his half brother. Courtesy of the Paul Green Foundation and the Paul Green Papers, Southern Historical Collection, Library of the University of North Carolina at Chapel Hill.

Unidentified cast members of the Carolina Playmaker's 1931 production of *House of Connelly*. From left, the characters Patsy with former Connelly slaves Big Sis and Big Sue. In the Group Theater production, Big Sis and Big Sue were typecast as figures of comedic relief; in Green's original script, as well as in his revisions for Playmakers and the Iowa City production, Big Sis and Big Sue were tragic figures of scale, proportion, and murderous resolution. Courtesy of the North Carolina Collection, University of North Carolina Library at Chapel Hill.

Green, at the top of his artistic game, on the steps of the Playmakers Theater on the UNC campus in 1931. From left, mentor and advisor Barrett H. Clark, then of the Samuel French agency; playwright Lynn Riggs, author of the play that was revised and titled *Oklahoma!*; and Paul Green. Courtesy of the North Carolina Collection, University of North Carolina Library at Chapel Hill.

Erma Lamprecht, Tante who took care of the children on the Guggenheim tour in Germany and who was then rescued from Hitler's Germany by the Greens and the Samuel French Company. Lamprecht is shown here in Chapel Hill, 1931, with Nancy Byrd Green (seated), Janet Green (on lap), and Paul Green Jr. (standing). Courtesy of the North Carolina Collection, University of North Carolina Library at Chapel Hill.

Lib Green and the children in 1932. Standing, Paul Eliot Green Jr.; on floor, Nancy Byrd Green; on lap, Janet Green; seated with Lib, Elizabeth McAllister Green. Courtesy of the North Carolina Collection, University of North Carolina Library at Chapel Hill.

Green with Frederick "Proff" Koch in 1937 at the newly opened Forest Theatre on the UNC campus. Courtesy of the North Carolina Collection, University of North Carolina Library at Chapel Hill.

Green and Richard Wright, at work during the heat of July 1941 on the playscript for the Broadway production of *Native Son*. They defied Jim Crow laws by working together in Bynum Hall on campus. Wright also spent some working time at the Green home on Greenwood Drive but spent evenings with unidentified African American families in nearby Carrboro, literally across the railroad tracks from the segregated Chapel Hill. This print appeared in *Raleigh News and Observer*, 27 July 1941. Courtesy of the North Carolina Collection, University of North Carolina Library at Chapel Hill.

Jonathan Daniels, circa 1940s. In his family's *Raleigh News and Observer,* Daniels was generally reliable in the crusade against Jim Crow, although Green occasionally had to goad and scold him to take editorial stands. Courtesy of the Jonathan Daniels Papers, Southern Historical Collection, Library of the University of North Carolina at Chapel Hill.

Scene from *The Lost Colony,* circa 1950s. Queen Elizabeth blesses Sir Walter Raleigh and his mission. Courtesy of the Samuel Selden Papers, Southern Historical Collection, Library of the University of North Carolina at Chapel Hill.

Paul and Elizabeth Green, circa 1950s. Losing status as a creative playwright, Green is entering his period of intense political campaigning against Jim Crow. Courtesy of the Paul Green Foundation and the Paul Green Papers, Southern Historical Collection, Library of the University of North Carolina at Chapel Hill.

Jonathan Daniels and Paul Green, circa 1950s. Onetime Carolina Playmakers, these two, with Thomas Wolfe, formed a tontine sealed with a fifth of sour mash liquor. Courtesy of the Jonathan Daniels Papers, Southern Historical Collection, Library of the University of North Carolina at Chapel Hill.

Portrait of Green, circa 1960, working on a
set for production. Courtesy of the North
Carolina Collection, University of North
Carolina Library at Chapel Hill.

The Old Warhorse rests during a season
of troubles on the steps of his cabin
behind the house on Greenwood Drive in
1972. He is with Mark Sumner, left, who
was vital to the staging of *The Lost Colony*
for many seasons. Courtesy of the North
Carolina Collection, University of North
Carolina Library at Chapel Hill.

Sam Ragan, circa 1980. Loyal Green protégé, the newspaper man from Raleigh and Southern Pines carried on Green's services to young writers and continued the campaign for racial justice. He encouraged and sponsored the writing of this biography. Courtesy of the Sam Ragan papers, Southern Historical Collection, Library of the University of North Carolina at Chapel Hill.

True to the end, in the final weeks of his life, Green spoke in memory of Thomas Wolfe at a gathering of the Thomas Wolfe Society, 11 April 1981. Courtesy of the North Carolina Collection, University of North Carolina Library at Chapel Hill.

Paul and Lib Green in 1978, after forty-six years of loving, campaigning, and sacrificing. Courtesy of the North Carolina Collection, University of North Carolina Library at Chapel Hill.

A set from the outdoor drama *The Lost Colony,* 1981.
Courtesy of the Samuel Selden Papers, Southern
Historical Collection, Library of the University of North
Carolina at Chapel Hill.

7 : TAKING AN EARTHLY PRIZE
1926–1928

    This most idealistic of men in the years 1926 and 1927 had his eyes turned to a very earthly prize, one having nothing to do with grand goals of racial integration and social justice. This was the Pulitzer Prize for the best original American play performed in New York, and he was told by his new friend the Samuel French agent Barrett Harper Clark that he could win it. To do so, he must become a "true pro," one dedicated to writing for the sake of writing, he must grant interviews and say certain things the right way, and he must let Clark and other prominent theater talkers do the rest. The much-labored-over *In Abraham's Bosom* was the likely candidate, and Clark was convinced that if the one-acter could only be gotten onto a New York stage, even off Broadway, it was good enough to sweep the prize. Now the difficult part: Paul Green himself had to be exhibited in New York circles, and he had to charm and win critics and reporters and sponsors and producers; and all of this must be accomplished without costing him his family-supporting job in the Carolina philosophy department—and without turning his head even as he turned his eyes. It was his caring and his sincerity that made his art work, and these qualities were easily lost on Broadway and even off Broadway.[1]

    Paul Eliot Green Jr., now deep in the phase of life styled by the pediatricians the terrible twos, grew and flourished, and, as his father said, he yelled a lot and ate a lot. On 25 February 1926 a sister had been born, and this no less healthy (and no less demanding) baby was christened Nancy Byrd Green. She, thus honored with the cherished name of Bettie Lorine Byrd Greene's Virginia folks, was called by that family name rather than Nancy. The male breadwinner had to be gone often from the home—indeed, the more often gone, the more bread won. These children became largely the mother's responsibility, for Paul Green was away from them for long stretches of time. His enforced absences worked some hardships on Lib Green, although she would be spared the abhorred cooking, cleaning, and other housework by that series of maids and cooks already marked.

    Of course, these were very typical patterns for an ambitious man of that era. Such a man "on the make" saved his wife from some work to leave her more time to be his helpmeet—performing tasks that included childrearing, book-keeping, household management, and, most important, playing host to the unremitting stream of eccentric guests. Leaving *The Reviewer* had not altered the young couple's status among regional writers, and leaving the editorial of-fices had not changed the status of Greenwood Road as *the* writers' gathering spot on the Hill. Lib Green remained the hostess for the many gatherings, including some convened when her husband was traveling and thus unavail-able as host. Paul Green did not want things to be this way; he agonized over Lib's lack of time to think and to write and to be herself, and he resolved to work harder and to earn more to give her resources. But that very resolution, in taking him farther from home for longer stretches of time, only aggravated the centrifugal forces that pulled him away.

Thus for the children Paul Jr. and Byrd, the father they called Doogie was often not there. Sometimes, it was said, he was not there in a more disturb-ing sense of the same phrase. The long working trips for the Little Theater, for university workshops, for Broadway and off Broadway, and eventually for Hollywood, put this man constantly in the company of talented and energetic young women. These were not more talented or energetic—and certainly not more attractive—than his own wife; but unlike her, they were unencumbered and unattached. That sort of company, Caro Mae Green told Lib with a nettled edge, suited her brother very well. In the fashion of the 1920s, he could play the role of the male victim, the small-town boy captivated by the songs of the big-city sirens of the Flapper Age. As Caro Mae marked it, pushing the stinger in a bit farther, this particular victim was not about to cover his ears to protect himself from such allure; and unlike Homer's hero Odysseus, he was not about to lash himself to the mast to avoid responding to the Sirens. Eventually Lib Green would reconcile herself to rumors about various women.[2] Perhaps noth-ing was happening; if it was, then she could only trust that they were sharing something "purely" or "merely" physical, and she could only trust that any trysts, if happening, were not becoming something spiritual, that such things were of the flesh and not lovemaking with mutual commitments. Too often doubts lingered. It hurt, and the reconciliation carried its own pain. In the fashion of the day, Lib Green achieved the reconciliation privately in her own soul, in her own way, and she did so without discussing it.

Trips to New York to discuss the routine of the professional play-wright forced him to confront the actual size of his ego and to be frank with himself about his emotions. Dining with Barrett Clark and sipping tea with publishers or drinking sour mash with New York playwrights, he heard how brilliant he was. He recorded that more than once he heard, "[C]ome here and be the great American playwright in two or three years." He tried to stay levelheaded, but he confessed to Lib Green, "It is so much fun to be where you can hear and see what you want, *ain't it*?" And besides the rush of blood to the brain provided by Broadway and Times Square and the resources of the New York Public Library and the experiences of Greenwich Village, there was the logistical and practical consideration that New York was the real show for anybody with a show: "[A]fter poking around it does appear the only thing to do—come here and work awhile and get into the swim." What a contrast to grading essays and preparing lectures and talking to an interesting, but small and very parochial, group of intellectuals back at the Hill: "And then the teaching," he sighed, "and staying in the hollow!"[3]

Whatever he did, he simply had to make more money at it. Mailing a royalty check for one hundred dollars, half of which was already spoken for in an arrangement with his brother Hugh to start payments for a used car and the other half of which must be proffered to the loudest of several hollering creditors, he sternly warned his wife not to write any more checks. And then he promptly changed tone: "Oh, me. I wish I could make a lot of money for my gal so she could have servants and write and enjoy the world more! I do!" He could not work any harder, but, as the professors say to M.B.A. students, he could work smarter; and working smarter inevitably entailed some moral compromises, some kowtowing and other politic game playing, some crowd pleasing, and some leavening of artistic will. And if he was very clever, and if Fortuna's wheel spun his way, he might well be a successful pro and still be the kind of man he wanted to be. "I will," he declared; but this resolution involved a lot of tension, and he knew where tension made itself manifest: "I will if my stomach doesn't kill me off too soon"; and he also kept his bottle of Luminal phenobarbital at the alert to sedate himself so that he could sleep during those evenings when severe headaches suddenly attacked.[4]

In the summer of 1926, William Archibald Green passed on out of Buies Creek and this world. At the time, his son Paul was in New York City, in the offices of the Samuel French agency, on 29 June, when the telegram about the death reached him. Crushed by the news, Green had soldiered on as a theater pro all the same, meeting his assigned rounds to discuss sets and legal matters and preparing for a trip to the Peterboro Writers Colony. Funeral arrangements were managed by others back home.

Everyone at home and in New York understood that Green could not drop everything and go home, but their kind assurances did not help him when he at last fell into a fitful sleep. On the twenty-ninth he endured a terrifying dream about Papa's returning from the grave to the farm. In the dream an obviously dead but irresistible Papa forced his way into the house demanding his supper. Berating his sons John, Hugh, and Paul, he actually smote daughters Caro Mae and Erma, marking the rebellious artistic women with an irreparable ghoulish disfigurement. Perhaps Papa's ghost could not take his rightful rest with Bettie

Green until Paul Green took his rightful place back on the farm. Perhaps Papa's ghost needed nourishment. There were many ways to apprehend this thickly layered nightmare, but however one puzzles it through, it does shout at us that Green was hardly at peace with his father's death, and that he was especially unresolved in his own choices made and actions taken during and immediately after that death.[5]

"Here, catch this casket, it is worth the pains," Jessica says in the playwright's *Merchant of Venice*.[6] That casket was both a small jewel box and a symbol of a funereal box; and everything theatrical now seemed a casket in those multilayered senses. Paul had caught the casket, and he now had the pains. His new friends the pros would help him decide that it was worth the pains.

Of all the new friends, it was Barrett Clark who was the truest pro and the truest friend. Clark became the mentor and the exemplar of the theater pro. Although never technically his agent, Clark was the man who ran Green's career in its early phases, and he was the man responsible for the critical notice that Green received almost at once after turning pro. After all, it was he who knew well—and who knew how to talk to—the important New York critics and publicists Brooks Atkinson and Robert Burns Mantle, both of whom became early and loud champions of Paul Green. In the most redolent of ironies, this pro's pro was himself at heart the amateur, the lover of art for the sake of art, and a man who would eventually decide that his own Samuel French casket was not worth the pains.

The Samuel French agent had first taken up correspondence with the promising writer in June 1925. That note began with a pro forma announcement of the pleasure that the Samuel French Company took from publishing Green's script *The Man Who Died at Twelve O'Clock* in an anthology of plays by new authors. The anthology paid each contributor twenty-five dollars, a tidy sum in those days; and, more to the point, any subsequent production, even by an amateur and nonprofit troupe, carried a five-dollar fee to be split evenly between firm and playwright. There followed an equally formulaic request for patience because "The Director . . . is asking you to give him a few more days regarding the play 'In Aunt Mahaly's Cabin,'" which the Carolinian had recently submitted. But then came a very different message:

> And now I must tell you, on my own behalf, and not as a publisher's reader, how deeply impressed I have been by your plays. The two I have recommended to French's are recommended on the grounds of being quite unobjectionable from the point of view of sex. The "house" must be particularly careful in this regards [*sic*] as the play must appeal to churches and schools. In regard to your plays, I find in them qualities discoverable in few other American plays known to me: a poetry, and sense of situation grasped, and a mastery of technical means which are in the possession

of only half a dozen of our best native playwrights. My enthusiasm for your work is absolutely sincere and I beg you to believe me when I say that works like "The End of the Row," "Sam Tucker" [an early version of *In Abraham's Bosom*], and "The Hot Iron" will make their mark in our contemporary theatre. . . . Any publisher who publishes these plays should consider himself very fortunate indeed. Whether the plays can be widely acted or not is, of course, a practical consideration. One thing is sure: they cannot fail to make interesting reading.

I hope if ever you are in New York that you will look me up, and meantime that you will be good enough to send me any other manuscripts you happen to have.[7]

These kind words were followed by actions that came quickly after Green sent in a package of manuscripts. Eight days later, Clark reported that he had arranged for Guy Holt of Robert McBride (then a major trade press) to take a serious look at Green's collection of "Negro" play scripts. And no less a Broadway producer than Arthur Hopkins was looking at *Sam Tucker* (by then renamed *In Abraham's Bosom,* but the rechristening was so recent that it was unknown to the agent) for presentation under the biggest of all theater lights in New York. In less than a month's time, Clark had arranged publication of two play scripts by French's, publication of a volume of plays by Robert McBride, and a "read through" of a script by Arthur Hopkins. It all reminded Green that Clark was not only hard-working, earnest, and sympathetic, but also a very successful pro: "Making a living," the agent said in a subsequent letter, "is something of a job (as *I* know) especially when one is doing the splendidly sincere sort of things you are doing. I don't know whether it will encourage you or not, but I prophesied the success both of Eugene O'Neill and Sidney Howard some years ago, when very few people had heard of either one of them."[8]

It seems likely that Green already knew about Clark's early sponsorship of and continuing friendship with O'Neill and Howard. In any case, he already knew other things about Clark, enough to appreciate that this was a man accustomed to getting things done by finding and nurturing writers or, in the language of the trade, stroking the talent. Clark came by these skills through a regime of paternal instruction, for his father, Solomon Henry Clark, was deadly earnest in the mission to develop a popular national culture of artistic expression.

Clark *père* collected baccalaureate degrees, but it was his studies at the University of Chicago that had most affected him. The University of Chicago was in the 1890s a place where humanities and fine arts faculty members were always engaged in teleological "conversations" that brokered classical traditions and liberal visions. Solomon Clark taught public speaking at his alma mater for a while, but by 1896 he had become a major force in the Chautauqua School of Expression. This institution, which he served as principal on its secluded campus retreat in the New York countryside, was dedicated to educational sessions in which the most sturdily optimistic Western authorities were taught. One did not graduate with a baccalaureate degree after one of these retreats, but initiates did leave with a certified purpose to read and discuss Great Books. In addition, Chautauqua provided a so-called circuit of lecture tours, often conducted in the first person, by presenters who functioned at once as scholars of biography and as actors. Solomon Clark took great pains to dissociate Chautauqua presentations from any connotations of frivolous entertainment. Presentations and lectures, never called shows, were usually monologues, occasionally staged dialogues, and were always followed by accompanying explanations or guided discussions. Shakespeare says it is a wise father who recognizes his own son, and Solomon Clark was surely wise, at least in that vein, for by 1926 he was offering a series of Paul Green dramatic dialogues with discussions. Father and son both assured the new pro: "[I]n every case he mentions your plays and who publishes them."⁹

For his part, Clark had also earned a baccalaureate from the University of Chicago, and his course of studies had included a year abroad at the University of Paris. After some work as an actor and as a stage manager, Clark taught at his father's Chautauqua campus for eight years and also served as the editor of *Drama Magazine* while publishing a number of drama studies. In 1918 he became literary editor at Samuel French. Despite, or perhaps because of, his heavy involvement in scouting and brokering talent for the agency, he continued a steady production of drama studies and was elected to the board of directors of the Drama League of America. In all those roles Clark not only scouted the talent, not only stroked the talent, not only pumped the talent, but also pushed and pulled the talent, holding up a high standard: Write your best, and worry about good readers rather than large audiences. And more: Take chances, write different things, build a solid base of intelligent, committed readers who will only over the long run fill up the theater seats. Following his own counsel, Clark told about his personal speechifying on the circuit: "I no longer attempt to give 'popular addresses' but I am always interested in talking shop to those who are interested in the things I like." But yet, Clark said, *hold onto your wallet!*

He scolded Green like a proper Dutch uncle: Stand up for your professional entitlements and prerogatives, and don't let sweet-talking Little Theater people in Peoria or tough-talking producers on Broadway steal away any of your pro's earnings.¹⁰

One aspect of turning pro, and turning tough, was made manifest soon enough. The Gilpin Players, a black troupe in Cleveland directed by Rowenna Woodham Jelliffe, was using *The No 'Count Boy,* and they hoped to perform other Green plays. The troupe, named for Charles Gilpin, the first black actor to gain critical notice and a modicum of commercial success in the United States, was performing for residents of a settlement house and for their social workers, and they were charging no admission fees. Almost no other playwright in the 1920s was writing serious material for or about black people, and Green's plays of the era appealed to talented African Americans not only because they offered black actors and directors serious and challenging work, but also because the settings and themes were of obvious, intensely relevant, interest for black audiences. This was especially the case in settlement houses, where many newly arrived residents had come from lowland Carolina share-cropping. That a black troupe was "doing" Green, and for black audiences, brought ideological and personal gratification. Unfortunately, there was this rub: the Gilpin Players had not written to the Samuel French Company for permission to stage the play until after performances had already begun.[11]

Jelliffe had written, perhaps naively, to the Henry Holt Company after she had read *The No 'Count Boy* in a Holt volume of plays. She informed the publishers that the Gilpin Players was a nonprofit troupe performing for residents of a settlement house who were charged no admission fees; and she suggested that the author and his agents could waive claims on any royalties. She did promise full and fair credit to author and agency for the comedic creation. Eventually, this letter was forwarded to Samuel French Company, and their attorney got in touch with Jelliffe. She made sure that Green was informed fully about all the correspondence so that he would understand the nature of the performers and this theater crowd. With some pain, Green allowed the agency to seek its ten-dollar royalty fee; and he supported the company's insistence that no one could produce the play without permission secured on a royalty basis through the agency before performance. Jelliffe wrote again, pointing out that the Gilpin Players had been following the printed Henry Holt guidelines in the book of plays, had tried to secure prior permission from the published copyright holder of record, and had not at all tried to deceive or defraud anyone. In reply, with Green's concurrence, the agency sent its invoice for ten dollars. In time, a ten-dollar check was written to French's, and still later the Gilpin Players performed more Green, now according to the pro's rules. The skin was toughening, and Clark's admonition to let the agency worry about the business details Green took with deadly earnestness.[12]

The pro's work began to pay off by the summer of 1926. Until that season, there was much disappointment born of equal parts false starts and bad luck. Although Green was the committed reformist who wanted to put African Americans on stage, and although Clark was the canny pro who counseled a "big" play about "white folks," it was Clark the old pro and not Green the rookie who actually *knew* the handful of black stars. More, Clark even had to identify for Green who was the biggest, in some ways the *only,* black star after Charles Gilpin's descent into alcoholism during the middle of the decade. "Paul Robeson," Clark explained to Green, was "one of the finest negro actors" on Broadway, and "he ought to see a copy" of the revised *In Abraham's Bosom.*

Of the multitalented Robeson, Clark said that his interest and support "would mean a great deal"—even more so for Green's "black play" than would help from the legendary producer Hopkins, for, if Robeson was available, and if Hopkins could not use the play, then "I'll try other managers."[13]

In any case, Clark insisted on personally handing Robeson the script, and he had succeeded in doing so by early August 1925. Robeson was "confined" to singing after the commercial failure of *Black Boy,* a play about the rise and fall of a boxing prizefighter (not to be confused with Richard Wright's later novel of same title). As his biographer Martin Bauml Duberman relates it, Robeson demanded serious roles for and about African Americans, but he also longed for commercial success; and these two goals, as any pro could understand, often got in each other's way. Duberman writes, "Robeson's vision could occasionally be compromised by his desire for commercial success, and further distorted by the sanguine Harlem Renaissance lens through which he viewed his art. When he was offered Paul Green's new play, *In Abraham's Bosom,* . . . late in 1926, he turned it down, fearing it was too negative thematically and too risky commercially: 'there's hardly a note of hope in it. I'm afraid it wouldn't be popular and I can't afford to be going into plays that are foredoomed to fail.'"[14]

After the painstaking effort to explain Robeson's relevance, the actor's refusal was devastating to Green, but Clark had soothing words: "Things like putting over a full-length play for production have a way of not turning out the way one wants them to, but the effort must be made." He reminded Green of the need for faith as well as works, telling him that, "In your case I am sure that success will come eventually. Meantime, it is a pleasure to be able to offer an actor or manager a play like yours." Clark kept at it, dispatching a friend, Charles Kennedy, to talk with Robeson at more length about the play's prospects. Yet Hopkins, and three lesser figures, turned the play down. Then someone at Samuel French held up Green's money advance, most of which he had already spent on pressing expenses. And thus the fall of 1925 dragged by, followed by a bleak January of 1926; but Clark remained optimistic, and, despite the atmosphere, his enthusiasm was catching.[15]

In the midst of Broadway bad news, plus economic hardship on the Harnett farmlands and microeconomic doldrums at the house on Greenwood Road, Clark quoted the Hungarian playwright Andar Garvay, who "puts you next to O'Neill." And to shine that quote up a bit more, the agent added, "This means quite a deal coming from him, because he considers O'Neill to be the very acme of perfection." And, again, Clark came through at the material level, by the end of January solving the problem about the delayed advance. The agent did have to compromise, working cleverly and tirelessly behind the scenes to effect an arrangement: Green would give up a higher percentage of the "take" to Samuel French than a pro normally would give up, but in return would receive the five-hundred-dollar advance laid on the barrelhead. Clark reminded Green about the agency: the manager, T. R. Edwards, "takes the position that he is gambling & therefore he deserves as it were a higher rate of interest. Not unreasonable & good business. He also adds that many an unknown today is willing to *sell* a good slice of his play for $500. Remember, he is a businessman." Remember too, Clark conceded, "my interest in this case is not in accord with the businessman's." Thus, Clark shielded his friend and student, but certainly did no damage to Samuel French in the process: "[P]rotect yourself to the extent of putting say a 3-year termination to the agreement, saying that while you have no doubt the relationship will be friendly & beneficial, you believe that by that time you will have proved (1) either that you *are* a good business bet—in which case the advance will be covered by receipts—& therefore deserves to make a 10% contract; or (2) that you are not, in which case the whole thing ought to be ended."[16]

Clark also arranged for Green to spend the coming summer at the Peterboro Writers Colony in the high, wooded hills of New Hampshire. Knowing that the Greens had no money, Clark found him a scholarship and, through Samuel French, arranged to cover the cost of the train trip up and back and the cost of any travel back and forth between Peterboro and New York, just in case Clark could offer Green the happy interruption of a conference with a Broadway manager to close a deal on some play. Packing up his grade books and lecture notes, Green "figgered" and "refiggered" and decided to go to Peterboro. He took with him *In Abraham's Bosom,* less to revise than to have as the talisman representing his Broadway hopes; and he took *Supper for the Dead,* which he intended to "size down" for production. But mostly he took his big bound diaries and workbooks and his troubled mind and his racing heart. Far from bill collectors and the babies and the wonderful but energy-absorbing characters on the Hill, Green could relax in the woods and focus himself and do what Clark commanded: *Write.*[17]

It was there, in the summer of 1926, that Green learned of his first break as a pro. Clark wired a message to him that the Provincetown Players were set to produce *In Abraham's Bosom.* Other good news followed. Stuart Rose of Robert McBride, who was anxious to publish all of whatever Green wrote about black people, at once arranged a $250 advance against royalties on a promised manuscript; and he was almost as solicitous as Clark was. Too, he learned that the drama critic Edith J. R. Isaacs was the person that Clark had approached to arrange his Peterboro scholarship; and that sub rosa she too was arranging a number of other financial matters to help him.[18]

In a few days that seemed like months to Green, his New York friends had worked out a production contract; and this group, with Lib Green's full encouragement, packed the playwright up to go back to Peterboro. Lib did have her misgivings, which she did not declare to her husband, about Frances

Newman's presence there. She pushed to one side the memories of the snide remarks by Caro Mae Green, who had pointedly described Fanny Newman as a very dangerous woman—and Paul Green as a most willing victim. As always for Lib, the playwright's career was the thing above all things, and she desperately wanted her husband to get some significant writing done there, away from all the distractions at home and at the university. Some year, her own chance would come, when she could stay at a writers' colony and do her own writing her way for herself; but even if such a day never came, she wanted her husband to have his day. For his part, Paul Green wrote his wife—in ignorance if not exactly in innocence—about her anguish: "[B]ehold, there sat Frances Newman talking away." But he also wrote, "[I]t is wonderfully quiet. The air is fine and bracing, front last night, they say." And he was writing and rewriting, permitting himself no excuses about grief or about anything else. If Clark found anybody in New York who wanted to read something else, Green vowed with his old spirit, "[I will] have plenty to shoot to them." [19]

It was good that he had plenty to shoot to people on Broadway, because all at once he was wanted there. Moreover, Provincetown Playhouse, the very people who had introduced Eugene O'Neill to the Broadway circle, were the ones who would first take him there. The happy reports poured in by the autumn of 1926. The Provincetown Playhouse wanted *In Abraham's Bosom,* and they wanted to look at another play, *The Field God.* Eugene O'Neill had actually read both plays and liked them; Robert McBride wanted rights to a novel and to two more sets of plays; and the professional guild of dramatists wanted Paul to pay up his monetary dues now that everyone officially recognized he had paid his dues in the blues singer's sense of that phrase. [20]

Money remained an overwhelming concern, for despite winning critical acclaim, Providence Playhouse (P.P. to their followers and coworkers) did not enjoy solid financial backing and did not always follow sound business practices. Nevertheless, the irrepressible Clark was generally optimistic, and he was soon reporting that Eleanor "Fitzie" Fitzgerald, part of the brain trust at P.P., had picked up five thousand dollars' backing specifically for *In Abraham's Bosom.* Even more, Clark reported almost breathlessly, Fitzgerald had some hopes of further backing from Otto Kahn, a philanthropist active in support of African American art and a risk taker who loved a long shot if the target included civil rights. The finance people and the publicity people, then, were doing their jobs, all of which left the playwright with the strong suggestion that he for his part do his own job and write away. [21]

Clark invariably followed up such fussings with money and with encouraging words, and in this case he again practiced those habits. *The Field God* he had sold to the versatile and risk-taking actor/painter/director Edwin R. Wolfe for production at Werba's Theater in Brooklyn. The New York theater critics would get to see two Paul Green productions in the same season, and just in time for their deliberations about prizes and recognitions. Although Wolfe was offering his traditional low advance of $250, Clark suggested that the money might come in handy on Greenwood Road. Too, he mused in his note, adopting the tone of one professor mumbling to another in the faculty club, in the normal course of things Samuel French would credit such an advance to the author's account balance (especially one like Paul Green's, with outstanding debits carried over from the previous season). Perhaps, however, a meeting among the old boys could be arranged in order to send the advance along shortly. The word *shortly* in this case was defined as the same day: a second communication came that the French agency would send Green $200 at once, along with a contract. Clark would have to wag his finger again over these issues, reminding Green later that the new pro had New York performances for two plays in one year, something that other good playwrights waited for as long as ten years. Since both pros appreciated word symbols, Clark then pointedly said that he was speaking philosophy and *not applesauce*. Then he broke his own longstanding rule about the jinx of mentioning specific awards and prizes too soon: he told his charge to write away on *The Field God* and expect to walk away with the Pulitzer. It was the first mention of that prize, and Clark spoke of it only after talking with influential and important theater people, including the handful of critics who would be voting. Most prominent of those voters was Burns Mantle of the *New York Daily News,* then the dean of Broadway critics. Mantle was overwhelmingly impressed with the North Carolina playwright and indeed planned to include Green in his annual collection of "ten best plays" for the production season of 1927.[22]

He wrote away all right, but first with still more revisions of *Abraham*. He worked to draw out certain subthemes within the obvious controlling theme of the quest by the mulatto hero Abraham McCrannie for knowledge and justice. Knowledge Abe McCrannie obtains, and he attempts to share it with his African American people; but the same knowledge and the same effort to teach it damns him in the judgment of his white relatives, and he is for those reasons denied justice and finally denied life. The playwright is a voice on stage and in the audience, a voice of one who believes in political justice and who wants to believe in social equality. Green's voices emerge in the old-time call-and-response rhythms of the African American spiritual: "Men are mens," calls Abe McCrannie from the stage. And people of color are people, responds the audience as they leave the theater. No wonder that the response came most loudly from labor groups and Jewish tolerance groups and civil rights groups and critics and theatergoers with a social conscience. And no wonder *Abraham* has never played in the South. Indeed, even outside the South it has seldom played far away from a major urban or university center with traditions of social protest.

In revising, Green grew franker and bolder, perhaps because Clark kept comparing him to the incomparably frank and bold O'Neill. It was the fact of sex, of miscegenation, of physically crossing those forbidden boundaries of color that gave the McCrannie family such a poignant tragedy. If Abe McCrannie were a black man with no hint of whiteness in him, then there would be an external tragedy of white/black race relations. But Abe was brown, was mixed-breed, was miscegenated, was in fact directly related to the white paterfamil-ias of the plantation community and was the brother, albeit half brother and even wrong-sheetside shadow brother, of Mr. Lonnie, the heir apparent to the role of paterfamilias for both races. It was no magician's trick and certainly not any professor's abstraction that had made Abe *mulatto* or *new person* or *half-breed* or *high yellow* or any of the other regional terms for his ethnic identity: it was sex, sex between white man and black woman, that created this brown man, and Green probed the issue of sexuality with special and sensitive attentions.

Sex, the act, as for O'Neill, has its own destructive as well as creative qualities; and Green here follows his characters around in a painful display of the effects of unbridled sexuality, in this case the white male's lust for the black woman. Unlike classical treatments of deep emotional distresses, however, Green offers nothing particularly cathartic. To be the child of miscegenation is not Abe's fault, but society so clearly regards his very being as a sign of primordial sin that there is nothing that he can do on his own behalf. Moreover, the cathartic potentiality, the possibility that Abe's suffering and destruction could inspire racial and ethnic equality and harmony, is a distanced potentiality un-likely to be realized even among the most liberal of the audience selves. Indeed, a complete sense of racial equality is not firmly grasped even in the self of the well-meaning Green. Still and all, the prize of racial integration remains out there, lighting a pathway—and who else among white Broadway playwrights spoke so in 1926 and 1927?

There is no less poignancy in the treatment of the play's McCrannie women. They are fleshly and plump and sensually acute and sexually active. Their cooking and their singing and their playing and their dancing and their lovemaking and their farm working and their childrearing fuse the identities of the female generations. Muh Mack, the original object of Master McCrannie's desires, in her seventies remains an intensely sensual being. In much the same way, old Aunt Zella, her huge breasts dominating the horizon of the cotton field, expresses this unremitting and irresistible sensuousness. But these women are not only physical: while each, no matter how old, exudes a sexual conscious-ness, each also, no matter how young, exhibits tenderness and genuine concern for those in need. Too, Abe's tragic dimensions are matched in these women, and especially in the mulatto women, who are intelligent but futile, deeply troubled by their own sense of primordial doom sealed by the previous generations who made their own unenforceable rules and then broke them and thereby punished the offspring.

Even the normally optimistic and hopeful issue of education is a matter of tragedy and something close to pathos. Of course, that issue was virtually the holy grail for the sandhills kid who read books while plowing back in Harnett County. Characters praise schooling, but something always defeats those who are educated. It is not only the racist antagonisms of the white forces, but something in human nature itself that mocks and flouts and then smashes reform. After his beating by Mr. Lonnie, Abe's "book l'arning" drops from his broad shoulders like a worn-out and useless jacket, and he kills his brother in an effect that is class conflict, yes; economic oppression, certainly; racism, obviously; but also a preternatural fate: "Blast me Lord in yo' fiery furnace!" The duty is called forth: try, try, try, try to change; but always it must be understood that finally one cannot change even one's self. One must join the struggle exactly *because* the struggle is hopeless. *In Abraham's Bosom,* then, is all about the seamless characteristics of stoicism in the eastern Carolina countryside. Standard Judeo-Christian tenets with their hopes for salvation come a cropper in this land, and pagan deities rule. As Green said in several notes, some to himself in his diary, some in correspondence with friends, people must save themselves. Jesus, Green believed, was misunderstood: He was not the Christ divine but a pagan man, and Jesus did not show us how to gain heaven but how to live bravely and truly a doomed struggle here.[23]

The same pagan's understanding of God, that is, a powerful supernatural force acting on each of us here on earth instead of in an afterlife, informs his plans for *The Field God,* his "white" play, and such a rebellion against organized religion found ready acceptance among modern humanists of 1927. Actually, however, Green's paganism is a very different thing from the self-consciously avant-garde humanism of the late 1920s. His paganism is rooted in tradition, and its pessimism is a judgment on human nature rather than a modernist's questioning the authority of the Enlightenment or the authority of the Age of Science or the authority of liberal rationalism. Above all, he remains a deeply spiritualistic man, a sincerely religious man, and he still longs, much as had the lonely young soldier, for a church that will, in Horace Williams's words, "take a new view of religion." Moreover, Green is actually less anticapitalist than precapitalist: he is not so much unhappy with contemporaneous materialism as he is separated from it, not even yet a member—protesting member or approving member—simply not yet part of the modern culture of materialism and consumerism.

As it turned out, Green benefited from humanists' misreadings of *The Field God,* as he benefited from the historical and financial accidents that brought this play to Brooklyn while the little circle of decision makers was assessing his best "negro play," *In Abraham's Bosom,* and judging nominations for the Pulitzer Prize. Moreover, Green and Clark were themselves involved in the good luck of the misreadings, and they were both aware that it was a great advantage to have humanist thinkers and critics talking excitedly about two of his plays at one time at a moment when southern writers were gaining real attention for their literary work. *The Field God* was moved from Werba's in Brooklyn to the Greenwich Village Theater, and as Charles Blackburn notes, even the unkind notices and the generally "cooler reception" for the second play helped in the campaign for the Pulitzer.[24]

In *The Field God,* Green set the pagan conception of God against the dominant contemporaneous cultural assumption of a rural white community in which Calvinist precepts reign. He is here remarkably close to a description of Papa Green's conception of a pagan deity whose fatalism and severe judgments and demands for hard work seem to be, but are not, the dominant assumptions of limited atonement professed by New Light Presbyterians and fundamentalist Baptists back in the ancestral valley. The protagonist's pagan approach to suffering is related to that of the Reverend Tom Long, but the suffering reveals the existence of an earthly morality, an earthly goodness, and a salvation by and through human love infused by God, that is, immanent, but not transcendent: the saved pagan lives a saved life here, then dies, and is gone. The salvations come one by one and do not transcend time and space, although it is possible that the memories of one salvation may inspire surviving generations to save themselves through the agency of their own human love. Both views involve fate and doom and a pervasive, often punishing, supernatural force; but the nature of sin is different, and of course the site of salvation, mortal earth for one, immortal heaven for the other, is very different.

To play out these theological conflicts, Green establishes two sets of love triangles, one among a dying Calvinist woman, her pagan husband, and a favored niece, another among the pagan husband, the favored niece, and her rejected suitor. Two deaths from disease ensue, followed by an accidental self-wounding, a community scourging, an ironic backsliding into the Protestant faith, and then the pagan couple's saving by the mortal grace of their own human and physical love. Few people "got" the pagan message, although they did hear that people can save themselves through love for one another and that they can be brought to such love through physical suffering. To get across such immanence in the concept that suffering can bring wisdom and then love was a lot to accomplish; and if no one was going to understand that there is a supernatural force, a pre-Christian and pagan God, moving all of those things, then so be it.

The tone of this play is very stoic, and the death and suffering have to be treated just right to avoid making it into a series of shocking events with no purpose other than the sort of gratuitous outrages that lure large crowds to the site of car wrecks. Especially in later years, when he consciously hung about with worshipful fans, Green often spoke of writing *The Field God* in four days of intense work. That bit of exaggeration belies the clear evidence that he revised it extensively many times in 1926 and 1927 (and at least three more times after 1927, when he expanded it to a three-act drama). He rewrote a great deal after Clark critiqued it admiringly but unsparingly; extensively again after Clark's friend the agent Winifred Katzin with her shrewd eye critiqued that revision; still again during the early fall of 1926 in close work with the producer/director Edwin R. Wolfe, who came down to Chapel Hill to express his concerns about problems with the script; and once more in a major collaborative revision with Wolfe at the Brooklyn site in the late winter of 1927, right before production began at Werba's. All of these people forced Green to rethink and rewrite his depiction of the central theological struggle.[25]

Nor was bringing the play before the public any less a struggle than what was depicted in the many scripts. Between money problems and artistic problems, production was delayed from the hoped-for January 1927 until April. Yet again Fortuna spun her wheel to Green's advantage. Theater people all over New York understood that *The Field God* was an ambitious production involving a serious playwright, a serious producer, serious actors, and serious, if necessarily small, audiences. In the end, the various rewritings did not bring forward Green's pagan theology, but theater people did appreciate the sense of struggles, and if they heard it with modernist and humanist ears, they still liked what they heard, and they rewarded the playwright with kind, even generous notices.

Preoccupied as he was throughout 1926 and 1927 with *The Field God* and saddled with a full load of courses to teach, Green permitted the self-styled Experimental Theater people of Providence Playhouse to develop *In Abraham's Bosom* with relatively little auctorial interference. In subsequent years, with other plays, Green was often a director's—and an actor's—nightmare, and some of his plays would be produced only after he agreed to stay away from the rehearsals. With *Abraham,* however, he came to trust the intentions and the skills of its artistic directors, Kenneth Macgowan, Fitzie Fitzgerald, and Jasper Deeter. In any case, he really had almost no time to spare for the long trip to New York to monitor daily doings on the set. Too, Fitzgerald often wrote him flattering notes to win his approval for changes.[26]

It went well that he let the troupe alone, for they produced a wonderful play, and one certainly true to his script in detail as well as true to its larger tragic vision. Fitzgerald was well connected with excellent black actors: for instance, when Jules Bledsoe, a superb baritone and usually an effective tragedian, performed indifferently as Abe McCrannie and then left the play, the Experimental Theater quickly brought in Frank Wilson, who performed Abe brilliantly and in many ways made the play. Rose McClendon and Abbie Mitchell had featured roles in a cast of ten African Americans and two whites. Bledsoe's performances—on-again, off-again, and out—were much commented on by the cast and in the Harlem community, but the written reviews, if noting his problems at all, tended to blame the baritone and praise his replacement, Wilson. More important, the Harlem arts community, like other reform communities in New York in the era, formed a consensus of warm enthusiasm for the troupe, the producers, the directors, and of course for the white playwright.[27]

Both Fitzie Fitzgerald and Kenneth Macgowan had worked and played with sensitive and often egoistic talents as different as O'Neill and Gertrude Stein in the white ranks of the avant-garde; and the Experimental Theater people were good talkers in the best New York manner. All-night sessions in the right coffee shops and bistros and artists' flats were filled with talk about Paul Green's play: it was regarded as part of the Harlem Renaissance by the artist/activist James Weldon Johnson and the trend-spotting critic Carl Van Vechten (already a fan of Green's from the late *Reviewer* days). The African American sociologist E. Franklin Frazier, a tough critic and no-nonsense commentator on such things, pronounced the project a "genuine appreciation of the character of the Afro-American." In fact, Frazier suggested that the full development of Green's kind of drama would help to create a culture "that will be unique but not in opposition to [African American] growth and wider participation in American life as a whole."[28]

Fitzgerald did get the play uptown, at least in figurative sense, to the Garrick Theater with its capacity of 215 seats and its high profile among important critics. It should be marked how many and what kind of reformist groups bought out the house for performances, for example, the Teachers Union, the Socialist Party, Young Israel, and the Mohegan Modern School. It seldom filled to capacity except on such occasions, but the small groups who did come listened, loved it, and talked—and talked. Now the talkers included not only Green's longtime supporters Van Vechten, Burns Mantle, Brooks Atkinson, and Edith Isaacs (and of course Barrett Clark himself, one always as much an influential critic and commentator as an agent), but also Montrose Jonas Moses, a southerner who had developed a popular New York radio show devoted to theater. Even those who did not like the play at all, such as the important critic John Anderson, made their complaints with a combination of respect for and resentment of prevailing critical reactions. In fact Anderson loudly conceded that the play was likely to win the Pulitzer Prize. He may have been playing the old trick of reversing the patterns of good and bad luck: if the mere public mention of the Pulitzer could jinx a nominated author, then Anderson was happy to mention it in order to provide the jinx. It seems, however, from the sincerely scornful tone of his remarks—emphasizing with ham-handed adjectives that the play was "tedious" and "monotonous" in its emotions and "impotent" in its impact (some of his problem evidently being a racist doubt that African Americans could properly *be* the stuff of serious tragedy)—that Anderson was in unhappy agreement with Green's supporters that *Abraham* would take the prize this season.[29] Whatever role he chose to play in his interviews—ploughboy, professor, pro—Green had quite captured the attention of the Broadway pros even if he could not gain much attention from Broadway audiences.

Paul Green received the Pulitzer Prize for 1927, still another affirmation that his friend Fanny Newman was right to describe a southern literary renaissance rising into national consciousness after 1924. Fellow writers were thrilled, although Green's old Carolina Playmaker friend Thomas Wolfe reported that he went on a drinking binge—and not fully in celebration—when he learned the news. In any case, the recognition brought much-needed cash, one thousand dollars of it, a fact that Green noted with rueful appreciation in an acceptance statement when he first learned of the award. Little additional money came in, however. There was not even the indirect boost in attendance usually associated with the prize. Gate receipts at the Garrick continued much as before, with special groups buying out the house on occasion, but with few legitimate sell-out performances. The play ran on its critically acclaimed, reformist-celebrated, and commercially ignored path until its closing in the fall of this long year of 1927. It did not come south then, and has not subsequently, and probably never will. But *Abraham* and the prize certainly brought Green favorable notice at home, and especially among the Real South southerners he wanted to reach artistically. The words of the citation read: "For the Original American Play, performed in New York, which shall best represent the educational value and power of the stage in raising the standard of good morals, good taste, and good manners."[30]

1928–1929

Project: To study at first-hand the theatre and drama of Continental Europe
for the purpose of gaining technical training in creative dramatic work.
Period: Twelve months from the Summer of 1928.
Stipend: Twenty-five hundred dollars ($2,500).[1]

It was only an application, of course, but the mere act of filling it
brought excitement. Lib Green had pushed her husband to compete for a
stipend to support travel and study offered by the Simon Guggenheim Foundation. With help from her and from Barrett Clark, Green filled out the forms.
Colleagues on the Hill, all of whom supported the project with an anxious
hope, were no less excited.[2]

Horace Williams was enthusiastic about the opportunity, but it should be
marked that he expected his philosophy professor back in harness for the department by beginning of fall quarter 1929, as the application specified. Too,
Williams thought his colleague—his hope for "real" philosophy and for "a new
view of religion"—was also to read and reflect on philosophy, although nothing in the application suggested any such plans. The department now included
the bright scholar Katherine Gilbert, and both Williams and Green hoped for
much from her. Assistant Professor Gilbert could teach Green's classes in addition to her own, should he win the award. She was, in fact, happy to take
on extra work on behalf of her young older colleague and in tandem with her
ancient older colleague, both of whom she then admired. Frank Porter Graham, dean of the liberal arts faculty, and Harry Woodburn Chase, president
of UNC, were both delighted by the prospects for Green. Graham and Chase
were beset with institutional financial woes during a regional agricultural recession and a period of declining profits for the textile industry; but the national
economy was still expanding, and the two were infectious optimists who assumed progress and who wanted faculty members to dream dreams and to take
chances. Dean and president would find the money for such an endeavor, even
if finding the money involved giving up something else among the academic
budget items. Even UNC Press editor William Terry Couch, who had Green
writing manuscripts, editing manuscripts, and scouting out authors, even this

feisty and demanding Bill Couch could imagine work without Green. In fact, he was willing to take care of the house on Greenwood Road for a year, a task that would include proxy representation before the many creditors pressing for their just deserts.[3]

In March came the happy news from Henry Allen Moe, granting officer of the Guggenheim Foundation, that Green would be awarded a fellowship for study of folk drama in Germany and other parts of Europe, with funds and travel starting in the summer of 1928 and continuing through summer of 1929. Too, he was eligible for an extension beyond that summer of 1929, a possibility welcomed by all of his colleagues on the Hill, though the mention of it did give a long pause to Horace Williams, who began to worry about building a successful department around a hope who was gone for long spells at a time. In quick order Gilbert rearranged her teaching schedule, and the legendary mentor was mollified, at least for the coming season. Proff Koch sent his blessing, delighted that the hope of the regional theater would be coming back with still more ideas, not to mention his delight with the prestige that could rub off on all Playmakers by association. Graham and Chase were quick to square things with trustees and obtain an official leave of absence, something not hard to do since great honor was coming to a faculty member while someone else paid his salary.[4]

And so to Europe, the 1923 trip that was postponed when Oxford University graduate studies were displaced by Cornell University graduate studies. Many established patterns went right along with the Green family. Paul Green would rise early in the morning and stay up late at night. He would drink strong coffee in the mornings, horrible evaporated milk in the late afternoon, strong spirits most evenings; and always he was reading and writing. The daytime writing would be both vigorous and sustained, both intensive and extensive, and in every genre, from poetry to playwriting to novels to diary keeping. There would be many visitors, especially long-staying visitors, to the small adoptive Green homeplaces, and there would be many visits to people and places, some of these sorties being solo trips by Paul Green, as to see George Bernard Shaw, Thomas Hardy's widow, Leo Tolstoy's widow, Sigmund Freud's personal secretary; but there would be family trips too. The activities would always be paced a little too fast, and there would be emotional tolls on the body and the spirit, including periods of clinical depression for Paul Green and periods of overwork for Lib, Paulie, and Byrd Green, such periods alternating with troughs of ennui. Much excitement and joy was broken by dread and even by acute fear. Lib Green would run the family and manage finances and plan trips, both family and solo trips, and oversee the playwright career. She would doctor her husband, baby him, scold him, help him in all things. He would see Europe, and Paulie and Byrd would see Europe, and this was because Lib Green saw to it that each of them saw Europe. It wasn't quite the trip that she had hoped for since 1923, but it was quite a trip.

One thing that this heroic and multitalented woman was not going to do was cook and clean. She didn't have time, but she never had taken time for such tasks in any case. To do their necessary menial tasks and to help with the children, who sometimes could be lost amidst the cycles of the action and the inaction, she hired Fraulein Lamprecht, a young German women who would soon demonstrate that it was not only African American peasants down on the Buies Creek bottomland who ran into difficulties that ultimately produced the stuff of art and the stuff of heroic cooperation. In many ways, during the bad spells on this European tour, Paul Green would never be worse; but Lib Green would never be better, and thus she could make her husband look good regardless of how he felt.

Barrett Clark too, although not there, was available by the long arm of correspondence and telegraph network to help in all things. Already he had talked with Green about folk traditions in Germany, with special emphasis on the folk who were the best raconteurs and who had endured the most in the region, the Jews of central and eastern Europe. Clark had talked a lot and Clark had listened a lot, and the long and the short of it was that the pro again followed the mentor's coaching, this time to win a fellowship to teach himself about the German denizens who had their own speech, their own ways, their own light, their own memories, their own dreams, but perhaps the same truth as Green himself had. The itinerary for the year's work Clark had helped to draw up, with wise advice about the people you *had to know* and with instructions about the great things to do and see for knowledge's sake.

An introduction for Arnolt Bronnen illustrated the mentor's help in building *networks* before the term became a verb. Clark described Bronnen as "one of the most original and distinguished of the younger generation of German dramatists." He continued, "I wrote a long article about him in the *Stratford Review* some years ago. Herr Bronnen is living in Germany and has many friends among the people you would be glad to meet. He speaks English, in case you have not yet learned German." And that intricate spider's web of "people . . . you would be glad to meet" would indeed capture for Green some of the masters of Jewish lore, as long as he did learn German and as long as he applied himself to the search as diligently as he had worked the sandhills.[5]

Work the old world, he did, though that work involved such a combination of library research and the actual doing of the folk plays that he developed and expressed a profound ambivalence about how in the world to accomplish a task with two such different facets. The man who had boasted of simultaneously riding the two horses of philosophy teaching and playwriting had chosen, after all, to ride the playwright horse and only go through the motions of riding the philosophy-teaching horse. But no such resolution seemed possible here, for one had to master the theory of Jewish folklore and folk plays, but that theory was useless unless put into practice in plays. This dilemma of ideal versus practical was the very dilemma of pragmatism limned by Charles Peirce and William James, and that dilemma Green had dealt with by denying it while studying at Cornell. After months of tormenting himself, he characteristically abandoned the intellectual and scholarly side of this business and focused himself on learning Jewish folk theater by doing Jewish folk theater. To his diary he confided that Aristotle was right about actualization, that is, drama must be *done* rather than studied in the abstract. He convinced himself of this Aristotelean truth with an image: he said that a lion at study is no lion at all. [6]

Choosing to study Jewish folk art in general and Jewish folk theater in particular enmeshed Green in the gravest and most complex of emotional dilemmas. Plainly put, Green was prejudiced against Jews. He would struggle with his prejudice, and in an important distinction, he would never act on his prejudice, would never *discriminate against* Jews on the basis of these feelings. Too, he would support another awful world war despite the antiwar passions engendered by his personal nightmare of the Great War, and he would thus defend World War II largely because of the evil discrimination and genocide practiced by German Nazis. [7]

For all that, however, he would remain prejudiced against Jews. Very late in life, acutely conscious of his public standing and anxious for the right "place" in history, he would even break his strictest personal rules about full and frank disclosure by attempting to edit out of memory—and thus existence?—diary entries in which he had made snidely prejudicial remarks. Much like the Yiddish street theater he so admired, there was in these actions a seriocomic element, since he was using the clumsiest device—a white liquid cover-up or "correction fluid"—in globs on typescript in such a way that the "deletions" all but scream at the reader; and in any case, the handwritten originals he never touched at all, leaving them safe for scholars to examine in the Paul Green Papers of the Southern Historical Collection in the library named for his friend and colleague Louis Round Wilson. [8] By the end of his days, he had seen enough to know that a little prejudice goes a long way, especially when played on and redirected by evil demagogues. Even so, these awkward and fumbling efforts to undo the personal past were essentially to preserve his reputation. Sadly, the efforts were not the experience of an epiphany. He felt bad about how he felt, but he remained prejudiced. He sought then not to remove the emotions, but only the record of the emotions.

How could someone, especially one who wrote with such passion about what he loved, how could such a person study and write about a people whom he prejudged to be inferior? He had evolved out of regional racist patterns and then self-consciously rebelled against those patterns, and in any case he was constantly asking himself and his friends if a given act or statement or even thought was in some way racist. Yet, in the very years of studying Jewish folk theater, he talked and wrote in a prejudicial way about Jews with no contemporaneous regret for what he—and Lib Green and his friends—were saying. Is this antisemitism? What kept this prejudiced man from celebrating with, even marching with, the Nazis already on the scene in Berlin and already promising the final solution to the "Jewish problem" of their own devising?

Gavin Langmuir, a close student of antisemitism, offers insights that explain Paul Green in this context. Langmuir distinguishes between two kinds of prejudice against Jews, one a "realistic hostility" grounded in misunderstanding of an ethnic out-group and its actual behavior, the other "an unusual kind of human hostility" based on an abstract image of Jews and dedicated to the eradication, that is, genocide, of that out-group. Hostility between ethnic groups is "well-nigh universal," says Langmuir, and such hostility is generally the result of misunderstanding about what the out-group actually does. The misunderstanding and prejudice are "realistic" in that the starting point is real and observed differences in food, clothing, speech, manners, and other habits as practiced by the out-group. The prejudice can result in discrimination, or choosing to exclude a particular person on the basis of an observable difference in a group's behavior. Such prejudice and discrimination in tandem can indeed produce at the least emotional wounds and property damages, and at the most they can produce physical harm and even killing. Nevertheless, this ethnic prejudice is susceptible of amelioration, especially with some social and cultural interaction whose processes can dispel some of the misunderstandings. This "realistic" prejudice, while tragic at the personal level, does not result in the societal catastrophe and world-stage tragedy of genocide.[9]

On the other hand, antisemitism has no relation whatever to anything that Jews actually *do*, and is thus abstract and "unrealistic" and "irrational." Grounded in imagination rather than in misperception, this antisemitism is murderous in its inception, and its death-talking elements will be compounded into an inevitable genocide unless forcibly arrested. Langmuir traces antisemitism from the twelfth century, specifically between the years 1150 and 1250. He finds that German Christians were in that period making laws that set Jews apart as a group completely different in kind, rather than in degree, from other sorts of German peoples. These laws were accompanied by the development of unique tales about Jewish behavior. No rational approach can stop antisemitism, since the out-group never does anything that is imagined and the talebearers themselves *never* claim to have personally *seen* a Jew *do* these things, for example, stealing babies, cannibalizing, torturing victims in ritual settings. The antisemite believes without seeing that Jews do these things, and he or she cannot be resisted with reason at all. Awful as prejudice is, antisemitism is worse, is indeed different in kind, and it is appropriate, in fact the only solution, to persuade the persuadable (that is, the merely prejudiced) to help keep the antisemites from killing off all Jews.[10]

Green's prejudices against Jews were thus in Langmuir's sense "realistic," that is, he misunderstood things that he actually saw, and he prejudged all Jews on the basis of these misperceptions. The misunderstandings are well documented in his diary and correspondence, as some examples can show: he told one friend that Jewish boys will do almost anything for sex or money; he used the phrase *jew down* in suggesting to Lib Green that she bargain for a lower price on an item; he declined at least one Hollywood dinner invitation from a Jew because he felt that Hollywood was being all but overrun by Jews; and he regretted the displacement of farmers from an area by Jewish capitalists. In his army days he had made wartime notes about a trench mate to the effect that one must never trust a "silent Jew." By contrast, he also noted with admiration the ways that Jews look after each other, their "charitableness"; and he specifically praised an agent because he was unostentatious in a "plain Jew" way that should be admired. All of this, even the nice things, are of course stereotypes and involve prejudice.[11] None, however, is in Langmuir's sense antisemitic, and Green was shocked by the idea of destroying a kind of people, any kind of people, any kind of out-group, African American, Jewish, *any kind*. Prejudiced indeed, he was not genocidal in the antisemite's way. Finally, in the dusk of his long day, he worries that his prejudice, even in the diaries, will be misread as antisemitism, and he tries to fix his antisemitic references, not because he is no longer prejudiced but because he does not want to be confused with the antisemite.

By the third week of October, Green was deep in funk, suffering grave self-doubt about his artistic capacities and enduring the only spell of clinical depression that family legend admits into existence. His diary, as it does on many other occasions, sketches a picture of one "too blue" to work or play, of one virtually immobilized by emotions that sadden and then enervate. The expressions are often those of Anatole France, whom Green was then reading, and that notation marks the influence France once had on young southern writers. The novelist Shelby Foote, who studied at Carolina in this era, recalled that France was de rigeur for the aspiring authors on campus, and presumably throughout the campuses of the region. Green, for his part, took up France's voice for several entries, lamenting Germany's, and particularly Berlin's, resistance to reform. Letting that voice speak a little longer, and a little louder, Green extended the lamentations back across the ocean to his own United States, also fat and happy and evil and self-satisfied, although the first two adjectives badly described his region in that time. At other moments, however, the joined facts of oppression and reactionism did not depress him; they angered him. Generally, when so angered, he responded with vigor, with a prophet's denunciations tempered by a fatalist's humor. Now, facing the same forces, he went into one of the spells that his sister Erma could remember from his childhood, but this spell ran longer.[12]

Lib Green saved him, and not in any metaphorical sense. She prodded and pulled him into physical exertion, hoping thereby to wear him out enough to produce an honest night's sleep instead of the emotionally draining unrest of many of his depression nights. Nor would she allow him to lose sight of the larger purpose of this trip. Regardless of what her father intended or whatever she had once hoped, the purpose of this trip was exactly that filed with Henry Moe in the Guggenheim offices, namely, to study and then *do* folk theater, especially Jewish folk theater. Focused work on the foreign techniques that he must master in a period of only a few months would go far to cure those blues. To that end, she helped him reorganize. Herself an intrepid follower of lists, Lib Green encouraged her husband to write down an imposing catalog of plays, movies, concerts, readings, plays, exhibitions, and lectures to go see in this Berlin. Even these two at peak levels of efficiency could not do all the things in the list, which covered more than forty pages, but the act of making the list helped immensely. Other women might pull Green away, but only this one could focus him and center him on task.[13]

The depths of greatest clinical depression cannot be treated so, as the couple would discover in the 1970s, but Lib Green had the prescription for this particular run of melancholic inaction. She got him out of the apartment and down the streets to meet his appointed rounds, especially with the Moscow Theater, directed by Alexander Granovsky, the genius of Jewish folk drama. That man's infectious enthusiasms, plus the sheer spectacle of how much Green did not know about this form of art, combined to snap him to attention and to recharge the battery cells. Too, a note at Lib Green's urging sent Barrett Clark into action. If the public university and the private foundation had underestimated the budget for a family in Berlin, there was always the Samuel French Company, and by mid-November Green had signed contracts for German productions of some "Negro plays," with advances of five hundred marks, sufficient to buy groceries and even splurge a bit (the playwright bought himself a volume of Arnold Bennett, a change of pace from Anatole France). After Lib Green's intercessions with Clark, the diarist wrote that he was safe now: Byrd and Paulie were no longer crying with hunger, philosophy made more sense, and his stomach disorders were relieved.[14]

Philosophy, stomach, and presumably psyche as well were best in the presence of Alexander Granovsky, director and originator of Das Moskauer Jüdische Akademische Theater. Actually, Granovsky was a pseudonym for the man born Avrom Azarkh in Moscow in 1890. His eventual effect on Green could hardly have been foretold by the diarist's first recorded responses: he is there described as around forty-five years old, considerably older than his actual thirty-eight years; and he is described as fat and bald with the tired eyes of a middling-level American businessman. Yet subsequent meetings developed the most powerful devotion, and contemporaneous records show that Granovsky's Yiddish troupe had enjoyed recent theater successes in Leipzig and Frankfurt, despite the rapidly crescendoing antisemitism there. West of Germany there was notice too, opportunities for filmmaking and dramatic presentations in Paris, plus a contract with First National for a film, and a feature study in the *New York Times,* whose arts and theater people were interested in the troupe after Otto Kahn (also a benefactor of the Harlem Renaissance figures) agreed to back Granovsky for a tour of New York, Boston, and Chicago.[15]

As a youth this man had studied in Saint Petersburg (Petrograd), had traveled to and studied in Munich, and then had returned to his native city during the Russian Revolution. In the second year of the revolution, he organized a small Yiddish theater; then popular with Soviet officials, he developed it into a studio in Moscow, and in 1919 he was granted status as director of the State Jewish Theater with sanctioned repertory and his own troupe, which was permitted to travel into non-Communist Europe. He also made silent films for the state, including *Jewish Luck* (*Yevei Schastze,* 1925), based on a story by Sholem Aleichem, a Yiddish writer whose fiction would later gain notice in the United States. But it was Yiddish folk drama, performed live and largely in the difficult and fast-moving dialect of the vernacular, that was his forte. Yiddish theater was by then in its second full generation of performances, and Granovsky intended to move well beyond its origins as "primitive" folk tales or commedia dell'arte. He wanted a theater still playful with language, as Yiddish speech was by its nature, but ironical in tone, with thoughtful treatments of significant issues. He wanted drama with serious authors, serious actors, serious staging before audiences no longer there just to be there, but there to let the art engage and exercise their minds. Featuring such presentations in a 1927 tour of Germany, he had resigned his state directorship to work unfettered by any government restrictions (which had been minimal to that point), but also because of the great opportunities in Germany and France. His Moskauer Jüdische Akademische Theater was thus unsanctioned by the Soviets, but he was still esteemed back home, and memory of him would remain officially fond until Josef Stalin initiated purges of Jewish artists and academics after World War II.

Though hardly a proper Soviet, Granovsky could play the role of the didactic mentor. He sat Green down. Pulitzer Prizes did not cut much ice with him, and he had here a pupil who needed to be drilled in the basics. The basics were quite different from anything the diarist recorded hearing from anyone else. Do not, the master lectured, confuse folk theater with puppet shows, even if "authentic" peasants are doing the puppet shows. The master himself did *not* model his theater on puppet performances. In fact, he had never seen a puppet show. Women actors Granovsky disliked working with and cautioned about

the problems, though for certain roles he found them necessary. Formal training in classical theater, and certainly in some avant-garde techniques, was not
always helpful, and could even be harmful, for the purposes of folk theater.[16]

He could be and was often unconventional and unpredictable; and certainly
he was often trend-setting. When he dramatized I. L. Peretz's *Night in the Old
Market,* he provided minimal dialogue, and he experimented radically with
what he called "the art of silence" to force the audience to think about the action
and the themes. Too, that play's lighting was self-consciously artful, aesthetically challenging in and of itself, and charged with the additional task of actually
telling part of the story. Whether Granovsky was performing as a specialist seeking the historically accurate or as a generalist attempting to cross over between
cultures, he had his troubles with audiences and occasionally with authorities.
The cruelest, because most unavoidable, dilemma was at the moral level for this
practicing Jew in the historical context of violent antisemitism: sometimes Jews
themselves objected to his work, which many considered to be a caricature, or
which in any case brought up memories too painful for some.[17]

After this thorough and unsparing "talking to," the director packed his overwhelmed student off for proper instruction in theories about German drama.
And he was generous with photographs and passes to shows so that the pupil
would have a record of examples for his own use and to share with other American theater people. In the process of these reinvigorated studies, Green met two
more academics, Berlin's Plessow and Frankfurt's Pringhorn, who in separate
dinner conversations insisted that he involve himself in contemporary German
criticism, then in quite a stir. According to these two professors, the great stir
involved two more figures: Heinrich Wolflin, a critic who spoke effectively to
and thereby educated the "middle-brow" audience, and G. F. Fechner, a theorist who instructed the masters in his golden sections theory of aesthetics.
Although Green did not meet Wolflin or Fechner, he read their works with
appetite, took notes on their ideas, and brought some of their ideas and techniques into his own teaching and writing.[18]

Wolflin emphasized context, seeking an appreciation for a particular form
of art *as it fit an age,* Green wrote in his notebook. The goal of the producer
or other exhibitor is thus to restore dramas, songs, sculptures, choreographed
dances, or other works of art to their own original, contemporaneous settings,
and to do so as naturally and as congenially as possible. Green himself was
very much in an experimental mood, especially in this season, but he still felt
some allegiance to classical forms. Now he was thrilled to see and hear this
historicism: he liked this insistence on preserving what was as it was because it
was. Finally he could codify the difference between classicism, which preserves
ideal forms forever in timeless style, and historicism, which faithfully preserves
the concrete form of a particular moment for its own sake, in such processes
acknowledging that time changes everything. He too wanted his artistic ex-

pressions to "fit an age" faithfully rather than fit an unchanging form. Like Granovsky, Green could expand radically the subject matter of the theater, to include not only peasants but Jewish and black peasants, and here was Wolflin saying straight out: Classicists who demand a timeless standard for subject matter and timeless treatment of such subject matter are creating monuments, that is, dead things. Wolflin's art preserver and art presenter, rediscovering and representing context, deals in history, where time and its patterns of change are everything. At last, Green had a good theoretical rationale for his profound but previously unexamined urge to gather things: he was collecting folk tales, folk sayings, maps, recipes, and local-history documents, checking carefully what kinds of trees and bushes grew where and what sorts of storms blew when, and all because he needed an aesthetic of context, of history, not of classical philosophy. Too, Wolflin offered a standard of behavior in these tasks: Professor Pringhorn insisted to Green that Wolflin was popular without sacrificing scholarship. That was good news indeed, for the best of German high culture agreed that the arts must "speak plainly" in an aesthetic of context instead of classical form. Plain speaking was of course Green's own hopeful term for the artists of his Real South. [19]

But there remained another issue about form and its cousin structure, especially in language, something so crucial to the poet and playwright. That issue was resolved and codified for him by Fechner, the other force in the great stir in Germany. Should an artist experiment with form by developing brand new structures, or even by abandoning structures? Question all things, proclaimed the self-styled modernists; but should one step farther out and question the questioning, question the very structure with which an artist, or any other human, questions? Perhaps, as postmodernists do, one should even question the concepts of artist and audience, and thereby argue that things are so completely subjective and relative that art is strictly in the eye and the soul of each beholder, that the number of possible forms is virtually uncountable, and that any efforts to categorize are essentially political acts by the powerful attempting to stifle expression by mislabeling it. Late in life, when Paul Green encountered the postmodernism of Samuel Beckett, he would have the chance to speak to these concerns directly, and he then denied all the movement's claims very bluntly. Of course structure matters, he said then; and without it, he implied, there is neither audience nor author and no art at all. As he once noted for a fellow writer, "I know you don't want to say that you have a message, but isn't there something that kind of *seeps* through?" [20]

In 1928, he did not confront a full-blown postmodernist and poststructuralist theory, if one existed anywhere in that day to confront. But he did find in Fechner a foursquare justification for formalism. Fechner said to pay close and conscious attention to structure. Indeed, without structure, how could one form any context at all? Without authors to keep track of it—and without self-conscious audiences to appreciate those authors—how could one understand the historical development that provides the context crucial to an appreciation of art? Two decades later, another, more accomplished regional poet and playwright, Robert Penn Warren, would more artfully say what Paul Green was trying to say in his diary in 1928. Penn Warren in 1946 would say that we may not be able to find the truth, but it is out there, and we have to search for it. During the search, conducted in what Warren called a "spiralling process" back and forth across the imperfectly known events, we must show the untruth that surrounds the hiding truth, and thus there must be some *definition by negation* in order to move toward the truth. And the truth, for Warren and for Green, was a singular thing, never a plural thing. It was subjective only in the sense that people had a hard time finding it and because individual humans had imperfect judgment; it was *not* subjective because of its nature.[21]

Since Green was predisposed to defend structuralism, he was pleased to find in Fechner a firm defense of the movement. In fact, Fechner even worked it out in a geometrical expression of the old golden mean or *aurea mediocritas* with his golden sections theory for artistic form, especially the form of language. Among other things, Fechner said that an experimental analysis of "psychic facts" would locate the "elementary aspects of the appeal [of] figures such as fragments, lines, squares, rectangles." The theorist described in precise German manner a rationale for "empirical" art that finds out and then expresses a moral "aesthetic from below," that is, moral values expressed in art as those values flow upward from the common people in their lives.[22]

From Wölflin, then, Paul came away with a formal statement, plus lecture notes for drama classes, about the vitality and morality of a historical approach to theater that dramatizes an event from another era: actors, dialogue, clothes, sets, all must be accurate for a time and a place, or else the art would be inauthentic. From Fechner, Green came away with a precise, geometric proof of the need for structure in the language of the theater. Some contradictions are suggested by the things said by the spokesman for historicism and the spokesman for formal structuralism. As usual, however, Green did not puzzle at length over this Gordian knot. Instead, he borrowed eclectically from each man, and he used their arguments as he needed.

Whatever else, he now regarded that period of depression as less a clinical experience (especially since he went to no clinic and avoided any professional diagnosis) than a period of strategic retreat. Perhaps he thought it was like Achilles sulking in his tent before going to avenge Patroklos, or like the Prophet Muhammad on hegira before undertaking jihad. At any rate, by late November 1928 he had what he came to Germany for, and he was going to use it right.[23]

The winter of 1929 was a bitter one in Berlin. Years later, the Greens would still be talking about it. Even with cash advances from Samuel French, it was hard to find the resources to stay warm. Each member of the family took cold, then took fever, then grew terribly ill, and everybody but Lib Green spent spells in the hospital, in a sanitarium for a deadly influenza or perhaps pneumonia. Too, throughout the period of February, March, and even April, the long-staying ice and wind were matched by economic problems in the American theaters that Paul Green served and was served by. Every production troupe associated with Green's work, from celebrated Theater Guild to amateur performers in settlement houses, asked to renegotiate contracts to pay Samuel French smaller advances and smaller commissions, all of which suggested smaller revenues for the playwright, who had been granted relatively large advances. He would be in the same deep debt, but the expected stream of income to cover that debt was bound to slow; he would be deeper in debt, then. Lib Green began to handle much more of the family finances, and she was at times virtually the Berlin agent for Samuel French. Yet, in the midst of such troubles, Paul Green was tough and resilient, occasionally even buoyant. He was happy with his family, happy with his work, happy with his European friends. He grew more confident during this period, and he even wrote a warming letter to buck up Hugh Green back home, postponing some of his brother's own debt payments to the Greenwood Road household and giving advice about cutting and selling juniperwood, apparently a kind of red pine, for market to supplement the low returns on cotton and tobacco. In the correspondence Lib Green and Barrett Clark emerge as tough and no-nonsense negotiators, both watchfully protecting the playwright during a difficult economic season, both true to a sense of the playwright's artistic vision.[24]

How striking that in these very hard times, there is none of the "funk" and "blues" and "melancholia" that beset him in other times. The evidence from this period of late winter further suggests that Paul Green's earlier depression was a serious clinical problem and not a funky dip in spirits during a bad spell. When he was not afflicted with the disease of depression, circumstances could get pretty rough without sending him into the blues. By contrast, when he was afflicted, as documented in 1975 correspondence, he could be depressed even when circumstances of the external world appeared to be favorable, if not sunny. At any rate, the evidence is also unmistakable about the kind of roles that were played by Lib Green and Barrett Clark. She was wife, lover, friend, and counsel; Clark was agent, mentor, and friend. The public statements Paul Green consistently gave on behalf of each of them sometimes ring of the rhetorical; but in the context of the diary and correspondence, anything favorable he or anyone else might say about these two is hard to overstate. In their different ways, they saved his life.

As noted, the word *depression* was not one that Paul Green or his family or his friends in the 1920s used much. He was far more likely to speak of blues, funk, melancholy, or melancholia. After October 1929, that word *depression* would be capitalized, and it would take an article and the modifier, also capitalized, *Great*. More, after the stock market crash and bank failures were marked as unmistakable and irreversible, the phrase would be used exclusively to describe a grand economic malady for an entire society.

And for once, the "poor professor" would be relatively better off than most of his family and friends who were not academics. Over the first months of the Great Depression, which the Greens lived through in England, Paul and Lib Green came to see that their microeconomic status was actually improving relative to everyone else's, that is, relative to those who were losing jobs, losing land, losing savings, all but losing their lives in a macroeconomic catastrophe. As a shrewd history professor at Carolina recalled the era from his own youth and from his painstaking research, the Great Depression was proof that "there are worse jobs than an academic one," for in this era a college professor, even one at a poor southern school, did enjoy a job security unavailable in almost any other profession or trade.[25]

The state of North Carolina itself was clobbered, and perhaps more palpably than other states in the former Confederacy. Neighboring South Carolina, still overwhelmingly rural, was already in deep agricultural recession, and the broader national calamity brought most South Carolinians a sense that the country had "joined them in the ditch." And indeed Paul Green's native Harnett County was like that, as he and Hugh Green had been sweating the details of cotton and tobacco production for depressed sandhills and eastern markets since 1925. By contrast, however, the North Carolina piedmont cities had been enjoying business expansion, and for Greensboro, Charlotte, and Durham, the late 1920s had been boom times, and the crash in 1929 was thus a hard one in both relative and absolute terms.[26]

The word that came in by post from Broadway, Buies Creek, and Chapel Hill confirmed for the traveling Greens how bad things were. Contracts were yet again renegotiated for plays and performances, and this time Paul Green was given to understand that only by such severe cost-cutting—on the back of the playwright author—could his art be displayed *at all*. Lib Green, the tough negotiator, and Barrett Clark, the protective mentor, reached a working agreement that she could bargain as hard as she wanted without hurting anyone's feelings—as long as she worked in the context of dramatically reduced expectations. The playwright's debit account thus grew still more, but Lib Green was assured, and through her the playwright himself: Paul Green enjoyed a big credit limit at Samuel French exactly because the agency was confident that he would produce still more material, that that new material would be marketable, and that the agency would collect its money with something to spare for its own profits, and even something left over for the Greens beyond the playwright's advances. He was told that he was a good risk, even and especially in bad times, and he should consider himself so. Above all, Clark and Lib Green always insisted to the playwright: *Write!*[27]

As for the Buies Creek farmlands, Hugh Green had more than he could say grace over. The nature of the farm was that the Green family members there could always eat, and they could revert to barter with neighbors to gain some services that they needed; but credit was hard to come by at a time when an already depressed subregion fell afoul of an international depression. Hugh Green had only brother Paul to go to when the farms had to have cash. Of course, that was still Paul Green's farmland too, and that was still his family, and the cash went there as quickly as the playwright could get hold of any himself. But the Buies Creek Greens and the land operations could get no cash from the Chapel Hill Greens until after the travelers came home, for there were simply no spare nickels that Lib Green could find. Thus, the Buies Creek farmlands, for which Paul and Lib Green remained equity holders, cash creditors, and attenuated family members, were now by extreme degree what they had always been in kind, that is, *land-poor.*

And so the Greens shivered through the lingering winter of 1929 reassured by university tenure and publishing house credit but threatened by everything else, from the bad weather in Berlin to the worse market conditions on Broadway and on the farmlands. Then came an encouraging call suggesting security and prestige, from nothing less than Harvard University. Late in April, Carleton Parker wrote to Paul Green that students and some alumni associated with Harvard University's drama productions were prepared to offer the Carolinian a guaranteed three thousand dollars per annum to teach playwriting and otherwise develop the drama program at Cambridge. This call came because George Pierce Baker—Proff Koch's own teacher—had done the unthinkable and had abandoned the crimson of fair Harvard for the blue of Yale University, the bitter rival in unlovely New Haven. According to Parker's note, members of the stunned drama department had then taken a great deal of time for full discussion of the crisis. Result of the consultations was a frantic call that Paul Green save them. Carleton indicated further that it was students themselves who were especially eager to have this particular playwright to fill this large void.[28]

Although the salary was firm, teaching duties, possible directing and producing duties, and other expectations all seemed a bit open-ended, and Paul Green's general accountability in the proposals seemed a bit vague. The appointment did not seem to carry full-time faculty status on any track for tenure, and it did not otherwise bear the imprimatur of President Abbott Lawrence Lowell. Withal, the jobs appeared to threaten the precious time for his own writing. Flattered in any case, he politely demurred, citing commitments to the University of North Carolina: they had been kind enough to grant him leave, and then an extension, and he owed his own colleagues something for their kindnesses.[29]

Of course, loyalty was only part of his reasons for declining this call, but it was a genuine part, and that quality was soon strained by some of the folk back home on the Hill. The sheriff sent a bill from the county, with pro forma notice of foreclosure and property sales as the final way to collect taxes in arrears. Paul Green was convinced that he had actually paid these taxes, and he was able to get the Reverend Lay and Bill Couch to confirm his records for him and then to call off the authorities. It was a minor, and short-lived, annoyance, but the complications of long-distance wrangling, combined with a sense of unappreciated sacrifice to stay in Chapel Hill, certainly rankled.[30]

The bad news of this official's notice, however, was as nothing compared to what his young philosophy colleague Katherine Gilbert told him in her springtime note. Gilbert sent word that Horace Williams disapproved of an extension of leave for Green; furthermore, the legendary mentor was expressing his disapproval by trying to have the Chase administration fire Green. This communication, in Green's words, *floored* him, and he wrote to Gilbert and to Williams demanding explanations. Gilbert's explanation came at once, but Williams's would not arrive until the following autumn, and by that late date it was so unsatisfactory that the two men would never again be as close as they once were. As noted, some years before, Green had come to realize that Williams was not after all a great scholar; and Williams had come to realize that Green was hardly the proper hope for a revitalized and modern department of philosophy. Yet, until this incident the old affections between mentor and master had remained strong and sincere, and in their different Hegelian ways, each had counted the other an ally in grander causes. Now, each man was convinced that the other had attempted something clandestine, had betrayed a trust, and above all had displayed deficiency in what they both called *virtus*—and what their parents had called *character*.[31]

In retrospect one could see it coming: Horace Williams at the end of his long career finally realized that his planned legacy of a modern philosophy department was in jeopardy because his hope for philosophy was no pro in philosophy—and thus no hope at all. Always uneasy with the idea of the extension of this Guggenheim sabbatical, Williams was outraged when he came to understand that Green had done no systematic study of philosophy abroad and in fact *never would do any such systematic study*, at home or in Europe or back at Cornell or anywhere. Green's self-image of riding two horses, his infectious enthusiasms for broad-ranging discussions, his popularity among students, his personal attractiveness to Williams, perhaps even the accomplishment of "stealing" him away from the English department, all these things had blinded Williams to the fact that he was losing Green as a real philosopher, that in fact Paul Green had never intended to be a real philosopher.

Horace Williams's reaction, while draconian, was logical: Green was not keeping his end of the contract to make a modern philosophy program—*and so out he must go!* Laying aside for the moment the legal niceties of academic tenure, the part that was regrettable—and low—was that Horace Williams never communicated these things directly to his favorite pupil but instead let Green find out after the fact. On the other hand, Green himself—Thomas Wolfe's student philosopher of the cotton patch—had not really played it straight and aboveboard with his favorite teacher.

But if these things seem logical and even inevitable to us at a remove of decades, they did not seem so to the two wounded lions. The old lion wanted to kill his deceiving son, and the young lion called for help from the rest of the pride: Horace Williams might be a legend, but he was not after all king of the current jungle. Green thus wrote to his younger colleague Katherine Gilbert to see what the powerful reigning lions Harry Chase, Robert B. House, and Frank Porter Graham would do and say about this dispute.

Part of Gilbert's lengthy reply to his query was reassuring. She could report that the UNC administrators, especially President Chase and Executive Secretary Bob House, were completely on Green's side in this dispute, as was historian Doc Graham, dean of the liberal arts faculty. Extension of Green's leave was granted for academic year 1929–30, and he would be welcomed back joyfully in fall 1930. Those same officials agreed with Green that Gilbert was doing a credible job as his replacement, and that the department could function satisfactorily for another academic year with her continuing to teach Green's courses. Despite those reassurances, the letter was devastating: it was her characterization of Horace Williams as untrustworthy that stung—and it stung with special pain because Green had come to agree with that characterization.[32]

Gilbert declared her surprise, even disbelief, that Green had not realized Williams was treacherous as well as discontented. She also called the old legend two-faced, indeed thousand-faced. She urged Green not to trust his philosophy mentor at all, particularly because Williams was saying kind things to Green's face while trying to fire him behind the scenes. She reported further that still another junior colleague, Stephen Albert Emery, was teaching some philosophy and was handling the administrative details of the department because Williams was not efficient nowadays in those matters. Gilbert urged that Green enjoy his leave, and rest assured that there was good will for him at Carolina and that competent people, despite Horace Williams, were holding the fort in philosophy. Finally, she noted that her soon-to-be colleagues at Duke University, folklorists Frank Brown and Newman Ivy White, also declared their own good will for Paul and Lib Green. Everyone, in short, said that this couple was much the best of the Chapel Hillians.[33]

From President Chase there came a telegram, "Leave granted—Chase," and a letter almost as laconic. In the letter Chase said that he and Horace Williams had talked at length and that the administration then announced its complete support of Green's extended leave, with return to regular appointment in philosophy, effective fall quarter 1930. Williams, in his own much-delayed communication with Green, mentioned two letters that he had written, but Green does not seem to have received either of them. In the surviving, last note, Williams said tersely that he and the president had talked, and that Chase supported Green's extended leave and his return, exactly as Green requested both things. Williams indicated that, after that discussion, he was displeased, but there was nothing else that he could do but accept the administration's power and prerogative. He declared that he had been aboveboard and frank in his statements of concerns about Green's abandoning philosophy, and he said that philosophy at Carolina stood at low ebb, with inadequate faculty and lack of student interest. He described the cause of philosophy as suffering from blows, blows coming from within and from without. Presumably the blows from without were financial and budgetary, but he certainly implied that the blows from within came from Gilbert, Emery, and from Green himself. He closed this letter with the lament that the Chapel Hill campus was generally in low spirits, with good people leaving because of bad pay, and with reduced prospects for those who remained behind.[34]

During his extended leave, Green wrote many things, among which the most important, and most interesting, was *Potter's Field*. This one-act "Negro play" is in many ways as experimental as anything he ever attempted. He shipped the finished version to Clark, who was wildly supportive, and the playwright also showed it around to people in Europe, including the risk-taking producer Maurice Brown of London. Brown and others were almost as appreciative as Clark, and some preliminary steps were taken to produce the play in Moscow of Petrograd, although finally it was not presented in the Soviet Union. Sidney Ross put it on with Jasper Deeter at the Hedgerow Theater of Rose Valley, Pennsylvania, after balking at least once, and after it was turned down by Arthur Hopkins and by the Theater Guild. As Green had long feared, the Provincetown Playhouse group went inactive; and that dreaded result cost him one troupe predisposed to accept his offerings. Still, the Hedgerow was a very sympathetic company, especially the rather self-absorbed but very innovative director Jasper Deeter. The Hedgerow group, which had also dramatized some things for Sherwood Anderson, was self-consciously left of center in ideology and experimental in technique; and they would produce *Potter's Field* at least once more with African American cast. The play thus took its place, along with the already-celebrated *In Abraham's Bosom* and *No 'Count Boy,* as one of the reasons that African American actors of the era needed Green, since he was giving black performers original, challenging, and above all serious roles to play.[35]

Potter's Field has no scenes and is a lengthy one-acter, with important narrative and thematic developments coming through interior dialogues while other significant aspects of the plot are carried forward in vernacular conversations in dense and challenging dialect. There are original songs and some clever and ironic new uses of old folk songs, and this music, as Granovsky would will it on his own stage, becomes itself a kind of player in the drama. There are many characters, all of whom emerge from a black version of the extended Abramic family, and only strong acting can differentiate the players. It makes few concessions to the audience, or to the actors. As Clark wrote in several letters, it is no more a one-acter in the ordinary sense than *Oedipus* is a one-acter; and the agent opined that in this modern era his friend Green had again, and brilliantly, demonstrated that a tragedy need not be divided into acts.[36]

The blues singer and his songs are both crucial to this play, and the author is careful to get what he called the "rightest" interpretation of that music, that is, to allow minimum room for audience interpretation of a message in the blues on stage. It is piedmont blues, with an insistent, compelling, unstopping rhythm as steady, slow, and irresistible as a long freight train. Blues songs borrow from black gospel songs, especially in the call-and-response interplay with the audience and in the biblical themes that they develop. They are, however, nonreligious and are even considered diabolically antireligious by the churchgoers of the Carolinas and Virginia, for they are touched with a sense of malevolent power. One line of dialogue says that the blues singer "makes dem songs ag'in God." At a crucial point, the aged character Ed Uzzell, once bootlegging Bad Ed of Memphis, takes the gospel song image "rainbow round my shoulder" (a favorite of the liberals Howard Washington Odum and Guy Johnson of the UNC Regionalist school of science and reformism). He sings it ironically, after first describing how an angry congregation that he had bilked put a "window frame round my shoulder." The message is one of a cruel fate and an unavoidable tragic resolution for the black men in Green's script.[37]

None of what Green does in *Potter's Field* is waste motion, despite the length of the play, and none of it is ostentatious or "showing off," despite the self-conscious experiments. The audience must learn a few things from Old Ed Uzzell about his youth as Bad Ed, and it does so through the agency of that timeless and troubled elder's memory; the blues songs and a construction crew's percussive dynamite blasts set a pace of unhurried and inevitable destruction; and the female character Seeny in her external dialogue with Ed completes a thematic circle begun by Ed's interior thoughts. The blues words not only complete a circle, but also draw a snare around every character on the stage.

To drive home the message of doom for the inhabitants of the hogdump, as Green called the place, he gives a remarkable twist, more a thematic than a plot twist, to the ending of *Potter's Field*. A chain gang is working, and the leading or "pace" hammer in the crew is the devil-preacher Bad Man Bolis, the same man who had cheated gullible believers and one who had committed other crimes against his people. Now Bad Man Bolis sets the pace for the work by chanting relentlessly while swinging the rock-busting steel as the gang breaks a path for a road right through Potter's Field. This convict not only had pretended to be a preacher in order to preach evil "ag'in God," but he had also taken the name of the folk hero John Henry, the steel-driving man—and thus had posed as a laborer's hero. But a finishing irony in the Bad Man Bolis/John Henry character is that by the play's conclusion he is legitimate: he is the lead steel driver, reliable, strong, better than a machine; and he is the prophet who sees the moral disorder in things. Bad Man Bolis/John Henry chants, the *hanh*-grunt of the downswing punctuating for him:

> Sing on—sing on—beaten—darkness—night—God sits on high, his face from the
> Negro. The poor and needy cry
> in vain, the iron palings hold them—hanh—The steel
> and the iron divide them—hanh![38]

Ed Uzzell sees everything, understands everything, and thus takes up a convict's pick. He has no other choice in what remains of his life. The chain gain digs on to heaven, the displaced shantytown residents dig on to the end of the world.[39]

Green did some other fine writing during "Lib's trip," including travel reports from Thomas Hardy's very heath, an interview with George Bernard Shaw, and early work on *Tread the Green Grass,* still another experimental folk play influenced by Granovsky, Wolflin, Plessow, and other contemporaneous continental thinkers.[40] The little family had weathered the dragged-out Berlin winter, unexpectedly high expenses in London, academic shenanigans back on the Hill, worsening agricultural recession on the Harnett farm properties, and the collapse for piedmont cities when the Great Depression struck. Lib and Paul Green took account of themselves in the autumn as they began to realize that this economic downturn was not a bad spell, but indeed a depression for everyone.

The accounting listed plenty of happy things on the credit side. Play productions were moving along nicely, with *In Abraham's Bosom* showing in Frankfurt, *Potter's Field* being positioned for a New York run after a Hedgerow performance in Pennsylvania's Rose Valley, and agents inquiring about rights to existing plays as well as rights to planned plays. Certainly, Green had plenty of material, plus a satchel of new playwriting techniques for still more plays. Barrett Clark said that Hollywood was a possibility, and Green already knew how different was the money in California, a relative difference even grander during economic downturn. Green had manuscripts for Bill Couch, and he had plenty of information about rights to translations and rights to American publication of other manuscripts. Horace Williams was at bay, and professors Gilbert and Emery were set to teach fall quarter, with everyone, including Williams, assuring the traveler that the Department of Philosophy could make it without Green during winter and spring quarters of 1930.

Away from the professional level, there were still more credits. Green was now fully back in his usual resilient energies and enthusiasms and again able to work very long hours and to play very late hours. Paulie and Byrd Green were healthy once the weather finally warmed up and dried out, and Lib Green was recovered from her own bout with sinus infection. She was ready and in fact excited about doing England and the western Continent as thoroughly as they had done Germany and the central continent. With the Guggenheim imprimatur renewed on all that he might do, the poet in Green was ready to stay until summer of 1930, perhaps even "figger out" some way to stay until August of 1930. And of course the judicious side of Green comprehended well that "Lib's trip" had been one of nonstop service to family, business, and his own career, followed by her own turn at serious illness. The result was few chances for her to do any of her own creative work and not even as much sightseeing as they had planned. Poetry and justice spoke, and each said, *Stay*.

There was, however, also the bookkeeper inside Green, and ledger-book values were constantly revised downward in this Great Depression. Knowing that he must sound ridiculous, but not then knowing how ridiculous, he dropped a note to the hard-pressed farmer Hugh Green warning that the Chapel Hill Greens might need a little financial assistance during the coming winter of 1929–30. The Samuel French people could not extend much more credit, and revenues after November 1929 would make the low revenues of the previous year look good by contrast. Bill Couch and the Reverend Lay may have straightened out the Orange County taxing authorities for 1929, but paying one's just dues in 1930 would be a difficult challenge. Debits were piling up, and Sidney Ross was reducing his terms of payment for *Potter's Field*, plus delaying its production; and Ross would not allow Green to publish the play until after it had been performed in New York, thereby delaying publishing royalties on which the playwright had long ago drawn an advance. Green explored the possibility of using some of the Guggenheim money at home in spring of 1930, but the people in that agency made it clear that the money was to be used in Europe for the stated purpose of study. When he came home, the stipend would stop.[41]

Weighing these things, Paul and Lib Green decided to come back in December. Then, upon "refiggering," they determined to come home the first week of November after a quick visit to Paris. So reckoning, they saw how very few days they could enjoy in England and in Paris. Within a few weeks, even the short time allotted for England seemed like too much. As October wore on, it became harder for Paul Green to do creative writing, Lib Green was mostly a hostess, and they found themselves for different reasons exhausted as well as broke. Green wrote to Proff Koch with the disappointing news that the London theater was not especially interesting—wonderful acting of course, and knowledgeable audiences, but no director or playwright half as innovative as Granovsky, and certainly no performing troupe half as interesting as the Berlin remnants of Moscow's traveling Yiddish group.[42]

Still, there was an inspiriting trip to Hardy's homeplace, with visit to family survivors, Green having just barely missed the realization of his dream to meet the novelist and poet himself, for Hardy had died about the time that Green won the Guggenheim stipend. Tramping the heath, Green drew maps and with help from Hardy family members and other Hardy scholars, figured out where the characters had done things; in most cases, he could place the major fictional events of the novels on a real map. Then the wartime engineer could go and stand on that very spot. And he had an evening with George Bernard Shaw, being careful to assure the Irishman that current British theater might sometimes be dull, but never one particular host playwright. Writing up that interview a little exuberantly and sounding perhaps a little too much the cheerleader, Green was at least careful not to repeat the error of his colleague Archibald Henderson, biographer of Shaw, who liked to tell people that he had "discovered Shaw" and who was mightily embarrassed both by Shaw himself and by H. L. Mencken when these claims were exposed as wild exaggerations. Green had the good sense to listen carefully, and then he kept his essay focused on the subject, with himself barely there at all.[43]

The man could feel good about his studies, about the people whom he met and learned from, and about his writings while abroad. It was time to go home and set to work there. Lib Green agreed, but there was a final piece of most complicated business to negotiate, and she had to put it into motion before they could leave.

Erma Lamprecht had been a godsend to the Green family in Berlin. It was not only that Lib Green detested cooking and cleaning, and it was not only that Paul Green's period of clinical depression followed by respiratory ailments for all four Greens had given Lib Green so many new duties that such domestic help became a necessity instead of a luxury. Although these considerations were hardly small, the larger thing was that *Tante,* as the children called her, and *Fraulein,* as Paul Green called her, was a wonderful companion to very young children of very ambitious parents at a time when Doogie and Mother were not always able or willing to give them a lot of attention.

As the family prepared itself to leave Berlin, Lib Green insisted that Erma Lamprecht go with them to England. At that moment, in the summer of 1929, Paul Green thought only that Lib Green wanted guaranteed help with the abhorred household duties. [44] What he came gradually to understand was that Erma Lamprecht was important to his family, and that someday the Greens would have to get her permanently out of Berlin, not so much to help them in the kitchen as to help her escape Adolf Hitler's awful new Germany.

In fact, the postscript to "Lib's trip" was recorded a full year after the Greens had resettled on the Hill. Then in December of 1930, Erma Lamprecht, at Lib Green's invitation, attempted to leave her Germany at least temporarily as its economy worsened and as its politics became portentous with disaster. When she arrived at Ellis Island, however, Lamprecht's visa was marked "governess" for the occupation blank, much as it had been when she had traveled to England with the Greens. Unfortunately, immigration authorities generally did not allow governesses into the country, and in any case they were profoundly suspicious of Germans attempting to enter the United States during the second full year of the Great Depression. She was thus detained and warned of possible deportation. Lib Green thereupon ordered her husband to New York and, if need be, to Washington to take action. [45]

In events that the playwright could not have scripted, not even in an H.E. diary, Lamprecht was permitted into the country on temporary visa, stayed through several last-second rescues from deportation, and indeed eventually became an American citizen with her own chicken farm in the Old North State. It took more than Lib Green's will and Paul Green's actions, of course, and that is where several situational ironies transpire as the records are unfolded: Franklin J. Shiel of the Samuel French Company was especially useful, but most useful of all was Josiah W. Bailey, a Raleigh attorney and state senator from Wake County. This Bailey had first corresponded with the Greens in 1924 as an aspiring poet and subscriber to *The Reviewer*. And, if Chekov is right and no playwright should ever place a pistol on the mantelpiece in full view of the audience in one act unless some character shoots the pistol in a subsequent act, then Clio the Muse knows these dramatic procedures and follows them in the spinning out of history. Not only is the good attorney introduced in 1924 as eager poet, but he is brought down from the mantelpiece to help Erma Lamprecht between late fall 1930 and early winter 1931. Still more appropriate for Clio's production, Bailey was busy with other things besides helping Lamprecht. He was also working away as member of a commission charged to establish an appropriate festival and fitting memorial, possibly with annual dramatic performance, to commemorate the Roanoke Island settlement of 1584–87. [46]

Bailey said that he would need a playwright, especially one who knew something of local and regional history, to help with these very vague plans.

1930–1934

When they arrived back on the Hill, Paul and Lib Green found that the Great Depression was also called simply "hard times." How hard?

Edith J. R. Isaacs, editor of *Theatre Arts Monthly* and an early supporter of Green's plays, summed things up in a note to him: he was doing his very best work, but there was no commercial outlet for that fine work. Often she had helped Green, as with the early appointment and scholarship at the Peterboro Writers Colony and with publicity, and by talking to the right people at the right time. After 1930, however, Isaacs could do little more than write him encouraging letters and urge him to keep up his best work in the hope that something, somewhere, would break his way. He was a pro, and a pro has to work through the bad spells. Left unsaid but clearly implied was a postscript: This bad spell, these hard times, were so completely beyond the control of any pro that a playwright had to work not only optimistically, but idealistically, almost *gratia artis.* [1]

Of course, if one were really to work *gratia artis,* then why be a pro and write for the marketplace at all? This sort of tension was always there in such a high-risk endeavor as Broadway and off-Broadway playwriting, but the depression exacerbated the risks while removing most of the rewards. In such circumstances Green was fortunate indeed to be a professor of philosophy, uninteresting as the scholarly pursuit of that discipline had become for him. Despite hard times, the people at Samuel French were confident enough to advance Green another two thousand dollars against expected royalties from publication of the new plays, from planned publication of repackaged old plays, and from new productions. Thus again borrowing against the future revenues, he could pay part of what he owed brother Hugh Green in the overseeing agreement for the Harnett farms, and he could pay the most demanding of the suppliers and creditors in Chapel Hill. Writing to and talking with his brother, Green could reflect on relative poverty and relative ease. Unlike Hugh Green, the professor did have a reliable automobile that he could drive. And UNC proffered tenure rather than tenancy. [2]

But bad news did come for the Greens; and despite their relatively privileged position, the news was very bad, and it struck hard. It became painfully apparent that Sidney Ross was not going to bring *Potter's Field* to Broadway; and worse, he was going to make it impossible for anyone else to do so on Broadway by "sitting on" the play for the full legal time of his cheaply bought—and dearly sold—option for the rights to Broadway production. The deeply respected director Leo Bulgakov sadly informed Green that Ross and his people had no respect at all for the aesthetics of the play and that their machinations were ruining *Potter's Field* for the otherwise sympathetic pros in New York. And, after compromising the integrity of the play, Ross had no intention of ever producing it. It was, then, a rich man's toy in hard times.[3]

By late October 1930 Green gave up and accepted Bulgakov's verdict. He wrote Ross and told the producer that he wanted the rights to the play at once, as it was apparent that the financier intended to delay until the contract expired in January 1931. The note is frank but conciliatory and courteous. Between its lines is Marcus Aurelius the Stoic, perhaps less appropriately so for a modern philosopher than for a man holding responsibilities for family lands in eastern Carolina. Ross did not hew to the letter of the law and relinquished his rights amiably enough—it had, after all, cost him very little, and he had had his fun. Among other things, ending the Ross production finally allowed Samuel French to publish the play, and there could be at least some revenues—or more properly, reductions in debts from advances—to gain from sale of the scripts. At least *Potter's Field* had been performed honorably by the Hedgerow troupe in Rose Valley, Pennsylvania, and friendly critics and fellow artists could read the script now.[4] In any case, there remained *Tread the Green Grass,* another experimental play with its own Broadway prospects.

Green described *Tread the Green Grass* as a folk fantasy in mixed forms, and he was frank that it is antireligious, that is, it unsparingly attacks organized religion. Although it is divided into parts, and it does have scenes, it too offers no siesta time and no opportunities for between-scenes audience-gabbling. As with *Potter's Field,* the audience must pay attention to dialogue, to music, to settings, and even and especially to the things explained during interludes between scenes. Anyone going to the bathroom or chatting or even paying less than full attention in those interludes inevitably and irretrievably loses the threads of plot and theme. It features specially designed sets, new music particular to the occasion, one entire scene in pantomime, other scenes in puppet dumb-show, and demanding roles for players who have to shift, often rapidly, back and forth between the comedic and the tragic and between a kind of intensely historical peasant realism and virtually timeless fantasies about everything from traditional Christology to Satanism to Mother Goose fairy tales.[5]

Working on the concept for American productions, Green became friends with the musician Lamar Stringfellow and the technical man and someday director Samuel Selden, two who became longtime *compadres* inside and outside

Chapel Hill. And the processes of attempting yet another Broadway run taught such bitter lessons about theater finance that the likes of Sidney Ross, William Dorsey Blake, and Lee Shubert drove both Green and Clark to look for new ways of being honorable pros in the arts-economics world after hard times not only hit but stuck.[6]

It is hard to do the play right, or as Green insisted, to do it *rightest,* and the audience is expected to work hard to get the point; but unlike postmodernist art, *Tread the Green Grass* does not permit the audience much interpretive room. Like most art of that modernist era, the structure that defines author and audience, and the relationships between author and audience, is a formal one, and an imposing one. Green demanded a director who would do the play Green's way. Meeting that charge entailed meeting some high standards for complex technology as well as dramatic techniques and expensive sets, all hard to manage artistically and all even harder to finance under depression-era budget constraints.[7]

One of the most problematical aspects of putting on this play is Green's concept that it be universally about peasant fantasies, and that it exist timelessly and in no particular place. Unlike his other plays, this one is not set in a specific place during a specific era, and its theme of peasant fantasies in conflict can be developed only by convincing the audience—always an urban, even urbane, one—that the emotions being played out before it are real because they are universal responses to the nonrational tyranny that comes when competing shaman-priests manipulate the symbols of the supernatural. There isn't any effort to be fair or balanced in dealing with the priestly leaders of the peasantry, and readers and theatergoers are given to understand that the evil worked by renegade anti-Christ people and other antichurch people is essentially the effect of an equal but opposite evil worked by established churches themselves. When the "demon" folk burn down the church building, it is obvious that the playwright thinks that what they have done is at least partly justified; and he is quite clear that the characters on stage and in the audience must be liberated from what he considered the superstition as well as the lies of the established churches. In his own notes Green says that the character Davie, who destroys a church building, symbolically frees at least some of the young members of the congregation from the chains of a narrowly binding religion.[8]

Other things about the play are difficult in terms of scenes, sets, and language. Ineffably, it looks and sounds southern, despite scrupulous efforts to keep cotton and tobacco and the Civil War and even African Americans off the stage. It is the southern Protestant structure of the music, the words, and the gestures that make it a Carolina peasantry and not a universal country folk. Green even writes stage notes for a production that the congregation in the penultimate scene is to move in a "Jewish" walk with "Jewish" gestures and is to bear a "countenance" that is "Jewish." The demon figure and antihero young Davie is to don a Roman helmet. The point of these non-Christian, European, and "Jewish" gestures and signs seems to be to pull the entire play into the fantasy emotional world of folk in the countryside in any land, any place. However, all of these gestures and signs occur after quite a great deal of singing and preaching that is pointedly Christian, and intensely Protestant, and specifically the bowdlerized Calvinism of the Baptists from Harvey Easom's and Paul Greene's youth. Audiences hear the voices of the Reverend Tom Long and the roaring Texas evangelist who came through the upper valley of the Cape Fear River and preached at the playwright in his youth. Thus, Green's own genius for the sound of the Calvinist southern fundamentalist makes it instead a play somewhere in the South with still more proof that Proff Koch was dead right: a Playmaker must stand in a small place and talk from that vantage point about large issues for everyone. In other words, *Tread the Green Grass,* whether it fails or succeeds, is very much a regional product, and Green here is just as much a Chapel Hill liberal, Carolina Playmaker, and even "Hegel in the Cotton Belt" as he is everywhere else.[9]

The judgment here is that *Tread the Green Grass* is less than Green thought it was—even when directed, staged, choreographed, set, acted, and *heard* rightest. Even so, it is so much more than the competing dramatic fare of 1930 and 1931 and 1932 that it certainly deserved support and study. In any case, there was a story behind the story, and the acting behind the scenes among directors, producers, financiers, critics, and theater talkers made a dark and fey comedy fully worthy of the playwright or the blues singer. The details are tedious, but summing up, they are that the play could not be performed in New York, not even off Broadway, despite the opinions of some very savvy theater people who insisted that it should be performed. Green's original benefactor, the noble Provincetown Playhouse, made the fairest effort, but it went broke in the depression. Eleanor M. Fitzgerald, Fitzie of the Provincetown Playhouse, was early and late and always loud in her support of *Tread the Green Grass.* With her troupe disbanded, Fitzgerald moved farther off Broadway, to the County Center in White Plains, New York, where she did eventually produce a fine version of the play.[10] Her efforts were sincere, and Green appreciated everything that she did; but he was bitterly disappointed that his most innovative play was performing only in White Plains.

He could not dwell on disappointment, however, for good things also came to the rambling house on Greenwood Road. On 14 July 1930 Lib Green delivered yet another fine baby, this one christened Elizabeth MacAllister Green and immediately called Betsy. And on 18 December 1931 she delivered Janet McNeill Green, always called Janet. Now there were four children in Doogie's household, in addition to whatever traveling artist or reformist might have stopped over. Among many other things, these depression-era births inspired

Paul and Lib Green to think again about finances. They agreed to swallow a portion of pride and to approach the monied men in New York again, with flexibility and humility if not desperation.

Thus putting aside his white-hot anger with "rich man" financiers of Broadway, Green went several times to New York in the depression so that he could meet in person technical people and finance people as well as the theater talkers of the newspapers and radio shows. On one such trip, Green came to see that many others suffered too, not least the canny and otherwise irrepressible Barrett Clark. The agent and adviser talked in confidence about eventually leaving the Samuel French Company in order to develop an artists' consortium to produce plays for profit at universities and in major population centers—but emphatically *not* on Broadway or even off-Broadway New York. For the year of 1931, however, Clark had to report that the Dramatists Guild was to cut its own budget, thereby ending his referee's commissions for critical readings of new plays. The very mentor had to confess that the loss of income hurt, for New York was a very expensive place to live and work. As for the playwright, Clark talked with the office people at Samuel French, and Green was extended still more money. However, the agency flatly refused his most humiliating offer: he suggested that they buy a large percentage of his plays, a much higher percentage than a frontline, Pulitzer-winning playwright would normally permit. The agency was not buying. In the long term he was judged to be still worth the risk of advances against future royalties; but as to ownership of experimental plays, Samuel French declined those longer-term risks.[11]

What finally happened with *Tread the Green Grass* was that in 1932 E. C. Mabie of the University of Iowa arranged to produce it with his school's troupe. Iowa City was already a writer's paradise, and good things were happening there for performance arts as well. Green went out in summer of 1932, taught classes for a fee of five hundred dollars, collected one hundred dollars from production royalties, and found himself subject of some very well placed and extremely complimentary articles both by Barrett Clark and by Brooks Atkinson. Mabie had money, modest but still a remuneration, to hire *compadres* Lamar Stringfellow and Sam Selden, and both men received much-needed credits in a good production. As noted, Fitzie Fitzgerald came out to Iowa City to see the performance, loved it, and brought her own faithful version of it to White Plains. Proff Koch next arranged to put on the play with the Playmakers, and Green was assured of complete artistic control over those doings. With financiers Ross and Shubert out of the way, Samuel French was legally able to publish *Tread the Green Grass* and *Potter's Field* in a volume of new plays that sold well enough to reduce some of Green's debits with the company.[12]

More important, the publication, plus the university and White Plains productions, put Paul Green in front of intelligent audiences once again. It wasn't Broadway, but he was back in business, and for that depression era, being in business at all, in Iowa City, in Chapel Hill, and in White Plains, was an accomplishment.

Green did understand that the financial afflictions of his theater productions were mere daydreams, and pleasant ones at that, if compared with the nightmares of the Great Depression as lived out on his farmlands in Harnett by his own tenants and debtors—brother Hugh Green and his family; an uncle, Thomas Green; and unrelated renters and croppers of all "three races" (that is, including the "Croatan" Lumbees). And besides the personal pain that he could feel for family and old-time neighbors, he understood that the majority of farmers in the broad coastal plain of the Old North State lived the same agricultural nightmares. He understood too about the hard lives in the textile mill communities in what had once been the prospering piedmont. And from his students, some from farming families but increasingly from the service sector of the petite bourgeoisie, he could learn about what the social scientists were calling the "new poor" as once comfortable white-collar workers scrounged for odd jobs as day laborers. And he understood too that the "old poor" and the "new poor" scrounged but failed and were denied relief by overstrapped charitable agencies. He understood because he saw and heard how they then turned to begging, trickery, prostitution, and sometimes outright stealing.

He was in this period of the Great Depression, 1930–34, still officially an academic, a philosopher trained to analyze, and so he attempted some diagnosis of this current history. However, in those days Green was even more so the social activist, and thus he sharpened his previously vague politics of the left. Always a neopopulist with a soupçon of French socialism, Green pronounced the Republican Party of the period hopeless, but he was also harshly critical of the Democrats, again and again scoring presidential candidate Franklin Delano Roosevelt for proposing programs that were too traditional, too timid. Although he admired Governor O. Max Gardner for many things, he was almost brutal with Gardner's advisers who asked for his confidential response to the administration's Ten-Year Economic Development Plan for North Carolina.[13]

Even when the famed One Hundred Days of "First New Deal" legislation was enacted in 1933, Green disdained it as too little, too late. In fact Green was white hot in his discontent with societal injustice, red in his artistic associations, and pink in his politics. Correspondence before, during, and after the election of 1932 with the leftist activist Miriam Bonner indicates that in that context Green voted not for FDR but for Norman Thomas of the Socialist Party.[14]

While his own financial difficulties explain some of his left-wing attitudes and actions, they do not explain everything. After all, he himself was *the* landlord in Buies Creek, he himself was the protected professor on the Hill, and he himself was the playwright who enjoyed a security and some amenities as one who could receive royalties and who could draw on a relatively generous credit line. He had much to lose if the entire Western capitalist system collapsed by implosion or it if was exploded by revolution. And yet the ameliorative actions of the FDR New Deal angered him, even though the legislation was designed exactly to save his middle class among the Chapel Hillians and his kind of landowners among the country set. His quasi-Marxism, then, cannot be explained too well by class analysis. There was also in there the rally cry of the Old Harnett populists from the long-ago days of his childhood when black and white farmers, if hardly claiming to be brothers in society, yet declared themselves to be economically "in the ditch together" and so for that reason cooperated politically to protect their rights as agrarian workers.

During the darkest days of the early years of the Great Depression, Soviet Russian experiments in aesthetics interested American and European artists, as seen already for Green when he first tasted the fruits of Granovsky's formerly state-supported theater troupe. It may be that Green and his contemporaries in the early 1930s exaggerated the freshness of Russian artistic experimentation; and it may also be that he and others exaggerated the openness of the Soviet bureaucracy to such experimentation and risk taking in that period, for certainly by the late 1930s the USSR had become infamously rigid, with numbing censorship and literally mortal punishment for would-be innovators and experimenters. But in the hard times of the early 1930s, it was the economic de facto censorship of show-business financiers/producers Sidney Ross and Lee Shubert and Jed Harris that playwrights such as Green most noted. Thus, Green's leftist reformism in the era (something of an embarrassment to younger friends and family members looking back on it decades later) was hardly unusual, and certainly not hard to explain, when it actually happened.[15]

Paul Green was not by temperament a man of moderation, and if leftist campaigns were not then unusual, the degree of his public support of them was unusual. After all, he seldom entered into any campaign lightly or quietly. An inveterate signer of petitions and manifestos, he was in the 1930s purposively activist on the left side of the stage of political and social issues. In later years, when he was by no means radical in politics or in art, his continuing support of free speech was so prominent that some scholars believe that he lent his name to socialists and other left-wingers of the 1930s only as a sign of his commitments to free expression of ideas as modeled for the academy by John Stuart Mill.[16]

For Green aesthetics and politics had always intersected in terms of racial justice, but during the Great Depression economic questions seemed to be more obviously of a class nature; and he often found racial injustice to be a part of an economic determinism and class oppression. In correspondence, in his diary entries, and in some playwriting and scriptwriting, he then seemed to hint that racism may develop out of economic systems of injustice. In any case, that was certainly the message of the proletariat art movement, and Green was loudly and proudly involved in that movement as it first emerged.[17]

This movement, its literature and dramatist phase universally styled "prole lit" by detractors and proponents alike, was quite the rage, and it quickly developed a school and then subdivided itself into subschools and camps, and withal was subject of much warm discussion and some hot debate. Most of such discussion and experimentation was unorganized and uncoordinated, for prole lit was essentially a gestalt, that is, an attitude shared by many that art must serve the laboring classes. With exceptions, it was, like things labeled gestaltic, a broadly held but vaguely stated attitude rather than a systematic program. One program, however, did emerge, and Green joined it for a while: *Revolt in the Arts* was a published manifesto that attempted to state in aesthetic terms how differing forms, whether painting, acting, sculpting, singing, or writing, could express economics as an "independent consideration" in any subject of art. *Revolt* said that the Machine Age had created a "new interrelationship" between economics, aesthetics, and morality, with economic factors foremost in a way that they could not have been in the 1920s, when popular art had to serve the prospering middle class; now, with the Great Depression in force, most of that middle class was itself "new poor," and popular art had to serve the poor in order to serve the majority.[18]

The *Revolt* manifesto insisted that artists could still perform as craftspeople working as creative and autonomous individuals, even though all industrial productions must be standardized on the assembly line. Indeed, *Revolt* claimed that mass production, properly managed and controlled, could provide technological resources, such as radio and cinema, that made highly individualized artcraft free or at very low price in many places and all at the same time. Arts people whom Green admired in the era were prominent in the movement, for example, Robert Edmond Jones for scenic art, George Pierce Baker for drama schools, Maurice Brown for Little Theater, and Arthur Hopkins and David Belasco for drama production. Green signed the manifesto with enthusiasm, especially when *Revolt* people began talking with him about a reconstituted Provincetown Playhouse, with its innovative plays and performances to be displayed in many places *other than* the money-censored Broadway of financiers Shubert, Ross, and Harris. He also contributed an essay, "Some Notes on the Playwright in Revolt," in which he walked through some garden-variety Hegelian concepts ("Revolt then is but another term for development or growth. . . . Thus any production is the production of something new from the old.") but generally spoke with more of a revolutionist's edge in his voice: "[I]f art, the drama, to consider once more, is beholden to gain, commercial enterprises and rents, gambling and exchanges, whims and fancies of its upholders, it is no longer art but a symbol of barter and vanity, in which beauty becomes a figment on an expedient currency." Although the *Revolt* program did not survive in its planned form, elements of it eventually reappeared, transformed and flourishing for several seasons, in the Federal Writers Projects. Specifically, there were the theater programs of the Federal Writers Projects, and these Green served and was served by.[19]

Green did find one artistic way to declare his sympathies with the *Revolt* movement, and at once: Russell Sedgwick of Masses Stage Guild produced a prole lit version of *Abraham* for London audiences in the fall season of 1930. Sedgwick was a man known well and admired by Paul and Lib Green, and he produced a version of *Abraham* with a largely black cast, not only with the Greens' full approval but also with the playwright's written suggestions so that this tragedy could be done *rightest* for the English masses. Sedgwick was not entirely happy with the results, but a review by the prominent critic St. John Ervine was enthusiastic, and playwright and producer were both cheered by the fine performance that the previously unknown African American actor Grace Walker rendered as Goldie. As for his opinion of the name Masses Stage Guild (obviously a self-consciously prole-lit labeling), Paul Green was emphatic and unequivocal: That is a *grand* name for your organization, he said flatly and repeated without irony.[20]

Among grand names, none was grander for artist-activists than John Reed, the only American buried in Russia with honors by the Soviets. Green eagerly joined the John Reed Club, an organization of writers and artists that included Michael Gold, I. Klein, Hugo Gellard, and, most famously, the then-leftist novelist John Dos Passos. In March 1930 Dos Passos and Green signed a manifesto that would haunt each of them in future decades, though they would have plenty of company in that haunting. That company would include not only the creative and imaginative writers but also the supposedly more levelheaded Ed Keen, vice president of United Press International news-service syndicate, and Walter Duranty of the good and gray *New York Times*. Indeed other signatures came from the ranks of the organized-religion groups thought to be especially vulnerable to the Soviets: a delegation of Minsk Jewish rabbis and Metropolitan Sergius, head of the Greek Orthodox Church in Moscow.[21]

The issue was a planned protest of a planned protest, showing just how convoluted could be political signs in those times. Pope Pius XI, the archbishop of Canterbury, New York Episcopal Bishop William Thomas Manning, and Rabbi Stephen Wise had organized for 16 March 1930 a prayer day on behalf of Christians and Jews denied their religious freedoms by the Soviet Union. The John Reed Club, drawing on reports from the newspaper correspondents of UPI and the *New York Times*, informed its members that the only Soviet prosecutions of Jews or Christians involved "activities against the State collectivization program, not for religious reasons." Too, the Minsk rabbis sent word that the Soviet Union alone in the modern world had taken official action against antisemitism; and Green himself could testify to Soviet sponsorship of

Yiddish folk theater and could assure those who wanted to know that Granovsky and other Jewish theater people came west because they were pulled by financial and artistic opportunities, not because they were pushed out by the state. Therefore, the John Reed Club petitioners planned to protest the prayer day because it would insult an unoffending government.[22]

Indeed, ran the petition as its authors warmed up to this task, the prayer day could well cause war! "Will the next war be fought," petitioners asked rhetorically, because of "the fraudulent slogan of 'making the world safe for religion?' " Yes, they declared, it could well become "the emotional basis for plunging the world into war against a country in which the creative energy of millions of people has been unleashed by a revolution against tyranny, corruption, and superstition." Signing this protest, petitioners concluded, was a declaration that one understood the aggressiveness of "meddling in the affairs of a people with whom we are at peace." Green sent in his name to be so published, and for good measure he wrote on his own copy of the "Dear Friend" circular that he *protested* the march.[23]

As the facts of Soviet persecutions transpired, the signatories looked ridiculous, producing such remorse and anguish in Dos Passos that he became a famously anti-Communist activist in his mature years. Too, other Old Left intellectuals and artists eventually produced secular and political versions of Augustinian confessions in which they renounced their wrongheaded, and wronghearted, old ways. Most prominent of those self-absolutions was a collection of cold war anti-Communist essays sponsored by Richard Crossman, a British member of Parliament, to which one of the contributors was the black novelist Richard Wright, whom Green admired and with whom Green would work on a Broadway adaptation of *Native Son* that received serious Pulitzer consideration. However, in 1930 most leftists—and in fact most moderates—had no idea the extent of abuses then taking place in Stalin's regime. When Paul Green insisted that war could result from praying in the United States for those who could not pray in the Soviet Union, he did so alongside many others in the avant-garde politics and art of 1930 and 1931.[24]

Closer to home there were leftists less well known, but equally dear to Paul and Lib Green. *Contempo* was an experimental small magazine run in Chapel Hill by Anthony J. Buttitta. Buttitta was charming as well as courageous, and the Greens certainly appreciated what he was trying to do with such a magazine, having their own bittersweet recollections of running *The Reviewer.* Buttitta's partner was Milton Abernathy, the village Communist, one of perhaps five fully registered members of the Communist Party (CP) on the Hill. The local party comprised Abernathy, who later became a wealthy stockbroker on Wall Street, and his wife, plus one artist, one literature professor, and perhaps another person. This academic village was notoriously tolerant, even proud, of Abernathy, who was best known for running Ab's, a bookstore on Franklin Street that featured new literature and leftist political tracts. Ab's prominently displayed *Contempo* on its shelves, and the bookstore also featured evening ingatherings of activists and artists—and the former and the latter in the 1930s were one and the ilk. Paul Green himself was considered worth visiting by that time, and sometimes writers and thinkers such as Thomas Wolfe, Sherwood Anderson, DuBose Heyward, Lynn Riggs (author of the play that became *Oklahoma!*), and Brooks Atkinson came to Ab's *after* seeing Green; but many others, including William Faulkner, F. Scott Fitzgerald, and Gertrude Stein, came to Ab's, and Green apparently met these figures there because of Buttitta and Abernathy.[25]

These people at Ab's were not cocktail-party reformists who drank in sitting rooms and only imagined themselves radical operatives. Buttitta and Abernathy were activists, especially on behalf of civil rights for Carolina's African Americans and on behalf of labor rights for Carolina's mill workers. In the autumn of 1931, Ab's was abuzz with protest over a series of incidents that became *the* case of black justice in modern U.S. history. The issues concerned a north Alabama trial in which eight African American men were convicted of raping two white women. The Scottsboro authorities probably thought that they were being liberal in actually holding a trial and providing a defense lawyer instead of permitting a lynching bee outside the jailhouse; but in fact the case suggested that southern injustices were growing more subtle and its racists more clever than in the old days of Green's youth.

Because in that day most southern whites pointedly called all black males "boy," and because several of the accused were very young, and because of the clever reverse-English of the radical chic, the defendants have always been called the Scottsboro Boys. The case wound through different levels of the courts for decades, with both liberal attorneys and Communist Party attorneys working for the defendants, and the Scottsboro Boys became the symbol of southern racism in the modern South until the early 1960s, when paramilitary assassins, bomb throwers, police dogs, and fire hoses came to the television foreground. The women's original testimony was oddly self-contradicting, and one of the "victims" subsequently recanted her original version, said she was not raped, and then even joined vigorously in the appeals campaign. Eventually all defendants were cleared of these rape charges, but only after such lengthy incarceration for some of them that prison-related accusations and injuries arose to bedevil them. Posturing by celebrants of damnable Jim Crow, by Communist Party propagandists, by moderate reformists, by Bib Graves, governor of Alabama, and by New Dealers was as rococo as anything that Granovsky might have scripted for a Yiddish dark comedy of wild and crazy words and barely believable actions. Its inherent drama has produced two award-winning scholarly studies and one movie, and certainly neither an artist nor an activist on the Hill was going to sit on the sidelines during the case of the Scottsboro Boys.[26]

Green in particular was exercised, and he told Buttitta and Abernathy that they should publicize the case. Initially, he told them that he would write a major piece for *Contempo*, but what happened instead was that *Contempo* persuaded Lincoln Steffens, then virtually *the* conscience of the American Left, to write a major essay, with poems by black poets of the Harlem Renaissance Langston Hughes and Countee Cullen. The magazine and the bookstore informed their patrons that Langston Hughes would come to the Hill to read poems and to speak against lynching and against other racist injustices, and that he would be staying at the home of Paul and Lib Green. Green was proud to be associated with this kind of activist art and with these kind of politically committed artists published in *Contempo* and displayed and discussed at Ab's.[27]

As noted, Green in this period often described civil rights cases as instances of class oppression and economic injustice. Thus it is not surprising that he was also very active in disputes about labor rights between 1930 and 1934, when there were some notoriously violent and divisive strikes, lockouts, and efforts to break the fledgling unions in the South. In 1932 he joined with Dos Passos and Theodore Dreiser in a protest of the treatment of striking and protesting coal miners in the bloody disputes of Harlan, Kentucky. In that same year, he joined with other leftist activists in supporting Henry Fuller, a Kentucky radical working in Alabama to defend black sharecroppers and small-scale farmers jailed for their resistance to foreclosure. And he kept up his correspondence with Miriam Bonner, whose Vineyard Shore School educated selected working-class girls. He gave Bonner signed copies of his plays so that she could sell them for her causes; he helped her to produce some of his plays in prolelit fashion at a reduced fee; and he happily took from her suggestions about things to read concerning the political economy of the factory for women in the 1930s.[28]

Yet if Green was very much a man of the Left in this era, and if he "fellow-traveled" with Communists on some protest journeys, he was not a full-fledged Marxist, even in this brief moment when so many American intellectuals were. Part of the reasons involved what he regarded as duplicity and other misconduct by the CP and its legal force, the International Legal Defense, in a number of civil rights defense trials. His complaint was echoed by the great southern historian C. Vann Woodward, then a young admirer of Green: both men were on record as insisting that the ILD attorneys were mishandling the Scottsboro case, a verdict partly substantiated by Dan T. Carter in his own study of the proceedings. Indeed, early in 1932 Green and Woodward began complaining about the ILD, and both continued to complain throughout the dragged-out processes. The point is not whether Green was *rightest* about the conduct of the Communist Party and ILD: the point is that he became convinced that CP members were more interested in scoring points for a grand cause than in saving the lives of those young African Americans.[29]

However, it is unlikely that Green rejected Marxism only because of some misbehavior by a few of its agents, however awful he judged them or their actions to be. No, he remained on the near side of Marxism in the radical days of the early 1930s for broadly philosophical reasons, as appropriate for one trained in that discipline. He was likely forced to think these things through very systematically in August 1932, when he was confronted with a fairly complex questionnaire about art and politics presented him by editors of *Modern Quarterly*. At any rate, that moment is the time when he wrote down in most thoughtful way his reactions to Marxism.

Much as he admired the general scheme of *Revolt in the Arts,* he was developing profound doubts about prole lit. He saw no regional and no American historical development of a genuinely re-enfranchised proletariat, because he did not see a genuine radical revolution on the horizon; nor did he even think that the "new poor" would form the basis of a long-term proletariat who had permanently lost its place in society and thus must needs seek revolution. He wearied of the in-house debates about whether revolutions properly occurred in phases or not in phases, at once, or gradually, violently, or nonviolently. He just did not see it happening at all. There certainly was peasant suffering in the countryside, and he knew those stories well, but in his view nothing in the CP or any other American Marxist program was going to offer substantive assistance to the farming poor. As for the factory workers, various ameliorative programs would ease their lot in peaceful processes, and, for good or ill, American industrial capitalism would persist.[30]

Green was deeply skeptical about any justice emerging out of American industrial capitalism, and his recognition of its continuing success had more to do with the force of its overwhelming battalions than with any special belief in its intrinsic values. Young Vann Woodward called it, then and later, "unrestrained capitalism," and the phrase captures Green's feelings at the time: capitalism was a force that had to be restrained, but it was not a force that could be conquered in America. He remained thus what he had been, an agrarian radical with the oddly blended accents of the Harnett populists and the French peasants. Whether talking to a gathering of women at a Country Life meeting in his native Harnett County or corresponding with Elmer Rice, Theodore Dreiser, and Sherwood Anderson about political causes, Green was profoundly dubious about big-scale finance, nervous about a completely industrial structure for the national economy, and opposed to a consumerist society. He petitioned and he talked about and he signed manifestos that people should live simply; that everyone should spend some time working in the green grass of the fields;

that banks, railroads, communications lines, and suppliers of necessary things must be strictly regulated; that people must think collectively and communally; that a socialist welfare system must be put into place for the poor, the elderly, and the sick and the infirm; that the extremely wealthy classes must be taxed heavily and watched closely; that labor needed court protection and a meaningful voice in national politics. All of these things are certainly left wing, but of course none is full Marxist, and finally all are trademark agrarian radicalism brought up to date by the Great Depression. Too, the program is tightly bound by time and by place, and is thus as untranslatable and finally as inapplicable somewhere and sometime else as any other political thing of the moment, including the right-wing version of agrarian radicalism proffered by the dozen Vanderbilt men who wrote *I'll Take My Stand*.[31]

However far left he went, Green knew that there was one form of art with a potentiality that had barely been tapped by 1931. He had been fascinated by the possibilities that inhered in cinema ever since he saw the silent movie *Birth of a Nation* (1915), D. W. Griffith's evocative technical masterpiece of negrophobia. The diarist had written in 1928 that the great artistic future belonged to the movies: the mechanical devices, the greater range for perspective, the scale of the characters—including the chance to see their facial expressions so clearly—all these things could bring movies closer to duplicating the pure imagination than any other medium. There were, he said, new gods, new art, and new men.[32] By 1931, of course, movies not only talked but sang with orchestrated scores; and they looked even better, with photographic techniques that made Griffith's once-bold camera work into a commonplace.

At another level, not spoken in the academic's language but said in the talk around the feedstore's hot stove, writing for Hollywood *paid,* and it paid well. The depression was having some impact even out there, but nothing like the impact elsewhere. In nonacademic words, you could still make a killing there while everybody else was dying here. Talking and talking about these possibilities, writing to friends, and writing in his diary, Green was profoundly aware of the artistic risk in going there; but he was even more profoundly aware of the financial risks in staying away. As usual, he found a third path, a way to hedge the bets and protect part of the stake: he could request leave from the university, work for the Hollywood people for relatively big bucks, and then come back to the low-slung and sagging, but virtually impenetrable, safety net that Harry Woodburn Chase and Frank Porter Graham had strung for Carolina faculty. The money could pay off the many overdue bills, and, with luck, stake the playwright to a prolonged season of writing off-Broadway, with an eventual return to the Big Show still possible. And the exposure, the chance, in the cinematic west just might let Green do new and better things in the movies;

but if not, there was still the money, and it would spend well on Franklin Street.

Actually, Green was hurt in these processes, particularly as he began to see that Hollywood was no more interested in his concepts and ideas than was Broadway. In fact, he learned that the movie-script writer stood much farther outside the Hollywood command tent than did the playwright from the Broadway command tent. The playwright could at least write a full script complete with stage directions and instructions for the set and suggestions for casting. That fully shaped product might well sit around, ignored or rejected; or it might be distorted beyond the playwright's recognition. Still, a playwright could have the satisfaction of doing what the name *playwright* proclaims: the wright builds, crafts, creates, finishes every aspect of the play.

The Nation's critic Alexander Bakshy marked the contrast between Holly-wood and Broadway in 1932 (Green's first year of writing movie scripts): "[S]uch is the anomaly of the film industry. A film is not merely sponsored by a producing company, as a play would be, but is actually written and directed under the constant supervision of its producers. Under the Hollywood system, it will be a long time before the author and the director are free to say just what they want to say and in the way they want to say it."[33] Some of these tensions had been painfully apparent to Green in his own experiences on Broadway, but nothing to this degree. For Green, Hollywood was emerging as an enormity with its own evil challenges.

Hollywood, then, was just different. Difficult as Broadway was, writing itself was there appreciated as a real talent, and the playwright was there celebrated in proportion to his or her ability to do the writing for the commercially suc-cessful dramas and comedies. Any given writer, for example, Paul Green, could certainly complain with or without justice about *which* other writers should be honored; but it was a part of the Broadway game rules that *some* writer was going to be honored. That no writer would win much respect was a part of the Hollywood game rules. In 1932 this new game with its new rules and new relationships would be Paul Green's game—but not for every season. Above all, he was well paid, and there was no uncertainty in his own mind as to why he was there: get in, do their work, take their money, then get out in such a way that one could return, on a strictly part-time basis, sometime in the future.[34]

The script that he wrote in these first eight weeks was for *Cabin in the Cotton,* a film starring Richard Barthelmess as the main protagonist, Marvin Blake, and introducing in her first major role Bette Davis as Marvin's femme fatale. Green was to adapt the story from Henry Harrison Kroll's novel of the same name. Kroll's *Cabin* describes class tensions between Lane Norwood, the lord of this bit of southern land, and his tenants, including the Blake family. Norwood in his territorial-monopoly country store systematically overcharges his tenants, in the process binding them to him and to his land in long-term debt to be paid in cotton crops. For their part, the tenants just as systematically steal from the Norwood store and cheat in their deliveries of their crops when they pay this piper. This entire conflict of credit and discredit operates in a context of southern agricultural decline in which the price of cotton is falling so fast that neither landlord nor peasant tenant is going to flourish, if even survive. For Kroll, true to regional history, the peasants have the worse part of these misdealings, and their petty thieveries and misstatements are a part of being an unempowered individual in a culture of debt and dependence. When a number of the tenants come to realize what is happening to all of them as a class, they begin to protest as an organized group of cultivators. Kroll shows the complexities of the societal tensions among the tenants, who are slow to make common economic cause across color lines; and he adds a personal tension for the Blakes and the Norwoods by having the Norwood daughter, Madge, toy with the affections of the sharecropper Marvin, even though, and especially because, Marvin is already and very publicly pledged to the ever-true Betty Wright of his own cropper class. In still another devilish twist, Norwood the patriarch seems to develop a genuine fondness for Marvin, whom he hires to run the store, and Marvin returns the filial affection even as he rebels against the landlord and creditor.[35]

These themes, so often in Green's own plays, were of course dear to him, and he fought to write a script that celebrated the struggles of the commoners without portraying an ahistorically happy ending. In particular, the character Marvin fascinated Green, for Marvin is the only person who sees all the stories whole and clear. Marvin knows how kind Norwood can be, for Marvin is himself being educated at the patriarch's expense; and Marvin knows how his fellow croppers, even his own stepfather, steal away with cotton in the night and double-deal through the long days; yet Marvin knows as well how Norwood and all the other lords of the land use the tenant system to make cotton cropping an unfree system. Too, Marvin knows the trueness of Betty Wright, but he as sincerely wants the pleasures of Madge Norwood, even if those pleasures are only part of a dangerous game. Eventually, Marvin discovers that his own late father was cheated outrageously by his patriarchal benefactor Norwood; and during a scene of confrontation between the contesting classes, Marvin publicly reveals this knowledge as prima facie evidence in the case against all landlords. Fully joined in the characters' fights, Green was doubly joined in the fight to protect this script as something true to life and art and reform.

He won half of that fight: producer Jack Warner insisted that Marvin in the film *Cabin* emerge as a kind of regional ambassador of peace who would mediate between equally guilty parties to bring a lasting settlement—and incredibly, a lasting prosperity. Jack Warner's Marvin is to persuade both sides to quit cheating each other and develop together an honest and equitable farming system that pays both tenant and lord handsomely. Warner even printed a special introductory message disclaiming any intent to choose sides in a labor struggle, even though the film scrupulously avoids advocating for workers as it scrupulously avoids the historical fact that the tenant system paid no parties adequately by 1925—and was doing even worse by 1932. What Green did salvage was a believable image of the violence wrought by the hardships of this cropping system and a profound sense of the unresolvable sexual tensions among Madge, Betty, and Marvin. On the surface of the film's narrative, Marvin abandons the vampish and trifling Madge for his simple and true sweetheart, Betty; but Bette Davis's Madge steals the scene and reopens a story line with her close-up smile, at once omniscient and grand and very mean. As the credits roll, Bette Davis's knowing smile lingers in the memories of the audience, and moviegoers in 1932 and today realize that Madge still has her man, whether Marvin and Betty Blake acknowledge that or not.

Cabin in the Cotton, its very title derided by the editors of the *Motion Picture Guide* because it "sounds like a Gershwin tune for an obscure musical," was not great stuff, even as melodrama. Jack Warner got his way, and the film blurs the lines of class conflict and significantly understates the economic bankruptcy of the region's tenant system. Alexander Bakshy pointed at this diffusion and dissipation of historical forces in what could have been and should have been "a corner of human life simmering with passions and hatreds that now and then burst into flames of wholesale destruction." Bakshy complained about Warner's production decisions, but he announced himself "decidedly grateful" to Paul Green for showing as much of such conflict as he was allowed to show. Withal, Bakshy praised *Cabin* for "provid[ing] a welcome relief from the juvenile trivialities of the average Hollywood film." The far more influential New York film critics, especially the *Times*'s Mordaunt Hall, complained of overacting brought on by overwriting, a fair critique. As the film has aged, its critical stature has not risen particularly: latter-day audiences, not themselves living through the profound economic tensions of the Great Depression, see only the style of the protest melodrama, which is severely dated; and even in that genre, the sting is drawn because of Warner's ending, the heavenly contract drawn up quickly by Marvin to protect all sides in the labor dispute while improving productivity. Still, there are marvelous lines, not least Bette Davis's "I'd love to kiss you, but I just washed my hair." Barthelmess's veteran skills and Davis's emerging genius, along with a strong supporting group, make the movie endure, something of which Green came to be very proud. Davis's great one-liner is often credited to Green, but in fact the sentence comes directly from Kroll's

1925 novel, and in any case, the moment in the movie is not a writer's line, but the accomplishment of a great actress.[36]

The First National Studios offered him an extension, this time as a writer "brought in" to repair a script already written for a film about a Pikes Peak gold-digging silver prospector. Notwithstanding his many protestations to the contrary, Green "fell" for the lure of this work, deciding to propose a renaming, from *The Silver Dollar* to *The Shining Mountain*. He also called for a very different theme, one emphasizing the endurance and final triumph of human character, especially in women and half-breed men, through terrible but redemptive suffering. His political preference for leftist themes of commoner courage shines in his memoranda and his notes far more brightly than the original script's theme of the shining metal.[37]

Hollywood in those days was not unreceptive to leftist themes. In fact, by the time of World War II and its idea of a popular front, that is, a common campaign against world fascism, certain studios would become very receptive to leftist themes, including those of a very red cast. However, in 1932, and at Jack Warner's First National, the mood was at its very best only "not unreceptive." Green reworked the old script. Indeed, he essentially discarded it, writing with a quickening enthusiasm that confounded his own political passions with what was only the temporary enthusiasm of some studio officials for his ability to do "this" (their industry's dismissive reference to the writer's work). He forgot the newly learned lessons about how lightly writing—"this"—was regarded in the Hollywood community. Anxious to reshape things, Green tried to develop the theme of protagonist Haw Taybor as a halfbreed drunk with overweening ambition who overcomes the scorning "fullbreed" whites but then destroys himself. Too, he wanted to take the female lead, Agatha Taybor, and make her into a neo-Puritan, a sturdy rock of New England, thus building tension between husband and wife and also suffusing the scenes with a rich and dark fatalism.[38]

Perhaps most instructive in his lengthy memorandum is one line in section 8, for there Green says that a character could be allowed to die, as he is unimportant to the *play* now. Besides forgetting that he was not working on theater, but the cinema, Green was clearly stepping out of bounds and assuming that he could control more things than "this." He was not a playwright developing a play but was instead in the highly specialized role of the scriptwriter who had been "brought in" to finish "this"; he had not been summoned to write a new vision, for that was the purview of the producer. Whatever else, Hollywood officials did not tarry long in setting scores straight about role and station, duty and position, power and prerogative. Two days later, on 23 May, came an interoffice memorandum from Lucien Hubbard (significantly, it did *not* come from a higher officer): the officials were informing the writer that this interpretation of *Silver Dollar* (carefully noting the correct title chosen by the "concept" people) was too far removed from the direction that the creative people wanted it to go, and in fact there was not much more that Green could do usefully on this particular project. Having reestablished the Hollywood version of right reason, Hubbard closed with a note to the "hand" about "this": Please report at once to Mr. Wallis for another assignment.[39]

Thus restored to proper place, the scriptwriter returned to his appointed rounds as one "brought in" to do "this" for those with controlling vision. He also had to be honest about his work schedule and how much time there was in its interstices to work on plays. There were in fact virtually no such interstices permitting chances to do anything other than "this"; and doing "this," regardless of its lack of status or authority, was draining, full-time work. As he marked it, there were two Hollywoods, both real but involving very different people. One was filled with fine people who worked long hours from early morning to late night, with a hurried sandwich for a working lunch. The other, reported in the William Randolph Hearst chain of newspapers and including the scenes at the newspaperman's mansion, involved people at play and was the spectacular, seamy, extravagant image that outsiders had of Hollywood. As Green saw things, writers and even most actors could only occasionally play in what was called the *Hearsty* Hollywood.[40]

The playwright career thus waited until the summer workshop for *Tread the Green Grass* that E. C. Mabie had scheduled for him at Iowa City. For the nonce, there was a little time for recreation once the long workday ended, and during those moments of play Green combated loneliness, sometimes with enough success to feel a bit guilty. Always attracted to and attractive to women, especially "new" women in new places, Green may have been less than faithful to his own steady rock of New England, that is, not his Agatha Taybor of a memorandum but Lib Green of his marriage. He tried to be good and in any case discreet. By Hollywood standards he certainly was, but rumors of misadventures slipped out and back, bringing a little more hurt for Lib Green and compounding old guilt for a man who was after all "come of preacher stock" (as he had styled himself for the Pulitzer Prize interviews). He confessed that on the very few occasions when he had stepped out, he had stepped high and wide, and that once again Rome had stirred the yokel, as the Romes of the world had always stirred the country boys in town for a visit. Lib Green was concerned enough to write a letter of worried inquiry, and Paul Green solved things by scolding himself in his diary and by inviting his wife out to see the sights for herself, even telling her that she might have a chance to see cute Marian Davis or Norma Talmadge in a bathing suit at one of the Hearsty parties in the tinted swimming pools. She did eventually come out for a visit during one of his Hollywood sessions, and the edgy moment of doubt passed without more discussion in their letters.[41]

Sometimes the waste in Hollywood during those otherwise and elsewhere parlous times got his goat, and he kicked and brayed at some industry hosts. It was actually a moment on a sort of stage, and he took the opportunity to render a monologue for a dinner party at a Hearsty palace. He then spoke not out of turn pretending to be a concept man, which he was not, nor as a talent, which he was not, nor even as a writer, which he appropriately was. Instead, he spoke as Cato the Censor warning about the consequences of heedless extravagance. He was thus here in a fully acceptable role, for the actors and concept people were ever appreciative of a silver tongue wagging at table, and Green was in his cups and talking with spirit. With this intimate audience, Green asked rhetorically if they heard someone knocking at the door. He paused and asked again; then paused and asked yet again. Finally, someone played the straight guy and threw him the line, *Did he hear someone knocking, and if so, who was it?* Everyone permitted still another long silence, and then Green said in lowered voice that it is the *Niggers* of eastern North Carolina, and they're hungry and cold and they want in. All at table felt the poverty in the rest of the world outside the Hearsty community, and there was a meaningful quiet for a long while. But, at such table and in such company in the community, Green was after all only part of a larger script that he did not direct, and he could only change the mood and the tone for a twinkling. In tribute to his mastery of the moment, all raised their glasses to him and drank to his health and his soul.[42]

Then they drank much more and became again very happy and without cares.[43]

10 : ACTUALIZING ART

1935–1937

In 1935 labor strikes in several mills in North Carolina's central piedmont became a defining test of political and ideological allegiances. These walkouts and their attendant strife are collectively known as the Burlington strikes, although this is only a historian's shorthand label for a series of loosely connected disputes between textile-labor organizers and the management of the Love family's Burlington Mills factories in several cities and villages. Complicating the situation considerably was the involvement of Communist Party organizers from New York in what had been a strictly local—and certainly a strictly Protestant and capitalist—dispute.

As usual in such struggles, local law enforcement officials took the side of management, but this case was unusual in that the federal officials of Franklin Delano Roosevelt's administration tried to stay neutral, and if anything were sympathetic with the strikers. When a building blew up in Graham, the violence of the Burlington strikes obviously went into another level of seriousness and complexity. And when a handful of striking workers were summarily rounded up and thrown into the wet and dank jail cells of Hillsborough, just north of Chapel Hill, a line was drawn in the red clay of the region. Everybody had to choose sides.

In Chapel Hill the path-breaking social scientist Howard Washington Odum, who had founded the Institute for Research in the Social Sciences and who generally proclaimed himself a liberal and a reformist, was quick to distance himself from the fray and even quicker to warn young instructors and graduate students to stay away from the dispute. Odum still nursed second-degree burns from his own involvement in labor disputes of a previous decade—and those disputes had in no way involved any violence. His protector and benefactor of that era had been the often courageous president Harry Woodburn Chase, but Chase on that occasion had been careful to mollify textile owners who served as UNC trustees. The president otherwise celebrated for independence of thought had also been very politic with the general assemblymen who were allies of the textile owners. Chase specifically cautioned faculty members about involving themselves in controversies concerning labor disputes and the system of capitalism. Now the current president, Frank Porter Graham, although very much the self-proclaimed liberal, was in this instance more canny and cautious and clever than forthright. [1]

By contrast, Green at once chose the side of the striking workers. He began to collect around himself left-wing intellectuals sympathetic to labor. He also began to work on behalf of a fair trial, since the mill owners, especially James Spencer Love and his relatives, commanded plenty of resources, perhaps enough to bring a conviction in court regardless of the guilt or innocence of the accused. Green visited imprisoned workers, he publicly protested their living conditions in the Hillsborough jail, and he arranged their bail. He went to New York to publicize the case among his fellow practitioners of prole lit. [2]

Complicating matters still more was the fact that Green's coworker in this campaign, his friend and eventual brother-in-law Phillips Russell of the English department, was himself part of this extended Love textile family. James Spencer Love, the sometimes enlightened and always articulate boss, was himself educated in the Ivy League and in previous seasons had been forward-looking on some political and social issues. Now Love wrote to his sister Cornelia Love, who served in the brand-new library at Carolina named for Green's esteemed friend Louis Round Wilson. He wrote with sorrow more than heat, for she had defended their cousin Phillips Russell and she had defended Paul Green, the liberal she admired—and a man who came into the library to read books much more often than any other faculty member. He wanted to sympathize with her, but he wrote bluntly: "If Paul Green is not a communist he is certainly beyond the slightest question associating and affiliating with them in this matter." [3]

Once again, Green was going to go places that other Chapel Hillians who called themselves liberals would not go.

In that epochal year of the Burlington strike, Green recorded on at least four occasions major statements of support for the mill workers who were attempting to build a union. In the privacy of his diary, Green confirmed one thing that Spencer Love feared, namely, the more the playwright thought about conditions of work that led to the strike, the more thoroughgoing became his critique of the political economy that indirectly produced those very conditions. He even quoted the Marxist expression "the evils of exploitation," a very pink and in some cases even a red phrase. But Love was wrong on another count, as Green's correspondence and diary also show. The real members of the Communist Party in New York had little regard for Green, one of them even writing to him punningly to complain that he was "only pink"; but then their leaders grew serious in tone and scolded him for not being sufficiently radical in his protest of the Burlington strike. To the New York offices of the party, Green responded that it is easy to be red as long as the blood is only talk. [4]

The playwright knew how violent this labor dispute was likely to become, given both the anger of some striking mill workers and the determination of some in management. Finally, he stood foursquare against Love and his allies on the still-unresolved issue of who set off an explosive device during the struggle. He was convinced that the men in jail did not commit an act of violence but were instead activist strikers of varying degrees of prominence rounded up for exemplary punishment, and for Green the example of this punishment uncovered disquieting evidence of terrible abuses in Carolina's prisons.[5]

Although Phillips Russell agreed with Green's assessment of the trial, he was careful to dissociate the playwright from the university during the controversies, telling his relatives that the Carolina Playmaker was not a regular member of the faculty—less a disingenuous dodge than a lie. Besides this behind-the-scenes "help," Green stood alone during these controversies, with the exception of a few students like the future historian Vann Woodward and some of the literary hangers-on at Milton Abernathy's and Anthony Buttitta's bookstore. The campus newspaper, the *Chapel Hill Tar Heel,* editorialized on behalf of the mill owners and against labor organizers, and in this instance the editors spoke words that pleased most of the faculty, staff, student body, and townspeople.[6]

Even such a small and scruffy group was a good place to start, however, and Green built a following for this cause despite the warnings of Howard Odum and the dissembling of Frank Graham. Indeed, Vann Woodward, then a graduate student on a fellowship arranged in part by his onetime neighbor Odum, remembered that Paul Green fascinated the rebellious young men on campus. As for the admonitions from Odum that Woodward avoid "getting in with the wrong crowd"—meaning Ab's Bookstore, the *Contempo* writers and readers, and above all Paul Green—the historian recalled that such warnings only whetted the appetite for activism.[7]

Moreover, Green fully intended to recruit young dissidents among the students, whom he called "hero students." Such young fellows needed fittingly masculine models among their professors, he noted, thereby adopting the chauvinism of the era's socialists. A university, he insisted, must train its students to ask hard questions about what he called the evils in the economic system, and only real "manhood" could so teach, so learn, or so rebel. Deliberately contrasting his state university with Duke University—and forgetting how very few people on UNC's faculty were doing any such leading that day—he decried the lack of manhood in the Duke faculty and proclaimed his own intention to serve as the prime example for his own hero students.[8]

Still another chance for Broadway suddenly presented itself. It came from still another experimental outfit, this one the Group Theater. To follow the related stories, we have to back up a bit, returning briefly to 1931 to hear the resonances of Aristotle's phrase "actualizing art," as Green was attempting to do exactly that on Broadway and off Broadway in the middle of the 1930s. Since 1931 the Group Theater of Harold Clurman, Lee Strasberg, and Cheryl Crawford had been attempting a new approach that "would actually mean something in the lives of its participants." Declaring independence from the Broadway of Lee Shubert and Sidney Ross, the Group intended to be truly autonomous by avoiding debts to the major commercial investors in and backers of plays. Once Strasberg actually turned down fifty thousand dollars from a donor to preserve the integrity of his independence: he apparently thought that the gift was too large from one source and thus would give one donor too much stake in the play—and too great a sense of entitlement. By 1941 the Group Theater would be defunct, but some of its ideas, the technique of so-styled method acting and the broader concepts of actors' largely controlling their own material, would be transmuted into the Actors Studio, which did succeed. Moreover, the people brought forward by the Group Theater endured and finally prevailed in theater and cinema: teachers Robert Lewis and Stella Adler, directors Elia Kazan and Cheryl Crawford, producers Harold Clurman and Lee Strasberg, songwriter Kurt Weill, actors Franchot Tone and John Garfield, and playwrights Clifford Odets and Paul Green.[9]

Indeed, Green, by writing two of the most controversial of their many controversial performances in the 1930s, became as important to this group as Eugene O'Neill had been to the Provincetown Playhouse. Strasberg, Clurman, and especially Cheryl Crawford knew of Green's work, and in 1931 Crawford had persuaded the Group to put on his play *The House of Connelly*. Then she had to persuade Green, since the Group wanted to remake the tragedy into an optimistic piece, and since it wanted the African American actresses to play relatively unimportant roles; in particular, the black women were not to be allowed to participate in the give-and-take between directors and actors as the play was redefined and redirected by the Group. This was surely a "hard sell": The tragedian had to relinquish his dark vision with its stern warning about human excesses in his native Carolina in order to encourage Americans to be optimistic about the nation, and, for all his pioneering work to give African American actors real roles of substance, he had to accept a New York liberal's Jim Crow policy in which two major black actresses would stay strictly within roles defined by white actors, actresses, and directors. Finally, of course, the very concept, that actors would define the nature of the play, was not to Green's liking since he had very definite ideas about authorial rights in general and playwrights' prerogatives in particular.[10]

For all that, Green was ultimately persuaded by Crawford, that "sturdy girl from Akron" and a recent Smith College graduate who fully intended to be the first major woman director of serious drama in the United States. She told him that these "fervent years"—as Clurman called them—of the Group offered the best chance for Green to "extend his influence in the establishment of a native theatre" by producing a play "representing the traditions and various phases of present-day life of the people." Clurman's "sturdy girl from Akron" was there quoting Green's own words, and using them very affectingly. She told Green, and he agreed, that if the Group's mission "wasn't precisely the same" as the Carolinian's, "the two were certainly compatible." He was convinced, and he signed on.[11]

He had worried this play for a long time. His diary shows that he was writing it as early as 1926, originally in response to Clark's oft-repeated admonition that the playwright needed to do a play about white people. Of course, as he evolved *Connelly,* it became anything but a white-folks play. Its focus is on the elite of the Old South as that caste sinks into declension during the New South era, but it is as much about black-white relations, class structure, gender, and economics as it is a white-folks play. Indeed, for Green, an abstractly white-folks play disentangled from the social forces of his land is hard to imagine. He kept revising *Connelly,* producing a play script for publication by 1931, and he eventually saw at least five versions of it performed between 1931 and 1941. Philadelphia, Boston, and college-town productions received favorable notices, and Montrose Jonas Moses admired the printed version enough to ask about it for his planned 1933 *Representative American Plays.*[12]

Again, however, Green was most eager to see his play on Broadway, or at least along the New York perimeter of off Broadway, and he was concerned about negotiations with the Theater Guild, with whom he had signed a contract for production of *Connelly* during those tumultuous and finally futile negotiations with the tandem of Ross and Shubert and Harris about *Tread the Green Grass* and *Potter's Field.* The Guild had prestigious people and good taste but no money at all, and they had been vainly looking for backers while occasionally paying small fees to extend their option rights to produce *Connelly* in the little negotiating games by now quite familiar.[13]

So things dragged on until Crawford convinced her partners in the Group, then the Guild, and finally Green that she and her fellows could make *Connelly* work, and work well, on Broadway. Ideologically, Green found these people very comfortable, at least in that era. All were left-leaning, and Clurman, who tended to talk most and loudest, was a product of the Laboratory Theater, which self-consciously styled itself "Theater of the Left." Too, Clurman had studied and worked with the Provincetown Playhouse in the noble days of Robert Edmond Jones and Eugene O'Neill, and these two figures remained almost magical for Barrett Clark and for Green.[14]

His diary reveals the apprehensions that assailed him: his bookkeeper side doubted that the Group could make any money for the Guild, and a fortiori none for the author; and his artist side was concerned about Clurman's enthusiasm for the recently imported Constantin Stanislavsky Method, in which actors under intense interrogation and goading by their directors improvised lines for their characters until they could "feel" the legitimate "emotions" truly, so that the "spine" of the play could be toughened and "straightened" beyond the abilities of a mere playwright. Such reduced status for the writer sounded distressingly like Hollywood talk, but Green was promised opportunities to speak often and loudly to the attentive ears of actors and directors, and he was repeatedly assured that improvisation—also called "affective memory" drilling—was only a technique for actors during earliest phases of practice; no actor would be making up lines of dialogue on stage during a performance. Finally, a historian of the Group opines that Green "was moved by the actors' devotion to the play and willing to be swayed. He allowed the directors to sweep him up with their faith in human perfectibility."[15]

Connelly, as Green conceived it and as he wrote it, was not about human perfectibility, but he finally permitted that interpretation in order to get the play in front of New York audiences, critics, and talkers. The play takes chances at both professional and personal levels: The protagonist is William Byrd Connelly, and in such a name Green quotes his mother's family traditions about the Byrds of Westover. Too, the Connellys are Scots-Irish, and the scenes are obviously his own valley of the Cape Fear River. The Old South Connellys are successful in cotton, with the women long-suffering ladies and the men aggressive with their farm "bidness" but even more aggressive in their play with the slave women in the plantation shacks. Green's Old South is marked by the evils of slavery, racism, economic exploitation, and sexual aggressiveness, all the prerogatives of the men in the master class. Its intellectual attainments in the classics are noted, lest modern folk blame these sins on ignorance. The evils he depicted were committed knowingly by intelligent men whose eyes were wide open.[16]

In the postbellum era, Green's *real* New South involves a long and often painful slide away from greatness—even into an incompetency. Everything is in decay, but it is clear that the sexual depravity of the new era is not itself new: sexual abuse of dependent women is the thread of behavior uniting the Old and the New Souths. Paterfamilias Connelly is dead and gone, and his widow, as the materfamilias, presides over a decayed community, one whose members call for a man at the center to hold it together. Much old remains, including the Abramic family, and all extensions, black and white, of the large family still live off the disused land and in the misused big house. Her brother-in-law Uncle Bob, once a politician with some ideals, is now a drunken wastrel with a bad stomach who still lurches after women, eats piggishly, and withal constantly quotes maxims from the classics in Greek and Latin, not because he believes them any more, but because, as Montrose Jonas Moses points out, it is the failed aristocrat's way of excluding women, blacks, the poor, and even the up-and-coming business elite of the new era: Greek and Latin are the things that Uncle Bob still has that others do not have.

William Byrd Connelly, or Will, the paterfamilias apparent, is at play's beginning an idealist ashamed of the sins of the regional fathers. He doesn't drink, he wants desperately to be fair to the former slaves who are now working as renters on the same land, and he avoids the advances of the black tenant women who have been conditioned to present themselves to the paterfamilias in return for favors. Will, however, is no farmer, and his principled inactivity and passivity, while noble in their way, are in effect no better for the community than Uncle Bob's drunken abuses and the awful sentimentality of his aunts Geraldine and Evelyn. Mrs. Connelly, knowing her late husband for what he was, can only hope that her son can overcome his inaction and amount to something before the bank forecloses on land and mansion.[17]

Patsy Tate, daughter of the tenant Jesse Tate, decides to win Will and take over the Connelly estate with its potentially rich lands. She does win him, and under the guidance of the hardscrabble Tate family, Will reorganizes the plantation according to her plan. For a while, the plantation functions well economically, though in such processes the extended Connelly family falls apart. The old aunts with their passive sentimentality and the African Americans Big Sis and Big Sue with their aggressive sexuality remind Will that he is out of place and out of order, and thus doomed to fall. Materfamilias with her gestures and in the implications of her words makes it clear that sexual dalliance with Big Sis and Big Sue, as still practiced by Uncle Bob, is acceptable if done discreetly; but serious lovemaking with a white tenant is not acceptable.

Will cannot bear up under all the pressures and soon begins to drink and chase skirts in town, much as did his successful, albeit sinful, Old South forebears. In the harsher competition of New South agriculture, however, the paterfamilias must be actively on the scene to make the plantation work, and things slide economically as Will dissipates socially. In his notes Green makes obvious the extent of the tragedy he envisions: Patsy Tate really *is* about economic gain and raising her own social status. She, and all the other Tates, are a practical, unsentimental people. They are avaricious.[18]

Having set all this up, Green for nearly five years wrestled with the play, striving for the best ending for it. His preference, noted often, was to have Big Sis and Big Sue murder Patsy in order to end the tension and resolve things with an inevitable decline and fall for the Connellys: morals, land, big house, Abramic family all implode. What he actually developed was a different tragedy with a resolution that shows clearly the triumph of a new class of practical, but soulless, New South people: Patsy Tate gets her man, Will Connelly; takes over the big house; and cooks a dinner to confirm the conquest. But Uncle Bob kills himself, Geraldine and Evelyn depart for Richmond, and Big Sis and Big Sue accept banishment to the New South kitchen, while Mrs. Connelly becomes a virtually captive invalid. The House of Connelly endures, but only because it is really the House of Tate. There is no joy in the Tates' rise, for they are not good; but neither is there much regret in the Connellys' fall, for their eventual collapse was always innate in everything that they did and were. The regnant New South reflects the evils of the Old South with no saving virtues, and the curtain falls on a scene of uncompromising moral desolation. [19]

That was the version that Montrose Moses wanted for his *Representative Plays,* the version that black actors like Rose McClendon wanted to play, the version that Cheryl Crawford liked. But the Group Theater, or at least Clurman and Strasberg, insisted on changes. Listening to the white actors answer their fast-coming—and loaded—questions, Clurman and Strasberg decided to make Big Sis and Big Sue much less important parts of the play; and of course the directors made it clear that only the white artists were to be improvising and discussing. So much for any version in which the black women kill Patsy. More, Clurman and Strasberg were determined to have an optimistic ending, one in which Patsy and Will say *goodbye* to a "dead" and "awful" past in order to embrace a real and hopeful present. Patsy in their version is certainly practical, but now with the idealism of buoyant hope: she grows to love Will, as he can grow to love his proper work. Clurman announced that his Group "had shown Green" some things, namely, the past doesn't matter, *buckle down to your work,* be optimistic about America. [20]

Green was not quite the dutiful and pliant pupil Clurman thought him but was merely accepting a lot of rhetoric to get the play done. Crawford for her part recalled that people in the Theater Guild (unfortunately not identified) were outraged over the alterations, even if they were made with the playwright's knowing acceptance. She remembered that someone from the Guild said, "[Y]ou have murdered the play!" Clurman tried to respond that Guild members were under the misapprehension that only tragedy could be treated seriously in drama. The result was that the Guild withdrew its offer of five thousand dollars toward production costs and finally severed all ties with *Connelly.* Crawford tended to agree with Clurman, but she had her own personal tensions to contend with: the sturdy girl was completely excluded from any directing role, suggesting that Clurman's treatment of Rose McClendon and Fannie Bell De Knight may have been as much chauvinism as racism. Also, given the many promises to Crawford, and considering the crucial part that she had played in bringing a reluctant and mistrustful Green aboard, Clurman's treatment of her further suggests that there is not always honor among idealists. [21]

At any rate, the Group's *Connelly* was an aesthetic success, one that the audience of talkers and critics loved. The Group's historian records opening night this way: Crawford sat with Green "nervous" in the mezzanine, while Clurman and Strasberg sat "tensely at the back of the orchestra." It seemed to Crawford that the actors lacked energy, that some words were inaudible, and that the audience was inauspiciously quiet. At curtain fall, however, Clurman leaped up and cried *Bravo!* and the audience followed the director's lead. Crawford "counted curtain calls—when she got to sixteen she grabbed Green and hustled him down to stage to cries of *author!*"[22]

At a celebration afterward, Green drank a lot of bourbon and then spoke to directors, actors, and the critics and hangers-on who had come by. He started by quoting from Saint John the Evangelist about the *logos* that was God and is God and is with God. Then, "[a]s he read on about the law handed down by Moses, the truth and grace incarnated in the life of Christ," it is recorded that "tears poured down everyone's cheeks. He seemed to be talking about their own dedication, the quest for unity of form, content, and spirit that was The Group's reason for being. They had worked so hard, they had come so far. At that radiant moment, anything seemed possible."[23]

Critics agreed that artistically at least anything might be possible for this playwright and the Group, and they certainly liked *Connelly*. Brooks Atkinson and Montrose Moses, already in Green's corner anyway, were enthusiastic, but so too were Carl Carmer and others. Bookkeepers found that not quite everything was possible, as receipts pretty well covered expenses and paid everyone who should be paid, with a few thousand dollars of royalty for the Samuel French agency and a few hundred dollars for playwright. Too, Clurman and Strasberg and Crawford as they searched for another play, consulting often with Green, had to concede that financial limitations would make many productions impossible for them. By 1935 FDR had started a number of federal projects for the arts, with an ambitious one for the theater, and Green became deeply involved in some of those projects.[24]

If the Group had provided a special forum for the already celebrated Green, then it introduced for the first time Clifford Odets, whose epochal *Waiting for Lefty* likely could never have been performed without their sponsorship. Too, the great German songwriter Kurt Weill, once Bertold Brecht's partner but by the mid-1930s in exile and otherwise without work in the era, brought his sophisticated, thickly meaningful, and darkly comedic lyrics and tunes to the Group, which for several seasons became his own balm of Gilead until commercial successes came after World War II. Although Weill's talents seem obvious enough today, in that day he needed an American sponsor. It was Crawford whose passion for popular music injected Weill into the Group's plans. And she was convinced that Weill and Green could help each other in a project of some sort.[25]

By 1935 Clurman was talking with Green about the Carolinian's new play, *The Enchanted Maze,* but this play was going to be much too expensive a production for the Group to contemplate. By happenstance Clurman mentioned an antiwar play, *Good Soldier Schweik,* an unfinished series of novels by the Czech Jaroslav Hasek developed into a play by Erwin Piscator for Berlin theater in 1928 and then revised again with lyrics by Bertold Brecht and music by Kurt Weill; and he also mentioned that Weill was available to the Group for music.[26]

Green then began to tell Clurman about some of his own war experiences, his support for the League of Nations, his fear of another great war, and the tragicomedy of an army in modern "total war." Too, Green had learned after the Great War that his commander/professor (and occasional postbellum partner in land transactions) Joseph Hyde Pratt had been party to a scheme to collect the names of Chapel Hillians who refused to buy the fourth issue of "Liberty Loan" war bonds: Pratt's secretary had noted on the list, "Just what use will be made of the records I do not know. . . . Their names will be needed later." Such financial bullying of the Orange County farmers and small tradespeople back home raised still more questions about the nature of the war that made the world safe for democracy. The mistreatment of common soldier and of civilian rankled Green the more he thought and rethought the issues, and he discussed such incidents with Clurman.[27]

The men had obviously found common ground, and Clurman arranged for Crawford to talk with Green about an English-language, and more than that, an *American* version of *Good Soldier Schweik.* So it happened that for a second time, Green found himself writing a play about white people—and for the second time a play that does not involve race and is not set in his region. As he did his reading and his search work in his dogged way, Green discovered that more than thirty thousand Johnsons served in the United States Army during the Great War, and that more than three thousand of the Johnsons were named Johnny. Crawford apparently helped in this search work, and the two were struck hard by the coincidence. Just like that, the revised play had the name *Johnny Johnson.*[28]

Again, there would be only a little money and an awful lot of improvisation, but Green was fully engaged with the project despite these problems. He enjoyed Weill, who was experimenting with polytonal forms and with jazz, and he worked enthusiastically with Crawford. For once there was not a lot of chatter about optimism and forgetting history, since the play was a complex blending of satire, comedy, tragedy, and experimentation that was hard to categorize. Too, its antiwar message was in Green's style: there is no way that the play can be called optimistic, but it is much too complex to characterize it as pessimistic either. The warnings are clear, and Green's prophetic traditions are well served by Brecht's framework and even better served by Weill's clever

and challenging music. Throughout rehearsals Weill kept insisting to the actors that they abandon classical singing techniques and adopt the *sprechstimme*
technique, that is, sing in a style accessible to the audience, with an "organic
mingling of music." It was the seriocomic style perfectly adapted by his wife,
Lotte Lenya, a singer with a "gravelly instrument" of a voice and a very worldly-
wise past.[29]

The Weills, the writer/singer couple, had very different responses to Paul
Green. Kurt Weill, on first meeting Green in Chapel Hill, wrote back to his
wife: "Paul Green's a strange fellow, and I'm not sure whether he's able to
handle the project." Later, everyone moved north, to the Pine Brook Club in
Nichols, Connecticut, where the Group Theater had its summer work-home.
Soon Cheryl Crawford, Paul Green, and the Weills removed to an old home
about two miles away. There Kurt Weill was charmed, and he concluded that
Green could do the writerly tasks, provided that he followed Cheryl Crawford's lead closely. As for Lotte Lenya, she too was charmed, and "by the end
of summer Lenya had claimed Paul Green as her first American affair."[30]

There would be many more American affairs for her, and Lenya would report all of them to Kurt Weill, who accepted her adventures as a necessary part
of their life together, since he often grew uninterested in sex when he was in the
middle of a project—and since she never grew less than fully interested in sex.
How soon Kurt Weill learned of this affair from his wife, we do not know, but
in any case it seemed to make no difference in his relations with Paul Green,
and later with Lib Green, and still later with Paul Green Jr., with whom he
enjoyed playing tennis. With all of the Greens, Kurt Weill was companion-
able and affectionate, and with Paul Green he repeated the judgment that this
playwright could be very effective if given plenty of guidance, and especially
guidance from Cheryl Crawford.[31]

For his part, the playwright found all of this invigorating, and it was to Crawford's credit that she kept away from him the knowledge that Clurman and
Strasberg were unhappy with the script, with Clurman pulling out at the last
minute in September of 1936 in favor of Strasberg's direction. Again, the sturdy
girl was rejected for directorship but was employed instead to give suggestions
and to work with Green. The Carolinian himself was useful in keeping practice
sessions and read-throughs going after Clurman's abrupt withdrawal. Green
gave an idealistic speech to the actors about the need for a League of Nations
because of the horrors of war that he himself had seen. The Group, playwright,
actors, director Strasberg, songwriter Weill, and whatever title one wanted to
give Crawford, then went back into the 1936 production with enthusiasm and
courage.[32]

Unfortunately, this production did not work well. The sets did not serve the
complex humor effectively. For instance, in one otherwise inspired scene, three
huge guns of war appeared behind sleeping soldiers, "so ominous, but pretty

music pours out. . . . the seductiveness of war." However, the sets made the guns look silly rather than ominous, and thus the music in combination made the scene look surreal rather than seductive. Nobody liked the sets, only a few noted Weill's music, and critics expressed respect for the concept and the innovations but decried the results, most blaming Green's script, with some blaming the Stanislavsky method acting of the Group. Significantly, the knowledgeable Robert Benchley of the *New Yorker* and Burns Mantle, dean of Broadway critics, both noted all of these things, but they specifically exonerated Green and then insisted that audiences should give *Johnny Johnson* a chance. In fact, Burns Mantle wrote up the play as one of the ten best for the 1936–37 season. On this occasion, nevertheless, few people listened to Mantle or Benchley, and the play closed as a commercial failure with generally poor reviews. [33]

The Group Theater attempted a few more plays, but these productions produced dwindling artistic results as well as plummeting financial returns. Clurman, Strasberg, and Crawford continued to talk with Green, but he was never able to do another play with them, probably to his relief. To his diary he confided that he just hated the way Clurman treated actors and writers: he thought that the Stanislavsky method, at least as practiced by Clurman, produced psychoses more than innovations; and he had wearied of Clurman's preachments about optimism and how to learn to achieve that state. He pointedly redid *Connelly* at the University of Iowa, offering audiences the Group version one evening and his own version another evening, then giving the discerning Iowa City theatergoers the chance to vote for their choice of endings. He recorded with pleasure that the audiences overwhelmingly preferred the tragic ending of Green's original 1931 script. Whatever his private opinion of the Group, however, their public opinion of him could not have been higher, and the Group directors and actors continued to seek new plays, or the rights to old plays, from Green. Within a few seasons more, depression-era economics did its work, killing yet another experimental theater group. At the time of the Group's collapse, however, Green was so involved with Federal Theater Project work that he did not take immediate notice of its fate. [34]

One thing Green had seen and heard from way back was the chain gang, that is, inmates of prisons performing public works, usually road building, as a part of their sentencing. He had depicted such a gang under the direction of a "souldriver" at the conclusion of *Potter's Field*. Despite his use of it for dramatic presentation then, however, chain gangs were a commonplace sight, and often Green took no more notice of them than anything else commonplace on the landscape. But tucked away on a reel of recording tape was Green's own voice from a 1934 trip during which the playwright had all but cried over the sight of a coffle of black prisoners overseen by a white guard armed with a rifle. Some time later he had played that tape, listened hard, and then wrote down those words, bearing down, in fast, hard, driving cursive slashes, the ink cutting into the pages of his diary. And later again he paid someone to type those words. And then he again put everything away, the tape, the diary leaf, the typescript. After revisiting those recordings, he had endured a troubling visit by a small African American man from Richmond who was trying to sell his story of shackles that cut into his ankle bones and a bending-standing rack that had buckled and warped his body. Although Green shooed the worrisome visitor away without helping him to find a magazine publishing outlet, the visit itself sent the playwright back into his different records of the chain gang. [35]

Then, in April of 1935, Green learned that fifteen-year-old Booker T. Watson would be executed in the state's new electric chair. Learning about Watson's coming execution sent Green yet again to those different records about the chain gang, although the chain gang as such was an issue separate from that of capital punishment. The issues were united by race, for it was mostly black men executed and mostly black men working in the coffles. He drew up a petition, had it signed by a number of people, and appealed to the governor, John Christoph Blucher Ehringhaus, a man he had met and a man he thought to be sympathetic to penal and judicial reforms. More, Ehringhaus was a racial moderate, and on the Carolina scene in those racist days, that made him virtually a liberal reformist. This petition did no good, but Green throughout the spring and summer of 1935 redoubled his efforts on behalf of others on death row, as the journalists began calling the holding cells for those sentenced to capital punishment. In his mind the connection between the chain gang and death row was obvious: in his native state both were almost always done to African Americans and almost never to whites; and both were a punishment "cruel and unusual" and therefore of doubtful constitutionality. [36]

By 12 July 1935 Green's novelist and reformist friend Jim Boyd had brought news from a Charlotte trial that outdid the gory account of the little man from Richmond: a chain-gang member had been locked in a small box overnight as punishment for some transgression on the job. When finally let out of the box, the inmate was found to have gangrene, and it was necessary to amputate his feet to save what remained of his life in jail. That same day, Governor Ehringhaus again refused to intervene in a capital sentence, and not one but two African American men were electrocuted. Other liberal friends were comparing North Carolina to the Deep South and finding the Old North State to be far more liberal; but to Green it seemed that black people in North Carolina were faring no better than black people in Mississippi. [37]

As he continued to think about these issues, and to talk about them with his friends, Green became convinced that the chain gang and the electric chair were only the extreme expressions of the evil that was damnable Jim Crow racism. On 15 September 1935 he exploded with feeling, and he recorded in his diary his principled objection to capital punishment: it was racist, it was class oppression, and it was plain wrong. He determined to lead a public attack against capital punishment, and he determined to write a one-act play attacking chain gangs. Deus ex machina. A God of justice could be heard speaking from inside that prisoner's box. And Green intended to use the Federal Theater Project as the machine to let God talk, and talk as roughly as an outraged God needed to talk about an enormity. Much of that talk would be in action, the theater God disclosing people's injustices to themselves by showing them a mirror.[38]

For a credible source of such descriptions, Green had not only the testimony of the little Richmonder, but also what he had seen of chain gangs for himself. And he could remember incidents from the wartime army, one of which he had written up into an unpublished poem in which he took the voice of a toadying soldier denied the expected reward of extra rations usually provided for those who "brown-nose" beyond the call of the common soldier's duty. Wartime pontoon builders are not that different from chain-gang crews, Green reasoned; and he was confident that army cooks were likewise not much different from prison cooks. On one set of these poems and notes—by 1935 more than twenty years old—he had written some additional remarks, including a description of a toadying prisoner who is similarly denied his extra ration by an officious cook.[39]

Green decided to take the symbols of God and country and write an extended hymn: the play would feature a prison official offering a paean to the liberties of America while in the background a voice sings "America the Beautiful." A straight line runs from beginning to end with this hymn, a hymn at once sacred and profane, "God of Our Fathers" thoroughly confounded with the secular fathers and sons, religion symbols and nation symbols deliberately fused with few seams showing. And the end of the straight line of worship would be the promised goal of justice and equality.[40]

The action of the play moves in an arc that starts at the beginning of the straight line of the hymn: this is God's chosen land of freedom and hope and justice and equality. However, the action of the play steadily moves away from that starting point, and the arc gets far away from the straight line of justice until its path rejoins the straight line at its terminus. There, at the end, is resolution of plot, the prisoner's death occurring on the Fourth of July as the nation-religion hymn "America the Beautiful" is sung and as the prison official reads a nation-religion creed. In terms of the play's action, there is a certain and unmistakable move toward the prisoner's death, and a horrible death at that; and the conclusion of the play's action demonstrates the distance between the creedal statement and the actual treatment of a people.

On stage there is no resolution of theme, although a conclusion of its theme is left in the audience's lap. Americans preach one thing and do another, and here is a first level of irony, for we preach the one thing, justice, to the very man to whom we *do* the other thing, injustice; and we even require the man's fellow

prisoners to preach and sing hymns of praise while the man dies from wounds
that we give him. Those who are seeing and hearing this ironic juxtaposition
of preached justice and practiced injustice have to resolve it for themselves.
The alternatives are simple enough to see and to state, but the choice is not
easy at all: give up the creed, or give up the chain gang. We cannot have both
at once.

This is a political drama, and it owes great debts to prole lit, for the audience is moved to resolve the dilemma for themselves and then to act. The
play has a very clear purpose, seen obviously enough using its text alone, but
this purpose is even more obviously seen and heard in the context of the diary notes, other notes, correspondence, and things Green told people while he
was writing *Hymn*. Yet, for all its polemical nature, it departs from prole lit. For
Green, the problem with the genre was the formula of noble victim and ignoble
oppressor. He did not want icons, whether the icons were called stereotypes
or archetypes; instead, he wanted believable, concretely identified people. The
point was not the innocence of the victim; the point was the injustice done to
the least of us. Why the man was in prison, and what he had done while in
prison, even what kind of a man he was, none of these was the issue.

The issue was the treatment of human beings who were black, regardless of
how good or bad they were. To no less degree, he wanted the antagonists,
the prison guards and cooks and officials, to be believed and even sympathized with. These antagonists were not to be cardboard criminals, but ordinary poor white Carolinians with their own problems in the middle of an
enormity. Green's target was not the man with the gun who was *lower* than
the prisoners; his target was the people of the state that told the man with the
gun to manage the chain gang. That man with the gun faces a task involving
people who are rebellious and troublesome, and he has as many problems as
the souldrivers who went before him. No one can do this guard job correctly
or justly. Only by throwing out the entire system can justice be served. Green
thus injects a different strain of irony here, for the prisoner may well deserve
to be in prison; there will still be black men who do bad things, and there will
still need to be prisons for those men. For all that, no human should be treated
in this way.

Thus far, Green was still working within reformist formulas, although he
had moved far out on the borderline of proper prole lit. Even this deliberately
and self-styled *improper* form of literature had in the course of things established its own sense of propriety, its own lights by which properly to be judged;
and Green was about to pass beyond the pale even of that which *chose* to be beyond the pale. He jumped past prole lit and even outside reformist literature of
any recognizable kind. He offered a different kind of irony, one that mocked
the usual forms of irony. Irony can, and does, strip away delusion and thus is

often the tool of the revolutionary artist. But irony can turn on the ironist, as literary critic A. Alvarez puts it. This turning back on the artist and undoing the artist is demonstrated by the Polish poet Zbigniew Herbert in his art and by the southern historian Vann Woodward, the man who as a graduate student at UNC was inspired by Green in his reformism and scholarship. Green, in thus stripping away delusions with his character's language, begins to damage his own credibility as an author, because the reader and the listener listen to the language of the characters and realize that the writer's words do not mean what they seem to mean. A little later, the reader and the listener come to realize that the character's language may not even symbolize what the playwright means for them to symbolize. This sense of the writer losing control over his or her own ironic language is crucial to postmodernist theory, and Green is here experimenting with something that he would later reject. He insists that he, the writer, remains in charge of the characters and their actions, and he insists with no less fervor that the audience can be shown a usable irony that will lead its members to reform.[41]

The most controversial aspect was how he treated the prisoner victim, whom he named Runt in an echo of the disappeared little man from Richmond who had brought his *True Life* story of the bending-standing box. Rather than have Runt falsely accused of some transgression, and rather than have him guilty of something "pitiful," Green wrote that he was guilty of masturbation. That breach of prison rules was questionable as a crime, and it was demeaning in a way that reinforced all the exclusions as well as the lack of privacy on the chain gang. While his predecessor and hero Eugene O'Neill had revolutionized theatrical depictions and discussions of sexuality, Green was in this instant dealing with something much more uncomfortable, and almost no one liked it. He realized the audience response after he read the play to a circle of friends who gathered in his study in October of 1935. Those in the group were completely in sympathy with the playwright's demand for artistic liberty in expression and depiction, but *nobody* was enthusiastic about the aesthetics of the play. Too, some black actors who otherwise sympathized with Green's intentions, and who were otherwise delighted to have a chance to play in substantive roles, were put off by Runt's masturbation, and some of these actors refused to perform in the play.[42]

There was also the issue of publication: Percival Wilde, editor of a yearly anthology of one-act plays, very much wanted *Hymn,* but he also wanted a more pitiful and more innocent transgression for Runt. However, Wilde gave Green the chance to explain himself and his methods and assumptions, and Green, ever since Barrett Clark's coaching in the Pulitzer campaign, was a past master at this kind of putatively private letter that was always designed to be read by the public. Thus he wrote a personal note to explain himself to Wilde in a way that he suspected the editor could use in a foreword to a published version of the play:

> I agree that the chain-gang is the matter of concern in "Hymn to the Rising Sun," and not any sort of sex vagary. But precisely because that is true, I think it would be a mistake to have Runt's punishment come as a result of some minor infraction of rules. For then the darker, more disastrous nature of convict life would be once again illustrated by a pathetic and not tragic incident—and tragedy is what I am after in this piece, since the lives I am telling about are tragic. Suppose the Negro were put into the sweatbox because he had been caught smoking in his bunk, or talking back to one of the guards. Then the dramatic result would be to point the finger of accusation at the system the while it put an arm of sympathy around the abused individual. But this would be the old sheep-and-goat method now a little too dear to our younger radical writers and not true to the infinite complexity and shades of differences of human nature. Again, the Runt is what he is because the system is what it is, and the system obtains as it does because of such fellows as Runt. But—and here the higher reality comes in—the observer (you, others, myself) stands outside the vicious circle and sees that we must go back, far, far back, to start growing a different and happier society. And that is true, isn't it? And after all what better criterion than truth?[43]

Green thus, as usually the case, remained true to the traditions of the all-knowing author who is able to reach through the actors—those caught up in that "vicious circle"—to speak about higher truth, and to speak thus directly with the audience that stands outside the vicious circle. By such older formulae, the tragic character of the protagonist needs a fatal flaw that is both a source of strength and a cause of downfall. Runt's strength is his sexual prowess, his mastery of lovemaking in freedom days before consignment to the chain gang; now in prison he turns his strength inward, on himself, masturbating; and that is his downfall. Again, the *device,* masturbation, is shocking for contemporaneous tastes, but the tragic flaw itself is a classical convention.

Like others experimenting with modernist forms, Green consciously reverts to classical prescriptions, and, in fact, he is annoyed when the readers and the actors and the audience do not "get it," though he is equally annoyed by the very notion of putting across the message—the need to start growing a different and happier society—in more direct fashion, as would be done in prole lit. Green experiments with many things in *Hymn,* but he consciously backs away from some things: the likelihood of Runt's turning to homoerotic lovemaking Green never allows readers to consider. His modernism, again, would only go so far, usually adopting a form here, a technique there, in order to affirm a traditional pagan call for justice. And he is very much in the wrong place and at the wrong time, and likely he is the wrong person, to experiment with postmodern themes, especially with regard to empowering of the readers and hearers to decide things for themselves.

This play, then, shows Green pushing against walls of conventions and finding those walls remarkably weak; but then he consciously draws back and leaves them essentially to stand where they were. He, the author with a message, is going to deliver that message to an audience using conventions long agreed upon. Political courage and political effectiveness, he had—yes, beyond question. Stylistic innovation and experimentations, yes. But modernist theory is only partly his, and postmodernism not at all. What an irony that, when it was all over, it is postmodernist reader-response theory that best explains the political success enjoyed by his play that enjoyed few artistic and no commercial successes. A strain of postmodernism says that readers do have power to shape what they see and hear, and thus readers actively participate in any process of writing. It is that very power of readers that makes *Hymn* historically notable; but that is a power that Green consistently ignored, and finally denied altogether.[44]

He failed to get an audience in a New York or in a Chicago theater to hear him and to act. He failed to get readers of an anthology to see his point and to act. But he succeeded in getting the governor of North Carolina, the General Assembly of North Carolina, and one great author to read his words, to hear the words their own ways, and to act to get rid of the chain gang in particular and more generally "growing a different and happier society." Unlike all his other plays, this one moved an audience to act, but it was not the audience that he really sought, and he remained as frustrated by *Hymn*'s successes in the political sphere as he was by its failures in the commercial and artistic spheres.[45]

In any event, Green demonstrated a noble sort of stubbornness about *Hymn*. Wilde published the play in his anthology, and the editor gave the playwright the introductory space to use for his letter. That an author has to explain so much before a reader is permitted into a work is its own sign, and Green was ruefully aware of this sign. Generally, in a case where there is unintended ambiguity, a generous editor arranges for a self-styled disinterested playwright or perhaps an even more studiedly disinterested critic to write an introductory guideline. But Green had to have it just his way and still he had to be assured that the reader would not miss the message; even more, he had to be sure that the reader who got the message would not then mistake it for prole lit. He needed his own well-wrought words. Thus guided, the reader then follows this plot, gets the message, and can choose to act or not to act. Writing the note and preparing the manuscript, Green became even more convinced of the need to put the play on.[46]

This script is a strong one, with hard, clean lines of action matching hard, tense words, and the several levels of irony compel one in a reading of it. Whatever his friends said, Green could see clearly that he had written a powerful thing, especially if it could be displayed to eye and ear on a stage: black skin, white skin, big man, little man, basso profundo voices, tenor voices, crude acts of niggardly men, high and noble words. In early autumn of 1935 he got in touch with officials in the Federal Theater Project of the New Deal Writer's Program. Joe Losey of the Let Freedom Ring Troupe in New York City wanted *Hymn* and arranged to produce it in the city at the Civic Repertory Theatre in January 1936. Losey's direction was a good one, and there were strong performances by Charles Dingle as the Captain, Douglass Parkhurst as Bright Boy, and Gus Smith as Pearly Gates. Besides Smith, black actors shone as well in a baker's dozen of roles as supporting and as extra actors. Yet that first New York production went almost nowhere commercially, the common fate for Green's plays. He had to hope instead that Wilde's published anthology would spark interest in a new production.[47]

In the meantime, Green at his own expense arranged for Samuel French to print enough copies of *Hymn* for Governor Ehringhaus and for every member of the North Carolina General Assembly. He mailed the scripts along with a typed note to each assembly member, and he again wrote to Ehringhaus, playing shrewdly on the governor's self-professed racial moderation and on the governor's call for penal reform and for a generally more efficient and more honest highway- and road-building system. These things were all related, the governor must come to see, for the chain gang and the good old boy contractors and the sweetheart deals between suppliers in combination were making a mockery of North Carolina's Good Roads Movement. Often the roads were bad, and they were always expensive. And the chain gang was so unjust that almost everyone in North Carolina was unhappy. True, many, perhaps even most, were unhappy only because of the bad public image and not because of real concern for the rights of prisoners, but the fact remained that the governor's own rhetoric was moving him along to reform at a moment when the public was ready to proclaim reform as well.[48]

For these, and perhaps other, reasons, Governor Ehringhaus made the abolition of the chain gang the dominant symbol for his reform proposals, both for the prisons and for the roads. Green, the governor evidently decided, was right; and *Hymn* became the occasion and in some ways the direct cause of Ehringhaus's demand for the twin reforms. In similar fashion, *Hymn* became the occasion as well as one of the direct causes for many of the assembly votes for those reforms, which were passed in that session. Indirect causes, of course, abounded; and those had much to do with businessmen frustrated by the "sweetheart" contractor deals for road construction, with chamber of commerce officials unable to mask the bad and decidedly unbusinesslike news about the chain-gang system, and with industrial and farming producers unhappy with the network of roads. Nor should the historian pretend that the white citizens of North Carolina suddenly became liberal on an issue of race. What did happen, however, cannot be gainsaid: Green's play, delivered as it was to the politicians at the moment it was delivered, caught the attention of a political audience at the "teachable moment" that all reformists seek.

Hymn spoke to all the things that needed changing, and it put the chain-gang system center stage as the visible, undeniable evil that could be eliminated. Whatever the play did or did not do as art and commerce, its achievement in politics is signal, for it uniquely signified and named a problem; and it did so in a way that politicians could respond without losing much, while gaining a great deal. Given the way that things had started with regard to this "amputated foot incident," the abolition of the chain gang was genuine progress. And Green could be rightly pleased with his own part in bringing the reform legislation into being.

Of equal weight in Green's scales of self-judgment was the artistic effort in *Hymn,* and he was thus equally gratified in 1936 to learn that the great African American artist Richard Wright was developing plans to restage *Hymn* in Chicago with that city's Federal Theater Project. Wright later memorialized his part of this story in essays that focus on his estrangement from, break with, and eventual hostility to the Communist Party in Chicago. In picking one's way back through the many pieces that remain to us, we do well to remember Wright's strong sense of betrayal by the party, and we do equally well to remember his willingness to use his novelist's talents to tell a story to make his point. And making his point certainly included a generous amount of settling old scores; he intended to score many points in the old game of *apologia pro sua vita* as well as to make points in a moralist's debate. [49] None of these considerations diminishes in any degree the ways that *Hymn* became an element of historical drama where everything and everyone was "real" and where no one was "playing" in any ordinary sense of the word. And all of these considerations underscore the oddity that *Hymn* becomes important as historical drama in almost direct proportion to its failure to survive as art in the normal sense. The farther it got from stage production, the larger and weightier it became as a politically effective thing.

Keeping in mind the many things in the background, really the foreground, for Richard Wright in 1936 and 1937, it is fascinating to look at his account of the second effort to produce *Hymn* in a theater funded by the Federal Writers Project. He took the assignment with the Federal Negro Theater immediately after being forced from the South Side Boys Club by the Chicago Communist Party. Already injured by racism in Chicago's party cell, Wright had by then begun the long journey from left to right that would put him foremost among the angry writers of the influential anti-Communist essays in *The God That Failed.* [50]

Still smarting from the wounds inside the cell, Wright then encountered a particularly bizarre effect of racism in his own relationships with Chicago's black actors in the city's Federal Negro Theater. He recollects subsequent things thus: "I could not believe my ears. I had assumed that the heart of the Negro actor was pining for adult expression in the American theater, that he was ashamed of the [*sic*]. Now they were protesting against dramatic realism! I tried to defend the play and I was heckled down."[51] The upshot of this dispute was a threat to Wright from knife-wielding actors: "I telephoned my white friends in the Works Progress Administration: 'Transfer me at once to another job, or I'll be murdered.'"[52]

Quite a story, with its bittersweet redemption of Richard Wright and Paul Green as principled reformists in art and politics. However, other pieces of evidence demonstrate an even more tangled series of disappointments, with little of redemption involved, especially for Green. From a telephone interview with Green for her history of the Federal Negro Theater, Glenda Gill records: "The Mayor of Chicago sent to Paul Green a telegram stating that he was closing *Hymn to the Rising Sun,* a Federal Theatre play focusing on the chain gang."[53] Yet the play was canceled long before it could be closed. It was the dismissal of Wright—and the refusal of this particular Chicago African American troupe to play the roles for anybody—that ended the performances. The telegram from Edward J. Kelly, the mayor, is a politician's slick and devious way of taking credit for what already has happened, but it only adds an establishment New Deal coalition figure's clever and unprincipled affirmation to actions *already taken by the black actors themselves.*

It is interesting that it is the politician, Mayor Kelly, whom Green remembers as the heavy player; while in Wright's recollecting it is the actors themselves. Too, Green omits the *players* in his recollecting, while Wright omits the *mayor* in his. Most interesting of all omissions is the most likely cause of the dissatisfaction for both the black actors and the white politician: the issue of Runt's masturbation. Mayor Kelly complained of "indecency" and of "filth," not the chain gang. And the actors, despite one man quoted by Wright who defended Carolina's road building, also complained of "indecency," much as Percival Wilde had warned that audiences would do. Green's point about the nature of the tragedy (that Runt must not be a pure victim, but must have human flaws in order for us to apprehend the tragedy of the system) is valid enough, but he ignores it in his own remembering of this incident. The unconventional thing in *Hymn* was not a protest against the chain gang: no, the unconventional thing was the frankness about one aspect of sexuality; and that element of sexuality was absolutely crucial to Green's scheme in which the protagonist and the antagonists, and all other characters, have to be seen in the middle of an enormity. Yet, in recounting the story of the Chicago killing of *Hymn,* Green's description of the controversies, like Wright's, has much of the "sheep-and-goat" character that Green decried in his own carefully designed covering letter to Wilde for the anthology. He, like Wright earlier, defends himself as a liberal reformist attacking an awful institution instead of defending himself as what he also was: an experimental playwright attacking theatrical and social conventions.

Hymn would get one more chance, with a return to New York in 1937, this time at the Ritz with the Experimental Theater of the Federal Theater Program. It was noted with approval by Brooks Atkinson, a *New York Times* critic usually in Green's corner. But other critics were not much moved, audiences stayed away, and *Hymn* closed again, this time for good.

A number of things seem to result from the many stories that are *Hymn* and the efforts to produce it. One is a special relationship with Wright, who would choose Green to collaborate with him on a rewriting of *Native Son* for Orson Welles's production of the black man's autobiographical novel. The resulting Broadway play, *Native Son,* became an artistic and a commercial success, in its production again involving Wright and Green in interesting dramas and comedies offstage. Another result is a kind of high-water mark for Green in terms of artistic experimentation. Nowhere would he again experiment so boldly: even and especially in the self-conscious experimentation of the Group Theater, Green would compromise his intentionalities because of the producers, the directors, the actors, and the audiences. Too, as we have seen, Green's otherwise interesting work for the Group Theater was finally not very experimental at all. Another result, likely related, has to do with audience. Green could not reach an audience with a genuinely radical and reformist message in a way that he considered true to his own art and aesthetics. He would not write prole lit, despite the ready audience for those conventions; and he could not get people into the seats for his own new and modified conventions of production.

Despite the successes enjoyed by *Hymn* offstage—the way that Governor Ehringhaus, the North Carolina General Assembly, and Richard Wright had each read and responded by acting vigorously as *equally real* reading audiences—Green longed for audiences of a more traditional kind, a kind that actually came in, sat down, and listened and laughed and cried at a production on a stage. In order to connect himself with such an audience of conventional theatergoers, Green would likely have to offer people a message less radical, less threatening, a message more compatible with the expectations of those relatively comfortable, liberal but hardly radical, and certainly middle-brow bourgeoisie that bought—or refused to buy—the tickets to his shows.

II : NEW DIRECTIONS

1937–1941

Defeated again commercially and artistically in New York, Green after 1937 entered an entirely new phase of playwriting by adapting theories of German and Russian people's dramas to venues strictly off Broadway. Indeed, for many of his productions, he moved far away even from the university and little-theater sites, where he was still a king. From this change in strategy came his quintessentially liberal play, *The Lost Colony,* the one Paul Green production that has survived and flourished at all levels. Also from this change in strategy came his quintessentially liberal action, the integration, however briefly, of the professor's work space at his state university, the Jim Crow law and the racist prophets to the contrary notwithstanding.

The first change in this period of his life and career was his status at the university. The decades of his on-again, off-again relationship with the legend and the legacy of Horace Williams in the philosophy department were finally ended. He was offered, and accepted readily, an appointment as professor in the dramatic arts department; now he was officially the obvious successor to Proff Koch and no longer the dubious successor to Horace Williams the Legend. This appointment was effective for fall quarter of the academic year 1938–39, and it shows the fine hand of the wise administrators Frank Porter Graham and Robert House. Prickly and overly personal, even catty, as he could be, Horace Williams had been right about one thing, and Green and the university administrators finally acknowledged that thing: in the modern academic world, philosophy the discipline in its own department fully deserved a serious scholar of philosophy. In that venue Paul Green was a charming enough anachronism, what with his renaissance catholicity of interests and his pointed moral commitments; but he had never even completed the master's degree in philosophy, and he never showed very much patience, and certainly little acumen, in developing philosophical arguments. It was time, and indeed past time, for more narrowly focused but also more sincerely dedicated philosophers to come aboard and bring the department, finally, into the new era. When they did, there would still be Paul Green on campus and in the community as a wonderful case in point for their students; indeed, Maynard Adams, the most influential of modern-era philosophers at UNC, would be the practicing, publishing, professional scholar, but he would also be among the most committed of liberal reformists, and always he would credit Paul Green as the inspiration and example.[1]

Another way to look at the new appointment was from the point of view of Proff Koch's own competing legacy: the dramatic arts deserved their own past masters to lead the way as mentors to new playwrights in a new era, and in that venue, why would Paul Green need a doctorate to present bona fides for some accrediting board of visitors? After all, he was a Pulitzer Prize holder, he was several times listed among authors for the best plays for a given season, and he was an acknowledged leader in the now full-blown and fully self-conscious southern literary renaissance. He clearly deserved this appointment, and no one would ever gainsay it. Even so, there was a problem, one as portentous as any of Green's early-hooting screech owls: drama students, no less than philosophy students, needed some mentoring and some close-hand coaching in the specifics of techniques, and a professor of dramatic studies who was often gone away to superintend the script for a play or a movie could not provide that kind of attention. After all, Proff Koch's genius had never been in his own creativity, but in his inspiration of his charges achieved through personal attentions—all of which was extremely time-consuming and energy-draining. Only a very clever, and very lucky, admixture of forces, events, personalities, and circumstances could guarantee that someone else at UNC would offer the young students the close attention that they needed while Paul Green provided inspiration and example from a greater distance. And, as noted often, this man was not often clever or lucky, being perhaps too sincere and too driven to pick up and use the odd chances that came his way. For all that, however, the new appointment had closed off one fascinating part of his personal drama and set up a new set of scenes far more appropriate to the research university and to his own talents and inclinations.

As to strange admixtures of forces, events, personalities, and circumstances, the most recent personal and institutional histories had featured the most unfortunate combinations that had conspired against the Federal Theater Project production of *Hymn*. Even and especially so, that government institution FTP remained an important outlet for Green, plus a special sign of the American people's support for the performing arts. For his own production needs, but also for the principle of such public support, he needed the FTP. He wrote about it, talked about it, and fought to protect it.

In the late 1930s, nevertheless, things began to happen to the program, and by 1939 a successful attack had been launched against it. Most of the missiles came from the Old North State, indeed from a United States senator with whom Green once had friendly relations and warm correspondence. Robert

Rice Reynolds, a man of the mountains formerly considered a kind of neopopulist Carolinian, by the late 1930s had determined that he would destroy the theater program, and he chose the right moment, when New Deal social legislation was given less consideration because of the possibility of another world war and when economic recovery (itself related to the military spending that came along with concerns about the possibility of another war) was taking away the edge of the reformism that once moved broadly across many areas of national life.

Hallie Flanagan, director of the FTP, wrote to Green and other sympathetic playwrights in hopes of mobilizing support for her besieged program. Founded in 1935, the FTP was up for review, during which time it was attacked by Senator Reynolds and by Representatives Everett Dirksen of Illinois and Clifton A. Woodrum of Virginia. These men adopted the clever ploy of reading aloud the titles of plays, in process emphasizing the "salacious" content and the "Communist" tone of the fare. Forecasting stratagems in hearings of a later day, the congressmen sometimes read names of plays *not* sponsored by FTP; and of course, since context is everything, many titles can be made to sound salacious or ideological by tone of voice and other tricks. Congressman Woodrum claimed that "every theatrical critic of note" had expressed his disappointment in these productions; moreover, Woodrum said that most of the actors lacked talent, but the federal money lured in people who would otherwise go find employment at something closer to their training. Also, Woodrum was delighted to find in the FTP an Austrian-born actress who boldly proclaimed free love and described her passion for lovemaking with African American men. After the Virginian introduced this testimony in the House, Reynolds drew the attention of his fellow senators to it, with emphasis on his own hatred of interracial sex and miscegenation. Finally, the FTP was, the congressman stated and the senator quoted, "a grand dramatic recreation program—combined with a school for actors—but [it] can truly not be called the legitimate theatre."[2]

Flanagan tried to respond to the legislators with facts, although of course the issue was not facts at all but symbols. To answer Woodrum's charge, Flanagan introduced into the hearings a statement of support for the FTP signed by many prominent critics, led by Burns Mantle, Brooks Atkinson, and Joseph Wood Krutch. As to the claims of salacious content and Communist—indeed specifically Stalinist Russian—direction, Flanagan responded by noting the preponderance of mainstream playwrights involved in the huge and sprawling program that claimed audiences of more than thirty million for about twelve hundred plays performed over a period of four years. She emphasized the strength of control by local communities—which certainly could be attested ruefully by Paul Green and Richard Wright in the case of Chicago's FTP and its local Negro Theater—and she celebrated the fact that 65 percent of the plays were free to the public, while others cost no more than pocket change.[3]

Green realized that the FTP was in serious danger. He wrote letters in its defense. Of course, he never needed encouragement to write letters for such a cause, but in this case he did so with a sense of ineluctable doom.[4] For one thing, there was no denying that leftist impulses ran through the theater. That after all was the gist of the revolt of the arts and of prole lit, and such things had been politically acceptable, even in some places de rigeur, in 1929–35 when economic times were especially hard, there was "thunder on the left," and the midwestern Republican Wendell Wilkie had wryly quoted George Bernard Shaw that any man who had not been a socialist before he reached the age of thirty must have no heart—but any man who was still a socialist after becoming thirty must have no head. By the latter half of the decade, everyone except the writers and actors suddenly seemed to be thirty years old. In one sense, then, the FTP was hoist with its own petard: politically supported by the Left when leftwingers had some power, the FTP had to expect problems from opponents of the Left when the political mood of the country shifted.

And on the count of salaciousness and indecency, of course that was the charge leveled against *Hymn*. Salaciousness is in the eye of the beholder, and Green had already seen that the middle-class mentality of audiences that controlled Broadway was not going to pay to have its emotions probed on issues concerning sexuality, Eugene O'Neill and liberation and flappers and new morals and all of that to the contrary notwithstanding. It was this class who paid the taxes, and it could hardly be surprising that its members were not willing to pay indirectly through government subsidies for something that they did not want and had resolutely closed their wallets against. Even within the operation of the FTP, real innovation involving genuine artistic risks was far to seek. But without FTP, there would be only Samuel Goldwyn's "en-tuh-tanement" in Hollywood and Sidney Ross's plays on Broadways. And so Green wrote his letters.[5]

Congressional discussions and the political debate about the FTP were as wild and entertaining as several colorful figures could make them, and the end was easy to see, even and especially for the tireless writer of letters and drawerup of petitions Paul Green. The program was destroyed. When it was all over, Green had not only seen a principle defeated, but he had also lost yet another outlet for his artwork. The public, whether buying tickets or responding to government programs, was not going to accept ideological art, nor was it going to accept art that explored the most troubling, and least controllable, of human emotions.

Could he make yet another attempt to create some new outlet for serious experimental art? Few in his era had tried so nobly to do truly innovative and risk-taking things on the stage. Now only the university stages and some strictly local off-off-Broadway stages lay opened to him. Perhaps it was time to change the way that he approached this core audience of a middle class that was comfortable and fully intended to stay comfortable.

As early as 1921, he had written to Lib Lay to tell her about his efforts to dramatize the story of Virginia Dare, the first child born in North America to English settlers, or at least the first child for whom there was a church record of baptism.[6] That settlement subsequently aborted, the settlers vanished, the English sponsor, Sir Walter Raleigh, was discredited and even imprisoned, and the whole "plantation" experiment was subsumed under the excitement of the defeat of the Spanish navy. Finally, even the memory of the colony was overwhelmed by the later successful development of Virginia after 1607. In time, the failed Roanoke Island venture, romantic and mystical and engaging to many North Carolinians, became yet more proof that the Old North State would be perpetually the "valley [or vale] of humility between two mountains of conceit," poor Carolina between once wealthy and still prideful South Carolina and Virginia. As the ironic but unrepentant cavalier James Branch Cabell remembered it cruelly, North Carolina was the kind of place where an aspiring gentleman buys a book telling him about proper manners—and then actually displays the book in his parlor.[7]

But to Green the Roanoke Island effort remained connected to grander strivings, and one of the strands of continuity that especially caught his attention was the Croatan (Lumbee) "tri-lateral mixed" Indians who had some black ancestry but who obviously also had much white ancestry, or in the old terms, a lot of white blood. These Croatans claimed descent from the Roanoke Island settlement, and that claim continued to draw Green in, even as it put off, even angered, the region's social scientists. Sometimes in his youthful diary notes, he had spoken a little disdainfully about the "wandering Croatan," borrowing the old biblical phrase "wandering Aramaian." As noted often, he was prejudiced against Jews, and thus "wandering Croatan," as he first used the term, was damnably clever, since it condemns the mixed-blood Croatans by association with the despised Jews—and uses a Jewish term to do so. However, as we saw, his thoughts evolved and matured, and he developed greater respect for Jews and Jewish culture, even sufficient to celebrate Yiddish folk in his studies in Germany and to emulate their genius in his folk drama. As his respect for Jews grew, so did his respect for the Croatans and their stories and their claims, and he came to say the same phrase with an extremely different meaning. By the late 1930s he had found a biblical and even a supernatural and heaven-inspired element in his phrase: certain peoples, Israelites in one day, Croatans in another, had been chosen to wander, and suffer, until that very wandering and suffering brought about an earthly salvation. The Hegelian was being lifted up to Horace Williams's "new view of religion" by his own higher thoughts until he came to deny and to defy the old lower thoughts of prejudice![8]

Drawing on his North Carolina, the scorned state, and the Croatans, the scorned people in the Cape Fear valley, he dreamed up a play. He wanted to have John Oxendine, Croatan, come to the state university archives to examine a ship registry for the Roanoke Island settlement, to prove that he is a white man descended from English whites. The character, recognized as Croatan and thus of mixed race, is denied admission to the search room, although the archival registry does indeed bear the name of an Oxendine. Green knew that by 1889 Croatans were given legal status as a group separate from white and black, but he wanted to set this scene in 1888, so that Oxendine would be treated as a black man attempting to use the resources of this proudly white state university. This personal tragedy of lost identity he would put into larger ethnic context of an entire group's lost identity. Thus, everything was circled and doubled and entrapping: a colored man of the Cape Fear valley seeking a grander identity for himself in the Old North State, itself identified as the Valley of Humility. It would make a strong tale, and as cast in his notes after a talk with Phillips Russell, it would be very much a Paul Green tragedy, with a resolution of self-knowledge close to the sad wisdom of the Preacher in Ecclesiastes: Vanity, vanity, all is vanity.[9]

But what about yet another Paul Green tragedy? Again he could probe the uncomfortable worlds of emotions about status and class and caste and identity, again he could end things in a realistic resolution of defeat and probably death, again he would simultaneously raise the consciousness and dash the hopes of the audience. Could such another tragedy *go*, even as a university experimental production? Much more, would it *sell* on Broadway? Given commercial responses to the best work that he could do over the past ten years, the answer seems obvious. What then if he approached the ethnic and racial issues more obliquely? What if he left broad implications about caste and class and regional poverty, but otherwise gave that broad middle class of late-1930s North Carolina something to cheer for? What if he used all the techniques that he had studied and mastered from Germans and Russians about folk drama, and what if he behaved like a symphonic conductor blending many elements of art into a grander performance of uplifting hope in which the prophecy was not about a justice of retribution, not about chickens coming home to roost, but instead about a justice of prospects, with a telos showing the rewards for going the right way? What if he—the original Hegel of the cotton patch—drew on the master philosopher for a large-scale prophecy of justice in the land of milk and honey, and what if he taught the same lessons about justice and equality with hope instead of with fear and trembling? And what if he offered the whole orchestrated symphonic artistry first for his own North Carolina, with everyone else, most especially Virginians, getting their moment on stage in American history *second?*

      To find and hold this new tone, Green changed the nature of the verse that he wrote. Always powerful stuff, his verse in former times was predominantly dark, with a comedy also dark—and with comedy that might not provide traditional comic relief from tension but, as in *Johnny Johnson,* would instead envelop theatergoers in humor so perplexing that tension is heightened rather than relieved. A Paul Green play of the period 1922–37 was an emotionally exhausting experience that made one think. There was a determinism, even a fatalism, in his drama, and it came from some combination of the plural Calvinisms in his upbringing and a sense of doom that was sui generis. He would retain in his new verse after 1937 a sense of foreordination and a feeling that huge forces were at play, with a human agent basically empowered not so much to control those forces or even get out of their way as to recognize their existence and live thereafter an examined and responsible life. Ever Hegelian, now he looked farther away, up toward the rising—and expanding—spiral of the great dialectic. Up beyond the Jamesian pragmatism that still served other intellectuals of the era but for Green was only useful because of its rationale for reformism. Up beyond the Marxism that now seemed only one more necessary phase in the intellectual and moral development, up, up, and out. *Aufhebung!*

He was again thinking through this Roanoke Island dramatization whose specific artistic requirements had worried his mind since 1921 and the sweep of whose broad themes he had felt before his birth. In so doing, he returned to the powerful, relentless, and optimistic idealism of Hegel's three-step progress through history. The story of democracy must be told in the very face of the totalitarianism on the move from left to right and from east to west in Europe. That story had a three-part beginning, and the artistic prelude must, in Hegelian fashion, open up and out, expanding the possibilities rather than closing off and narrowing down possibilities. Telos, a moral direction, yes; a specific program, a particular goal, no. The three-part prelude was *in* America, and the possibilities opened up and outward, *aufhebung, from* Americans *for* the entire world. His three-part structure of beginnings must be large. It must contain diverse elements, even contradicting elements. The first spiral in the search began at Roanoke Island, and it was not completed; but neither had it failed, nor had it ended.

The Lost Colony would chronicle men and women who were physically lost to the Old World but who themselves were not lost at all, not in physical sense and absolutely not in moral sense. The colonists' ideas would survive to prepare the way for the second great spiral, which was *The Common Glory,* and that scene would shift to Williamsburg to look at democratic institutions being built—but only *after* the necessary engagement, including the necessary suffering, of *The Lost Colony*'s first spiral. The third phase was itself "the end of the beginning," as another wordsmith described democratic struggles in the 1940s. That third phase was *The Highland Call*, in which the ancient freedoms of the disdained but still defiant Celts of the Highlands "beyond the pale" and outside the Wall of Antoninus, are drawn upon for a great battle of independence fought against old, worn-out, and morally exhausted Great Britain. [10]

Entangling ironies were everywhere, for the marginal people—those who were Indian and mixed-breed, those who were savage Celts banished to poor Carolina—are as much a part of his story as the Enlightenment titans Jefferson and Madison and Franklin. The spiral of the Hegelian synthesis got wider and wider as it moved up, thereby bringing the marginal people to our attention. The most marginal, African Americans, would inevitably be drawn into Green's spiral, and he spoke also of a fourth spiral (or fourth chapter) not even yet engaged, in which black people would be brought fully into participation in our society. The Hegelian synthesis as Green spelled it out is integrationist and egalitarian, and in fact he came to dislike the word *synthetic,* which he found less satisfying than *symphonic.* The latter implied not only an ingathering of all the disparate elements of artistic expression, but also a harmonious bringing together of all disparate elements. [11]

The change in his verse was stunning, and the playwright after 1937 is quite different from the already well established playwright of 1921–37. He became lyrical as his themes broadened in sweep. The effect is magisterial, a result for an author who senses himself in complete command, and this sense would increase each year and each decade from 1937 to 1981—exactly of course the opposite of the direction taken by other art and artists as modernism gave on to postmodernism in the same decades. There is protest, but the protest suggests hope: it is, as Wystan Hugh Auden puts it, angry *and* optimistic; indeed, it is angry *because* it is optimistic. The brooding tragic vision is gone, not so much from the man as from his art, and the long view is bracing: a banker, a teacher, a small-time farmer, some average Carolinian fed up with hearing about Virginia and the Commonwealth statesmen of the planter elite, could leave the amphitheater bucked up and inspired and invigorated, moral lungs filled with the sharp, cold, awakening air of the democratic telos that the commoners' ancestors had set in motion; and that average person of the modern world was by Green's art charged with maintaining that very struggle for liberty. Most prominent of the many champions of the ordinary person in that era, *the* New Deal liberals Franklin Delano and Eleanor Roosevelt were themselves pointedly in attendance to affirm this political message when Green's symphonic drama had established itself. [12]

For these plans Green obviously was not thinking about Broadway or even what is normally called off Broadway. Barrett Harper Clark was leaving the Samuel French agency to attempt a new kind of decentralized theater that would not be hostage to the high cost, financially high-risk, but aesthetically low-risk world of Broadway's backers. Green had himself joined several such experiments, and he was helping Clark out by reading some manuscripts and suggesting names of potential writers and directors.[13] Still, he was here working on something different, something different even from the innovations that Clark envisioned. He was not even thinking of taking his art to the boldest university groups at Chapel Hill or in Iowa City. Instead, he was talking about taking art to the site where the dramatized events actually happened, in context of consciously putting the form of art *second* to the facts of history.[14]

The people of the community involved would have to finance many things themselves, but he also demanded a lot of local talents and other local resources to apply to the grand project of a symphonic drama. He was now thinking on a physical scale bigger than he had dared before. He thought about an amphitheater set on a score of acres and laid out by a real bay with real boats floating in it. He thought about regulation-sized cannons loaded with real powder (albeit without actual shot or shells), and he was not going to forget the skimping on sets that hurt *Johnny Johnson,* when those howitzers looked merely funny instead of sinister. Every set on this stage would need to be very big and very heavy and even hefty, and some things needed to be *permanent* as well.[15]

He thought too about a very large cast, perhaps more than a hundred, and these would primarily be amateurs. As Green put it for a program note in the souvenir program that attendees could buy to identify the players: "They're not theatre people. Most of them have other jobs to do and they act for the pleasure in it." Nor could he resist taking a poke at the pros: why not hire local and amateur people here, "when you consider the thousands of young people wearing out their fathers' shoe leather tramping the fruitless pavement of Broadway, and think of the fine things they might be doing back in their home neighborhoods or towns."[16]

In fact, far away from Broadway—far away even from an established university theater or big-city little theater—one could think grandly because economics has always involved costs as well as revenues. Rent in the countryside was cheap, labor was cheap, space was cheap, time was cheap. And it was time in particular, not so much a lengthy production (although any of Green's plays tended to test an audience's endurance) as how long the production would run: Green wanted to run all summer, and every summer, without break. Such commitments of time would be unheard of even for little theater, but it might be possible on eastern Carolina's barrier islands, in western Carolina's Blue Ridge, in lots of remote places. There would be expenses of course, but these could be covered by a combination of public and private resources. And if people could be persuaded to think in terms of a long, long time, developing a symphonic drama on the same site for generations, then such costs could be legitimately amortized in a way undreamed of on Broadway where huge front-end or start-up costs had to be fearfully weighed against the likelihood of an early closing. And for the audience, one could travel to many such off-off-Broadway sites for the cost of one trip to Broadway, and even trips to the little theater in a medium-sized city were expensive compared to such sites.

Space too was both cheap and grand in Green's conception. One play, or spiral, in one place was to enter into a dialogue, or even a dialectic, with another play in still another place, until eventually Green would see some eighteen symphonic dramas going on in small towns, and each of them in some way related to every other one. Locality by locality, the people would be engaged in focused thought about the unfolding story of democracy, and all of it starting with the three-part beginning set in motion on Roanoke Island.[17]

To underscore his own commitments, Green the pro for whom the Samuel French attorneys once stoutly enforced royalty and other permission obligations on settlement troupes here foreswore royalties for these early seasons, in order that his own normal "take" of the proceeds not get in the way of starting the project. Unforeseen consequences would entangle the playwright off stage as well as actors and audience, and when the symphonic drama actually began to realize major returns, Green was not able to collect much revenue because of his original grand gesture to get things started. Thus the play that really brought him commercial and popular notice made little direct impact on his income, while the films, which he did not like doing and for which accurate script credits are in any case elusive, produced commercial success without due notice; and of course neither the films, for which he was well paid for his commercial part, nor the project of which he was the underpaid aesthetic creator and nursemaid drew critical acclaim. As North Carolinians came to know more and more about him and to venerate him, outsiders knew less and less, until a new generation of Broadway critics became almost cruel—or more typically, they simply focused on other playwrights and other projects.

Besides the sheer size and scope and length of operation for *The Lost Colony,* Green put in some very wry touches. And behind the wryness was guts. There is Old Tom. This character, prominent as a town drunk in the Old World and initially almost a vaudeville comedic role, evolves into a solid citizen who stands guard at a moment of great threat and thereby permits John Borden a moment of respite. It is Old Tom who delivers the memorable Jacobean, almost Shakespearean, line: "Roanoke, thou hast made a man of me." Too, Old Tom is also a device for Green to start raising the issue of interbreeding and ethnic identities: a young Native American woman follows Tom devotedly from a time early in the second scene of act 2 in the New World. At first her fealty is funny, and the possibility of an ethnic slur slides uneasily along the edges of the set as she, slavelike, even almost dumbly, follows the drunken fool.

White women from England laugh mirthfully, along with the audience, at the hapless drunk attended by the "squaw" whose devotion seems so misplaced because so futile. Perhaps an Indian woman cannot do any better than this? But as the play develops, Tom "who was lately nothing am become somebody." So evolving, he appreciates the support of his woman, bestowing on her his own reciprocating affections. Most significant, he shows her respect and love.

There is a chorus that echoes the classic Greek chorus in its technical devices of explaining the action as well as setting the tone with its melodies. Granovsky had said to use music so, and he had also remarked that such techniques were not by any means anticlassical. But this Greek chorus is not only not Greek; it is Protestant, indeed Episcopalian, intoning hymns much as the onetime Baptist playwright now heard in the Chapel of the Cross, the Episcopal church that gave the name to the host town for Green's state university. The chorus, featuring Lib Green's and Lamar Stringfellow's versions of Thomas Tallis, William Byrd, and "Agincourt" tunes, could have been performed in the New England high church where the Reverend Lay had brought up Lib Lay and his other children. The effect is bracing, and fit, since such music is both optimistic and magisterial by design, and works well; but deep beneath all of it is a subtle joke, for the chosen music of comfort for the prosperous bankers and bond traders serves a function and fills the task of the ancient, even chthonic, pagan Greek chorus.

Other religious symbols are significantly used, and there too with gentle and hidden humor. A Native American corn god is placed at an altar early, and a dance performed in his honor. Like Old Tom's pursuer, this icon is initially humorous, and the humor brushes against racism. The Christian priest places a cross in front of the corn god, seeming thereby to bring right reason to things, but it is important that audiences never really forget the corn god or the impressive dance done for him. Indian spirituality, not materialism, has fed the colonists and will save them. Behind the cross Green had the colonists place a Madonna, and therein lies another story. Nell Battle Lewis, Raleigh's longtime liberal, protested that the symbol should be clearly Protestant for this mainstream audience. But the Madonna remains, clearly visible behind the cross in the important scene when leader John Borden is fed soup to be revived.[18]

What seems to be going on in such settings with these mixed icons is more Hegelianism. Green sometimes spoke as a pagan, and he certainly disdained organized religion in his mature years. However, he continued to attend the Chapel of the Cross, he wrote occasional verse for those Episcopalians, and in his correspondence with his father-in-law, as in his plays, he reveals himself to be deeply spiritualistic, though there is no heaven and the salvation will be won by men and women here on earth. Again, he is consistent with Hegel, in what theologians once called the Idealist heresy. There is here a progression: first the primitive religion, then the more sophisticated, then the most advanced;

that is, corn god, then Madonna, then Protestant cross, and each in its turn points toward the audience, wherein resides the most advanced possibility of salvation, God's spirit, or *geist, in* people. The physical symbols follow Hegel's plan, for symbols move forward, and then up *into* the amphitheater seats.

There is the final stroke at play's end. John Borden has told his fellow settlers that the Spanish are soon to attack, and that their only hope is to go with Manteo to the village of Croatan. Earlier, Borden, joking, teasing, lightly asked if he would be a good Indian chief; but, as with Old Tom, the joke is actually as serious a sign as any of Chekhov's pistols laid on the mantelpiece. Such a pistol must be shot later in the play, and John Borden in leading his people toward Croatan is to become an Indian chief, or at least a leader in a village comprising red and white peoples.

The settlers in Green's version are not butchered by Indians, nor are they starved by the privations of the New World. Instead, their destruction is threatened by the Old World, by the Spanish, and at the very moment when the Spanish are being defeated back in the Old World by Queen Elizabeth's navy. But New World Indians save things, at least for the nonce. The ending is left ambiguous: it is possible that the settlers all perished, and that their dreams live only in strictly metaphorical sense to be connected with the next two spirals, *The Common Glory* at Williamsburg, where the ideals become a precise creed, and at Cross Creek, site of *The Highland Call,* where the precise words become revolutionary actions. But it is equally possible that some settlers do survive in physical sense too, producing new people: a white chief John Borden, mixed-breed children of Old Tom and his Indian spouse, perhaps even the once scornful English-born women taking Croatan husbands. It seems probable that someone survives in the village of Croatan, and whoever does would still be a product of the original colony, now miscegenated, blended, interrelated, interbred—*and made better by the blending,* even as Old Tom in his comic way and John Borden in his noble way are made better by Indians in the New World. Too, the Indians, not noble savages of wilderness purity, but humans evolving by cultural interaction, are themselves new, as the historian James Merrill has noted of Amerindians. Tom says, "Roanoke, thou has made a man of me," and his case is most spectacular, but he is not alone at all.[19]

Green's Hegelianism by its nature is integrationist, and he is here expressing it with almost palpable physicality. He says it in terms of blood, bone, and skin, as well as in the German's sweeping dialectical metaphors. *The Lost Colony,* then, is radical in one sense in particular: it is all about races mixing together. In other ways, especially its absence of class conflict, its ignoring economic forces, its self-conscious celebration of an orderly American middle class, *The Lost Colony* is hardly radical and even a bit too indulgent of a satisfied liberal consensus. Nevertheless, in his dramatic portrayal there are no races, culture is a polyglot process without timeless canons, and history is not only the unfolding story of the pursuit of liberty but also the story of disparate peoples coming together. In saying such things, Green was certainly being radical, and as brave as one could be in the Carolina of that era of damnable Jim Crow. Whatever else, everyone knew that the twentieth-century Croatans/Lumbees, who were at least partly white, were also partly black, and in Green's youth, legally *Negro*. In his metaphorical device, the playwright says that Carolina starts with the Croatan, and thus we are all in a poetic if not physical sense Croatan. *And the Croatan is all races.* Young Paul Greene had joked, with an afterthought, about wandering Croatans in Harnett County. Now, with a forethought, he shouted it: My father was a wandering Aramaian. My father was a wandering Croatan. Green had found the Lost Colony, and he had redefined his own liberalism for the next great fight, the one that would finally end legal segregation.

Green had said, and now repeated very publicly, that the fourth phase, or fourth spiral, in the unfolding story of democracy would involve black people. Damnable Jim Crow had to be destroyed. In a dialogue with a straw-man critic, the playwright in one staging of *The Lost Colony* indicated that he might still try to do something again on Broadway: *"Oh, I hope to continue writing plays for Broadway now and then."*[20] The commitment to decentralize a people's theater did not divorce one forever from Broadway, certainly not in the way that a full commitment to Broadway seemed to divorce one from little theater and from Green's symphonic dramas. In fact, Green did go back, and with a commercial and a critical success, and he did so with the same message of Hegelian integrationism and radical idealism. *Native Son,* both as a production on Broadway and as a process publicly displayed in Chapel Hill, was a statement about the fourth phase, the next and most steeply pitched and most difficult of the upward spirals set before us that would catch up and redefine this Chapel Hill liberal during and after World War II.

This Broadway association with Richard Wright did not come by happenstance for either man. As marked earlier, Wright had *read* Green's works, being especially taken with *Hymn to the Rising Sun,* and Wright knew what other African American artists of the 1930s knew: if you wanted a serious role that treated thoughtfully of black issues, then there were Paul Green plays. Even the great Eugene O'Neill's *Emperor Jones,* pathbreaking as it was and welcome for that, had such moments of stereotyping and otherwise playing to racism that it—artistically, aesthetically, writerly a better play by a better playwright— was yet inferior to any of a half dozen Paul Green plays as a chance for several African Americans to act and interact in challenging roles. Wright knew this thing, and he also knew that Paul Robeson had passed up more than one opportunity to play Abraham McCrannie in the Pulitzer-campaign play because the great polymath found the whole thing too spirit-dampening at a time when

Robeson wanted to portray hope and promise through exemplary success in the *character* seen on stage as well as in the career of the actor seen there. Robeson knew that he could win accolades for himself as a tragic character, as he had already done, but he wanted audiences to remember a character who offered his people some real hope.[21]

By contradistinction Richard Wright entertained no such assumptions. For one thing, he was done with optimism and its inspiring examples as a strategy. His political radicalism was once grounded in communism, with its promise that a classless society could not a fortiori be a racist society; but by 1941 he had proclaimed racism and other psychic and emotional injustices to be forces largely independent of the political economy, albeit certainly exacerbated by the capitalist system. Indeed, Wright was already angry, if not bitter, over the racism in the American Communist Party, which he was leaving. For the short term, the only solution that he could see to American racist injustices was dramatic portrayal of what he called in his memoirs the black *hunger* for the promised but excluded American dream. And one could not portray such hunger optimistically, at least not during this first phase of awakening people from moral slumber. Thus, Wright had consciously chosen *Hymn* as the thing to wake up audiences; only he found that it was his chosen fellow artists in Chicago who most resolutely avoided his planned wake-up call.[22]

Wright never forgot any of this, nor much else, and his long memory helped account for some of the raw, bitter, unremitting power in his art. Finally, he would not need another artist, no matter how emphatic or how brilliant, to write what needed to be written. His own resources of anger, resentments, thorough empirical observations, and great evocative powers would serve him better than anyone else's vision or skills. His own doomed character Bigger Thomas, set down in Chicago with its false liberal promises and its new racial colonialism, was all he needed; and Bigger's mock apotheosis in the manifestly racist but otherwise strictly *fair* trial was a masterpiece of bile-driven denunciation of a rotten system made the more rotten because of the great self-satisfaction that came to a liberal do-gooder who hired an African American slum dweller to drive her to charity functions in a limousine. No, Bigger himself, *the* Native Son, was a lot better than anything anybody else had dreamed up—or remembered—for the theatrical wake-up call.[23]

But Wright would need help to carry over the novel's Bigger and his angry evocations into a form of expression suitable for the theater stage. And he remembered Green as a craftsperson fully able to make the words work on the stage. If he could not dramatize a play for Green, then maybe Green could dramatize a novel for him. At any rate, he wanted Green to help with this work. He needed the playwright for Green's writing skills even as he needed Orson Welles because that white polymath at that time had a virtually unmatched ability to catch the public's attention.

Green readily agreed, and he invited Richard Wright to Chapel Hill so that the two could work together efficiently without the distractions of Chicago or New York. Too, Green had his teaching duties to perform, and so he wanted to stay on the Hill. Actually, of course, neither of those perfectly reasonable statements had much to do with his reasons for bringing Wright to Carolina. Always attuned to symbols, the playwright was manipulating them for all they were worth in another grand, and brave, campaign. Certainly, the nation's first and second cities could be distracting, but each did have its hideaway crannies and nooks, and of course the essence of the modern city is its sophisticated ability not to notice things, sometimes even racial things. In contrast, the distractions of the village that were attendant on having an African American at one's home and, more important, in Bynum Hall on the university campus, made the metropolises look almost secluded. As for getting away from professorial duties, Green had mastered that art so thoroughly by this phase of his career that he had become a legend on the campus: he could depart from the dramatic arts department for entire academic quarters, or for long spells during one of those "teaching" academic quarters. No, he was bringing Richard Wright to the Hill for the same reason that the historian Howard Kennedy Beale in 1946 would bring over John Hope Franklin, then at North Carolina Central College: some Chapel Hill reformists were in process of kicking themselves free from their kinfolk the Regionialists, who as a group had always been notoriously skittish about actually confronting racism. Paul Green was all set to sock damnable Jim Crow right in the snout.[24]

Actually, in the era between the two world wars, some at the university had been quietly defying much of Jim Crow in any case. Several weekend conferences, particularly one concerning art in modern society, had included African American students and faculty from nearby institutions. The dissident crowd associated with Ab's Bookstore and the *Contempo* magazine, led by the Regionalist sociologist Guy Johnson, had arranged in 1932 for Langston Hughes, godfather of the Harlem Renaissance, to read his poetry in Gerard Hall on campus, and that reading had proceeded without interference. And there had been other practices less formal but no less legitimate part of the academy and its pursuits. The Regionalist couple Guy Johnson and Guion Johnson regularly had black scholars visiting in their home, as did Bill Couch of the UNC Press. In fact, Couch eventually arranged for Benjamin Franklin Bullock, an African American farm agent from Atlanta University, to work in the campus offices of the press to revise his manuscript "Practical Farming for the South" for publication. The editor assigned a staff copy editor to help the author in the extensive rewriting. As Couch observed, "It's simply a superb book. . . . [t]hough the language is such that we had to put an [editor] with him to rewrite the whole thing. The [editor] was a white woman and they worked together in the office of the [Press]. That was at a time when if certain people, especially from eastern

North Carolina, had seen a white woman and a Negro man working together: I don't know what would have happened!" For all his own rebelliousness and courage, however, Couch was still much "relieved" that no segregationists observed Bullock and the female editor at their work in his offices.[25]

And that was the rub. One had to sneak around and dodge around and slip by damnable Jim Crow with tricks and through indirection. Green wanted a direct confrontation with the monster. He repeated that American democracy had been through three chapters of development, and it was now time "to write that fourth chapter," the one where African Americans received full social and political equality. The last person at UNC to attempt such a public facing-off with racism was Erik Eriksen, a left-winger in the English department who in the middle of the 1930s had breakfast in a public restaurant with an African American scholar. Subsequently Eriksen left Carolina, and most people, certainly Couch and the Johnsons, presumed he was forced out because of his actions, which had been very publicly criticized in the *Raleigh News and Observer* by Jonathan Worth Daniels. Daniels was an old friend of Green and Thomas Wolfe from their student days at UNC; among them the threesome had bought a bottle of liquor to be cracked open and drunk by the survivor in a final toast to his mates. In September 1938 Daniels had helped Green to carry the pall for Wolfe at the novelist's funeral in Asheville, and the sad experience had drawn the two a bit closer together. Moreover, Daniels had marched with Green on many campaigns, including some on behalf of civil rights. The journalist was, however, erratic on the issues, and sometimes could be harmfully, damagingly, racist in his widely read editorials for the daily newspaper styled "The Old Reliable."[26]

This was the regional and personal history in the background when Green brought Wright to campus, and the two worked on the play script in a very public way so that the campus and the community knew all about it. A great deal of the work was done in a log cabin that Green had bought in the countryside and set up in the back of the Green house on Greenwood Road around 1939 (perhaps in a conscious copying of his friend Sherwood Anderson, who had set up his own log cabin for a writing study in his adoptive Virginia highlands). This road was close to campus, and people could come by and look in and see the two men working. But Green also brought Wright onto the campus proper, into Bynum Hall, which was a building passed by almost every student sometime during a typical day of classes. Bynum, once a gymnasium and now a classroom, had oversized windows through which passersby could very plainly see the black novelist at his labors alongside the white professor. Too, Green was careful to give a spirited interview for Hoke Norris of the Associated Press. The session featured full attention to the concept of a fourth chapter of a democratic campaign, and Norris published a feature story about the whole affair. Those looking back on these events of 1941 generally remember with a warmth and gratitude how the student body reacted: the two writers worked away with a lot of onlookers, most of whom acted a little as if they were visiting a spectacle at the circus, but it was apparently a performance that the audience approved and even enjoyed.[27]

On the other hand, there were limits to what could be attempted: Wright actually stayed with a black family in a drafty and damp house off campus, apparently in Carrboro, a former mill village literally across the tracks from Chapel Hill and a place that supplied many of the custodial and physical plant staff for the university. For all that, there were threatening murmurations from segregationists, and Green had to stand guard in figurative if not literal sense to protect his visitor. The historian Frances Saunders in her own investigation of this series of incidents finds a complex intermingling of fact and fable that makes it hard to let the history transpire for us. She concludes reasonably after painstaking research that the whole thing certainly took much courage, that there was always the real danger of violence, but that Green had no face-to-face encounters with vengeance-seeking thugs.[28]

There is a photograph surviving from that 1941 summer season, and it is reproduced in the picture section of this volume. It shows a youngish Wright typing on an Underwood machine while Green stands before him. Both men are in shirtsleeves, in fact short sleeves with open collars, and each man has pulled his shirttail out of his trousers. Script revisions in galley form are all over the table, and a copy of a book, surely *Native Son,* sits atop a set of galleys. Green's reading glasses lie on a pile of still more galley proofs near Wright's hand, as if to be available to the novelist, although he is wearing his own spectacles while typing. Wright, belying his reputation as a Communist and rebel and the rumors of his social excesses and hard partying, looks very much the thoughtful scholar. Green mops his brow with his right hand, and his left hand is at his side, big fist clinched as if gripping a baseball.[29]

Both men liked to pose, and perhaps this is still another pose. If so, it is a good pose that captures something entirely believable, for it is a marvelous picture of two writers, intimate and accepting of each other, thinking about the same tasks, and awfully hard at work. It is a visual image that fits the spoken image Green liked to use: *Plough and Furrow,* the work of the farmer and the work of the playwright (and Green was self-consciously both) is essentially the same work involving related skills.[30]

The successful collaboration in Bynum Hall may have been a phenomenological revelation for Wright, for New York theater people, even for Green. Unfortunately, however, it was only a sunny start for what quickly became a very stormy period of teamwork once the script was returned to Broadway for the final phase of rewriting, casting, and production. The dispute became hottest between director John Houseman and Green, but Wright ended up agreeing with Houseman and disagreeing with Green. The playwright wanted to take Wright's main character, Bigger Thomas, and show his internal tragedy, a rewriting that would entail a trial scene in which the audience comes to see Bigger as a grandly tragic agent rather than a mere victim of class and caste in a racist and aggressively capitalist society that cannot offer justice to a black man of the laboring class. Houseman's reading, namely, *Bigger as victim,* is of course true to the conventions of prole lit, true to the novel, and is in any case starkly dramatic on the stage, since racism and class oppression themselves become in a sense characters, even the main antagonists for the trial scene.[31]

Green had been through such debates before, notably with his character Abe McCrannie of *In Abraham's Bosom,* and of course with Runt in *Hymn to the Rising Sun*. Green remembered that Wright fully approved, even admired, the complex, fully rounded character Runt, who had his own internal dilemmas as well as the external oppression of racism. The playwright hoped that the novelist could accept something on that order for a stage version of Bigger Thomas.

However, Wright did not accept such a revision, and he lined up with Houseman in the disputes. Green, miserably abandoned on the sidelines in Chapel Hill, felt disengaged from the Broadway production. For a time he seemed to detest Houseman, and the latter seemed to return the scorn, although the two eventually had—and took—the chance to be very gracious to each other in public three decades after these facts. At any rate, as 1941 Broadway talk grew excited about *Native Son,* Green occasionally declared his unhappiness. At one point, he even said that he could not really share any of the accolades since he had not really shared in the production as it evolved. For Wright he retained an admiration and affection; and the novelist for his part, while disagreeing with Green on the set of issues, also seems to have judged his partner favorably.

Regardless of Houseman's feelings about Green, and regardless of Green's sense of disengagement, critics gave Green instant and full credit for his share of the writing, and they certainly gave Orson Welles, Richard Wright, John Houseman, and Paul Green maximum credit as a team that had produced a superb play. Welles in that period could do no Broadway or Hollywood thing wrong, and he had brought his own master touches to the production. Even better, the African American actor Canada Lee gave a performance of such tightly focused anger that he knocked the socks off the New Yorkers' feet. To *Native Son,* unlike Green's other "Negro plays," people actually came in good numbers, and the playwright collected royalties from this production. Besides a successful Broadway run, *Native Son* did well in San Francisco, Chicago, Cleveland, and other cities. Most critics agreed that everything about the play was good, but the consensus was that the writers held the key to *Native Son*. Burns Mantle, still very much in Green's corner, started another Pulitzer campaign and worked to secure recognition from the New York drama critics. Other major figures jumped aboard his bandwagon, despite the fact that Lillian Hellman, the eventual winner, had written *Watch on the Rhine,* an anti-Nazi play of great power and certainly a play whose time *was* 1941. There were some negative responses, the most predictable being that of John Anderson, who had been roundly outvoted in 1927 when Green won the Pulitzer for *In Abraham's Bosom.* Too, the Hearst newspapers were publicly hostile, even running front-page denunciations of Wright, Welles, Houseman, and Green in their widely circulating dailies. Generally, however, Mantle won this fight with Anderson, despite the fact that Hellman won the entire war.[32]

In looking back, *Native Son* must rate as yet another of those odd admixtures for Green, in some ways his most satisfying play but in other ways an immensely dissatisfying piece of work. It showed his most mature artistry, it won critical acceptance, it made a commercial success, its script has survived in form readily accessible to today's readers—and phenomenologically it involved a courageous interracial assault on injustice, with the boldest actions staged at Green's own state university. But of course Houseman, already building his marvelous reputation as director and actor, had overruled Green on the crucial issues of interpretation, and then Wright and Welles—and the critics however unknowingly—had then ringingly reaffirmed Houseman's judgments.

To some degree, *Native Son* marked another change in Green's career. He would never again enjoy such critical recognition, but the money would become good, and his regional fame would grow thereafter. As noted, through yet another of those personal anomalies in a most vexed and complicated life and career, he would make a name from *The Lost Colony,* and he would make a comfortable living after the symphonic drama began its long run—but he would not actually make much money from *The Lost Colony* itself because of the contractual arrangements, and he would not make much of a name for himself from the lucrative Hollywood work because of the low place where writers stood in that industry in that town. *The Lost Colony* grew on its own, developing a life and a career independent of the playwright, and as a tourist attraction became something with an identity almost divorced from its author:

Paul Green?
No, I never heard of him.
The Lost Colony?
Yeah, sure!
Did he write *that?*

He kept at the playwriting, and he would attempt a return to Broadway with an ambitious, but not particularly well received, effort to carry over Henrik Ibsen's *Peer Gynt* into American-style English-language production. Mostly, however, he wrote symphonic dramas, with one in Texas and one in Ohio enjoying longevity, though of course nothing equal to *The Lost Colony*.[33]

The judgment here is that Paul Green's artistic accomplishments were done with by 1941. Indeed, a number of the symphonic dramas are so tedious that some critics dismiss even the pathbreaking artistry of the period 1923–41, if they indeed know of it at all. The work from that early period, with its experimentation, especially in dialect and dialogue, no longer seems very accessible to theatergoers and so is largely lost from view. What remained in full view in the decades after 1941 was the political courage and the outspoken support for racial integration that established him as the force for liberalism in Chapel Hill.

12 : THE GOOD WAR
TESTS THE IDEALS
1941–1946

The era of World War II was by any account a horror. The Episcopal hymnist says that Christ is "God in man made manifest"; and Adolf Hitler appeared to be the devil in man made manifest. As Green learned from eyewitnesses and from journalists about what Hitler was doing to Jews and others, the troubled playwright grew more troubled still. Worse, by 1941 Hitler seemed in a fair way to win the day unless the United States intervened. This Nazism of thoroughgoing antisemitism and thoroughgoing racism, this Nazism of war for the sake of war itself, this Nazism of power for the sake of power itself, all these things in the force of Hitler's Germany, Green recognized as early as 1934 to be something evil. By 1939, and perhaps earlier, he was publicly telling people that Hitler must be stopped.[1]

The snide remarks that he and his friends and his family members had passed among one another about Jews—whether about moguls in Hollywood such as Samuel Goldwyn, fellow workers such as Stella Adler of the Group Theater, almost forgotten acquaintances like Private Bittemann of another war long ago, or even the more abstract "Jewish boy" who is said by the diarist "to love his money and love his sex"—all the snide remarks indulged out of earshot of the Jewish friends and coworkers themselves, now these pained Green as if aimed at himself. The remarks had never been launched with intent to wound, and certainly never with intent to kill. The half-thinking prejudice that formerly lay on one's mind and soul as casually as the dew of a humid morning now suddenly stank. The very same words were being used now by the Nazis who were stoking the crematories. This Nazism must be stopped, and Green was pleased that the United States was funneling arms and other materiel to England when the island stood alone out there under the Luftwaffe's barrage.

For all that, however, World War II *the fight* itself was no less the devil in man made manifest. Green referred to this fighting as "war and its chilling shadow of evil." No cause could glorify the extreme misery being visited on people by the total war that was outdoing the horrors of Green's own war: the unspeakable terrors of the trenches were, incredibly, gone one better in the current global conflict. More than ever, Green deplored the failure of the United States to join the League of Nations; more than ever he resented the internal American politics that made the league powerless in the face of the Nazi quest for power for the sake of power. After all, as the Chapel Hillian understood it, the real damage of Hitler and his followers was their worship of war as a good thing in and of itself. And, after all, even the *final solution* could have been stopped in the early phases of its execution by a cohesive and committed League of Nations supported by the money, materiel, and military potential of the United States.[2]

Yet another world war, applying the most awful of weapons against the entire citizenry, Green did not want to countenance. He was after all the man who had inscribed PEACE three times in his diary on the day of armistice, 11 November 1918; he was after all the man who skipped out on a troop audience with European royalty, but who made special efforts to see Woodrow Wilson in the triumph of the president's peace processional through Paris. Above all, he was the man who had fired the imagination of the Group Theater actors with his writing—and with his ex tempore speeches—about the awfulness of any war because of what it did to the Johnny Johnsons of the New World and the good soldier Zweiks of the Old World. His leftist reformism—especially in his role in the *Revolt of the Masses* publication and in the prole lit movement—included a hefty antiwar component that insisted that preoccupation with war drew attentions and energies away from the domestic struggles for justice when the peacetime foes were poverty and racism.[3]

During 1940 and 1941, in fact right up to the moment of the bombing of Pearl Harbor, the Chapel Hill campus and community in particular was to large degree an antiwar place. The YMCA had become a center of international justice on campus, and much of its ethical teachings involved a sense of the global responsibility of rich nations to assist poor nations; but an even bigger part of Chapel Hill YMCA teachings was antiwar. The YMCA building, immediately south of historic South Building in the center of campus, included a coffee shop where ideas were exchanged enthusiastically in an informal forum, and it also included a good-sized auditorium that served as a more formal "bully pulpit" for the presentation of ideas. Student body funds for YMCA activities were administered through an elected president, and these young men in 1939, 1940, and 1941 tended to sponsor programs and speeches that were both internationalist and pacifist.

Nor was this combination of activism and pacifism unusual on the campus. Indeed, former history professor Frank Winkler Ryan, one of many graduate students who would eventually leave the Hill to serve in the army or the navy, recalls signing a gigantic petition urging that the United States stay out of World War II; and he recalls that the petition was so big in scale and bore so many signatures, perhaps several thousand, that transporting it to Washington,

D.C., for President Roosevelt's attention was something of a logistical nightmare. Many such petitions came in, and New Deal and presidential scholars
assure us that FDR did not dare bring the United States into this war, but must
needs wait until—and if—provoked by attack.[4]

Green supported such dramatic antiwar symbol-making, and through most
of 1940 and 1941, he hoped and hoped—and prayed at the Chapel of the Cross,
where his family regularly communed in town—for a peaceful end to the conflict. He hoped and prayed too that the United States could stay out of it in
any case, even after the Nazis proved victorious in his beloved France.[5]

With the attack of 7 December 1941, however, the mood changed completely
on campus and in the community. The student body in general responded
much as Green himself had when he was their age in "his war": they left their
books and joined up in the fighting, briefly depopulating the campus. This
time, however, the military came *to* the campus soon thereafter, repopulating
it with training facilities established at the university for soldiers and sailors.
Green was profoundly shaken by this Japanese attack, and by the third week
of December, he had changed his mind, now supporting the war effort.

Part of the bombing's impact was immediate and personal: There
could be no 1942 season for *Lost Colony* now. The exigencies of wartime economics, especially the need to preserve gasoline and rubber, all militated against
staging a symphonic drama on an island at remote distance from the population centers. Too, some of the actors would need to serve in the military
overseas, and others would need to work in the factories stateside that served
the army and the navy; and this war would famously involve the female cast in
both venues. There was even the worry that large-scale outdoor events could no
longer be held on the coast, what with the Japanese air force said to threaten the
west coast and the German navy said to threaten the east coast; fetched as far as
those worries now seem, given what is now known about oil and coal and other
supplies missing from the Axis arsenal, those fears then were palpable enough
to move the Rose Bowl football show all the way from California's Pasadena to
nearby Durham, North Carolina. Underneath all of these wartime necessities
of course was another problem, and one that Green did not choose to address
on this occasion: art takes a back seat to everything else during wartime, and
at such times it is revealed to be strictly ancillary to the real business of the
American people. Above all wartime concerns was the fact of Nazism: If Hitler
prevailed in war over the United States, and prevailed so completely as to bring
his forces to march in triumph before the Lincoln Memorial, then there would
assuredly be no such theater permitted at all, wartime, peacetime, any time.

Yet this dense tangle of reasons only explains why yet another Paul Green
theatrical experiment was postponed and possibly ended. There remains the
issue of how the playwright himself responded to world war. The long and the

short of it is that Green in a space of a few weeks went from opposing entry to supporting it. His pathway was traveled quickly, but it was by no means straight or simple.

His characteristically pained correspondence shows when Green changed his mind, during the third week of December in 1941, and it also helps us to understand how he came to explain himself over the next ten months. The correspondence and his diary do not fully explain *why* he changed his mind, but it does seem that the general context of the Popular Front provides most of the answers in his personal case. Perhaps more important, the broad cultural implications of the Popular Front also help explain Green's turn from the radicalism of leftist reform—revolt of the masses, prole lit, his attacks on capitalism, his complaints that FDR was too socially conservative and too easy on big business—to the mainstream and so-styled consensus liberalism of his mature years. The uniqueness of his role in the Popular Front movement also helps us to see the distinguishing feature of his postwar liberalism, that is, his fervent, if not perfervid, commitments to racial justice and especially to integration, as other, broader concerns about socioeconomic justice were deemphasized.

First, the pained correspondence:
He had to write to his sister/mother, Mary Green Johnson, when her son William left the UNC student body to enter the army at the same time that the dying Proff Koch's son Robert left the same student body to join the army. He told his old maternal confessor that he was "sad and worried" about "Billy" Johnson's and "Bobby" Koch's enlistments; but he also declared his pride in them and in their willingness to make sacrifices. As he wrote to her about the diminished but continuing antiwar campaign on campus, he was even more revealing. He noted that all good people begin with an aversion to war; but he said that this war required of the antiwar people some "positive suggestions" about how to stop the Nazis. He said vaguely that there remained some people, whom he would not name, who persisted in antiwar demonstrations. He was probably thinking of the historian Howard Kennedy Beale as well as some of his friends in the YMCA. Beale traveled to California to help German-born professors retain their positions in state and private universities and colleges, and he continued to work on behalf of public school teachers who questioned the war. As for the YMCA, it remained a courageous, and sometimes lonely, center of pacifism. While he still liked and admired these unnamed associates and friends, Green had in the space of a few weeks lost patience with them. He told his sister that good people had to support the war effort now—or they would never have the right to make suggestions about the nature of the peace to come. Similar notes saying much the same things, he had sent to Lib Green earlier during a stint of Hollywood writing.[6]

Continuing to confess to sister/mother Mary, he went on to say that his "whirl-around of words" reflected the fact that he was in "the full thriving of the dilemma" between a profound aversion to war and a profound desire to eradicate Nazism with its racism. His use of the word *thrive* is interesting; an Old Norse word, in English it becomes intransitive and usually means *to grow robustly* or *to prosper.* At its root, however, the word is transitive and means to *grasp.* This most sensitive of wordsmiths and most assiduous of word collectors was here choosing to describe himself as all but physically held, grasped, in a dilemma. Yet it is also characteristic of him that he said, "I don't plan to stay caught" in the dilemma; and of course, ever since he declined to finish his philosophy studies at Cornell University, he was willing to resolve such problems with more regard for moral earnestness than for logical consistency.[7]

Green then told his sister/mother that much of history is tragic, and that tragedy by its nature produces "a result different from itself." That was a Hegelian flourish, one of the Hegelianisms adapted as a universal rule for Marxian science of society, namely, that one movement necessarily negates itself—and then defeats itself—by creating its antithesis. Furthermore, such internal contradiction was necessary for the expanding dialectic as Marxists understand the working out of history. Adapting the Marxians' Hegel, Green could then say that by fighting this war one was actually fighting against fighting and thus fighting for peace in the long run. In his diary he had noted in related vein that a true internationalism could only come out of the crucible of such a tragedy; and now he took parallel words and offered them to Mary Johnson as she watched her son Billy Johnson enter a world war much as she had watched her brother/sons Paul and Hugh Green do long ago.[8] This war too must be fought, and good men must fight it.

So resolved, he then acted without looking back. He even suggested, incredibly, that he might rejoin the army himself, at age thirty-six and with four children. Instead, he chose a more realistic wartime role for himself, as president of the National Theater Conference, which provided entertainment of morale-boosting kind for the troops through sponsorship of radio drama. He thus chose to join the so-styled Popular Front of all those fighting against Nazism abroad, even though many of those had no interest in working for socioeconomic justice—and in fact some of them were themselves decidedly part of the problem of damnable Jim Crow and related indecencies at home. At the same time, there was a self-proclaimed United Front of committed leftists who kept up a broad-based campaign for socioeconomic justice at home, even and especially if that domestic campaign led to disputes with allies in the Popular Front. This distinction between the Popular Front and the United Front could lead to some strange results, as we will mark it, but it was no insignificant distinction at all. Others, especially FDR, spoke of "Doctor Win the War" taking precedence over the doctors of social engineering; but Green and his fellows in the Popular Front, who were always lukewarm about Roosevelt in any case, could stand with New Deal people to stop Hitler while continuing to push those same politicians to face up to injustices at home.

On the international scene, the impact of this Popular Front alliance on the playwright's art and activities could be a bit surprising. By the spring of 1942, he went so far as to rewrite the character of Johnny Johnson, bringing that former antiwar figure into World War II. Invited by Raleigh's Nell Battle Lewis to contribute to her column in his friend Jonathan Worth Daniels's *Raleigh News and Observer,* he accepted and took the occasion to recast his character. He actually had Johnny Johnson declare flatly that one must fight in this war because "then the new world of federated states will have a chance to be." In a twinkling he had not only rendered his tragicomic protagonist guileful instead of guileless, but also made him heroically prowar instead of antiheroically antiwar! By Christmas of 1943, Green even wrote "Christmas Prayer," a religious commemoration of student sacrifices in World War II. Celebrated at Christmas services in the Chapel of the Cross, the litany included these rolling lines:

> Seventeen hundred and ninety three
> Nineteen hundred and forty three
> Sons and fathers, fathers and sons
> And sons again
>
> In their name, O God,
> Help us find the way.[9]

This piece, however, is in no sense an antiwar chant or song. Although it is concluded with a prayer for peace, the peace sought demands victory over the terrible foe. Just as the tyranny of Great Britain must be broken by the colonists, so must the tyranny of the Nazis be broken in what this worshiper clearly regards as a just war. Green thus entered the Popular Front from the left side of the stage, still grumbling that Roosevelt was too conservative, that American businesses were being allowed to earn indecent profits from the war, that New Dealers were flagging in their duties to black people and to the working-class poor.[10]

Indeed, he wrote to Lib Green and noted in his diary that the American system was corrupt, and he specified capitalism as the corrupting component of the system. In the midst of wartime sacrifices by workers, Green was incensed to read of profiteering, and he pronounced such unjust profits born of soulless opportunism to be endemic to the political economy of industrial capitalism. Although he never officially joined the United Front, Green certainly marched with them in a number of domestic campaigns during the Good War, and in these specific campaigns he provided a wartime definition of southern liberal as he was redefining himself.[11]

Green broke rank with the Popular Front on almost all domestic issues and traveled instead in fellowship with the United Front, most prominently on the issue of labor relations. Roosevelt's people apparently had crafted a remarkable domestic diplomacy in which the right of labor to organize and to strike was recognized and supported, but for their part, organized labor did not agitate much during the war and thus seldom exercised the dearly bought right to strike. Employment levels were high and wages were good, and at least for skilled workers, there was little to strike about during the war: it could legitimately be said that Hitler was the worse—and certainly the more pressingly immediate—part of evil than any boss of any corporation, and the right to strike could be held without using it for the nonce. In fact, *not* using the right to strike at this time actually strengthened the claim to strike at another time.[12]

Such reasoning was true enough for skilled labor in the workplace in 1942 and 1943; but it ignored southern history, and it specifically ignored the low-skilled and poorly organized textile workers and their travail in the Carolina piedmont since the period 1929–35. By contrast with New Deal officials and politicos, Green could remember all of it, if only because textile entrepreneurs such as Spencer Love continued to regard him as "red of the deepest dye." As marked, the United Textile Workers Union had shown a new militancy in trying to organize and to bargain collectively; and when mill owners had responded with predictable violence in related episodes between 1929 and 1935, the textile workers had literally fought back. The upshot was that the owners had the bigger battalions and so prevailed. As the scene shifted from strike sites to the courtroom, the owners enjoyed even greater advantages in legal counsel battalions, and most strike leaders were penalized heavily for labor's share of the violence, while the corporation management portion of violence went unprosecuted.

As noted, Green and a few other academics on the Hill, notably graduate student C. Vann Woodward and the editor of the UNC Press, Bill Couch, had been active in the period 1934–37 on behalf of the striking textile workers; and these three had even organized some "mass demonstrations," although insufficient numbers came to make the campus protests truly "mass." For a time, the leftists on the Hill and on other college campuses treated the Carolina piedmont strikers in Burlington and Greensboro and Gastonia as main characters on an important stage. But, as leaders languished in jail or in exile outside the region and as the Good War seized attention in its own theaters of action against the Nazis, supporters of labor were generally in step with the Popular Front, and little was said about the leaders and the followers of that particular lost cause. Woodward took his doctorate degree and left the Hill, Couch became notably quieter, and others drifted away from the cause of labor activism in Chapel Hill.[13]

Of course Green could not forget and so could not in good conscience drift away from the cause of labor, and he was especially concerned about Fred Erwin Beal, an activist worker still in prison for his union activities at Loray Mill in Gastonia in 1929. Beal had been convicted of murder and sentenced to twenty years in prison during a series of trials that Vann Woodward called "a pretty raw sort of thing, with not even a half-hearted regard for the formalities of legal decorum." Slipping bail after conviction and before sentencing, Beal had run away to the Soviet Union for asylum and stayed in Russia almost nine years. However, by February of 1938 Beal had seen enough of Stalin's communism, and he returned to the United States to begin serving his sentence at Caledonia Prison in the eastern part of North Carolina. Green kept in touch, visiting on a number of occasions; on one visit in 1940, he found that Beal was still the reformist on assignment, in this case attempting to rehabilitate his fellow inmates as they faced their eventual reentry into free society. Generally, Green found that Beal did not show outward signs of bitterness or even much sadness about his plight.[14]

Green was never one to mask his own feelings about injustice, and he tried hard to make others pay some attention to Beal in his cell in Caledonia. As he had in 1937, when the issue was North Carolina's convict-leasing system for road construction, Green wrote letters to state officials. As was the case with Governor Ehringhaus then, Green—and Beal—were fortunate that the sitting governor in 1942 was a moderate on social issues and a man with a conscience. This governor, J. Melville Broughton, did pardon Fred Beal in February of 1942.[15]

Many had been involved in trying to help Beal at different times, but it was Green who never forgot him and who stayed consistently on the case in this drama that ran for fourteen years, a point demonstrated amply by Laurence Green Avery in his own studies.[16]

As winter gave into spring, Paul Green unburdened himself of his multiple unhappinesses with the modern university. He had moved into his "natural" position as professor of dramatic arts, but this assignment actually left him no happier than when he squirmed and fretted in the "unnatural" position as professor of philosophy. This dreamer who had "ploughed the furrow" with a book propped on the handle before him and who had argued with Papa Greene about attending university, this dreamer who had willed himself through the trenches of the Great War in order to return to university studies, this dreamer who had defied damnable Jim Crow to give African American scholars their chance to visit the people's university, this dreamer at last awakened to the fact that he now resented the modern university for which he had sacrificed and suffered personal loss.

Indeed, the very sacrifices and the very losses added an additional burden to, and certainly deepened, his frustration and his anger. Het up with such steam, he kept a firm hand on the throttle as he let it all out in an essay of some considerable force. His greatest complaint was that the modern university had no soul, no place for spirituality, no acknowledgment of commitments to anything beyond the mind and its mental constructs sporting about for the fun of it in the marketplace. The university would not acknowledge God, and in this creedal statement Paul Green marked off his southern liberalism, and perhaps all southern liberalism in this era, from the predominant national movement. His liberalism was informed by a Supreme Being who transcended time to sit in absolute judgment and to speak one truth in one voice. Whatever else this deity was or did, Green's God had no interest in the pragmatism that the Cornell professors had tried to teach him—the same brand of pragmatism that the New Deal liberals of the Popular Front alliance were putting into practice. Instead, he declared that the students in their desks before him did not need to know what was going to work, or how to measure material success and failure in practice: youth needed to know what was right and what was wrong. None of this brought Green into organized religion, and none of it said that he conceived of a heaven for departed souls; but he shouted quite plainly that God's justice must be acknowledged and served. [17]

Finally, Horace Williams's student was taking the mentor's "new view of religion," although the master still could not bring himself to name the legendary professor as the obvious touchstone for this believer's manifesto:

> [W]e did not teach them that the firmament sheweth the handiwork of God and that there is a benignity among the stars and a peace dropping therefrom like the gentle dew of evening. [18]

and furthermore:

> In short and simple terms—we professors, we keepers of wisdom, following the pragmatic bent of the times, not guiding it as we are sworn to do—have lost our religion, our inspiration for living, and with us lies the responsibility most for what our young people are and may be. If this is true, and I believe it is, then are we not responsible also for much of the present tragedy in the world itself? [19]

This current generation of scholars was failing to keep up the mission begun by Horace Williams's generation of men who actually professed belief. In thinking back on his legendary teacher in another era, Green quotes his Episcopal liturgy as it instructs directly from the Bible: "And I live again that rich eternal hour, *know again that my redeemer liveth* still, beyond the reach of time or clutch of tool, or blood and war, and formulated circumstances."[20]

From his writing desk in his studio-cabin, this attack on secular human-ism and modern research made its way into a major springtime address before Carolina students, faculty, and alumni gathered in assembly on 25 May in cer-emonies before commencement. Moreover, it was printed up and distributed to every member of the university faculty by authority of the administration as the following autumn academic quarter of 1942 was convoked. Exactly who thought to feature Green thus prominently in speech and pamphlet it is hard to say, but there is no question that Frank Graham, president of the consol-idated UNC campuses, fully approved its message, as did Robert B. House, then dean of administration and soon to be first chancellor of the Chapel Hill school. Graham and House espoused the same values of faith-based—indeed Protestant—reformism unabashedly called liberalism; and each in his way was somewhat suspicious of pure research and disinterested scholarship. Thanks to Graham and House, Green's address to the professors was laid out before a student body that adored all three men, and it was pointedly distributed to every member of a faculty whose members were considerably more ambivalent about all three men.[21]

In particular, George R. Coffman of the English department wrote a note in protest to Green, pointing out that serious research and social consciousness are not antithetical and that inspirational teaching and spiritual commitments were marked in many of their colleagues. Indeed, Coffman implied that Green was hacking away at a straw man, letting his rhetoric overwhelm his own re-search and reason, neglecting the fact of the marvelous dialogues involving pro-fessors and students developed on this very campus over the five most recent decades. Coffman called it, with perhaps unintended aptness, a "jeremiad," that is, a scolding sermon in the style of the prophet Jeremiah. Green, on receipt of the letter, made the usual polite Carolinian demurrers and apologies, but he accepted the term *jeremiad* as entirely fitting, for he was in the role of a prophet calling the once faithful back to the true way of right belief. Despite the letter's conciliatory tone toward Coffman in particular and their colleagues in general, Green was in fact finalizing his own act of secession, preparing himself to resign from the university but also putting Chapel Hill the place on notice that this impassioned prophet would be very much with the community forevermore, telling them things that they might not want to hear at all.[22]

Green's message in his speech and the reprinted pamphlet provoked the professors for a season but otherwise had little influence in the university. However, his friend and nemesis Bill Couch saw possibilities for much wider influence by publishing a number of prophetic essays in two slender collections aimed at the market of the generally educated middle-brow concerned citizen.

One set of essays Couch collected and arranged under the title *Hawthorn Tree,* and he released that volume in 1943. The other volume, really one extended essay, Couch released in 1945 under the title *Forever Growing.* Both volumes enjoyed critical success among reviewers writing for liberal newspapers of the era; and both are period pieces of the time when American educators began to make a serious reconsideration of teaching moral values to the very large student bodies that would overfill classrooms as the Good War ended. Many others wrote about the moral responsibility of the serious scholar to catch the fervor in youthful students and direct it to make a better world; and many others wrote about the great need for a general education as a necessary counterweight to the technically trained specialist who might become a Nazi. As a matter of fact, Bill Couch himself would in a few seasons move to Chicago to establish such a focus on the *World Book Encyclopedia* — and also to observe and follow at first hand the curriculum developer Robert Maynard Hutchins.[23]

Two things set Green's essays apart from other such period pieces and make them distinctly his own. First is the Protestant spiritualism and Christian reformism in the moral absolutism and transcendent idealism so at odds with the pragmatism of the post–World War II intellectual. Second is the way that he goes straight to racial issues and really defines a regional liberalism in this era. Pragmatist intellectuals seeking social reform and neoabolitionist reformists focusing on racial injustice would both salute Green in the period during and immediately after World War II, so that his star among generalist thinkers and activist reformists rose to full crescent even as it was past its peak and indeed fading among serious dramatists and actors and critics. The distinctive regional and personal feature that sets him apart from his admirers outside the South in between 1943 and 1946 is the fervor of his spiritual convictions in moral absolutism created and sustained by a good God, even and especially if no organized religion could explain that deity successfully for him. These same features that once made him uniquely attractive in that era later contribute to his descent in a society more and more and more secular, relativistic, cool, self-absorbed — and also one that grew bored with talk about racial injustice.

The title of his essays, *Hawthorn Tree,* is an image both odd and old, and it quotes his folklore collecting and Scots songwriting from his earliest days in the upper valley of the Cape Fear River. Hawthorn trees are sometimes little more than bushes, but they bear a red berry in winter season and lend brilliance to a flat and even sere landscape of beige soil and trees and grasses and gray skies and clouds. An ancient Scots ballad that he had collected featured a beautiful maiden, in her own springtime of fertility and lushness, mocking the humbled hawthorn; but the hawthorn informs her that she too will enter a season of drying up and withering and that he for his part will reenter another season. The song in its message, tone, and tune catches some of the eastern Scots fatalism as well as the wryness seen in Green and his ancestors, but it also makes clear the sturdiness and enduring nature of his people in their land. He had played with the images often, especially in the Harvey Easom shadow diaries and poems, and it sounds the tocsin for the prophet who insists at the same time that there is a season for justice, but that that season will come in its own time and not on any human timetable.

There is even an ironic slyness in the very arrangement of the essays, for one of the main pieces, "Artist in Time of War," is itself bound by time and season so thoroughly as to be almost meaningless except in the context of that very moment. The essay tells creative persons, most of all perhaps himself, that Nazi victory will destroy all creativity and artistic endeavor, and thus art itself must bend to the immediate task of beating the evil foe. After all, he himself had warped his character Johnny Johnson out of all meaning in order to serve the war effort, and he is here telling all artists that this is almost a season to lie fallow, for the "only way you and I can guarantee the return of our lives into the full flower and fruitage for which they were meant" is with military victory over the Axis powers. [24]

The artist and the intellectual and everyone else thus were required to give up much in order to fight the Fascists, but there was one campaign that was heightened rather than lessened as one fought the Good War: racism and its damnable institutions of Jim Crow. Beyond the extreme power of the state and the necessity of war, definitions of fascism were vexingly vague, and perhaps designedly so; for all that, however, fascism built much of its power and authority on racism, and to fight fascism one really had to fight racism as well. That part of the Popular Front Green could accept and even embrace, and his artistic talents could find full expression in the continuing wars against racism.

In *The Hawthorn Tree* he concludes with "Evening Sun Go Down," a dramatic dialogue about race. The setting is an eastern Carolina grinding mill, and the "I" voice is unidentified, but it is clearly young Paul Greene, really Harvey Easom, in a role that the playwright took on naturally. There is an antagonist speaker, the miller who grinds corn for local farmers; and there is Claude, a crippled African American farmer who speaks with his actions and even with his afflictions. Dialogue starts with the miller complaining that "the greatest mistake" for America was bringing "the Negro" over here from Africa. His complaint is not with slavery and its enormity, but with the physical presence of black people of whatever status in the upper valley of the Cape Fear or anywhere else. The "I" voice moves the speaker along, until at last the miller draws the conclusion that the only real solution is to wipe out the race. There is an inevitable outcome of logic coldly followed from the assumptions of a starting point in which African Americans are said to be inferior and known to be unwanted in this land. Although the language is colloquial Carolina, the syllogism is professorial in the elegance of its abstraction. [25]

At the moment when these two common folk have constructed between them the apparatus of racial genocide, they are interrupted by Claude, a local black farmer who is physically unable to load his sack of meal once the mill has ground his corn for him. This is of course the social Darwinian moment, the Hitler moment, when the "uselessness" and vexing burdens of the so-styled "inferior" and even doomed dark race makes appearance on the stage. But the miller and the "I" voice cannot fulfill fascist logic; they respond to deeper instincts of country folk, rushing to help with the task of filling and then loading the sack, all the while communicating in that country man's austere and yet very warm talk. By episode's end, it is obvious that profounder currents in southern rural life will move Claude and all other black people into the middle of the river where everyone else is. Warmer instincts of the nonrational and kinder habits of being will combine to defeat the logic of genocide and someday those same forces will combine to defeat the logic of less deadly but very damaging racial prejudices. The evening sun thus sets not on Claude and not on black people and not on decency but on fascist notions that roil and moil in a good country man's mind but cannot rule his heart.

These essays so collected did what they were designed to do, with sales that more than covered their modest costs, and with critical acclaim from the nation's liberal dailies, such as the *Cleveland Plain Dealer* and *Chicago Sun* and from Jonathan Daniels's *Raleigh News and Observer* and the statewide syndicated review column "Literary Lantern."[26] Bill Couch could show off the slim volume as another uniquely University of North Carolina Press production, virtually unimaginable in that day and time from the better funded, and probably technically superior, university presses in Charlottesville and Nashville. More, Couch could show the volume on his distinguished backlist when times changed everywhere as proof that once Carolina really was different from other schools in the region, at least in its press publications.

A sign of Green's maturity was his relationship to Betty Smith, a political and aesthetic disciple who became intensely identified with the social reformism and the literary style in Chapel Hill. Coming to the Hill largely because of the exigencies—and the opportunities—of the Great Depression, Betty Smith stayed on to become in the 1950s the most obvious good example of Green's influence on North Carolina writers. When she arrived in town in 1937, she was already an accomplished writer and already one who had seen much, heard much, paid attention, and learned much. Yet her ripened talent still needed just a little more mentoring from an astute master of the literary pro's world, and Green functioned for her in that role much as had Barrett Harper Clark for him two decades earlier. In addition, Green functioned as a political tutor to this one who was already mature politically in her native Brooklyn but quite the novice in wartime North Carolina.

Smith had graduated from the University of Michigan, had then studied playwriting under George Pierce Baker at Yale University, and had worked in the Federal Theater Project before its demise at the hands of southern congressmen. Author of six full-length plays and more than fifty one-act plays, she had already earned the Avery Hopwood Award for excellence in dramatic arts, a Rockefeller Foundation fellowship, and a Dramatists' Guild–Rockefeller Fellowship in playwriting before she came to know Green. In 1937 she was on the road in North Carolina in a traveling production of a play called *Post Road* when that play disbanded; rather than return to Brooklyn, she came to Chapel Hill and established a relationship with the Carolina Playmakers, where she met Green.

A determined as well as a talented person, she credited Green with important encouragement of her concept for her first novel, a kind of sociological study of her Brooklyn featuring the hard life and good times of a blue-collar Irish family in the depression-era borough. The concept and her techniques for realizing it in a novel sound somewhat like Green's Harvey Easom stories, but mainly Green gave her advice about what publishers to talk to and a lot of warm encouragement to keep at her writer's task. He also did some blue-pencil editing of her manuscript, as he is said to have done for many young Carolina writers. For all of that, the protégée was actually considerably better at the writing tasks than her mentor was at his own writing tasks or at editing her work, and there is withal an odd echoing of Proff Koch, who was never as good at the writer's techniques as his students were. In 1943 *A Tree Grows in Brooklyn* was published by Harper and Brothers, and it won immediate acclaim. Orville Prescott, writing in the *Yale Review,* called it the best novel of the year, and the *Atlantic Monthly* reviewer called it "poetically written." Katharine Jocher, longtime Regionalist in service to Howard Odum's social scientists, dutifully noted its superb social notation and brilliantly turned sociological features for readers of *Social Forces.* Indeed, some critics were a little puzzled what to call *A Tree Grows in Brooklyn,* and thus *The New Republic, New York Times,* and *New Yorker* reviewers all concluded that it was some new sort of autobiography or fanciful memoir, all of which they heartily approved as long as it need not be classified as a novel.[27]

Whatever critics called it, the novel was a commercial success, and in time it was turned into a successful movie, establishing Betty Smith as a reigning literary figure on the Hill. In a subsequent decade, her superior place, supplanting her benefactor and mentor Green, was completely established after *Joy in the Morning* (1963) became even more wildly successful as both book and movie. Even so, John Ehle and others describe her as personally loyal to Green and ever insistent that he was the greater creative figure for Carolinians.[28] Above all, Smith stood with Green in the political stands that he took; and in fact her novel is very much a reformist's celebration of the innate goodness of the common folk as she found them in the Brooklyn tenements, instead of where her coach and confidant found them, in the farms of the hollows and valleys.

The remainder of the years of the Good War Green dedicated to making money writing for Hollywood cinema. He was by then pretty discouraged about any real chances to be creative for the film industry, and there were few serious prospects on Broadway. But the Hollywood industry was a mighty machine releasing a lot of film, and the machine needed writers all the time. Their pay indicated how much their work was needed, even if they were otherwise held almost in disdain. Much as did William Faulkner, Green took it, in equal portions, the matchless compensation and the lack of respect.

One thing for sure, he was done with the academy, as if there were very much doubt after his *Hawthorn Tree* essays. In 1944 he formally resigned from Carolina in order to devote himself fully to his writing—and of course to declare again his radical disappointment with the shape and direction of the modern university. Now he was in position to publish some things, even and especially if he was not then writing anything particularly new. In 1945 he brought out the essays *Forever Growing,* another sharp blow aimed at modern education, but now he was truly an assailant attacking from the outside and no longer a colleague/prophet working from the inside with some hope of making friends change their behavior. In 1946 he brought out *Salvation on a String,* a set of short stories that dated back to his Harvey Easom days of the shadow diary sessions.[29]

Forever Growing completes his definition of art, and especially of regional art for his Real South. Beauty is in truth, and truth is in action, and even the outwardly ugly has a beauty vouchsafed by the sincerity of effort, a fine self-description of his creative works in any era: "Geographically, industrially, meteorologically, sociologically, we are one of the most active, yeasty and turmoiling regions of the earth, and vastness, power and daring reach are our middle names." Of wartime, but really of all times, Green insists, "there is no time for confusion, frustration, and despair." To be absolutely sure that no one looks for guidance from the academy, he draws on more biblical language to say:

> (And why do I not say, yes, have converse with the professors and teachers in this land, the keepers of wisdom and inspiration and the holy grail of youth? Why not? Because it is written that the son who asks for bread should not be handed a stone.)[30]

Why he put those sentences in parentheses is hard to understand, for they ring loudly in support of his actions and attitudes as he leaves the academy. In any case, he proceeds back into the Bible to conclude these essays by quoting his namesake Saint Paul, another prophetic visionary of the Hebrew wisdom traditions, and all the idealists who instructed him, not least Horace Williams: "Moreover, it is written—that with faith a man thinks. Faithless he cannot think. And he worships God as the great King milks heaven and drinks it day by day. His food is never exhausted . . . 'And he shall be like a tree planted by the rivers of water, that bringeth forth his fruit in his season; his leaf also shall not wither, and whatsoever he doeth shall prosper' " (Green's ellipses). [31]

Despite the language about growth and newness, Green attempted to prosper by recycling some old short stories, shown in the publication immediately after the war of *Salvation on a String*. As noted, most of the fiction dates back to his youth, especially the Harvey Easom days of the early 1920s. Although Green rewrote the stories, as indeed he conscientiously rewrote almost everything that he ever produced, there is nothing particularly fresh or "growing" in the volume. These pieces then are light if not fluffy, uniformly charming and humorous, especially the title piece, which describes a church sexton whose trouser string breaks as he stands on ladder—the string breaks at the very moment a young member of the congregation was about to make his testimony and seek salvation. The resulting hubbub of laughter breaks the energy of the boy's own intentionalities and also turns the mass-conversion experience into a farce, made the more so since the minister had been talking about how the salvation of sinners hangs by a string. The irony, if not sarcasm, is that the boy and all the others in attendance are most likely "saved" by *not* being saved in a false ceremony presided over by a minister of dubious motives. Again, native good sense and good humor intervene to prevail against manufactured malfeasance. His own brand of southern liberalism is more impressive as a theme in the stories than is the quality of the art, and none of the pieces functions as well as the comedy of other works such as *The No 'Count Boy*. It was politely reviewed, and he earned royalties from the commercial publisher Harper and Brothers, but he in no way "prospered," neither in modern capitalist sense, nor in the biblical sense of God's recognition for serving the spiritual. [32]

As the Good War ended, Green was far more important to liberal reformists than to those in dramatic arts circles, and among other things his evolving role enmeshed him in the confusing and contradictory inner politics of the Popular Front and the United Front. With the Fascists effectively eliminated, at least on the battlefields, there was little to hold together in the always tenuous connection between the Popular Front—again, simply meaning all those opposed to fascism—and the United Front—those committed to serious fundamental and structural reform of society. United Front activists believed that they had postponed serious reform in order to fight the greater evil of fascism, and Popular Front people, many of whom were quite conservative and in the South even segregationists, believed that they had tolerated allies who were at best eccentric and at worst real menaces.

For Green the break came quickly and irrevocably, and it centered around Harry S. Truman and his decision to drop the two atomic bombs in order to end the Good War. The playwright, always tepid in support of FDR, was instantly hostile to Truman, and he was incensed over the explosions of the Fat Man bomb over Hiroshima and the Little Boy bomb over Nagasaki. In October, President Truman announced that the United States would not share information about the atomic bomb, and of course Truman was generally a more dedicated foe of communism and specifically of Josef Stalin than was his predecessor, FDR. On 18 October 1945 Green sent a telegram from Hollywood to Truman, and he sent copies to selected newspapers and to his onetime confidant, and continuing ally in the *Lost Colony* project, Josiah William Bailey, senator from North Carolina:

> As an American citizen I earnestly beg you to continue to do everything in your power and to the uttermost in these darkening and dangerous days that the principle of international cooperation may prevail before it is too late and before some explosive incident has hurled us into a third and final global war. The news for instance that the administration refused to share the atomic bomb with certain of our war-torn and weary allies seems if true once more an example of mistrust working to harden the hearts of our allies against us and us against them and making more difficult the mutual control of their own atomic bomb when they too have discovered it as they certainly will. We have no corner on scientific brains here in America. But we do have at the present hour one of the priceless chances of history, and we should seize the chance and once more assume the moral leadership of the world and hold to it this time with all our might until peace and trust among men are accomplished or accomplished as nearly as possible. . . . Such a chance will doubtless never come to us a third time. And it is terrifying and unthinkable that so many of our political representatives and leaders should still bullheadedly try to meet this divine opportunity in terms of a Missouri mule trade. To do so is not only to assure the ultimate death of the trader but the certain killing of the mule and along with it the likely destruction of nearly every customer in the environment, to wit civilization itself.[33]

The sarcasm about the Missouri mule was sufficiently barbed to show that Green was uninterested in actually persuading the president, but rather was writing to an audience that could protest against Truman and his actions. It is doubtful that Truman took much notice of this telegram, if he was aware of it at all, and in any case the Missourian was already deep into his own struggles with a recalcitrant Congress and a dangerous Russian antagonist. With this president, as with all of them except for Woodrow Wilson, Green took a stance to the left of the chief executive, and after the Good War there would be no overarching causes that would bring him into an even temporary and tenuous support of their actions.

Thus the Good War ended for Green much as had the War to End All Wars. As before, he declared that no war was good, that all war ends in disaster because the quest for social justice is always lost in the enormity of the wartime deaths, especially the enormity of civilian suffering. As before he had to admit that he himself had supported a "total war" at the important moment of decision making; once fighting vigorously on the line, later calling vigorously for young men to fight on the newly formed line—and as before, he had to admit that during the fighting he had been dismissive and even disdainful of the pacifists who tried to demonstrate the horror of the giant conflicts. With unsparing self-scrutiny and rigorous honesty, he admitted that he himself could not find reasonable ways out of the moral quagmire of two total wars, and therefore he and everyone else needed a structural protection, the institutionalization of Woodrow Wilson's international peacekeeping mission. Only a new sort of League of Nations could possibly resolve differences in such a way that injustices like the invasion of another Belgium or another Poland could be stopped by reasonable discussion in parliamentary processes of debate.

Never at peace with himself on any issue, Green characteristically resolved the philosophical dilemma about war and social injustice by pronouncing it to be over: there could be no more such wars and no more such social injustice. As the Popular Front disbanded, the United Front also melted away, and Green seldom again talked about either movement. Instead, he again charged at the nemesis that most beset him, damnable Jim Crow and its excesses in his beloved countryside of rural Carolina. In these contests he occasionally considered himself almost alone, especially in the university academy he once loved in Chapel Hill. His editor friend Bill Couch set off for Chicago, much to Green's profound dismay, since he feared that the UNC Press would never again be as bold in fighting injustice; and Frank Porter Graham went off to the United Nations, appropriately enough for Green's passions for international peacemaking but costly to domestic struggles for racial and economic justice on the campus.

What he knew he could do was to focus on a more popular and more accessible form of dramatic art dedicated to reform, and his vehicle for that mission was again *The Lost Colony*. Teaching could occur with meaningful and spiritual art on the stage of the symphonic dramas; those warm instincts and the kinder habits of being that he finds in the country folk must be stirred, even and especially now that country folk have left the river valley and gone off to the piedmont cities. They must be recalled to their better instincts, and the best of their instincts in their history is the integrationism that Green finds always there culturally; again he locates the genesis of this cultural integrationism and physical integrationism through miscegenation in his mythic portrayal of the Lost Colony.

After all, the uneducated are at least not yet miseducated, and the *Lost Colony* production could again be a marvelous didactic tool to focus on miscegenation, integration, the defying of class barriers, and the expanding horizons available in North Carolina. The careful scholar Laurence Green Avery demonstrates beyond question that Green by January of 1944 was working to restart his outdoor drama, even meeting with Governor J. Melville Broughton as well as businessmen and politicians who were sympathetic.[34] Bankrolled by Hollywood writing assignments and supported by key figures, Green by 1946 was able to see *The Lost Colony* again in production, as it has remained ever since.

13 : VICTORY IN CIVIL RIGHTS
1947–1965

If Green could no longer wow the Broadway critics, he could still perform in public in effective ways. Marion Fitz-Simons, a veteran of the *Lost Colony* performances, recalls an occasion when the playwright himself took center stage and acted:

> Finally, the house lights went down, the spot lights came up on the center stage, Mr. Green was introduced and walked out into the light . . . [author's ellipses] and nothing happened! He just stood there, saying nothing. We had all crowded closer to the stage, puzzled, wondering. Was he ill? Had he forgotten what he had come to say? Paul continued to stand silent staring out into the audience, so we looked too; and pretty soon every eye in the audience was following his gaze. He was looking at a rope tied to the top tier of seats and running all the way down the theatre to the first row. On one side of that rope sat all the black people; on the other side were all the other colors.
>
> Well, Paul stood there, and he looked and looked. Finally he spoke, and this is what he said. He said: "I'd like to say that my play won't be done in this theatre until that rope is cut, but there's a law that says that rope has to be there. It's a bad, bad law; and before I die, my plays and the plays of all other people will be done in theatres where there is no rope of any kind."[1]

This heroic stance is of course theatrical in a strictly literal sense, but Green was just as often theatrical in a more figurative sense. Indeed, he was effective in political reform after World War II exactly because he was so theatrical. While his artistic courage flagged and his playwriting fell into a formula, there was still another kind of courage: that of the Public Man who was Chapel Hill's Liberal. In those roles, Green was if anything more gutsy than he had ever been before.

Public Man has been defined by Richard Sennett as an essentially seventeenth-century sense of theatrical presence. But Sennett insists that the self-conscious role-playing can be and should be brought forward and used again, especially in a democratic culture. It is Sennett's contention, demonstrated with care in his monograph, that politics and other civic efforts are best served by the Public Man who takes a consistent political stance for an audience, adapting certain stylized gestures and phrases that are theatrical and "artificial"; however, these techniques actually communicate more honestly than do modern politicians and other leaders who claim some kind of personal relationship with each voter or citizen, so that *character* becomes as large a question for people trying to make decisions as do the issues about politics.[2]

The problem with *character* as an issue in political and other settings is that a leader's character is often unknown, and likely unknowable, and therefore it becomes yet another image to be manipulated, only now not on behalf of any outcome—that is, things to *do* in the public sphere—but only on behalf of gaining and holding power. Sennett insists that politics is better served by a theatrics in which the roles are well understood and the gestures immediately comprehensible by the voting public. Whether Sennett is right about this prescription for all modern public figures is of no particular concern here. Rather, he certainly is right in describing Paul Green in his mature years. What Green did in particular was to take the same consistent stance as the public antagonist of the stylized and anthropomorphized character Jim Crow. Unlike previous years and previous campaigns, he was seldom specific about pieces of legislation but was generally the advocate of racial integration within a context of a broadly liberal sense of human dignity. If one looks for more recent analogy in terms of style, Green after 1946 resembles no one so much as Ronald Reagan, for both men mastered the grand and very general rhetoric and both men made the theatrical gesture on behalf of the largest themes without filling in many details about how to get there from here—and without making the character of their enemies or their own character an issue in the public staging of the political campaign.

By 1946 Green was Doogie the archetypal paterfamilias of a sandhills family now extended far beyond the upper valley of the Cape Fear River. Appropriate to his personal family history, his wealth was still in land, in Harnett and Orange Counties, and in traditional fashion he borrowed heavily against the real property to give money and presents to his four children, to his relatives, to his political causes—and to his own acquired taste for expensive suits and the latest model and largest-sized Cadillac. The Hollywood money he spent buying up land, especially near the University of North Carolina, which was poised to expand itself in all directions in southern Orange County beyond its historic campus site. He continued with more and more success to manage the finances of the Green family in his native Harnett, and he continued, with less and less success, to suggest career routes for his beloved sisters Caro Mae Green Russell and Erma Green Gold, each of whom established herself as an artistic critic and literary savant. Each sister for a season removed herself from the Old North State and from the entire South, but each remained fascinated with the now full-blown and nationally acknowledged southern literary renaissance. Caro Mae and Erma each returned home, married, and settled in North Carolina; Caro Mae married the UNC English professor, sometime reformist, and full-time family friend Phillips Russell. Above all, each sister remained fascinated with her brother Paul, and neither spared him any criticism on those rare occasions when he fell beneath their high expectations.[3]

Lib Green for her part was too much the New Englander and too much the independent artist to consider (or to be considered for) the role of southern materfamilias for the Greens. That role remained in the capable and willing hands of sister/mother Mary Green Johnson, and she insisted that Paul Green answer to her for decisions about the extended family, for she was the undisputed keeper of the family conscience; furthermore, she was the undisputed keeper of the family history, setting straight—and also occasionally editing for public consumption—the often tangled family stories. Lib Green, not burdened with the materfamilias duties, instead maintained an extremely hectic schedule supervising dinner parties and the impromptu drinking sessions for visiting literati, reformists, and interesting personalities at Greenwood Road. As noted, that house since the years between the world wars had served as a kind of salon for the region's up-and-coming writers, but now the hosting was a bit more formal and even a bit more heroic, despite the continued assistance of a series of kitchen helpers and housecleaners. As the novelist John Ehle, a Green protégé, marked it, the Greens did not come to *your* place to dinner, but rather you were summoned to *their* place.[4]

Green's beloved cabin still sat in its own honored place in back of the house on Greenwood Road, and it was still expected of Lib Green that her husband be left alone to his diary writing and his formal writing and rewriting until time for his official appearance at the special hosted function of the evening. Some days he might be working in the yard, perhaps operating a tractor or some other machine on what was virtually a small farm; but he was also not to be interrupted in these emotionally satisfying tasks. Between these duties as hostess extraordinaire and traffic cop, Lib Green was still able to do some creative writing, such as lyrics for the symphonic drama, and quite a great deal of editing, that most distilled form of creative writing, for her constantly writing and rewriting husband, especially in his mature years, trusted very few people to edit him.[5]

The children were no longer kids. All four were well educated, not only in formal schooling with advanced degrees but more significantly from their unique family experiences among all those guests and from the extensive travels. By 1946 Paul Green Jr. and Byrd Green had moved out of the house to set off on their own careers as successful leaders who could manage their own business affairs in the complexities of a very urban and sophisticated technological society. Yet Paul Jr. and Byrd not only remained conversant with literary and artistic matters but also became critics and connoisseurs. Still at home for the nonce were two precocious daughters, Betsy and Janet, now in their late teens and each of them firmly established as a brilliant student and determined individualist. The four children, then, were much in the mold of Lib Green the autonomous Yankee go-getter, with generous portions of the Lay family's toughness, iconoclasm, and lust for wandering. Yet all four, even and especially as they moved far northward physically and psychically, relied for decades on Doogie to help them with financial difficulties and to console them, and sometimes to scold them, as they launched themselves on their ambitious careers and travels of all kinds.[6]

The years between 1947 and 1950 were given over to two campaigns, each of which famously failed. Artistically there was the effort to bring forward two more symphonic dramas, *The Common Glory,* which was set in Williamsburg and featured Thomas Jefferson, and *Faith of Our Fathers,* which was designed for performance in Washington, D.C.; and politically there was the effort to reelect Frank Porter Graham to the Senate in the southern liberals' fateful year of 1950.[7] In each campaign the cause in retrospect looks a bit dubious, given the heroic effort expended. In each campaign too Green was more the Public Man fighting for his conception of southern liberalism than he was the creative artist or the political activist. The costs of these failures, financially, psychically, and otherwise, were high, and on occasion he could appear ridiculous, especially to the coolly discerning eye of later generations of literary theorists and political scientists. Yet for all that there was in each campaign a magnificence, in the high, old Greek sense of greatheartedness, on behalf of a struggle fully examined and fairly engaged; and in such perspective, the cause, the cost, and the consequences are finally not relevant at all.

The symphonic dramas were both essentially Virginia stories of the eighteenth century, and it may be that the time and the place, those touchstone categories for Paul Green, were all wrong. This man, whose beloved mother was a Byrd (though distantly, if at all, related to *the* Byrds of Virginia) and whose second child was christened with that family name, had grown up with many spoken tales and many more unspoken emotions about the Old Dominion and its role in the founding of the country. He was of course quintessentially a North Carolinian, and specifically a sandhills kid, and he was thus in thoroughly unfamiliar territory in Virginia, a land and a people almost as daunting as that of Olympus and its Greek gods, about whom he attempted a play in college days. He had struggled to produce his Virginia play in the 1930s, at that time hoping to do so for the Federal Theater Project, and with music by Kurt Weill, both of which collaborations failed largely because Green could not write effectively about the subject.[8]

He confided further to his diary and to some friends that he simply did not like the eighteenth century, especially the men of powdered wigs, silk stockings, liveried servants, and fine china. He much preferred the pioneers of the late-sixteenth-century and early-seventeenth-century Virginia colony— and the frontiersmen of any era anywhere. Indeed, Green had attempted to write a play set in Jamestown to commemorate the spirit and spunk of Captain John Smith and others who followed the noble failure of the lost colonists who preceded them. Members of the Jamestown Foundation were helping him on the endeavor, but he was persuaded to shift the site to Williamsburg, which changed the subject matter to the writing of the Declaration of Independence and the struggle to build a nation. Jefferson he admired of course, but apparently he was too much in awe to write about his hero believably; and other Virginia leaders, whether portrayed on stage in Williamsburg or Washington, D.C., were too much swans and dandies for his personal tastes.[9]

As Laurence Green Avery documents superbly, the story of the production of *Common Glory* is itself, in Green's own words, "plenty of commonness and little of glory." Norfolk journalist and editor Robert Mason, then associate editor of the *Norfolk Virginian-Pilot,* notes the bitter resentment among locals in the tidewater, especially among the "literati and intelligentsia" of the colleges in the area, the College of William and Mary and its branch campus in Norfolk (today's Old Dominion University, now independent of its parent). According to Mason, these figures, and their friends who supported the performing arts in the tidewater, understood that Green had "delivered a mint for a pittance" in his long-term contract for *The Lost Colony,* and they suspected that he intended to make large royalties on any contract arranged in their amphitheaters for the Virginia symphonic drama. These people did not intend that the playwright gouge out any large royalties from the hides of local artists or local backers of the theater. As for that successfully running *Lost Colony,* those operating it on the outer banks of Carolina were for their part anxious and apprehensive that Rockefeller and other "big-time" northern money could generate a lavish production of *Common Glory* that would outshine and eventually close down the original symphonic drama. Apparently unaware of such emotions behind the scenes at either production site, Green often wrote to people in Williamsburg, Norfolk, Newport News, and Carolina's outer banks on Jamestown Foundation letterhead stationery, an artless irritant that did nothing to allay the rumors and suspicions.[10]

When he at last completed his many revisions to the script, he displayed none of the clever Kurt Weill touches to which he had been exposed. Nor did he write with much of his own dark humor and brooding depths. The play does have its moments, and he took pains to present period music accurate to the times of the scenes. Basically, it is a play designed to make the solid middle class feel good about the origins of its solidity, and the glory that is common does not really extend to the black, red, or poor white denizens who made up his most fascinating subject matter in earlier drama. There is in it the sort of consensus liberalism that marks much of the cold war era; and withal the formulaic approach to a self-satisfied audience marks him as something of a Cadillac liberal artistically, though never politically.

After some initial enthusiasm in the summer season of 1949, audiences in fact did not respond well, and the play was in trouble financially almost from the start. It nearly failed twice, but was "rescued by Green's lobbying the James-town corporation directors and appealing to the public through the press," as Robert Mason reported from the scenes. As for *Faith of Our Fathers,* it was prof-fered to the audiences at the national capital in 1949 with even less success, and it closed after a season despite equally vigorous pleading from its author. He would attempt to dramatize his maternal homeland again, but the immediate results of Virginia stagings of outdoor drama were, as the Norfolk journalist noted, "disappointing."[11]

In 1949 he also brought out to slight notice *Dog on the Sun,* more rewrites of older stories based on eastern Carolina folklore and touched up by some per-sonal memories recast as detached fiction. That same year a special conference, "Culture and Collards," showed the Public Man standing proudly on behalf of the middling culture of those sturdy plain-folk who ate that most truly re-gional food, collards. Generally the more urbane North Carolina elite, many obviously arriviste and in any case pretty snobbish regardless of their tenure at the top, detested collards exactly because of their common and plebeian ori-gins. But for Green, the common collard was a part of the common glory, and it did something good for Tarheel writers and artists to have their most public spokesman standing in Dunn, in his native Harnett County, with the up-and-coming novelist James Street and the future poet laureate Sam Ragan and a score of other North Carolina writers to celebrate the unique vegetable, especially as cooked southern style, that is, simmering for great periods of time until one's entire house reeked of collard greens, its very smell an ethnic marker for the regional archaeologist or folklorist. Here, he was not at all above embar-rassing those who aspired to rule the region without reference to their roots; and of course it was yet one more thing that united, rather than divided, black people and white people. Collards, he could declare convincingly, were there-fore one more pearl of his Real South.[12]

In 1950, then, he kept at his movie scriptwriting, he was able to keep *Common Glory* afloat, albeit barely, and he had brought forward some publications and some live productions. Having lost the attention of the Broadway critics and most academic authorities, now he was trying hard to gain the attention of the voting middle class in the Old North State, but it was a hard, hard sale. Nevertheless, if he could not win them to his art, there was still his politics, and the year 1950 loomed as a year to conjure.

In several southern states, especially North Carolina, there were cru-cial senatorial campaigns as Harry Truman and the liberal remnants of the old

New Deal sought to erect a permanent structure of a welfare society that featured some social reform. Frank Porter Graham thus emerged as a significant figure in the year's campaigns. Much as Green disapproved of Truman's foreign policy with its cold war language and gestures, he supported the Democrats' domestic social agenda, and he was personally beholden to Graham in any case. The longtime UNC administrator, appointed U.S. senator by Governor Kerr Scott in 1949 upon the death of J. Melville Broughton, subsequently finished first in the 1950 Democratic primary, in a four-way race that included the redoubtable clown Robert Rice "Our Bob" Reynolds and a hog farmer whose wife reported, "[H]e's not much of a husband and he won't make much of a [senator], but don't think he won't get it if he goes *after* it."[13] However, the fourth candidate was the distinguished attorney Willis Smith, chair of the board of trustees of Duke University, former president of the American Bar Association, and former speaker of the North Carolina House of Representatives. Smith was a very different candidate, an intelligent fellow and one with his own deep pockets and with conservative supporters who had even deeper pockets.

As soon as Smith had announced his candidacy, he received assistance from Jesse Helms, then a radio personality at Raleigh station WRAL and a man who formerly supported "Dr. Frank." Helms brought a technological sophistication, a knowledge of demographics, and a shrewdness bordering on romantic genius to an old strategy in which Willis Smith took the high road while his supporters advanced rapidly down a low road. Their anonymous literature attacked Graham as a Communist. Doc Graham in predictable fashion never replied to any attack, but instead kept expounding on a complex and somewhat dense platform of fifteen proposals. In the first primary contest Graham benefited from the formidable operations of Governor Kerr Scott's Democratic machine, which dutifully got out the vote, and he won a substantial plurality, although he did barely miss an outright majority that would have let him avoid a runoff with the dangerous Smith team in a two-person race unclouded by the presence of a hog-farmer and a clown.[14]

Apparently Willis Smith was reluctant to pursue a runoff, but persistent persuasion, especially by Jesse Helms appealing to listeners over the radio, drafted the jurist for a late-season runoff, scheduled for 25 June and announced only a couple of weeks before the voting. This time Smith's managers shifted tactics, moving away from communism and back to the perennial Carolina preoccupation with race relations, that ploy labeled "Mr. Nigger" by Green's youthful hero, the sandhills poet and journalist John Charles McNeill. Smith himself was widely reported to hold moderate views about race and sometimes was even said to be little different from Doc Graham on the race issue, that is, he would peacefully accept inevitable federal action on behalf of civil rights instead of actively resisting in a way that might foment violence. However, Smith explained in some detail later that the North Carolina black people who could vote (and some could in 1950 in the Tarheel State) had voted overwhelmingly for Graham; the attorney considered such "block voting" to be antidemocratic and dangerous and offensive to his sense of fair play, and so he had to run.[15]

Whatever his actual views about race relations, Smith certainly had a race-baiting team working on his behalf. With Helms aboard, these issues took on an electronic sheen as the popular entertainer found ways to reach folk with a simple negative message focused tightly on Graham the man. After all, as Vann Woodward once noted, even the notoriously reformist Howard Kennedy Beale was not *left* of Graham, but only *north* of Graham. Helms's insight was to remind voters that Graham was down-home eastern country in speech, dress, demeanor, and style, but otherwise foreign in ideology: the UNC administrator believed in world peace and in racial equality. Smith's Know the Truth Committee distributed the flyer

WHITE PEOPLE WAKE UP BEFORE IT IS TOO LATE,
YOU MAY NOT HAVE ANOTHER CHANCE[16]

Pictures circulated showing a black man dancing with a white woman on whose head was cleverly superimposed the face of Doc Graham's wife, Marian Graham. School buses were stopped in one county, and men climbed aboard to warn children that if Graham was elected, they would soon be sitting next to "nigger kids" on the same bus and in classrooms. Voters were told that Graham had "appointed a Negro" to the United States Military Academy at West Point (the recommendation was actually for an alternate position, but Graham was clearly on record that "academically qualified Negroes" deserved admission to the academy).[17] Where communism could be dismissed as something of an abstraction and in any case unbelievable for one so folksy as Doc Graham, these proofs of his decent regard of African American people struck many white voters in a different place, angering and alienating them as Smith's people expected.[18]

It is the testimony of Pou Bailey, later a superior court judge, that Jesse Helms personally saw all of these anonymous advertisements and personally approved all of these clever tricks, and indeed contributed to most of them. For his part, Helms himself has always insisted that he took no part in such stratagems and that Smith was completely innocent in the campaign. The meticulous study by Burns and Pleasants makes it clear that Smith *knew* what was going on and that Helms *did* much of what was going on. But Burns and Pleasants also make it clear that "Dr. Frank" was a poor, unfocused campaigner, damaged only in part by his age and health (the septuagenarian during the contest suffered a severe bout with pneumonia that laid him out for crucial days and then left him weak and drained). More damaging was Doc Graham's own failures to show up on time or at all for rallies and appointments, his professorial and inaccessible stump speeches, and above all his stubborn refusal to deny the wilder charges against him, which he could have refuted without attacking the character of Smith at all.[19] For all this scholarly wisdom, it should be remembered of course that the most damaging charge, that Frank Graham wanted racial equality and economic justice, was entirely on the mark: it was Paul Green stuff, and such desiderata, whether the playwright or the politician wanted to admit it, were offensive to most white Tarheel voters of the day.

Barely defeated in the runoff, Graham was damaged more than he allowed himself to concede.[20] Doc was nearly broke, he was physically worn out, and he was emotionally drained. Truman, who had been counting on Graham to support his beleaguered Fair Deal programs in the Senate, was initially outraged with the Smith people. Even when the president recovered his customary pragmatism and accepted the new senator on his team, he remained deeply sympathetic with Graham and appointed him ambassador to the United Nations. The post was partly to recognize his skills in personal diplomacy (as distinguished from knowledge of foreign affairs) but mostly to reward a faithful liberal Democrat down on his luck. Although Doc would persevere another two decades, he grew physically smaller and in some other ways smaller, and he became more a living memory than a living presence in the contemporaneous political and social discourse. Not only were these election results saddening to Green, but also he received an unmistakable sign from the success of yet more race-baiting techniques with the very middle-class audiences that he was attempting to persuade into integration. The white middling and plain-folk classes made it quite clear that they just hated the very mention of integration, no matter how softly Doc Graham had tried to pedal on those issues.

With Frank Porter Graham thus lifted to a new—and more removed—place, it would fall to Green himself to lead racial reformism in Chapel Hill after 25 June 1950. Yet he remained a most resilient and determined figure, for he knew what political scientists since Valdimer Orlando Key have often observed about North Carolina, namely, that the Senate often features rather odd characters from that state, indeed often features very reactionary ones; but its governors have since the Civil War tended toward the pragmatic and racially moderate. In other words, at the state level there were still men who often did listen to Paul Green. Losing at the national level in a most embarrassing campaign that showed new rules were at play, Green could still play the Public Man in more local and statewide contests involving Jim Crow.

And there would even be another fling at great art and experimentation on Broadway.

The final chance at Broadway came from old acquaintances and in a familiar venue. Cheryl Crawford, that "sturdy girl" of the old Group Theater, arranged to produce an experimental folk play in ANTA Theater (American National Theater and Academy, physically occupying the old Guild Theater). The production company ANTA was chartered by Congress, and finally the sturdy girl herself was in charge of producing dramatic art of her own choosing. The director of her choice was Lee Strasberg, he of method acting and also one from the glory days of Group Theater; and her choice for lead actor was John Garfield, one of the few American actors then performing successfully both in cinema and on stage. Most enticing of all, Crawford wanted to use Green's imaginative revision of a complex and controversial folk drama by no less than Henrik Ibsen. As noted, Green's record of working with the Group Theater, especially with Strasberg's directing, was not an unalloyed success; but he admired Crawford, and he was most anxious to attempt something truly challenging on Broadway and in the Guild Theater, for he remembered well the efforts to create that institution, as he remembered well the efforts to create its successor, ANTA.[21]

The Ibsen play *Peer Gynt,* both in Ibsen's conception and ANTA's operation, was the kind of bold experiment that Paul Green and Barrett Clark had attempted to Burns Mantle's and Brooks Atkinson's enthusiastic celebration in the bravest days of the 1920s and 1930s. There was a caution flag, since some important supporters and advisers were now unavailable to help in this risky venture. Clark—agent, sponsor, coach, friend, confidante, and the pro's pro—was long gone from Broadway and gone even from off Broadway; he was the victim of the unblinking and unmerciful economics of the theater that he served. And Burns Mantle—the longtime dean of New York drama critics who had twice campaigned for a Pulitzer Prize for Green and who had five times ranked Green plays in a given season's best ten plays—had died in 1948. Brooks Atkinson of the *New York Times* was still around but was lately more respectful of Green's past accomplishments than truly interested in the playwright's current work. It may well be that either Clark or Mantle might have pointed out to Green that his best writing was always rooted in the rural Carolina countryside and that some of his worst writing was literally rootless, concerning folkloric characters farther afield. Whether they would have said suchlike, and whether he would have listened to their counsel, is of course impossible to know.

In any case, this play was pretty far afield for Green, despite his infectious enthusiasm for a Broadway performance and his almost supererogatory approach to folklore of all kinds. Critic Margaret Marshall notes that the character Peer Gynt is a man "with a passion for power and an incapacity for love" who commits two sins: one is something along the lines of classical hubris, trying to step outside his assigned role and position; and the second is something along the lines of romantic egoism, focusing too much on self to the exclusion of others. Nevertheless, the results of both sins in combination—personal hurt to individuals in particular and disharmony and discord for society in general—are not classically tragic, but rather seriocomic. In the end the mythic Buttonmolder must simply melt down the badly fitted Peer Gynt and recast him as someone who buttons better into the fabric of society. It is thus not Christian, and certainly not Calvinist. Nor is the play classically pagan. Rather, it is a very Norwegian folktale of power and wit with some pathos and some low humor. Unlike Ibsen's later work, there is here very little social notation and nothing at all of social relevance or political prescription. Various authorities, especially Norwegian critics, are not of one mind as to how well Ibsen himself performed in attempting a poetic rendering in his own language of this extremely dense and tangled admixture of themes and techniques. Any translation, then, was bound for unsympathetic and even hostile reading by a variety of critics who were in no accord at all about the original master's intentions—and some of whom never considered *Peer Gynt* to be in the Ibsen canon.[22]

Green himself, of course, always essayed social notation and political prescription in muscular and accessible poesy as the poet and prophet of his self-styled Real South. He thus attempted a topical and realistic play designed to wake up the contemporary American middle class to their responsibilities, albeit by shocking them with mythic and folkloric images from the timeless—and thus ungrounded—Norwegian tales and characters. He wrote the script with lean and clear lines, some of which read very well, and the sets were designed brilliantly, even stunningly, by Donald Oenslager. Crawford remembered ineffective sets from the days of *Johnny Johnson,* and thus she gave Oenslager money and means to render sets that did full justice to a serious production. For his part Strasberg got strong performances, especially from Garfield as Peer Gynt and by young Karl Malden as the Buttonmolder who must concede that this button does not work and must be recast. On the other hand, the music was ill suited to this "mélange of realism and fable," and the forgettable score and its forgettable performance were further damaged because of inevitable comparisons to the unforgettable score produced for New York audiences in the 1920s by Edouard Grieg.[23]

Opening on 28 January 1951 to a full house that included many intelligent and sympathetic people who for different reasons admired Green, Crawford, and Strasberg, the ANTA play that evening drew lukewarm responses from an apparently confused audience. Thereafter it drew poor crowds, and it was panned by critics writing in the *New York Times, Nation, New Republic, New Yorker,* and other publications. Perhaps most painful was not the harsh criticism but the almost disdainful attitude of men in publications that once accorded Paul Green maximum respect. John Chapman, successor to Burns Mantle for the *Best Plays* series, said dismissively that "Paul Green messes around with Ibsen's 'Peer Gynt.'" Brooks Atkinson, who had so often celebrated Green as a luminary in the southern literary renaissance, lambasted the music and even Ibsen for this "lifeless play." And Wolcott Gibbs, writing in the *New Yorker,* a venue that had always given Green full serious attention with long and thoughtful reviews, was snidely dismissive: "Altogether I had as artistically gruelling an evening as I have had this year."[24]

After thirty-two performances at ANTA, *Peer Gynt* closed down, and Paul Green departed Broadway forever. As Thomas Stearns Eliot had put it in another poem of the era about another mythic representative man of the era, he had gone, not with a bang, but with a whimper.

The remainder of the decade of the 1950s featured Green as the Public Man par excellence after the civil rights movement had finally gained enough traction to win notice from the white middle class, especially in North Carolina's self-consciously progressive piedmont cities of Greensboro, Winston-Salem, Durham, and Charlotte. By the end of the 1950s Green's artistic star would be even further dimmed, but his political star would be bright indeed. Not all the people in the growing ranks of racial liberalism were literary-minded, and certainly many literary-minded people were apolitical or even segregationist; but in North Carolina in this era there was an interesting connection between literary figures and those who were liberal on racial issues, as seen in people such as John Ehle, James K. Boyd, Betty Smith, Thad Stem, Walter Spearman, Sam Ragan, and Betty Hodges. Almost all of this small but prominent group were in some way protégés of Paul Green. They invariably admired him for what he had accomplished artistically in the past and were themselves emboldened politically by his continuing activism in the 1950s.[25]

At the national level, some of the Harry Truman liberals knew of and appreciated Green. If President Truman even saw the playwright's angry letter about atomic bombs, then he deliberately forgot all about it as he and his people searched for southern allies for his civil rights program. Green was in many ways ideal for the beleaguered Truman liberals, because he was down-home and plainspoken and yet still a respectable intellectual. Thus in 1951 Green was sent to lecture on culture and democracy in Japan and other parts of the Far East. The Truman administration also appointed the Chapel Hillian to the U.S. National Commission for the United Nations Educational, Social, and Cultural Organization (UNESCO), a post that gave the Greens the chance to travel yet again, this time to Greece. At long last Lib Green got her trip as befitted a true daughter of the New England Lays; and this trip abroad was mercifully unmarred by bouts of emotional depression, terrible weather, grinding poverty, looming fascism, or financial disaster in the entertainment industry. In fact, the correspondence, the diary entries, the preserved family photographs all record a very contented Green couple joyfully making their rounds.[26]

It was of course cold war stuff as much as civil rights stuff, and Green was likely helping Truman and Secretary of State Dean Acheson in the cold war campaign more than he was helping the cause of world peace and international governance. If he marked these ironies, he hardly dwelled on them, but instead stood proudly for the cause of American integration and racial justice while gratefully appearing in ancient sites of public and civil honor from Epidaurus to Tokyo. In all of these designedly staged travels the Public Man played this role perfectly, assisted and supported ably, even brilliantly, by Lib Green.

These world travels for UNESCO and the Truman foreign policy ended for the Greens with the defeat in 1952 of Truman's would-be presidential successor Adlai Stevenson; and thereafter Paul and Lib Green stayed stateside. Yet the honors hardly stopped, or even slowed, as he became something of a monument for the extended family of literati and liberals back home. In 1952 Green won the Sir Walter Raleigh Award for Outstanding Literary Achievement, ostensibly for recent symphonic dramas, Hollywood scripts, and contemporaneous essays, but really for the career. The following year he produced *Dramatic Heritage.* These essays, brought out by his longtime publisher and benefactor Samuel French, were characteristically humanistic in impulse but marked by a most unmodern spiritualism, idealism, and even absolutism. Meanwhile, the symphonic dramas continued, successfully on the Outer Banks, less so from other venues, but offers kept coming in and he kept accepting the opportunities to write more of them, producing *Serenata* in Santa Barbara to celebrate California and *Seventeenth Star* in Columbus to celebrate Ohio. In 1955 he produced the symphonic drama *Wilderness Road* for a reformist academic community centered in Berea, Kentucky, and *The Founders* for Williamsburg, the latter still another effort to capture the elusive Virginians of his mother's ancestry. All of these symphonic dramas follow a formula of consensus liberalism for a middle class eager to find courageous ancestors, and all of them deal grandly if vaguely in themes of sacrifice for the common good. All of them "stabilize his income," as Laurence Green Avery notes and the records document amply; and all of them provided a bully pulpit for one preaching racial integration and an old-style New Deal social liberalism with nothing specific about economic problems.[27]

So buoyed was Green by the encouragement that he was receiving in the 1950s that he decided to try to dramatize that character who most allures and most often eludes white male southerners. He decided to write *the* Virginia play about Robert Edward Lee.

It was not only Virginia that still bewitched Green, but also the Civil War, and he was bound in determination to catch the full spirit of his Real South in that place—the Commonwealth—and in that time—the War. He told a regional drama critic that he was taken with the idea of dramatizing the losses of the Civil War, juxtaposing those losses with the spirit of recovery and resilience that to his mind marked the people of his Real South. To catch the moment when the civil rights movement was coming to crescendo, he wanted to commemorate the sacrifices of common southerners and combine that spirit of sacrifice with the same kind of spirit, in different form, seen in the movement that he served. The coming centennial of the Civil War was a special moment, he realized, and he understood that the centennial might well become an occasion for celebrating the Lost Cause and that that Cause might well include states' rights, the Ku Klux Klan, damnable Jim Crow, and all sorts and conditions of racism. As the decade of the 1960s loomed, then, Green set himself the task of capturing the goodwill and the right-hearted spirit of Real South commoners on behalf of peace and reconciliation between white and black in a literal integration of common glory. Painfully aware of the possible uses of the Confederacy by segregationists, he yet remained very hopeful that the same symbols could be set to serve the civil rights movement.[28]

Atlanta, the city "too busy to hate," interested him, and he spoke of a plan to start a symphonic drama with a General William Tecumseh Sherman character burning down a full-sized house on the outdoor stage—and after that emotionally pyrotechnic prologue, the drama of reconciliation, rebuilding, and racial justice could emerge. But it was Virginia that still enticed the most, for the real battleground and thus the major sacrifices were located there; and that of course brought back the figure of Lee, the man who, to Green's understanding, considered states' rights a bore, detested slavery, and thus freed his wife's slaves; who later sought to employ black soldiers in the gray ranks, and most important, at war's end, insisted on harmony and concord and thus rebuilt Washington College on a ridge in the Shenandoah Valley as a place to train leaders of a peaceful South that rejoined black and white and North and South. In Green's hands Lee was something of a protoliberal and integrationist on the issue of civil rights and race relations. Virginia thus, he kept deciding, was the place and Lee was the man for his play, *The Confederacy*.[29]

Thus far he was well within the venue and subject that he always handled ably, but two things hurt his cause. First, the best Virginia sites in terms of his theme were the Shenandoah Valley or Richmond; but his best Virginia sites in terms of available staging were Virginia Beach or Williamsburg, neither of which was Lee's territory and neither of which witnessed any of the great land battles conducted by the commander. The second problem was noted by Norfolk's journalist Robert Mason and by a local playwright, Ed Devaney, both of whom loved Green and loved his idea, Devaney even functioning as stage manager for Green's symphonic drama in Virginia Beach. But each man noted that Lee was probably the wrong character for Green, being too perfect in the eyes of most southern white men, even and especially the North Carolina playwright. Lee was too easy to lionize into unbelievability and thus dramatic immobility; and Lee was also too easy to parody into slapstick.[30]

In fact Green in writing *The Confederacy* did make Lee a lionized monument, while he also introduced some elements of crude "potboiling" action. Almost at once the Virginia Beach symphonic drama became the stuff of slapstick parody, some of the low comedy managed by Devaney himself on the very stage during off nights between performances of the play. Other aspects of the staging and presentation were as haphazard and seriocomic as had been Green's noble failure *Johnny Johnson* long ago. Devaney recalls that the jet planes of a nearby naval training base flew on a path directly over the amphitheater, drowning out many lines, that the wind and wave currents fetched up stormy interruptions, that poisonous snakes often blocked the entry of characters onto the stage. Devaney even says, "[W]hen we weren't being drowned out, we were being drowned." Withal, the cast was more interesting backstage than onstage, and Green's self-styled "Temple of Democracy" and his worshipful litany commemorating the nobility of the Common Man "was staffed with bawdy and irreverent priests and acolytes and had a congregation of potbellied Shriners and the like decked out in loud print shirts and straw hats slurping beer out of plastic cups, while Robert E. Lee strove to save the south from ruin."[31]

Yet for the Public Man the unkindest cut of all was the use to which Governor Lindsay Almond put Green's play. Almond had sponsored Virginia's massive resistance to school integration, and he had cooperated with a battalion of clever lawyers to close certain strategically placed public schools rather than integrate them. Thereby the Virginia segregationists at the highest level had kept things tied up in court as a much more effective forestalling of integration than Little Rock's or New Orleans's shouting and violent crowds. Almond's tactic worked well, and the governor was able not only to delay integration but also to deny any education at all in certain counties to the very denizens of both races. To Green, the celebrant of public schools who so desperately wanted proper schooling for the children of Abe McCrannie and Harvey Easom, Almond and his allies thus were especially noxious. Finally, Almond tied everything to states' rights and connected that theme back to the Virginia of the Civil War. In other words, Governor Almond was manipulating Confederate symbols, and especially the symbols of Lee, on behalf of segregation much more effectively than Green manipulated the symbols on behalf of integration. Most disastrous of all, Almond came to Virginia Beach to speak on behalf of states' rights, segregation, and *Green's* play, thus linking the playwright's own creation with the things Green most detested.[32]

It was a thorough drubbing in 1958 and 1959 in Virginia Beach, and Paul Green finally had both the Virginia venue and the Lee character pounded out of his system. Yet he was nothing if not resilient and determined, and he soon found a way to take Hollywood and dramatize integration in his Real South in his chosen place and in his chosen time.

John Howard Griffin was a southern newspaperman who could have been dreamed up by Paul Green or, better, by Harvey Easom. In 1959 Griffin decided to travel from New Orleans to Birmingham and describe for readers exactly what damnable Jim Crow was like for the black people taking that route. But Griffin was not content to look at the black experiences of segregation and racism as a detached observer. Instead, he intended to tell readers exactly what segregation *felt like*. He decided *to make himself black* and to write about the oppression from the victim's point of view, from the inside. Thus he underwent a process that dyed his skin dark brown and made him to outward appearance an African American. So disguised, he made his 1959 trip and thereafter filed a series of articles, which in 1961 became his shocking memoirs *Black like Me*. [33]

Here surely was melodrama fit to wake up whatever decency resided in the middle class. Here too was a like-minded spirit for Green. His very namesake Saint Paul had so described such faith and the prophetic courage it produces:

> Choosing rather to suffer affliction with the people of God, than to enjoy the pleasures of sin for a season; Esteeming the reproach of Christ greater riches than the treasures in Egypt: for he had respect unto the recompence of the reward. [34]

Surely Griffin had his newspaperman's eye on the prize, and just as surely the Public Man had his scriptwriter's eye on Griffin. The independent filmmaker Julius Tannenbaum eagerly approached Green about scripting Griffin's memoirs for the cinema. Green happily accepted and exchanged letters with the journalist and also with the writer Carl Lerner, Griffin's friend and the "chief contact" between the memoirist and the film producers. Throughout the late autumn of 1962 and into winter of 1963, Green worked hard but happily at this task, producing a lean and muscular melodrama, one not noted for its profundity but one certainly effective in pounding out its message. The film, and the phenomenon of its very being, were received eagerly by the middling folk everywhere, and Paul Green did preach effectively to a large audience, even and especially in pockets of the Old North State. [35]

Black like Me, the book and the cinema, are period pieces that do not withstand critical scrutiny as art over the decades, for they are melodrama about a particular sort of problem instead of drama about a condition or a character. As political statements they are no less period pieces bound by time and place, for the United States has moved well beyond the kind of de jure segregation documented therein. Yet Griffin and Green, each in his own way, certainly ran against a giant and slew him in biblical fashion, thereby changing the thinking of many a thoughtful Carolinian. The scriptwriting money spent well on Franklin Street and on Greenwood Street, as did the coin of respect from the liberal literati John Ehle, Sam Ragan, Thad Stem, Betty Smith, Betty Hodges, and Walter Spearman. For the nonce, the Public Man could celebrate a political coup and an entertainment coup, and it had been a long, long time since he could revel in such twinned victories. [36]

At the same time, Paul Green was getting special recognition in a different way, for his state university called upon him at age sixty-seven to teach and preach again in its academic halls for the school year 1962–63. William Brantley Aycock, chancellor of the historic campus at Chapel Hill, was one with considerably liberal inclinations on race relations, and he was also one who admired Green for his reformist career. Probably more important, William C. Friday, president of the entire statewide university system, was a longtime assistant to Doc Graham and also one who proudly bore the label Chapel Hill liberal in his own career; and Friday was instrumental in arranging this special appointment. While damnable Jim Crow still remained law, many native white southerners were beginning to question the morality and practicality of the system, and Green's was a particularly loud voice in that chorus. Bringing him back into the academic ranks at this time was a most important sign, and one well understood by Green himself—and by his enemies and allies.[37]

As visiting professor Green joined a reconstituted program called Radio, Television, and Motion Pictures, RTVMP. In a way its snazzy new label mocked an old-time classicist and Hegelian idealist, but it really did not matter. The people in the drama department, then and later, did not want to be hampered by the vision or the practices of a living legend whose own creative endeavors had entered a period of decline. The people in the philosophy department were of course in a completely new era of highly specialized disciplinary studies, none of which were at all compatible with Green's training or interests. Withal, the appointment was yet another of those career recognitions, and whatever else, Green did *know* cinema from the inside as a lucratively employed scriptwriter and one who was at that very moment writing a script for *Black like Me.* Above all, President Friday, Chancellor Aycock, and the young professionals of RTVMP were able to effect a rapprochement between UNC and Chapel Hill's most prominent public figure.

There is little evidence of dynamic teaching at this post, and in fact some murmuration that he performed rather poorly at the tasks; but as a sign and symbol of the university and of the Public Man, the appointment was very apt, very fitting, and indeed inspired. Most significantly, the timing of the appointment put Green squarely in the front line of the battlefield chosen by the hard-charging right wing led by Jesse Helms, for the onetime campaign manager for Willis Smith—who had delightedly pummeled Doc Graham in 1950—now intended nothing less than an assault on UNC and on Graham's proudest legacy, the freedom to discuss all things fully and frankly on the Chapel Hill campus.[38]

By 1962 A. J. Fletcher's broadcasting system, WRAL, had also established a successful television station in Raleigh to complement its radio station of the same call letters, and Jesse Helms was the star personality in both venues.

WRAL's television transmitter sent out a signal all over the fast-growing capital city and also deep into Green's own province, the eastern farm country of the upper valley of the Cape Fear River. Although Helms grew up in the piedmont, any rural setting was his natural territory too, and the television commentator bid fair to represent those folks, that is the white ones, much more successfully than native liberals Frank Porter Graham, William C. Friday, Samuel T. Ragan, or Paul Green. More, Helms brought the fight right into Doc Graham's university, and he made it clear that he and his high-riding right-wing boys fully intended to set the rules and the tone for academic discourse on the campus.

Right-wingers in the general assembly had passed a speaker ban that prohibited Communists from publicly addressing audiences at the university. The liberal governor Terry Sanford, yet another easterner born in the valley, had watched helplessly, because North Carolina governors then had no veto power and he had been too unprepared for this surprising attack to use his considerable "moral jawboning" powers on assemblymen. Although Sanford was himself a graduate of UNC, and he was proud of the university's nationwide reputation for fostering free debate, he acquiesced in the ban as UNC was officially muzzled. Indeed, Sanford eventually took other actions inimical to academic freedom on his old campus.[39]

There had been an uncharacteristic breakdown in communications between the university leaders and the general assembly and between the governor and the general assembly, and faces were red and moods blue on the Hill as a result. It appears that William Friday, president of the statewide consolidated university system, did less than he could have to protect his faculty and students and may have cooperated with some of the muzzlers. It may also be that UNC Chancellor Aycock was less effective than he could have been in the struggle, certainly much less effective than had been campus leaders Harry Woodburn Chase and Frank Porter Graham in similar controversies in the 1920s and 1930s, when Green was a student and later when he was a young professor. Of course, students and faculty and staff largely bypassed the ban, for instance holding speeches on city streets instead of in academic buildings.[40] Also, professors and students in the classrooms entertained visitors who espoused a wide variety of ideological persuasions. Nevertheless, the university could not legally host a speaker in a public setting on campus if the speaker failed that era's test of politically correct thought. On television screen and on the radio airwaves, Helms reveled in the development.

On 12 October 1963 Green was given the chance to make the University Day address. It was another bully pulpit if ever there was one, and the liberal champion came out to pound the opposition. Manipulating the twin themes of free speech and human dignity as only he could, he also manipulated that rich voice with its obviously eastern Carolina nuances. The combat veteran of one global war for freedom could remind listeners about the second global war for freedom and could allude to Nazi and Stalinist limits on speech and expression while also reminding the audience of the way that dissidents since the time of Socrates had necessarily irritated leaders of their respective states. Speaking as a onetime Cornell University graduate student of *the* John Stuart Mill scholar Ernest Albee, Green reviewed the tenets of classical liberalism and free speech. Then he reviewed the mission of all universities, but especially of UNC in this region. He clobbered the very idea of a speaker ban.[41]

In Chapel Hill that day, Green won over his audience, although of course he had been selected by that very audience to give them this very sermon. Three days later, it was Helms's turn, on WRAL television, and he addressed a much larger audience there. With that signature sneer and deprecating whine that only he could effect, Helms stated that Paul Green had "merely pulled the trigger on an overworked pop-gun." He gave the playwright his due, very perceptively noting that Green once *was* a very fine playwright and also that he had been "duly rewarded" for those plays. Thus Helms let everyone, not least Green, know that the television personality himself *knew* how Broadway critics had dismissed Green's *Peer Gynt* and that the playwright's creative efforts were largely finished, being replaced now by modestly successful commercial productions of light weight and slight substance. It was a telling moment, and proof, if anyone still needed it, that Helms was a shrewd observer of all things. The television man then linked Green with various Communist and liberal causes and characters, the former having nothing at all to do with the Public Man. Helms concluded: "If he should wonder why North Carolinians are inclined to turn a deaf ear to his voice, he might find it helpful to take a look at his own record. Sadly enough, it speaks for itself."[42]

This was good theater indeed, and WRAL owner A. J. Fletcher talked with Green about having the playwright appear on television to offer a *Viewpoint* program address, something also urged by station manager Sam Beard, a friend whom Green accused of suffering from "hardening of the spiritual arteries." The Public Man, however, suspected a trap and in any case could see a pitfall, whether that pitfall was consciously dug for him or not. Green could have his moment on television, but then Jesse Helms could have many more of his own moments to wham away at the liberal. What Green wanted instead of separate speeches was one debate on television. That, however, Beard would not let him have, even and especially after Green attempted an appeal through the Federal Communications Commission.[43]

So who won and who lost here? The speaker ban was never effective, and it was officially lifted in February 1968. Thus the university and its people were never in any way actually muzzled. On the other hand, far more people saw Jesse Helms on WRAL television than heard Paul Green in the campus hall, and Helms was able to reinforce for his large audience his oft-repeated charge that Chapel Hill was "a zoo." The visiting professor of RTVMP reestablished the primacy of John Stuart Mill's liberal rationalism for the university campus, and then Jesse Helms set the university campus apart from television land. Green could reach back to those television watchers through the film *Black like Me* and through symphonic dramas that appealed to their patriotism, but it was a slow go. While Green won the day on campus, Jesse Helms won the day across a much broader area, and the entire series of episodes by its nature put even greater distance between the university and state citizenry than already existed. At any rate, Green in the effort was certainly noble, and he reaffirmed something about a university and what it has to be. That the scholars' academy of the university and the ordinary citizenry would be distant from each other was likely unavoidable in such an anti-intellectual culture as the United States, and it hardly seems worthwhile to abandon Mill's guidelines for discourse on campus in order to mollify a public that hates ideas and their study.

From this high-water mark of liberalism on his campus, Green retired triumphant from UNC in 1963. In that year he published still more formulaic essays about drama, *Plough and Furrow,* and in 1965 he produced still another formulaic symphonic drama, this one called *Cross and Sword* and set in Saint Augustine, Florida. In keeping with the monumental character of his senior years, he in 1965 also was given career recognition, the North Carolina Award for Literature. [44] Still hale and hearty physically, he was buoyant emotionally as the people of his university and the self-styled progressive-minded business leaders in North Carolina caught up with him on the issues of civil rights. Life was at last materially comfortable, and, though racial and economic justice was far to seek, he could mark most remarkable progress on important fronts at this state university and in his adoptive piedmont region; and he could and did express the profoundest hopes for his native valley and points east.

The accomplishments of the civil rights movement rose to full crescent, and the community of Chapel Hill was to large degree in harmony with these times, as noted eloquently in the period-memoir *The Free Men* by Green's protégé novelist John Ehle. The Civil Rights Act of 1964 and the Voting Rights Act of 1965 were at least tolerated in the Old North State, but in Chapel Hill and at Green's state university these laws were celebrated. [45] While Green in a way had nothing to do with the passage of these landmark acts, yet he certainly helped to prepare the way for their acceptance. His had been the prophetic voice, sometimes almost alone, calling for justice. His was the personality that had been most particularly, even most peculiarly, associated with the condemnation of damnable Jim Crow for the long season of that philistine misrule.

When this remarkable era rang down its curtain in 1965, Green no longer needed to be the Public Man for civil rights, because the time and the place had become liberal on race relations. This task in his long career was at last accomplished. Above all, he could go quietly now to see his one successful outdoor drama, at the amphitheater in the Outer Banks venue, or he could go to less successful outdoor dramas of his in Texas, Virginia, and Florida, and he no longer had to make dramatic demonstrations about who sat where.

That law, that "bad, bad law," was rescinded now, and that rope was gone from all his theater sites.

14 : A TIME OF TROUBLES
1966–1981

The date was 22 March 1974, an early spring in Chapel Hill. The place was the Carolina Inn, and Paul Green was holding forth yet again as the Public Man. A visitor could readily agree that the place was filled with history, for it smelled musty; and a visitor could certainly understand that ghosts were hereabouts, for the dim light and dark corners encouraged their presence. The inn of those days was cramped and dusty, and its restaurant featured fare that even in 1974 was passé, being overcooked and often deep-fat fried. Indeed the very concept of the inn was of a unique liberalism and paternalism, for its income went to help support the university library, and for that reason UNC operated the inn. Lately there was no money to help the library from this source, because the inn then operated at a loss, and that too was because of special arrangements and special relationships that were uniquely liberal and paternal. The dining-room attendants and lodging staff were paid better than workers at similar facilities in the county, and thus costs were relatively high. At the same time, prices could seldom be raised, for the faculty took their lunches there at a greatly reduced rate. People in town also took meals there at that reduced rate, as did visiting researchers and sentimental alumni. There were ballrooms for wedding receptions and football celebrations and poetry readings and conferences, although all of these things could be done with more style other places in Chapel Hill. The visitor, or some more objective historian, could well judge things harshly in looking at this inefficient Carolina Inn with its outdated board and its small rooms and its red bottom line.

But to the surviving liberals in 1974, the Carolina Inn was alive with the best kind of ghosts, the ones like the late Frank Porter Graham, who while fleshed and breathing had led Edwin Mims to pronounce the state university and its community in Chapel Hill to be leaders of the advancing South.[1] Indeed, many of those heroes of a pioneering era were still breathing and, more, still *advancing*. The proudly self-styled Regionalist social scientists Guy and Guion Johnson, now emeritus, might be there, and they could tell you humbly about entertaining black scholars in Jim Crow shops downtown and in their home. One might also find Bill Couch, editor of the UNC Press in its bravest days long ago, who was back from Chicago now and still talking about reform. Too, there were currently serving professors who had marched on picket lines protesting the war in Vietnam or the treatment of the kitchen help in the university's food service. And there were currently serving professors and administrators who were arguing in private and sometimes in public about whether UNC—a pioneer among southern institutions in integrating so many things—was now failing to keep pace with its own established racial advancing.

The very arguments and the protests proved that much was still wrong at UNC and in Chapel Hill, but at the Carolina Inn on this evening, everybody was a liberal with a glorious cause, and everybody insisted that their South was still advancing. The occasion for Paul Green to speak was a meeting of the Institute of Outdoor Drama, and everyone knew that Paul Green had invented outdoor drama. *The Lost Colony* was that rarity, a commercial success that pleased the chamber of commerce folk but also a piece of drama produced from the most radical impulses of political reform and artistic experimentation. Everyone knew also that the evening was an opportunity to recognize people. For the event Green was dressed in expensive linen, but he sounded as if he were wearing a farmer's soiled overalls and a straw hat. He was in any case deep in his bourbon, and his voice rolled steady and unremitting as the Cape Fear River in his ancestral sandhills. He stood grandly at the dais, a tall man with broad shoulders but right then looking impossibly large. He lay aside his reading glasses—on such occasions they were more stage props than useful instruments—and he looked around the ballroom, or maybe he looked across the Jordan River.

"John Houseman," he said as he swept a long arm across the decades, "John Houseman had the wide reach, the far view." It was unction, and it was not at all insincere, because Paul Green was incapable of insincerity. He was interring an ancient feud. As chronicled, Green and Houseman had argued viciously back in 1941 concerning the script for *Native Son* that the Chapel Hillian had produced in tandem with Richard Wright, author of the novel that inspired the Broadway production. Houseman, as director, had won that day by altering crucial scenes; and he had later attempted to expand his personal victory in his memoirs by claiming writer's credit for parts of the play that Green could demonstrate he himself had written with the African American novelist in Bynum Hall on a legally segregated campus in full view of the student body. There had been harsh words indeed, and it had become quite a row.[2]

All that was behind Paul Green now. John Houseman had fought for civil rights, and he deserved credit for that fight. No fight was more important than the civil rights fight. Much more, Paul Green needed to do the right thing, the grand thing. He had to close the breach and restore everyone to his broken circle. His kind words told allies and friends that John Houseman belonged. His words also reassured attendees that there still *was* a circle of liberalism even though the Reverend Martin Luther King Jr. was dead and new players were going in unfamiliar and threatening places on routes that were hard for veteran integrationists to follow. The troubling times called for graciousness and grandness, and above all they called for reconciliation. On that stage in the Carolina Inn on 22 March 1974 Paul Green graciously and grandly reconciled himself with John Houseman.

In this final season the lion would not always look so grand, not always be so gracious. This season would include quite a time of troubles, as his Bible called it, and he would find himself as powerless before that fate as were any of his characters on stage when they heard the portent of an owl hoot. The very success of the civil rights movement in 1964 and 1965 now militated against the campaigns that Paul Green demanded against a race-slanted capital punishment, against de facto segregation, and against a race-concentrated economic stagnation. After 1966 enemies were less starkly drawn, and the issues were more complex, even convoluted, and the solutions were more elusive. Public opinion polls gathered and interpreted by the UNC sociologist John Shelton Reed showed that everyone was liberal on racial issues; and yet, as he ruefully observed, "some of them are lying!" Richard Nixon could become president in 1968 largely by a self-professed southern strategy that relied heavily on racist appeals in a campaign that angered and frustrated Green in North Carolina.[3]

It was withal a very strange season, and no time for resting even though Paul Green was in fact weary of being the Public Man on the brightly lit stage. In 1965 he and Elizabeth Green had moved south of town, out on Old Lystra Road, where they established a handsome wooden frame home that they named allusively Windy Oaks. There was plenty of yard, really something close to a small farm, and Green could operate his tractor on the place and to some degree be removed from the vexations of a growing university and its growing host city. He had time and space to write and read and think, and to be with Elizabeth and with the grandchildren when they were brought by to visit. There were physical reasons to rest, too, for he was beginning to suffer some heart problems, and he was victim of attacks by an insidious and sometime acute clinical depression that he tried to ignore.

Despite the processes of aging and the passing of the tide of politics beyond Green's brand of liberalism, Paul and Elizabeth Green did not appreciably slow their efforts on behalf of any cause. The soirées in which young writers and young activists met established writers and veteran activists were simply transferred from Greenwood Road to Old Lystra Road. After all, the road to Lystra had biblical meaning to those people who had named it long ago, and the Greens knew their Bible and its allusions: it was in that Roman colony on the road to Lystra that Saint Paul had looked at the crippled man and commanded in a loud voice, "[S]tand upright on thy feet!"[4] And the namesake was still commanding that the morally crippled stand upright and march against injustice.

Letters to the editors of Carolina daily newspapers still rolled off the typewriter, and the couple still made many public appearances on behalf of causes. Too, Paul Green kept at his playwriting, which meant that Elizabeth Green kept at her editing and her supervisory bookkeeping; and the two traveled often to sites where new symphonic dramas were being opened.

No, it was not a good season for an old lion to fight, but this was after all still the boy who responded to his mother's call to serve by seeking the prize that still glimmered in the sky. It would mean looking ridiculous. It would mean continuing to run with one shoe off and one shoe on, running still on a mission that might well fail. The curtain could not be rung down on a player who had quit chasing the prize. He had written it down long ago, and it was still so: *He was Paul Green.*

There was one social institution that had always galled Paul Green, and that was capital punishment. In North Carolina, as in much of the South, the death penalty still smacked of damnable and undead Jim Crow: the inmates waiting to be executed were far, far more likely to be black than white. Racists might, and did, claim that more African Americans committed capital offenses, especially rape, but the data did not substantiate such a contention, because the percentage of rapes and murders committed by African Americans in North Carolina was always roughly the same as the black percentage of the Old North State's population. That is, the minority committed the minority of the capital crimes, and the white majority committed the majority of the capital crimes.[5]

Green's correspondence throughout his long decades was always filled with the issue of capital punishment, and the playwright seemed always to regard the issue as a racial one, although he campaigned no less passionately on behalf of convicted white men. Since 1934 Green had been officially on record in opposition to the death penalty. In that year he had cooperated with the North Carolina Interracial Commission to try to commute the death sentence of a black tenant farmer named Emanuel Bittings, who killed a white landowner, T. M. Clayton, while attempting to defend members of his family against an attack by Clayton on the front step of the Bittings house. The *Raleigh News and Observer* had covered Paul and Lib Green's activities in the unsuccessful campaign, and that episode is apparently the first written public record of Paul and Lib Green's opposition to capital punishment.[6]

In those early cases Paul Green tended to talk about the innocence, or the mitigating circumstances, of the convicted; and he then talked also about the cruel and unusual nature of the electric chair as punishment, consciously using the language of the Eighth and Fourteenth Amendments' guarantees of basic rights. However, by the 1940s Green was clearly on record in opposition to capital punishment even if the accused was guilty of an unmitigated, planned, and vicious attack, as he had said in an open-letter "op-ed" format in the *Raleigh News and Observer* in 1947. By then the gas chamber was in extensive use, and scores of men were being executed in certain years, with quite a list of condemned black men filing appeals and delaying their executions in processes often lengthy but only occasionally successful. Some defenders of capital punishment tried to make a case that the gas chamber was relatively painless and humane in contrast with the electric chair, but Green used his theatrical gifts to illustrate that the gas chamber "choked" and "strangled" a man in an execution fully as gruesome as "garrotte and rope and ax" of other eras. And he invoked Jesus Christ as the Savior whose divine law of forgiveness and redemption replaced an earlier "barbaric" Mosaic code of "eye for eye and tooth for tooth" vengeance. By the 1960s, with other aspects of de jure racial discrimination cleared away, the continuing executions of scores of black men reminded Green that merely removing some statutory discriminations would not end all racist practices.[7]

To demonstrate against the death penalty, the Public Man of course made a stage of the Central Prison in Raleigh. In 1967 he created North Carolinians against the Death Penalty, eventually organizing it formally under the aegis of Raleigh's Pullen Memorial Baptist Church, whose pastor, the Reverend W. W. Finlator, was a liberal in full sympathy with Green. Green raised money for legal funds and for publicity, and he was hard to turn down. As the attorney Marion Wright recalled, it was unwise to accept an invitation to stay at the Windy Oaks home because breakfast there included an irresistible call on the houseguest for one hundred dollars for the cause.[8]

True to his inclinations and habits, Green began the Death Vigils, originally called the Lonely Vigils because at first no one joined him. His ministerial sponsor, Finlator, recalls:

> He came repeatedly to Central Prison on the eve of an execution and stood alone all the night in silent protest to what he regarded as a heinous crime by the state of North Carolina against humanity. He knew, what most North Carolinians didn't know, or didn't want to know, that the death penalty was a relique [*sic*] of a barbarous past relegated chiefly to the American South, that only the poor and the minorities were executed, that it was something the state regarded as necessary for control now that lynchings were outlawed, that it didn't serve as a deterrent and that violence by the government can only brutalize the people. Those prisoners on death row were not strangers to him. They were fellow human beings facing cold blooded murder by the state.
>
> There he stood the long night through, this busy and gifted man of literature and drama, without media fanfare, the lonely conscience of North Carolina, yet surely awakening the conscience of North Carolinians to this atrocity. Of two clear legacies we may be certain: The Lone Vigil has proliferated into crowded vigils at the prisons

on the night before executions following noon day vigils on the Capitol Square, and the organization . . . of North Carolinians Against the Death Penalty.[9]

His Lonely Vigil by slow degrees was transformed into the Great Vigil, and Paul Green began to hope for political processes to change the law. To his surprise, in 1972 the executions suddenly stopped as a result of *Furman v. Georgia,* a landmark decision by the U.S. Supreme Court. Green had not expected this judicial result, because the famously liberal and activist court dominated by Chief Justice Earl Warren was gone and the chambers now housed putatively conservative nominees sent there by President Nixon. Warren himself had retired in 1969 as chief justice and had been replaced by Warren Burger, the president's personal choice. In fact, on this *Furman* case the chief justice joined conservative justices William Rehnquist and Harry Blackmun and moderate justice Lewis Powell in dissent, but the majority opinion, written by William O. Douglas, stated that "imposition and carrying out of death penalty . . . [is here in these three cases] held to constitute cruel and unusual punishment in violation of Eighth and Fourteenth Amendments." Although none of these cases involved North Carolina, the *Furman* decision for the time being stopped all capital punishment in all states of the republic. Perhaps missed by Green and others opposed to the death penalty was an important clause holding out the possibility that individual states could reestablish capital punishment if their statutes did not leave trial proceedings and sentencing so completely at the discretion of juries.[10]

There would thus be no executions for at least several seasons, and the vigils would not be needed for the year 1973. All the same, serious political action was much needed, for Green soon realized that right-wing forces recently empowered in this era of Nixon's "law and order" were working fervently to produce a new North Carolina statute that would be in compliance with the Douglas statement of the five-to-four decision. The state's invalidated law dated to 1949, when juries were given full discretion to decide the penalty for murder and rape cases; and the Supreme Court, not entirely unlike Green, had been struck by the way white juries generally executed blacks convicted while generally sparing whites convicted in capital cases. Thus, by 1974 the North Carolina General Assembly took the discretion out of the hands of juries: in the new law, murder in the first degree carried a mandatory death sentence. The new law guaranteed many more executions than ever before. Green and his friends were stunned by their inability to stop, or even significantly slow down, the passage of the new statute. The political phase of appealing to the legislature was quickly over, having failed utterly.

There remained the legal approach, through appeals in the hope that the new North Carolina statute would be ruled unconstitutional; and of course it was terribly expensive to attempt such appeals, bringing top-drawer attorneys to argue cases to superior courts and someday the U.S. Supreme Court. Green went to work at once, badgering friends for funds, and an appeal was filed on behalf of newly convicted men by several groups, including Green's Pullen Church–sponsored North Carolinians against the Death Penalty. As the costly and sometimes tedious lawyers' processes made their way through appellate courts, Green was almost perfervid in pushing friends and allies to give money on behalf of the legal campaign. These efforts were successful on 31 March 1976, when the Supreme Court invalidated the 1974 state statute in the case *Woodson v. North Carolina*. Yet this legal victory too sounded its own hoot owl's portent, for it was a split decision that rearranged the players and suggested still another statute that might well carry some future coalition of justices on a profoundly divided court. The majority opinion was written by Potter Stewart and was supported by Lewis Powell and John Paul Stevens, and now the complaint was that there had been an overcorrection for the problem of jury discretion, namely, that now there was no way at all for a jury to consider mitigating circumstances in capital cases. Only Justices Brennan and Marshall, who filed separate opinions, continued to speak as if capital punishment in and of itself constituted cruel and unusual punishment.[11]

Green realized that it was again time for political action, for pressure on the state legislators in case those who wanted a death penalty regrouped themselves to write yet another statute. This time the money raising was harder, for various public opinion polls showed that the citizenry of the Old North State wanted a death penalty. With a steadiness and a sureness that Green could almost feel, the legislators studied the court's opinions and in 1977 brought forward another statute, this one separating jury processes into two steps, one to determine guilt or innocence on the basis of facts, and a discrete process in which the jury then reconvened to assess mitigating and aggravating circumstances in determining a sentence within guidelines to be explained in detail by the presiding judge. This statute passed, and it survived judicial review without being submitted to the Supreme Court.[12]

Now Green and his odd alliance of Raleigh Baptists and Chapel Hill civil rights people and others had to expand the role and function of North Carolinians against the Death Penalty. Now it was necessary to fight in political action for statutory revision and simultaneously to appeal case by case in the courts; and those legal appeals in every case proceeded on two routes, one raising questions about a jury's decision of guilt or innocence, the other raising questions about the appropriateness of the given decision in light of its circumstances. These parallel campaigns cost even more, and the mood in the nation was changing as states outside the South began reinstituting their own capital punishment statutes, until a majority of states had a death penalty by century's end. The racial angle, the mark of Jim Crow that to Green was almost a devil's talisman, was certainly still there, for it was far more likely that a black man convicted of murder would be executed than a white man, only now that was not a phenomenon peculiar to North Carolina or to the South but was found as well in Illinois, Connecticut, and New York. [13]

In the twilight of his life, Paul Green found things much as Paul Greene had found them, and the black man in North Carolina was the one who would be choked and strangled as some form of social control. It was back to the Vigil from 1978 until his final days, but at least now he stood in a crowd and not completely alone in his protest as the gas chambers did the work to execute the will of the people whose grandfathers had had to rely on the Ku Klux Klan to accomplish this public act.

As he kept vigil against the death penalty and in that campaign season saw hope, victory, and then crushing defeat, he also produced dramatic works and essays between 1966 and 1973. Three symphonic dramas were brought forward in his formula for celebrating the courage and obstinacy of ordinary folk by setting those melodramatic vignettes before tourists in natural, outdoor settings that were physically stunning: *Texas* he produced in 1966 and proffered in the Palo Duro Canyon; *Trumpet in the Land* he produced in 1970 and proffered in New Philadelphia, Ohio; and *Drumbeats in Georgia* he produced in 1973 and proffered out on Jekyll Island. As with other symphonic dramas besides *The Lost Colony,* these three kept his name before at least a few people, kept his playwriting and creative energies in motion, and "stabilized his income," the latter a bit more important as the movie scriptwriting career ended itself (as had been the case for some decades, it was his investments in land, leveraged with local bankers, that provided the bulk of the family wealth and security). [14]

He also dipped into old texts of his to produce two more volumes for the University of North Carolina Press. In 1968, he brought out *Words and Ways,* a book of folkloric observations, some of which he had collected in the 1920s; and in 1970 he brought out short stories entitled *Home to My Valley,* some of which he had started writing in the Paul Greene/Harvey Easom days. Both books reflected, albeit from a distance of long decades, the sweat of serious fieldwork rummaging through abandoned buildings and decades talking with—and listening to—"old warhorses" such as Dan Hugh McLean back in his beloved and doomed upper valley of the Cape Fear River. He kept at the tasks of writing, considerably tinkering with each book and with all of his plays, and with his diary, whose daily observations and brooding musings remained a most strenuous vocation. [15]

He surely needed these labors, because among other things they kept his mind away from the emerging literary trends loosely called postmodernism and poststructuralism. For these purposes, it is not particularly helpful to go into detail about these theories, except to note that a whole host of fine southern writers were working under the aegis of postmodernism, and Green did not like it. One so conscious of the author's power and responsibility simply could not begin to accept these new theories about reader response and audience response and the creative, or "writerly," power of readers and the near impossibility of getting anything across to readers. More relevant to Green, the tendency of many self-styled postmodernist literati to be coolly apolitical angered him, the more so as he stood vigil—with no accompanying postmodernist writers—on the Central Prison grounds while black men awaited execution. In 1969, when Samuel Beckett won the Nobel Prize, Green was not grand or gracious and was even a bit petty, writing embittered letters to his daughters Janet Green Catlin and Betsy Green Moyer: Beckett's postmodernist experiments with seriocomedy and sexuality Green found childish, trivial, and worst of all, utterly irrelevant to political injustices—and all of this from an Irishman living in a land famously wracked by injustices. Green, as Public Man, did not exhibit this pettiness, bordering on jealousy, in writing or in public venues; but he certainly unburdened himself of his full emotions in his correspondence.[16]

In the gray and dank early winter of 1975, Green's dark moods, always part of the chiaroscuro in his art work, suddenly became the dominant mood, and he fell into a clinical depression for which he eventually sought treatment in early February. Lib Green did what she usually did, using her quick wit and her genius for affecting the home setting (down to the little details of her clever arrangements of bright homegrown flowers strategically placed), to counterweight the drab humidity of a piedmont Carolina winter; but this was not the sort of blue funk that she had held at bay back in 1920 or again in 1932 and often since those episodes. This was instead an energy-sapping, physically taxing illness, perhaps related to earlier such funks, but if so only a kissing cousin of those sad moods that had damaged friendships but never slowed writing, sports, reading, or manual work. Bad as were those days in 1920 when he had gone off by himself to rethink the Great War and the failed love with Renée Boiscelleur, the depression of this February was worse. Never one to sleep much and intermittently wracked by those nightmares from World War I and from his mother's death, he had still been able in the past to go into a very deep sleep for at least a few hours. Now, however, he tossed in his bed before stumbling into nighttime naps, even those brief respites occurring close to the surface of consciousness and with frequent interruptions. Getting out of bed exhausted in the early morning, he would all but stagger along, mind groggy and body drained of energizing juices, soul heavy.[17]

No jokes helped much, and in fact his own penchant for witty bons mots turned against him, some clever remark of his own, spoken aloud or thought or only felt deep down, could effectively negate anything he tried to do. Work, most surprising of all, was no solace, for he simply could not work, not intellectually or creatively, but also now not even manually, in the yard or on the house. The long set of tennis, the hard swim, the vigorous hike, the wood-chopping sessions, the carpentry, even cutting the grass in front yard, these things that he had counted on to exhaust his body and thus wear out the blues, all these failed now. He did not have the energy to attempt them. He was becoming a Samuel Beckett character, and the gall and the wormwood of that twist in his life's plot could not have been lost on him. Nothing that he did seemed to matter, and he was often paralyzed into inactivity by the emotional disorder: he who had listened so patiently to children and relatives and colleagues about their anxious times of ennui had never imagined what those emotions actually felt like until they shot a hole in his own soul.

At last he went to a doctor, was treated, and evidently acquired some antide-pressant drugs. More important, he began to talk, and Lib Green began to talk, with the children and with his sister Erma Green Gold. And that brought back Janet Green Catlin toward center stage, for at last he needed her, this often sick and troubled daughter, to tell him what was going on. By 1975 Janet Catlin was an accomplished academic married to Jack Catlin, a professor of the classics at the University of Oklahoma, and the couple were out in Norman. Warned by her sister Nancy Byrd Green that their Doogie was in clinical depression, Janet Catlin wrote to her father to let him know an insider's account of his near-term future. Her words are plain and the sentence structure as lean as any of her father's movie scripts; the message was powerful and yet touching too. Drugs would not actually help much, she warned, for their slightly meliora-tive effects were slow to come. The pain would be surprisingly acute; indeed, she insisted that the sharp stabbing pains she had endured while delivering Doogie's granddaughter Jennifer Catlin were nothing compared to the bodily aches and pains of clinical depression. Time would move at a plodding pace that defied credulity, and the wake-up bell of his internal alarm clock would sound itself earlier and earlier, leaving the victim no choice but to lie, sleepless and workless and afraid of the coming day in the darkest hours before dawn. Dawn itself, even on bright sunny days, would be a curse, bringing the frus-trating realization that the victim would not be able to lose himself even in activities that once he loved to do.[18]

Jan Catlin's words sank to the bottom of his gut and lay there heavy and troubling as a bad meal. She had accurately described the very things that were already happening to him, and he could review her own personal history. A bright and gifted student, she had had to postpone graduate studies during one especially difficult phase of clinical depression. Effectively, the damnable dis-ease had slowed and occasionally stopped her activities for years. Here he was eighty years old, and he might not have years in which to recover. Fortunately, Jan could offer practical advice from that insider's file of memories. But even as Paul Green came slowly out of the trough of depression, his daughter Jan was ever the little girl artist overwhelmed by the great man Doogie, who had often judged her harshly; and thus she stuttered these lines and halted her advice with apologies for those inadequacies of hers first and most notably marked by her father himself. It was much like the young and adoring artists who shied away from telling him that his symphonic dramas were not particularly good art. *Hanh!* as the playwright often interjected in his characters' dialogue. Here he needed desperately to receive practical advice, and his own past actions were intimidating the bearer of the remedies. Five previous decades had so intimidated this witness, this survivor. Crooked hand, crooked glove, the punitive sentence fit because of Paul Green's own nature.[19]

To these words of advice Jan Catlin's husband Jack added the briefest note, printed carefully around his wife's letterhead. The professor said that he hoped "Doog" would soon be well. He said that he and Jan would be down in May to visit. Jack even said that the coming springtime with its colors and fresh smells might be what his father-in-law needed to revive himself. This trivia! And from the classics scholar son-in-law who usually went volley for volley in word games and idea matches with the playwright. Could it be that now young scholars were intimidated not by his reputation and very presence, but because they *felt sorry* for him?[20]

Clinical depression cannot really be fixed, of course, because it is a disease and not a failure of will or a character flaw. It can be treated, and if Fortuna's wheel spins the right way, then the victim can emerge, bruised and numbed and still tired and weak but with the chance to do the next good thing on a daily basis if he can keep that perspective, much as is required of a recovering alcoholic. Green was reasonably well treated, and he needed those letters from his daughter, the survivor of this monstrous besieger. She even invested in a long-distance telephone call, a rare expense for the Catlin family in that day; she knew how good it would be for Doogie to hear everybody's voices, especially that of his granddaughter Jen. He was touched at the depths, and he saluted his child for her understanding and her compassion. Perhaps for the first time he took her ideas seriously; certainly it appears to be the first time he *told her* that he took her ideas seriously, and told her that he needed her. Bearing her advice, he was able to inform her in the early spring that he made himself write at least a little every day, and he understood now that that bit of writing was an accomplishment for which he must give thanks. He told her too of his pleasure in the now-flowering *Pirus japonica* that he and Mimi Lib Green had planted, as well as his anticipation of the modest garden—peas, lettuce, onions, and radishes—that the onetime champion cotton farmer had sowed.[21]

As his Bible told him in Ecclesiastes passages that he loved to read and to quote, there are seasons, and they do pass. By June he could return to playwriting and protesting and hosting the young writers and hosting the young reformists, and he was again the liberals' Public Man in North Carolina. It would never be the same, however, for now he moved about and had his being in a new world in which there were numbing reminders of how physically overwhelming clinical depression could be. There was a half-life to such episodes, and his dark moods would come back, but apparently never again with the stabbing, sapping, wracking agonies of February 1975.

Withal, he was loyal to his UNC despite his occasional harsh judgments that no one there worked for justice any more. Once his sister Erma had suggested that perhaps he could receive better treatment from the far more richly endowed hospital at Duke University than he was getting at his alma mater's university medical center. He forcibly told her that he was a Carolina Tarheel and was not going over to treated and handled by people at Duke.[22] Recovered sufficiently to get out of bed most days, he faced the challenges of his remaining years in a world that was artistically postmodern and disdained his work. More than that, this was a world that stood out toward social issues in a way not so much right wing as coolly apolitical. Now he knew that his ability to fight in that world could be withdrawn at any moment: by a heart attack and death, by the even crueler recurrence of clinical depression.

He climbed onto his tractor to plow, he swung the great ax to chop cords of wood, he wrote letters, he wrote plays, he made his Vigil at Central Prison. He argued with friends at his state university that Carolina was not doing enough to bring true integration to his campus, despite the storied accomplishments of some notable African American students. He did not sleep well, but he slept well enough. He did not feel well, but he felt well enough. He was still Paul Green, there were still problems in the land, and there was still a prize in the sky. Legal segregation was gone and dead and even forgotten. But real segregation, especially a segregation of color and wealth, was still in the land. Real integration, of real opportunity, was still far to seek, but it was harder to explain.

Some members of the family insist that there never was an episode of clinical depression, despite the telling correspondence and the hospital stay. Some friends too never talk of the episode. It was a different era, and there were still those who would look at the disease not as a treatable disease but as a cowardly retreat; and of course at some level the family and friends are right, for Paul Green knew nothing of cowardice. In any case, his trip to the hospital and his absence for a few months were followed not only by renewed activities of reformism and writing, but also by renewed career recognitions from allies and admirers. In 1976 the UNC Press issued *Land of Nod and Other Stories,* and the appearance of that volume of retooled short stories is both testament to his determined recuperation and to the respect he was accorded in some circles in Chapel Hill. In that same bicentennial year, the long-struggling *Common Glory* had disappeared from Williamsburg performances, but there were three more symphonic dramas, once again melodramas set for tourists in stunning outdoor environments: *The Louisiana Cavalier* in Natchitoches; *We the People* in Columbia, Maryland; and, in June 1977 *The Lone Star,* "a symphonic drama of the Texas Struggle for Independence," performed in the Galveston Island State Park.[23]

As for the official career recognitions, there were three very large ones. In 1978 the North Carolina Writers Conference, which he had helped to start, gave him their first NCWC Award. It was a marvelous evening, one that set the stage for the way other prominent writers would be honored in future years by that group. Writers read aloud from his plays to small groups, his many books were on display for sale, and in the evening a string of prominent writers and critics from Thad Stem to Sam Ragan to John Ehle to Betty Hodges stood to "roast" him for his various foibles but then concluded their remarks with sincere praise. All of them, of course, were saluting his political courage and guidance fully as much as his artistic achievements; but on this evening there were no postmodernists, only professionals grateful for the great art of another era.

In 1978 his university unveiled a large, somewhat pie-shaped wedge of a dramatic arts building, and this not particularly attractive thing thrust its way from the red-brick classical buildings of the old campus toward the cemetery where lay Frank Graham and Horace Williams—and a plot for Paul and Lib Green. Other new buildings in the same area were equally ugly, and what mattered here was that the building was acoustically sound, spacious—and named for Paul Eliot Green. No Paul Green plays have ever been performed there, and a modest exhibit of his hat and cloak and Pulitzer Prize has been removed, and so the tribute has its limits; but at the very least the most prominent playwright to emerge from UNC does have a building named for him.

In 1979 the North Carolina General Assembly, a collective body so often besieged by the crusading Chapel Hillian, designated Paul Green the North Carolina Dramatist Laureate in ceremonies that even his right-wing opponents were happy to join. If it was approaching the time to leave the stage, he appeared ready to do so with the crowd feeling good about his character if not his increasingly unpopular causes.

There remained one personality and one set of issues with which to conjure, and it was paramount for an eastern countryman: Would Jesse Helms and Paul Green necessarily be enemies as well as opponents? Was there one last chance to be grand and gracious and very southern with a foe? Certainly, they remained in opposition, defying each other in public even after the gunslinging showdown in 1963 about university speech and Communist visitors. Green had written several public letters about nuclear disarmament, and Helms the television personality had responded with heat in defense of a nuclear arms buildup. This debate and the public posturing between the two intensified after Jesse Helms won election to the Senate and could actually vote, and eventually sit as chair on committees concerned with foreign affairs. Yet for all their right-wing and left-wing opposition as Public Men engaged in controversies about policy and polity, they were yet each country boys and inheritors of older traditions. The general rule, quoting the Celts who could never practice it in Ireland, was to disagree agreeably, and the past master of such agreeable disagreement had been Doc Graham. Of course, if disputes became too personal—easy to do in a subregion where personal relations are everything—then very old codes of conduct suggested a relentless and escalating bitter contest of personal re-criminations. Many a political dispute had eventually become acrimonious and finally barbaric, and neither man wanted such a thing to happen in this case.

The two arranged in May of 1980 to meet out on Old Lystra Road at Windy Oaks. The announced occasion was a discussion about the enduring and long-lived things in their native Carolina countryside, the folksongs, the folklore, the habits, the food, the folkways that predated any real conception of politics. Jesse Helms was curious about some traditional ballads and about a short-story plot and what happened to the heroine of some old story. By 1980 the senator was in tall cotton indeed, leader of the rapidly ascending southern Republicans who were assured of presidential victory the following November; but more than that, he was symbol of intellectual conservatism, once beneath disdain on university campuses but now with its own think tanks and publishing houses and academic conferences and sessions. As for Paul Green, his art was not only passé, but his politics was musty and moldering, and the word *liberal* was itself becoming something beneath disdain.

The two could have talked about the sound and fury of recent North Carolina politics, for their leadership roles in respective wings of contending parties entailed much about which to talk. Indeed the blues singer reminded both that there were costs to pay for being the boss. More keen than any interest in discussing the day's politics was their intense desire to do the right thing by traditional manners of gentlemanly conduct. After all, each was now in Green's own words, an old war horse. They sang songs and looked at books and swapped tales and memories and transported themselves one hundred miles southeast and half a hundred years ago. If the blues singer reminded them of one set of realities, the playwright reminded them of still another truth:

> We two alone will sing like birds i' the cage:
> When thou dost ask me blessing, I'll kneel down,
> And ask of thee forgiveness: so we'll live,
> And pray and sing, and tell old tales, and laugh
> At gilded butterflies, and hear poor rogues
> Talk of court news; and we'll talk with them too—
> Who loses, and who wins; who's in, who's out;
> And take upon's the mystery of things
> As if we were God's spies.[24]

EPILOGUE

By the planting season of 1981 Paul Eliot Green had certainly fulfilled a prophecy. It was not exactly his mother's. It was yet again very different from his own radical prophecy that he conceived in the years between the end of World War I and the depths of the Great Depression. Rather it was the prophecy of Horace Williams that his student would become a new Isaiah and provide a *new view of religion*. The professor understood that this religion would not be particularly recognizable to those in any organized church, and he even understood that his chosen prophet would deny often that he was undertaking any such task. Horace Williams scarcely cared whether his chosen prophet gave him any credit or blame, just as Bettie Lorine Byrd Green scarcely cared whether her chosen prophet gave her any credit or blame. These two strong-willed people had chosen him and commanded that he act. They knew that he would do it.

Within the patterns of prophecy, it seems entirely fitting that Paul Green had rejected the call before. He has been as scornful of Horace Williams's call as Saul of Tarsus had been of the first call from the followers of Jesus. To Lib Green and to fellow writers, Green had insisted that organized religion was dead, and that it was *art* that was needed and art that deserved a new view. Indeed, over the decades, he had not only scorned Horace Williams's ideas; he had become disdainful of Horace Williams the man. For all that, the prophecy that he now fulfilled was none other than the Hegelian vision of his old professor and colleague, and the spirit of his late mentor must have been pleased to recognize that Green was doing what it seemed he could do way back in 1919. Despite his intentionality, Green could not move many people with his art. Yet he was the most spiritualistic force in the Old North State, and there was power indeed in his public campaigns.

In his public statements Green spoke most loudly and most often against damnable Jim Crow. He tried to preach against segregation in a number of plays, most notably *The Lost Colony,* but his best plays were no longer performed and his most successful play seemed to hit audiences in another place, no matter what he tried. Instead, he was more effective when he himself stood on the public stage and took a stand on a social issue, and he was most effective of all when the issue was the need for racial integration. When the de jure segregation was finally laid to rest, he realized that the de facto segregation that operated in capital punishment was fully as profound an enemy, and so he stayed on the stage trying to get the audience to understand.

His many public gestures, from the stand on the theater stage against the segregation rope to his Vigil at Central Prison, all brought off in the most melodramatic fashion, stayed in the memory of many people, not least then-young John Ehle, who memorialized the Chapel Hill civil rights movement in *The Free Men*. There were many other such writer-reformists in North Carolina who could recall Paul Green's preachments in the long wave of civil rights reformism in which he lived and moved and had his being, as he read the words aloud in his prayer book at the Chapel of the Cross and as he repeated at gatherings of reformist ministers who swore that this professing nonreligionist surely knew his Bible—and surely knew how to preach. Indeed, Sam Ragan, Thad Stem, Walter Spearman, Betty Smith, Betty Hodges and others joined Ehle in their dedication to their prophet, and these formed a talented and influential second generation of the state's literary renaissance—as they also formed a living and moving memory for the state's third generation of superb writers who have been less exercised about social reform.

Oh, Green's art had been honored well enough: the 1925 Belasco Cup; the 1927 Pulitzer Prize; five times in the book *Best Plays on Broadway;* the 1952 Sir Walter Raleigh Award for Outstanding Literary Achievement; the 1965 North Carolina Award for Literature; the 1978 NCWC Award; the Paul Eliot Green Theater in the same year; and in 1979 Dramatist Laureate of North Carolina.

More important than these celebratory awards was the acknowledgment by younger writers of his influence on them. And it was not solely the kind of acknowledgment that comes from gazing idolatrously at a living statue, although there was some of that and Green was not entirely averse to being so treated. No, there was also the recognition by masters that he was their mentor. Those bold experiments in drama in the 1920s and 1930s still worked their influence, and the aging craftsman could still wield a usefully mean editorial blue pencil.

The surviving correspondence, and the memories of his contemporaries, do not show any friendly critic offering Green such constructive help in his mature years. Perhaps that was the nature of his role after 1941. Indeed, in the fullness of time, it seems entirely likely that the literary critic will record Ehle, Smith, and the entire second generation of North Carolina literary renaissance figures as artists far, far more accomplished than Green—the discerning critic may even conclude that Green's very best path-breaking work of the 1920s and 1930s does not stand up well against *any* of the work of those who followed. Nevertheless, the historian must record that every fine Tarheel writer practicing the craft today has in some way benefited from Paul Green's going before them and attempting to do what he attempted to do.

On 4 May 1981 Paul Eliot Green worked on his correspondence, writing a note to Shelby Stevenson at Pembroke State University, an institution serving the Lumbees of Robeson County, whom Green still occasionally called *wandering Croatans*. He wrote in his diary. He dug around in the dirt of his small farm. He operated his tractor. He parked his tractor. He closed the shed door.

Every movement, every word written, every word uttered, was part of his routine. The routine could be a character's, or it could be his. Mostly the routines were from Harvey Easom, the creator creature of Paul Greene whom Paul Green was permitted by Lib Green to retain, probably because she still loved all three men. A theorist could say that he was thus living the life of the postmodern man, radically subjective, shaped as much by audience as by authorial self. He had dealt with binary and bimodal antitheses in his art, and these were now doubted, described as only things that he had created in his own discourse. His Hegelianism was not enough to capture and make sense of his own contradictions. He was told that his irony turned as often back on himself and on his causes as on his intended targets.

As it was marked before, there was in fact nothing that postmodernist Samuel Beckett—the Irish Nobel laureate whose work Green loathed with a truly impressive passion—there was nothing that Beckett understood that Green did not understand, and he hated that. Hated it enough to spit. Hated it enough, even, to whine. And the gentleman-farmer paterfamilias should never whine, as he and Senator Jesse Helms fully agreed.

And yet an idealist and an absolutist is never truly radically subjective. His actual being certainly has nothing to do with the opinions of theorists outside him. While postmodernism was moving forward, its practitioners and savants disdainful of Green's art, it is no less the case that he in his own being moved forward as if postmodernism was irrelevant to him. He did not have time for postmodernism. This man cared. This man fought. This man wrote, sang, loved, plowed, hurt, killed men in battle, stood up for causes. This man lost as often as he won, and in the classical sense of *arete,* he was fully joined in the honorable struggle in which the final score is not important at all, for it is not even kept.

This man created the role of Chapel Hill's liberal on behalf of civil rights. He acted it on stage, taught it to others, and left it there in the script if anyone wants to pick up the script and read it and act the part again. This man sought justice. Like his namesake, as his beloved mother willed it and as the much-resented Horace Williams willed it, he saw the prize in the sky and he staggered toward it. He never caught it, and the coolly discerning can now laugh at his clumsiness in the effort, for he was clumsy indeed. Some would say that there is no prize in the sky, and some would have it there is not even any sky. Yet these have no more proof for what they say than did Paul Green in his clumsy idealism. There is a nobility in his mighty, if futile, efforts that seems worth remembering because someone out there should imitate it. The script is left behind and is available for that day when others in Chapel Hill decide that injustice is wrong and that the prize is still there in the sky.

All of it, every bit of it, was with him on 4 May 1981. Ecclesiastes was even more true this day than most days:

> The river flows into the sea,
>   And the sea is not full.

He lay down to take a nap. He did not get up.

NOTES

INTRODUCTION

1 Jean A. N. C. de Condorcet, "The Progress of the Human Mind," 1790. I use the translation by Stephen J. Gendzier of an expanded version as reprinted in *Introduction to Contemporary Civilization in the West: A Source Book,* vol. 1, ed. Staff of Columbia College, 3d rev. ed. (New York: Columbia University Press, 1960), 1088–1102. The "special assignment" phrase comes from Max Ascoli (1898–1978), founder and most prominent editor of the quintessential liberal magazine *The Reporter,* published from 1949 to 1968. See Ascoli, "Farewell to Our Readers," *Reporter,* 13 June 1968, p. 18.

2 Interviews, Erma Green Gold (hereinafter EGG, 1 and 8 April 1991, John Herbert Roper Papers, Southern Historical Collection, University of North Carolina, Chapel Hill.

3 Betty Smith, *A Tree Grows in Brooklyn* (1943; reprint, New York: HarperCollins, 1993), and *Joy in the Morning* (1963; reprint, New York: HarperCollins, 1993); John Ehle, *The Journey of August King* (New York: Harper and Row, 1971), and *The Free Men* (New York: Harper and Row, 1965).

4 Phil. 3:12–16, 4:14.

CHAPTER 1. A HARNETT BOY

1 Interview, Laurence Green Avery, 25 August 1993, Roper Papers; Laurence Green Avery, ed., *A Southern Life: Letters of Paul Green, 1916–1981* (Chapel Hill: University of North Carolina Press, 1994), introduction. Interview, Mary Green Johnson (hereinafter MGJ) with Paul Eliot Green Jr., 14 July 1984, typescript in possession of Betsy Green Moyer (hereinafter BGM), copy in Roper Papers. U.S. Department of Commerce, Bureau of the Census, Manuscript Census, 1840, Cumberland County Northern District (N.C.); 1850, Cumberland County Northern District (N.C.); 1860, Harnett County (N.C.); 1870, Harnett County (N.C.). For purposes of this biography, the Greene family name will be Greene, and Paul Green will be Paul Greene until 1922, when he changed his own name and the family generally followed suit.

2 Eccles. 1:7.

3 Physical descriptions from Paul Eliot Green (hereinafter PEG) in PEG to George W. Lay, 6 December 1922, and in several versions of a poem concerning her death, original, first line "My mother sleeps upon the hill," and carbon copy of revision, numbered 22, both in "Book of Verses," Paul Eliot Green Papers, Southern Historical Collection, University of North Carolina, Chapel Hill. The original poem appears to have been written in 1918 or 1919, the revision in 1920. See also interview, MGJ, 14 July 1984, Roper Papers.

4 Interview, MGJ, 14 July 1984, Roper Papers.

5 "Order for the Administration of the Lord's Supper: Prayer," *Book of Common Prayer* (1789; rev. ed., Philadelphia: George W. Jacobs, 1929), 83.

6 PEG often wrote about God, spirituality, and religion, often with references to fundamentalists and Calvinists of the sandhills. Particularly revealing, especially of childhood experiences, is a lengthy and provocative, almost confessional, letter to his father-in-law, himself an ordained Episcopal minister and school administrator: PEG to George W. Lay, 6 December 1922, Green Papers.

7 Ibid.; "Paul Green: Cotton Picker, Professor, and Pulitzer Winner," *New York Evening Post,* 7 May 1927, p. 1. This clipping, preserved by critic and friend Montrose Jonas Moses, is a reprint of a letter from PEG to his agent, Barret Harper Clark, in response to a request for publicity information; it was published in full when PEG won the Pulitzer Prize and also published as the introduction to the 1927 printing of *In Abraham's Bosom.*

8 "Paul Green: Cotton Picker." Median slaveholding for this region of North Carolina in 1860 census was 25 slaves; the median for the entire state was 18.6. In 1860, 27.4 percent of slaveowners held 1–9 slaves; 24.4 percent, 10–19; 29.7 percent, 20–49; and 18.6 percent, 50 or more. Planters were considered to hold at least 10 slaves, and "large planters" or "big planters" held at least 20 slaves. Figures are slightly different for other regions in other eras. Lewis Cecil Gray, *History of Agriculture in the Southern United States to 1860* (Washington, D.C.: U.S. Government Printing Office, 1929), 1:530–32, esp. tables 9 and 10.

9 Gray, *History of Agriculture,* 520–32. Interviews, MGJ, 13 July 1984, Roper Papers; MGJ with Laurence Green Avery, 5 April 1985, typescript in the possession of Avery; Avery, 10 July 1990, Roper Papers. PEG to Lay, 6 December 1922, and PEG to James G. W. MacClamroch, 25 February 1950, concerning possible membership in the Sons of the Revolution, Green Papers.

10 Bureau of the Census, Manuscript Census, 1870, Harnett County (N.C.).

11 Ibid.

12 PEG, diary, vol. 6 [5], 13 August 1928; see correspondence with William Archibald Greene, 1916–22, Hugh Greene, esp. 1928–38, and Elizabeth Lay, esp. 1921–28, Green Papers.

13 It should be noted that PEG's surviving children, the scholar Laurence Green Avery, and two onetime executives with the Paul Green Foundation, Rhoda Wynn and Marsha Warren, all dispute any evidence of clinical depression in PEG at any time in his life; see esp. BGM et al. to Jack Roper, 11 January 1993, Roper Papers. Yet the evidence is very much there in the diaries and in the correspondence. For diary instances see vol. 2, 2 September 1917, 4 November 1917; vol. 6, April 1929; and numerous entries during the Guggenheim trip to Berlin, 1928–29. See also PEG to Elizabeth Lay Green (hereinafter ELG), November 1943; Jan [Janet Green Catlin, hereinafter referred to as JGC] to "Dearest Doogie," 12 February 1975; JGC to "Doogie," 16 February 1975; and PEG's response, 20 February 1975, Green Papers.

14 See diary, vols. 1–6, Green Papers; PEG to George Lay, 6 December 1922, Green Papers; and interviews, MGJ, 14 July 1984, and EGG, 1 and 8 April 1991, Roper Papers.

15 Interview, BGM, 31 October 1989, typescript notes, Roper Papers; interview, MGJ, 14 July 1984, Roper Papers; PEG to George Lay, 6 December 1922, Green Papers.

16 Interviews, BGM, 31 October 1989, and MGJ, 14 July 1984, Roper Papers; Moyer describes herself and the other children as thinking the story "a great bore," since they heard it often from their father; Johnson describes in some detail her sense of filling the role of the mother for the favored child after 1908.

17 Ibid. Roper, "Paul Green in Dreams and Diaries," address, PEG Centennial/UNC Bicentennial, 17 March 1994, Chapel Hill.

18 PEG to George Lay, 6 December 1922, Green Papers; interviews, Laurence Green Avery, 10 July 1990, and MGJ, 14 July 1984, Roper Papers; MGJ, 5 April 1985, in the possession of Avery. See also correspondence, esp. with Elizabeth Lay, 1920–22, Green Papers.

19 PEG to George Lay, 6 December 1922, Green Papers; interviews, Laurence Green Avery, 10 July 1990, and MGJ, 14 July 1984, Roper Papers; MGJ, 5 April 1985, in the possession of Avery; diary, passim, but esp. vols. 1–6; "Paul Green, Cotton Picker"; and Jonathan Daniels, "American Antaeus," *Pembroke Magazine* 10 (1978): 1–10, North Carolina Collection, Louis Round Wilson Library, University of North Carolina, Chapel Hill.

20 Interview, Daniel Stewart with Laurence Green Avery, 23 April 1988, in the possession of Avery.

21 Correspondence, 1916–22; diary, vols. 1–6, Green Papers.

22 Diary, vol. 1, passim, Green Papers; PEG to George Lay, 6 December 1922, Green Papers; "Paul Green, Cotton Picker."

23 *Campbell College Creek Pebbles,* 24 January 1931, Green Papers.

24 Ibid.; PEG to George Lay, 6 December 1922, Green Papers; Samuel Talmadge Ragan, "Southern Accent," *Southern Pines Pilot,* 12 October 1983, B1.

25 Ibid.; PEG to Hubbard Fulton Page, 4 January 1931, enclosure of manuscript with dedicatory letter; and Grayson Biggs to PEG, 8 June 1930, Green Papers.

26 See diary, vols. 1–6, Green Papers; "Harvey Easom Diaries," "Harvey Easom Poems," ca. 1916–26, Green Papers.

27 Mark 4:11a, 25a.

28 Interview, MGJ, 14 July 1984.

29 Ibid.; diary, vols. 1–6, esp. 1916, PEG.

30 Ragan, "Southern Accent"; PEG to George W. Lay, 6 December 1922, PEG; Noel Yancey, "A Hero Named Horace," clipping, n.d., in possession of Samuel Talmadge Ragan and shared with author.

31 Interview, MGJ, 14 July 1984.

CHAPTER 2. CHAPEL HILL

1 PEG to Mary Greene, [fall 1916], Green Papers; on young PEG's sexual escapades, see esp. first 6 vols. of the PEG diary. Concerning mature PEG's sexual escapades, see PEG diary, from vol. 7; observations about PEG by Kurt Weill and Lotte Lenya, *Speak Low (When You Speak Love): The Letters of Kurt Weill and Lotte Lenya,* ed. Lys Symonette and Kim H. Kowelke (Berkeley and Los Angeles: University of California Press, 1996); and interviews, Shelby Stephenson, 30 July 1986, 30 July 1987, Roper Papers; Alice Denham, in her unpublished memoirs, describes her relationship with PEG when he was her teacher in the 1950s: notes on "Shabby Genteel" (manuscript), Roper Papers.

2 Kemp Plummer Battle, *History of the University of North Carolina,* vol. 2, *1868–1912* (Raleigh, N.C.: Edwards and Broughton, 1912), 764–73; see also Moses' correspondence with PEG, 1917–1938, Green Papers; and Montrose Jonas Moses Papers, Manuscript Department, Perkins Library, Duke University, Durham, N.C., esp. Scrapbook, 1918–35. Specific quote in Noel Yancey, "A Hero Named Horace," *Southern Pines Pilot,* clipping in possession of Ragan; Cornelia Phillips Spencer, *Selected Papers of Cornelia Phillips Spencer,* ed. with introd., by Louis Round Wilson (Chapel Hill: University of North Carolina Press, 1953), esp. 218–21, 234.

3 Thomas Wolfe, *Look Homeward, Angel* (New York: Charles Scribner and Sons, 1929), 593.

4 Williams, "An Examination of Paul's Epistle to the Hebrews Compared to Paulinism," ms. copy of doctoral thesis, 1888, Williams Papers.

5 Williams, "Hegel's Philosophy of Religion," notes, ca. 1888; Notebook, ca. 1888; "Philosophy 10," 1928; "Notes for Graduate Students," 1935, Williams Papers.

6 Williams, "The Evolution of Logic," ca. 1910, typescript version of a textbook now out of print; "The Third Problem of Logic," 1935 typescript version of essentially same ms. he wrote in 1923; see correspondence with Ralph Moore Harper, 1923–35, including Harper's marginal notations concerning Williams's unwillingness to revise for publication, Williams Papers.

7 Yancey, "A Hero Named Horace"; Battle, *University of North Carolina,* 2:764–73; Wolfe, *Look Homeward, Angel,* 593.

8 Edward Kidder Graham Papers, President's Papers, 1914–17, University Archives, Louis Round Wilson Library, University of North Carolina, Chapel Hill (hereinafter UNC Archives).

9 PEG, diary, vols. 1–6, 1917–19; and "Notes on Paris," 1919, copybook, Green Papers.

10 PEG, "Notes on Paris."

11 Ibid.; cf. Laurence Green Avery, interview with Daniel Stewart, 23 April 1988, transcript in the possession of Avery. Stewart, who played on semiprofessional sandhills teams with young PEG, was convinced that PEG had enough talent to make it to the major leagues.

12 "Buies Creek Club" and "Harnett Club," college lists on envelopes in "Notes on Paris," 1919; PEG to Mary Greene, [spring 1917]; diary, vol. 6, 10 June 1935, Green Papers.

13 See chap. 1 concerning melancholia, the blues, and depression; correspondence with JGC, 12, 16, 17, and 20 February 1975, Green Papers; interviews, EGG, 7 and 14 March 1991. The PEG diaries, esp. the first five vols., often have passages in which he describes himself being unable to work or to do much else because of "the blues" or "melancholia" or "melancholy," his language for the early spells of what would become deep clinical depression in 1975. On Allan Dunn, see diary, vol. 2, 19 August 1917, Green Papers.

14 W. Aldis Wright, ed., *The Rubáiyát of Omar Khayyám, Rendered into English by Edward Fitzgerald,* 5th rev. ed. (Boston: Houghton, Mifflin, 1884).

15 Ibid., stanza 27.

16 Ibid., quotes from stanzas 25, 23, and 12.

17 Ibid., quote from stanza 8; diary, vol. 2, 19 August 1917 and passim.

18 Diary, vol. 8, [September] 1934; passage noted by Laurence Green Avery, Avery to Roper, with enclosure, "Introduction" draft, [June] 1991, Roper Papers. See also Avery, *A Southern Life,* iii–xxv.

19 Tennyson, "To E. Fitzgerald," in *Rubáiyát of Omar Khayyám,* ed. Wright, 323–34.

20 As cited in Fitzgerald, "Omar Khayyám, the Astronomer-Poet," in *Rubáiyát of Omar Khayyám,* ed. Wright, 37–64.

21 Ibid.; diary, vol. 2, 19 August 1917.

22 John Masefield, *The Collected Poems of John Masefield* (New York: Macmillan, 1916, 1917).

23 Ibid.; for Masefield's influence on PEG, see "Loose Poems," 1920s, folder, also "Notes on Paris," 1919; "Daffodil Fields," in Masefield, *Collected Poems.*

24 Phrases from verses by McNeill, "Sunburnt Boys." These phrases, and stanzas from "Autumn," "The Ploughboy at New Year," and "Old Spring Hill," are reprinted in *The*

Pocket John Charles McNeill, ed. Grace Evelyn Gibson (Laurinburg, N.C.: St. Andrews Press, 1990).

25 "The Ploughboy at New Year," in *The Pocket John Charles McNeill.*

26 PEG to Mary Greene, [spring 1917]; PEG to George W. Lay, 6 December 1922, Green Papers.

27 On Hegelianism in racial and other social consciousnesses, esp. on southern university campuses, see Joel Randolph Williamson, *The Crucible of Race: Black-White Relations in the American South since Emancipation* (New York: Oxford University Press, 1984). Such Hegelianism is especially apparent at the then-new University of the South at Sewanee, whose architecture as well as curriculum was designedly Germanic, see William Alexander Percy, *Lanterns on the Levee,* introd. by Walker Percy (1941; reprint, Baton Rouge: Louisiana State University Press, 1973).

28 Correspondence, 1914–17, Green Papers.

29 Comer Vann Woodward, *The Origins of the New South, 1877–1913* (Baton Rouge: Louisiana State University Press, 1951), 369–72; George Brown Tindall, *The Emergence of the New South, 1913–1945* (Baton Rouge: Louisiana State University Press, 1967).

30 See Joseph Hyde Pratt Papers, 1915–20, Southern Historical Collection, University of North Carolina, Chapel Hill.

31 Ibid., 1917, esp. boxes 12 and 13.

32 Pratt to State Councils of Defense, blind copy to files, 28 May 1917; Pratt to Yale Graduates, blind copy to files, 20 July 1917, Pratt Papers.

33 I learned this story authoritatively as PEG's own from Rhoda Wynn at a meeting of the Paul Green Foundation in 1991 in which we discussed the playwright's wartime diaries and verses. PEG often told Wynn, his personal secretary and executor of his papers, that he marched across campus to enlist immediately after hearing a speech about the war. See notes on foundation meeting, 1991, Roper Papers. However, the diary record tells a different story. Cf. diary, vol. 1, 1917, and also John Herbert Roper, ed., *Paul Green's War Songs: A Southerner Looks at the Great War* (Rocky Mount: North Carolina Wesleyan College Press, 1984).

34 Laurence Green Avery, editor of PEG's published correspondence and president of the Paul Green Foundation, told me in June 1989 about John Greene's role in this episode. Avery discussed John Greene's "shadowy" figure and his complex family role; Avery pointed me to areas of correspondence, diary notes, and particularly his own interview with PEG's sister MGJ: Notes on Dr. Avery, 1989–90, Roper Papers. Correspondence between PEG, Hugh Greene, and John Greene, 1917–37, corroborates this point, but only with the perspective gained from Avery thanks to his interviews with PEG's sister MGJ.

35 McNeill, "On the Cape Fear," in *The Pocket John Charles McNeill,* 31.

CHAPTER 3. THE GREAT WAR

1 Diary, vol. 2, 16 July 1917; vol. 2, 1917, Green Papers. For much more detail about PEG's wartime record, see Roper, *Paul Green's War Songs,* esp. edited poems and "Notes on the Poet Soldier"; see also Pratt Papers, 1917–20; the colonel kept his own notes but also filed a number of official reports of the campaigns, complete with maps and charts.

2 PEG plays: *Johnny Johnson* (1937); *Trumpet in the Land* (1972); *The Seventeenth Star* (1953); *We the People* (1976); *The Confederacy* (1959).

3 Diary, vol. 2, 24, 26, and 27 July 1917, Green Papers.

4 Diary, vol. 2, 27, 30, and 19 July 1917, Green Papers; BGM to Roper, 11 January 1993, with enclosure, photocopy of frontispiece of Greene's *Wooley's,* Roper Papers, volume itself is in family's possession.

5 Diary, vol. 2, 15 August 1917; see also diary, vol. 2, 2 August 1917, Green Papers.

6 See Roper, "Notes on the Poet Soldier."

7 "Thoughts and Verses in the Army," [probably December] 1917, Green Papers.

8 See diary, vol. 2, Green Papers; see Roper, "Notes on the Poet Soldier," 97–115.

9 Roper, "Notes on the Poet Soldier," 97–115.

10 Ibid.

11 Ibid; see also PEG to Mary Greene, fragment, winter 1919 and 31 March 1918, and diary, vol. 1, March 1918, Green Papers.

12 See "The Other Night I Saw a Little Girl in a First Class Metro Car (on a Paris Subway)," "Strolling along Boulevard Haussman," "The Making of a Bolshevist," and "Le Viel Omnibus," in *Paul Green's War Songs,* ed. Roper, 71–77; Roper, "Notes on the Poet Soldier," 136–37, 149–53.

13 Diary, vol. 3, 3 July–11 November 1918; notes on the war, boxes 12 and 13, 1917–20, Pratt Papers.

14 Paul Fussell, *The Great War and Modern Memory* (New York: Oxford University Press, 1975), 42–52; quotation on 45.

15 John Ehle, "Paul Green," address, 19 March 1994, PEG Centennial/UNC Bicentennial, Chapel Hill; Fussell, *The Great War,* 42–52.

16 General Orders, Citation, 10 January 1919, Pratt Papers.

17 Notes on war, 1917–19, Pratt Papers; diary, vol. 3, all summer 1918 entries but esp. 20, 25, 26, and 30 July 1918, Green Papers.

18 Diary, vol. 3, all September 1918 entries but esp. 28, 4, 6, 8, 15, 12, and 19 September 1918, Green Papers.

19 Diary, vol. 3, 28 September 1914; see also 24 September 1918, Green Papers.

20 Diary, vol. 3, 24, 25, and 28 September 1918, Green Papers.

21 Diary, vol. 3, 29 and 30 September and 1 October 1918, Green Papers.

22 Ibid.

23 Diary, vol. 3, 2, 3, 14–16, and 18–23 October 1918; vol. 3, 1918 sketch "H. L. Gallegly" and with PEG's notes in margin of sketch, enclosure, Herbert L. Gallegly to PEG, 27 August 1919, Green Papers.

24 Diary, vol. 3, all October 1918 entries but esp. 14–16 October 1918, Green Papers.

25 Diary, vol. 3, October 1918 entries, Green Papers; these episodes are developed fully in *Paul Green's War Songs,* ed. Roper, 132, 143.

26 Roper, *Paul Green's War Songs,* esp. poems on 48, 49.

27 Ibid., 146; General Orders, 2 December 1918, Pratt Papers.

28 Diary, vol. 3, esp. 11 November 1918, Green Papers.

29 See Roper, *Paul Green's War Songs,* esp. "Songs of the Metro," 69–82.

30 Ibid.

31 Ibid., 143–47, 49, 79. Note especially the evolution of the persona Uncle Joe into Comrade Joe. See also "Negro Poems," Green Papers.

32 Diary, vol. 3, 12 December and 18 February 1918; and vol. 5, [July 1919], Green Papers.

33 See Roper, *Paul Green's War Songs,* 155–57. Diary, vols. 3, 4, and 5, esp. 10 February, 8 May, 16 May, 26 May, and 27 May–30 June 1919. The never-published novel was "by" his persona Harvey Easom, and PEG provided a reader's key for the main characters, including identification of Ellen Cummings; see multiple H.E. diaries, poems, and novel, Green Papers.

34 Diary, vol. 5, 21 June 1919, Green Papers.

35 Diary, passim, but esp. vol. 5, 3 and 10–11 July 1919, Green Papers; notes on war and regulations form, 9 July 1919, Pratt Papers. See also correspondence with Hugh Greene, 1920–46, Green Papers.

36 Diary, vol. 5, 3 and 10–11 July 1919, Green Papers.

37 Diary, vol. 5, 11 July 1919, Green Papers.

CHAPTER 4. LIB

1 See Frederick Henry Koch correspondence with PEG, esp. Koch folder, 1919–29, Roper Papers; see folders for Carolina Playmakers and for Koch, 1919–29, UNC Archives.

2 Much of the biographical information, but not this interpretation, comes from a fine essay by Carolina Playmaker Samuel Selden, "Frederick Henry Koch," *Dictionary of American Biography,* supp. 3, 1973 ed., s.v. See also Koch to PEG, 15 June 1929, Green Papers. Koch's characteristic phrase, for example, see Koch to PEG, 15 June 1929, Green Papers.

3 Moses, "The Theatre in America," *North American Review* 219 (1924): 82–90.

4 Koch's lines quoted by Selden, "Frederick Henry Koch."

5 Moses, "The Theatre in America," 82–90.

6 Broadside, "Original Folk-Plays: *When Witches Ride,* 14–15 March 1919," North Carolina Collection; photographs by Mary Bayard Wooten, 14–15 March 1919, reproduced in *Carolina Folk-Plays,* ed. Frederick H. Koch (New York: Holt, 1922), photograph section.

7 See ELG, "The Paul Green I Know," address, [March 1978], North Carolina Collection.

8 MGJ to ELG, [November] 1931, Green Papers.

9 Ibid.; see correspondence between MGJ and ELG, 1921–70, Green Papers.

10 See correspondence, mostly undated but by context denoted winter, spring, and summer 1920 and summer and fall 1921; in particular, PEG to ELG, n.d., on auditor's stationery labeled "Thursday Night, Lillington," summer 1921, Green Papers.

11 Diary, vol. 6, 29 and 30 August 1937; photographs, Lay family, Green Papers; David Hackett Fischer, *Albion's Seed: Four British Folkways in America* (New York: Oxford University Press, 1989), esp. introduction.

12 PEG to George Atkinson Lay [hereinafter GAL], 6 December 1922; PEG to William S. Knickerbocker, 16 April 1931; Norman Foerster to PEG, 4 January 1932, Green Papers.

13 "Tonight, Dear Love," in "Poems," 1920; this is a carbon copy of the poem, with marginal notations addressed to Boiscelleur, and the original was evidently mailed to Boiscelleur, diary, vol. 5, esp. May and June, PEG to ELG, 1921; PEG to ELG, "Monday Night," 1921, with enclosure, Boiscelleur to PEG; and PEG to ELG, "Tuesday," 1921, Green Papers.

14 PEG quoted in Stahl, "A Paul Green Miscellany," p. 11. Greenlaw made a formal written offer of a scholarship to the student, but the person who approached PEG, and who talked of taking a chair to Williams's head, was more likely Hibbard, PEG to ELG, 1920, Green Papers.

15 Fragment of untitled play, 1920, Green Papers.

16 PEG to ELG, n.d., "Monday Night," summer 1921, Green Papers. Phrase is motif for Williams's lectures, Williams Papers, and PEG, Student Notebooks, Dr. Williams, Philosophy courses 10, 11, 12, 16, and 20, 1919 and 1920, Green Papers.

17 William Alexander Percy, *Lanterns on the Levee: Recollections of a Planter's Son* (1941; reprint, Baton Rouge: Louisiana State University Press, 1973).

18 William S. Knickerbocker to PEG, 13 April 1931; PEG to Knickerbocker, 16 April 1931; PEG to GAL, 6 December 1922; PEG Student Notebooks, Mr. [Norman] Foerster English, [1920?], Green Papers. Foerster quoted in Ragan, "Southern Accent." For concepts of modernism, see Henry Farnham May, *The End of American Innocence*: A Study of the First Years of Our Own Time, 1912–1917 (New York: Alfred A. Knopf, 1959); and Daniel Joseph Singal, *The War Within: From Victorian to Modernist Thought in the South, 1919–1945* (Chapel Hill: University of North Carolina Press, 1982).

19 Howard Mumford Jones, *O Strange New World: American Culture, the Formative Years* (New York: Viking Press, 1952).

20 President's Papers, 1918–19, UNC Archives. John Shelton Reed, *Southern Folk, Plain and Fancy* (Athens: University of Georgia Press, 1987), 68.

21 W. J. Cash, *The Mind of the South* (New York: Alfred A. Knopf, 1941); Bruce Clayton, *W. J. Cash: A Life*, rev ed. (Baton Rouge: Louisiana State University Press, 1997); Howard Washington Odum to H. N. MacCracken, 9 January 1937, and Odum to Newell L. Sims, 24 March 1937, Howard Washington Odum Papers, Southern Historical Collection, University of North Carolina, Chapel Hill.

22 Trustee Minutes, 1919, UNC Archives; Wayne Douglas Brazil, "Howard W. Odum: The Building Years, 1884–1930" (Ph.D. diss., Harvard University, 1975), and "Social Forces and Sectional Self-Scrutiny," in *Perspectives on the American South: An Annual Review of Society, Politics, and Culture,* vol. 2, ed. Merle Black and John Shelton Reed (London: Gordon and Breach for the University of North Carolina, 1984), 73–104.

23 See correspondence, esp. 1924–27, Odum Papers; Brazil, "Social Forces"; specific quotations concerning proscriptions cited in Brazil, "Howard W. Odum," 540.

24 Trustee Minutes, 1919, UNC Archives; specific quotations from Odum to H. N. MacCracken, 9 January 1937; Chase to Odum, 21 May 1935, Odum Papers.

25 PEG to ELG, "Monday Night," summer 1921, Green Papers.

26 Ibid.

CHAPTER 5. GETTING MARRIED

1 Diary, vols. 1–7, Green Papers; see correspondence, esp. Gladys Greene, Caro Mae Greene, Hugh Greene, and EGG, 1917–21, Green Papers; interviews, EGG, 1 and 8 April 1991, tapes, Roper Papers.

2 PEG, student notes, Philosophy 11, 20 February, 26 April, and 30 September 1920, Green Papers; PEG to ELG, [summer 1924], Green Papers.

3 See esp. diary, April 1929, and correspondence, 1929, Green Papers. Note in particular Katherine Gilbert correspondence with PEG, 20 April 1929, Green Papers.

4 Gilbert correspondence with PEG, 20 April 1929, Green Papers. Cf. PEG to ELG, [winter 1922], Green Papers.

5 PEG to ELG, [winter 1922]; PEG to ELG, [spring 1922], Green Papers.

6 Ibid.; PEG to GAL, 6 December 1922, Green Papers; interviews, EGG, 1 and 8 April 1991, Roper Papers; see also two undated letters concerning graduate plans and conversations with Harry Woodburn Chase and with Williams, PEG to ELG, each letter [winter?] 1922, Green Papers.

7 PEG to ELG, "Thursday Morning," [July?] 1922; diary, vol. 6, June and July entries, Green Papers.

8 PEG to ELG, "Thursday Morning," [July?] 1922, Green Papers. See also Moyer et al. to Roper, Roper Papers.

9 See two letters concerning his operation and recovery, [June 1922], Green Papers.

10 PEG to ELG, "Monday evening," 1921; PEG to ELG, "Thursday," 1922; PEG to ELG, [March] 1923; and PEG to ELG, [winter] 1923, Green Papers.

11 Williams seems to have mentioned William James twice in lectures to PEG, once on 5 March 1920 and again on 10 March 1920. He was actually talking about John Locke and the concept that ideas and ideals emerge only from the senses; but he did urge PEG to read several articles by and about James and pragmatism, Green Papers. PEG, "Philosophy 11," 1920, Green Papers. See PEG notebooks on philosophy, Cornell University, 1922–23, arranged according to courses taught by professors James Edwin Creighton, Frank Thilly, and Ernest Albee, Green Papers. In particular, see notes from Creighton on technical problems of the meanings and usage of syllogism in Hegel, "Philosophy Seminary; Dr. Creighton," 6 March 1923, and notes on technical meanings of *geist* and of *progress,* notes from Thilly, fall 1922, "Philosophy 26; Dr. Thilly," Green Papers. Both instances involved questions that Williams had noted but dismissed as uninteresting, Green Papers. PEG notebooks, 1919–21, Green Papers, and Williams notes, Williams Papers.

12 "Philosophy Seminar; Dr. Creighton," 28 May 1923, Creighton's notes and PEG marginal comments, and 25 May 1923 and chart, 28 May 1923; PEG notebook, "British Philosophy," 1923; PEG, "Philosophy 7a; Dr. Thilly," 23 May 1923, and "Seminary on Ethics; Dr. Thilly," fall 1922, Green Papers. Correspondence between Williams and Ralph Moore Harper, 1924–35, esp. marginal notations on copy of letter, 1 October 1935, in which Harper says that he could never get Williams to revise—or even permit Harper to pay an editor to review—an edition of a ms. that had been rejected at Yale University Press, Macmillan, and the University of North Carolina Press. Note too that the Williams lecture notes are far more interesting and much better written than this Williams ms., Williams Papers. See also an editor's comments about Williams: interview, William Terry Couch, 10–11 March 1980, Roper Papers. On southern intellectuals of the day and their tendencies toward conservative Hegelianism, see Williamson, *The Crucible of Race,* for the particularities of regional idealism. More generally, see Singal, *The War Within;* and John Herbert Roper, *C. Vann Woodward, Southerner* (Athens: University of Georgia Press, 1987).

13 PEG "Notes for Teaching," notebooks, 1923–26; PEG "Notes on Philosophy 13" [Williams], 21 October 1919; PEG notebooks on Thilly, Creighton, and Albee, 1922–23, Green Papers. The point about the hoot owl and other portents is made and illustrated effectively by the close reader Grant M. Herbstruth, "An Analysis of the Plays of Paul Green" (M.A. thesis, Iowa State University, 1949).

14 University Faculty Appointment List, UNC Archives, 1927–28. See also Katherine Gilbert correspondence with Charles Mills, Charles Mills Papers, Southern Historical Collection, University of North Carolina, Chapel Hill; and with PEG, Green Papers. See esp. PEG to Williams, [winter 1923], draft of note apparently never sent, Green Papers. "Modern British Philosophers; Dr. Albee" notebook, Green Papers.

15 See correspondence, Gilbert and PEG, 1929, Green Papers. "Notes for Teaching; Philosophy 16," Green Papers.

16 "Notes for Teaching; Philosophy 16," Green Papers.

17 "Notes for Teaching," notebooks, 1923–26, Green Papers.

18 "Notes for Teaching; Philosophy 16," Green Papers.

19 On the term *denizen,* see Marina Wikramanayake, *A World in Shadow: The Free Black in Antebellum South Carolina,* Tricentennial Studies, no. 7 (Columbia: University of South Carolina Press, 1973). PEG to ELG, [summer 1921] "Monday Night"; Koch correspondence with PEG, especially Koch folders, 1919–29, Green Papers. See also folders for Koch and for Carolina Playmakers, 1919–29, UNC Archives.

20 This shadow diary was gathered up, along with notes and drafts of poems to form "H.E. Poems," an uncompleted manuscript for a planned publication of "Harvey Easom Poems," hereinafter cited as "H.E. Poems," 1920; also, "Poems," 1920, folder; diary, vols. 6 and 7; "Map of Little Bethel," ca. 1928, Green Papers. C. Vann Woodward, "The Historical Dimension," *Virginia Quarterly Review* 32 (1956): 258–67. Woodward on several occasions in conversations with the author referred to PEG as "playwright of the New South" or as "the New South's playwright."

21 The phrase "sacred circle" aptly describes the sense of tight-knitting in a southern community in which even eccentricities are brought into, and kept within, the circle of common identity—and social control through sense of cohesion. The term is developed fully by Faust in *A Sacred Circle.*

22 Eccles. 1:18.

23 William Butler Yeats, "Under Ben Bulben," in *Selected Poems and Two Plays of William Butler Yeats,* rev. ed., ed. M. L. Rosenthal(New York: Macmillan, Collier Books, 1975), 193.

CHAPTER 6. THE REAL SOUTH

1 Interviews, EGG, 1 and 8 April 1991; BGM, 31 October 1989, Roper Papers. PEG diary, 1923–25, and correspondence, 1923–37, Green Papers. Edwin Mims, *The Advancing South: Stories of Progress and Reaction* (Garden City, N.Y.: Doubleday, Page, 1926). See also John Herbert Roper, "Paul Green and the Southern Literary Renaissance," *Southern Cultures* 1 (1994): 75–89. Quotations from PEG in that article appear here with permission of editors.

2 Roper, "Paul Green and the Renaissance." Frances Newman named the period in an influential essay, "The State of Literature in the Late Confederacy," *New York Herald-Tribune,* 16 August 1925; Newman was friend to both PEG and ELG, but the relationships were occasionally strained, since ELG was concerned that Newman might have designs on PEG and PEG for his part was sometimes overwhelmed by Newman's almost overbearing conversation; see "Frances Newman" folder, Green Papers. PEG, "Plain Statement," *Reviewer* 5 (1925): 71–76. PEG to William R. Kane, 22 January 1925; "Plain Statement" ms., *Reviewer* flyer, July 1925, Green Papers. "Plain Statement" was reprinted in full, with permission of the North Carolina Collection, in *Southern Cultures* 1 (1994): 80.

3 "The Hawthorne Tree," n.d., "Poems, 1920"; see esp. notes, "A Washerwoman Dead in September," "H.E. Poems," 1920, Green Papers. PEG, *The Lord's Will,* in *"The Lord's Will" and Other Carolina Plays* (New York: Henry Holt, 1925). PEG playscripts: *The No 'Count Boy* (1925); *The Old Man of Edenton* (ca. 1925); *White Dresses* (ca. 1925); *In Abraham's Bosom* (1926, 1927); and "Sam Tucker," *Poet Lore* 34 (1923): 221, "Sam Tucker" ms., 1923, Green Papers.

4 Barrett Harper Clark to PEG, quoting Andar Garvay, 14 December 1925, Green Papers.

5 "H.E. Poems," 1920, Green Papers.

6 *The Lord's Will;* Herbstruth, "Analysis."

7 Ibid.

8 PEG, *The No 'Count Boy, The Lord's Will;* Herbstruth, "Analysis."

9 Wystan Hugh Auden, ed., *Selected Poetry and Prose of Byron* (1966; reprint, New York: New American Library, 1983), i–iii.

10 Wyatt-Brown, *Honor and Violence in the Old South;* Orville Vernon Burton, *In My Father's House Are Many Mansions: Family and Community in Edgefield, South Carolina,* Fred W. Morrison Series in Southern Studies (Chapel Hill: University of North Carolina Press, 1985).

11 PEG, *Sam Tucker* (1923); ms., 1923, Green Papers; "Sam Tucker," abstract in Herbstruth, "Analysis," s.v.

12 "Sam Tucker," *Poet Lore* 34 (1923): 221.

13 Ibid.

14 *Sam Tucker* (1923).

15 PEG playscript: *Your Fiery Furnace* (1923); ms. "Your Fiery Furnace," 1923, Green Papers; "Your Fiery Furnace," abstract in Herbstruth, "Analysis," s.v.

16 For full details, see Roper, "Paul Green and the Renaissance"; PEG diary, 1924–25, Green Papers; correspondence, 1924–26, Green Papers; *Reviewer* files, 1924–26, Green Papers; see folders marked "Archibald Rutledge," "Du Bose Heyward," "Donald Davidson," "Josephine Pinckney," "Allen Tate," "Frances Newman," "Julia Peterkin," "Sara Haardt," and "Carl Van Vechten," Green Papers. A complete set of the *Reviewer* during Chapel Hill days and some of the Richmond days is in the North Carolina Collection. Laurence Green Avery owns a complete set of the *Reviewer,* Richmond and Chapel Hill, and was kind enough to share some numbers and to discuss the magazine.

17 PEG to William R. Kane, 22 January 1925; "Plain Statement," *Reviewer* flyer, blind copy, July 1925, Green Papers; "Plain Statement," *Reviewer* 5 (1925): 71–76; see reprint, *Southern Cultures* 1 (1994): 80.

18 Correspondence files, "Archibald Rutledge," "Du Bose Heyward," "Donald Davidson," "Josephine Pinckney," and "Allen Tate," 1925, Green Papers. See esp. Tate to PEG, 6 January 1925, and Tate to PEG, 13 January 1925, Green Papers.

19 Roper, "Paul Green and the Renaissance"; Brawley correspondence, B folder, 1924–25, esp. Brawley to PEG, 1 November 1924, and Brawley to PEG, 30 April 1925; Nell Battle Lewis to PEG, "Monday," 1925; Carl Van Vechten to PEG, 22 November 1925; Edwin Mims to PEG, 24 January 1926, Green Papers. Kathryn Lee Seidel, in a section of her carefully focused study of traditional uses—and misuses—of the southern belle archetype, notes emerging feminist perspectives among women writers of the era and pays special attention to pieces showcased in the *Reviewer:* see *The Southern Belle in the American Novel* (Tampa: University Presses of Florida, University of South Florida Press, 1985); see also Bradbury, *Renaissance in the South,* 280.

20 For full discussion, see Roper, "Paul Turns Pro," *Sandhills Review,* Paul Green issue, vol. 46 (1994): 85–108. Folder on Clark, esp. 1925. Clark to PEG, 21 January 1926, Green Papers.

21 See agreement, *Reviewer* files, 1924; PEG to Alfred Williams, 24 July 1925; *Reviewer* files with subscription lists showing perhaps three hundred subscribers and fewer than four hundred counter sales per annum—when PEG had planned for two thousand subscribers and store sales of at least six thousand copies; files also show around three hundred dollars in advertising revenues and donor gifts, when PEG had budgeted for one thousand dollars from those sources, 1924, Green Papers.

22 Roper, "Paul Turns Pro"; Clark to PEG, 13 October 1925 and 21 January 1926; "Samuel French" files, 1925 and 1926, Green Papers; correspondence with William Stanley Hoole and Jay Broadus Hubble, 1922–27 and some copies of the *Southwest Review,* Jay

Broadus Hubble Papers, Manuscript Department, Perkins Library, Duke University, Durham, N.C.

CHAPTER 7. TAKING AN EARTHLY PRIZE

1 For full description, see Roper, "Paul Turns Pro."

2 As noted, see in particular Caro Mae Green to ELG, 2 July 1926, Green Papers; Alice Denham, "Shabby Genteel," photocopy of page of ms., with notes, Roper Papers; Lotte Lenya's testimony and that of her husband, Kurt Weill, in *Speak Low,* ed. Symonette and Kowelke; interviews, Shelby Stephenson, 30 July 1986, 30 July 1987, Roper Papers. The Denham ms. details PEG's affair with her in the 1950s and his alleged efforts to get her to abandon her fiancé. See also Roper, "Paul Turns Pro"; and cf. note of protest written by PEG's daughter Janet to the University of Georgia Press, Janet McNeill Green (formerly JGC) to Malcolm Call, 5 August 1995; Call to Janet McNeill Green, 31 August 1995, and Call to Roper, with enclosures of above, 1 September 1995; see also correspondence between Foundation President Laurence Green Avery and Roper, 1994–95, Roper Papers.

3 PEG to ELG, 6 November 1925, Green Papers.

4 PEG to ELG, 5 July 1926, Green Papers.

5 PEG to ELG, [1 or 2?] July 1926, Green Papers. See also Roper, "Paul Turns Pro," and "Paul Green," address, 19 March 1994.

6 Shakespeare, *The Merchant of Venice,* 2.6.

7 Clark to PEG, 8 June 1925, Green Papers.

8 Clark to PEG, 16 June 1925, Green Papers.

9 *Who Was Who,* vols. 1, s.v. "Solomon Henry Clark," and 3, s.v. "Barrett Harper Clark"; Clark to PEG, 19 October 1926, Green Papers.

10 Clark to PEG, 16 July and 3 August 1925, Roper Papers.

11 Rowenna Woodham Jelliffe to Samuel French, 4 June 1926, Green Papers. See also correspondence with Clark concerning Jelliffe and Gilpin Players, 1926–27, Green Papers.

12 Jelliffe to Henry Holt, 24 May 1926; Henry Holt ["H.T."] to Jelliffe, 27 May 1924; Jelliffe to Samuel French, 9 June 1926; Charles Bayley Jr. to Jelliffe, 10 June 1926; Samuel French to Jelliffe, 29 May 1926; Clark to PEG, 2 April 1926; Jelliffe to PEG, 16 December 1927, Green Papers.

13 PEG to ELG, 29 June 1926; PEG to ELG, 5 July 1926; Clark to PEG, 28 July 1925, Green Papers.

14 Clark to PEG, 3 August 1925, Green Papers; Martin Bauml Duberman, *Paul Robeson: A Biography* (New York: Random House, Ballentine Press, 1989), 105.

15 Clark to PEG, 3 August and 21 November 1925, Green Papers.

16 Clark to PEG, 24 December 1925; Clark to PEG, 21 January 1926, Green Papers.

17 Clark to PEG, 21 January 1926; PEG to ELG, 29 June 1926, Green Papers.

18 PEG to ELG, 5 July 1926, Green Papers.

19 Ibid.; PEG to ELG, 21 June 1926; and PEG to ELG, 7 September 1926, Green Papers.

20 Clark to PEG, 7 September 1926, Green Papers.

21 Ibid.

22 Clark to PEG, 21 September 1926; T. R. Edwards to PEG, 23 September 1926; Clark to PEG, 1 November 1926, Green Papers. [Robert] Burns Mantle, *The Best Plays of 1926–1927 and the Yearbook of the Drama in America* (1927; reprint, New York: Dodd, Mead, 1948).

23 PEG, notes in "Book of Verses," 1918–19; PEG to ELG, 22 August 1920; PEG to GAL, 6 December 1922; PEG to Nell Battle Lewis, 16 March 1927; diary, vol. 6, esp. these passages: 11 June 1928, 30 October 1928, and 16 November 1928, Green Papers; notes, "Big John," unpublished script, composition book, [ca. 1943–44], PEG; interviews, EGG, 1 and 8 April 1991, Roper Papers.

24 For examples, see Joseph Wood Krutch, "Drama—A Folk Tragedy," *Nation,* 4 May 1927, p. 510; also, Montrose Jonas Moses, scrapbook, 1927, Moses Papers (hereinafter cited as Moses Scrapbook, Duke). Charles Blackburn Jr., "Paul Green's Pulitzer Prize and the N.C. Press," *Sandhills Review* 46 (1994): 113–20.

25 Clark to PEG, 23 September 1926; Clark to PEG, telegram, 20 March 1927; PEG, script notes, "G" folder, 1927, Green Papers.

26 John Ehle, "Paul Green: A Reminiscence," address, PEG Centennial/UNC Bicentennial, 20 March 1994, Green Papers. See also correspondence with Eleanor Fitzgerald and with Clark, 1926–27, Green Papers; correspondence with Jasper Deeter, Hedgerow Theatre Collection, Boston, Massachusetts.

27 Duberman, *Paul Robeson;* James Weldon Johnson, *Black Manhattan* (1930; reprint, New York: New York Times and Arno Press, 1968), 207; Glenda Gill, *White Grease Paint on Black Performers: A Study of the Federal Theatre, 1935–1939* (New York: Peter Lang, 1990). See also clippings, Hedgerow Collection.

28 Edward Franklin Frazier, "The Negro's Struggle to Find His Soul," unpublished typescript, ca. 1927, Edward Franklin Frazier Papers, Manuscript Department, Moorland-Spingarn Research Center, Howard University, Washington, D.C. This document was shown me by kindness of the historian Walter Jackson.

29 John Anderson, "Button, Button, Who's Got the Pulitzer Prize?" *New York Evening Post,* 19 February 1927, p. 8; see folder, "*In Abraham's Bosom,*" esp. clippings and Provincetown Playhouse box office receipts, 1927, Green Papers; see clippings, 1926–27, Moses Scrapbook, Duke.

30 Blackburn, "Paul Green's Pulitzer Prize"; Ehle, "Paul Green"; see Moses Scrapbook, 1927, Duke; citation, copy, "Pulitzer Prize" folder, 1927, Green Papers. The citation and the prize itself were for a time displayed in the Paul Green Theater on the campus of UNC in Chapel Hill but are now again maintained by the Paul Green Foundation.

CHAPTER 8. LIB'S TRIP

1 Application blank, enclosure, Henry Allen Moe to PEG, 13 March 1928; copy of completed application, [13 March?] 1928, Green Papers.

2 See diary, 1928–30; see also correspondence with William Terry Couch, Harry Woodburn Chase, Frank Porter Graham, and Katherine Gilbert, 1928, Green Papers.

3 Ibid; see also interview, William Terry Couch, 10–11 January 1980), Roper Papers.

4 Ibid.; Moe to PEG, 18 March 1928; Gilbert to PEG, 20 April 1929, reviews the arrangements as she remembers them when a dispute arose; Chase to PEG, 12 June 1928, Green Papers.

5 Clark to PEG, 31 August 1929, Green Papers.

6 Diary, vol. 6, August and September 1928; language about lion and Aristotlean actualization, diary, 10 November 1928, Green Papers.

7 On World War II, Avery explains PEG's anguish particularly well, *A Southern Life,* 360–442. See correspondence, esp. PEG to MGJ, 14 April 1942, Green Papers.

8 Interview, Richard Schrader, 18 April 1991, notes in possession of author. Schrader, then a research assistant at the Southern Historical Collection, saw PEG altering the

typescripts with correction liquid. After PEG left the collection, Schrader marked the passages in typescript with a note that the original ms. was unaltered. Examples of PEG's prejudice appear in his diary and in correspondence with ELG. Even after the rise of Adolf Hitler, PEG's prejudice is evident, expressed sometimes against Jewish directors and moviemakers in Hollywood. Examples: complaint about Jewish men, whom he trivializes by describing as boys who are Communists coming down from New York to study and prosecute the South and southerners, diary, vol. 6, 15 January 1936, Green Papers; he declared that Jews like sex and money above all other things, diary, vol. 6, 9–17 January 1936, Green Papers; he laments the loss of farming fields won by the sweat and blood of pioneers now gone, as Jews who talk too much buy up and dominate the land; he also complains about New York artists, Jewish or otherwise, who talk too much and who buy up the land once fought for and cultivated by courageous pioneer farmers, PEG to ELG, 13 June 1936, Green Papers; he asks ELG to bargain Mabel Bason downward on her asking price for her silverware, using the colloquial verb *jew* to mean "to bargain downward," PEG to ELG, 30 December 1941, Green Papers; on declining dinner invitation from Stella Adler in Hollywood, he says that he simply does not want to go; that the movies and the places where movies are produced are dominated now by Jewish actors, writers, producers, directors, whom he describes further as running over Hollywood. He says resignedly and with disgust that the movies will have to be Jewish in orientation and subject matter, since Jews write, produce, act, direct, and then offer to market the movies. The complaint is rather fey in tone, PEG to ELG, [December] 1941, Green Papers. By contrast, praising language about Jewish resistance to oppression and charitable nature to the needy, PEG to ELG, 23 January 1942, Green Papers; and positive language about the agent Geller *because he is* a good example of those good Jews who are as plain as old clothing, especially old and familiar headwear, PEG to ELG, [December?] 1941, Green Papers.

9 Gavin I. Langmuir, *Toward a Definition of Antisemitism* (Berkeley and Los Angeles: University of California Press, 1990), 351 and passim.

10 Ibid.; see also 6–12, 15.

11 See diary, vol. 6, 9–17 January 1936, Green Papers; also, on Bittemann, see diary, vol. 3, for 5, 7, and 8 February 1919, Green Papers.

12 Correspondence with BGM, 1993, esp. 1 February 1993, and attached comments, *"Paul Green's War Songs* Errata," June 1993, Roper Papers. She and other members of the family emphatically deny that PEG ever suffered any clinical depression, except during this trip to Berlin. Cf. diary, vols. 1–5, and correspondence with ELG, esp. [November] 1943, Green Papers; and, most important, correspondence with daughter Janet McNeill Green [then Catlin], JGC to "Dearest Doogie," 12 February 1975, in which she discusses her own bouts with clinical depression and gives advice about how her father should deal with the experience of depression, an experience that she describes as being exhausting and like punishment. It is a lengthy letter with specific references to clinical depression as a diagnosis and to antidepressant drugs prescribed for PEG. He responds on 20 February 1975 with warm thanks for her letter, which he characterizes as beautiful and as understanding. He says that she writes from personal experience, from the inside of such problems, and thus more authoritatively than others who write and who commiserate without understanding the experience of depression. Furthermore, he remarks that her letter provides more comfort than letters from others who have not experienced depression. See also: JGC to "Doogie," 16 February 1975. Shelby Foote, address, William Faulkner Symposium, 9 August 1974, Oxford, Miss.; diary, vol. 6, for 24, 30, and 31 October 1928, Green Papers. Interviews, EGG, 1 and 8 April 1991, Roper Papers.

13 Diary, vol. 6, pp. 66–110, Green Papers.

14 Correspondence between ELG and Clark makes it clear that by 1928 the agent was quite accustomed to dealing with her in money matters; diary, vol. 6, 1, 12, 14, and 15 November 1928, Green Papers.

15 Diary, vol. 6, 1 November 1928, Green Papers. Nahma Sandrow, *Vagabond Stars* (New York: Harper, 1977), 226–39; "Yiddish Literature," *Encyclopedia of World Literature in the Twentieth Century* (1984), s.v.; "Alexander Granovsky (Avrom Azarkh)," *Encyclopedia Judaica* (1971), s.v.; *Oxford Companion to Film* (1976), s.v., and *Oxford Companion to the Theatre* (1983), s.v.

16 Diary, vol. 6, 1 November 1928, Green Papers.

17 Ibid.; "Granovsky (Avrom Azarkh)," *Encyclopedia Judaica* (1971), s.v.

18 "Review Synopsis of *Kunstgeschichtlich Grundbergriffe*," 1928–29; and "Notes on German Aesthetic Theatre," 1929, Green Papers.

19 Ibid.; see PEG, "Plain Statement," *Reviewer* 5 (1925): 71–76.

20 "Plain Statement," *Reviewer* 5 (1925): 71–76; see correspondence about Beckett, PEG to BGM, 31 October 1969, Green Papers. Ehle, "Paul Green." PEG's remark about values or ideals or messages "seeping through" was almost a chestnut among North Carolina writers and was repeated often, both in formal speeches and in the gathering places at the North Carolina Writers Conference meetings that I attended, 1980–88.

21 Ehle, "Paul Green"; Robert Penn Warren, "Cowley's Faulkner, Part I," *New Republic,* 12 August 1946, 176–80, "Cowley's Faulkner, Part II," *New Republic,* 26 August 1946, 234–37, and "Faulkner: Past and Future," in *Faulkner: A Collection of Critical Essays* (Englewood Cliffs, N.J.: Prentice-Hall, 1966), 1–5.

22 The diarist is quoting Fechner, diary, vol. 6, passim, but esp. 1 November 1928, Green Papers.

23 Ibid.; also, note a long, reflective letter from PEG to Clark, 3 May 1929: there are ten points, and the ninth has been struck through, but it is still legible. PEG apologizes that Clark had to have a glimpse of the sicknesses and their attendant emotions; but at least this stay in Europe teaches more than rote lessons in history and culture. The revised version, point 9 of the same letter, repeats the phrase about Clark's having a glimpse of the emotional depression but says nothing about lessons from a stay in Europe, instead adding two lines about the cup of friendship and Clark's generosity of spirit. In other words, PEG did not strike out any mention of the illness of depression or of its devastating effects on him and on his work for a period.

24 Agatha Bullitt Grabisch, from a Chapel Hill family, was in Berlin with her husband during winter of 1929, saw the Greens often, and recalled the weather, the economy, and the hard but happy times, in letter of recollection, Agatha Bullitt Grabisch to PEG, 30 September 1930, Green Papers. Also, Clark to PEG, esp. 6 March 1929 (two separate communications), and 25 March 1929; ELG to Clark, 17 March 1929; PEG correspondence, December 1928–April 1929; and diary, vol. 6, December 1928–2 April 1929, Green Papers.

25 George E. Mowry, Kenan Professor of History and scholar of the Progressive Era, repeated these remarks about the Great Depression, almost as a litany: reading seminar, March 1972, recollections of notes, Roper Papers.

26 William S. Powell, *North Carolina through Four Centuries* (Chapel Hill: University of North Carolina Press, 1989); Lewis Pinckney Jones, *South Carolina: A Synoptic History for Laymen* (1971; reprint, Columbia, S.C.: Sandlapper Press, 1972); Lewis Pinckney Jones to Roper, 26 July 1998, Roper Papers.

27 Correspondence between ELG and Clark, 1929; see also diary, vol. 6, 1929, esp. October, November, and December entries, Green Papers.

28 PEG to Eaton, 15 April 1929; Carleton Parker to PEG, 26 April 1929, Green Papers.

29 PEG to Parker, 15 May 1929, Green Papers.

30 PEG to Couch, 26 April 1929; PEG to GAL, 13 May 1929; see retrospective explanation, PEG to Hugh Green, 15 June 1929, Green Papers.

31 Gilbert to PEG, 20 April 1929; HHW to PEG, 7 September 1929, Green Papers.

32 Gilbert to PEG, 20 April 1929; Harry Woodburn Chase Presidential Papers, 1928–1929, UNC Archives; hereinafter, HWC.

33 Ibid. Note that Gilbert's lengthy report appears to be in response to a lengthy letter from PEG, but I cannot locate that lengthy letter from PEG at Southern Historical Collection.

34 Copy of telegram, HWC to PEG, 25 April 1929, HWC. Original telegram, HWC to PEG, 25 April 1929; HWC to PEG, 22 April 1929; HHW to PEG, 7 September 1929, Green Papers.

35 Diary, 1929; PEG to Clark, 4 October 1929; Clark to PEG, 7 October 1929; PEG to Clark, 9 October 1929; Hedgerow Theatre [Jasper Deeter] to PEG, 30 October 1929; Clark to PEG, 29 November 1929; Clark to PEG, 19 December 1929; Sidney Ross to PEG, postal telegraph, 3 January 1930; Deeter to PEG, 4 January 1930; Clark to PEG, 7 January 1930 and 9 January 1930, Green Papers. Gill, *White Grease Paint;* Hilbert H. Campbell, ed., *Sherwood Anderson's Diaries, 1936–1941* (Athens: University of Georgia Press), 140–41; miscellaneous correspondence, 1925–36, Sherwood Anderson Archive, Smyth-Bland Regional Library, Marion, Virginia; *Potter's Field* folder and Sherwood Anderson Papers, Hedgerow Collection.

36 *Potter's Field,* in *"The House of Connelly" and Other Plays* (New York: Samuel French, 1931), 138, 137; references to text refer to pagination in this edition. PEG to Clark, 4 October 1929; Clark to PEG, 7 October 1929; PEG to Clark, 7 January 1930, Green Papers.

37 *Potter's Field,* 150. Horace Clarence Boyer, comp. and ed., *Lift Every Voice and Sing II: An African American Hymnal* (New York: Church Pension Fund of the Episcopal Church, 1993), esp. prefatory notes; lecture and performance, Clarence Boyer, 8 February 2000, Diocesan Convention of Southwestern Virginia, Roanoke.

38 *Potter's Field,* 163–66 and 222.

39 Ibid.

40 PEG to Henry Allen Moe, 5 July 1932, retrospective report on accomplishments during period of Guggenheim Foundation Fellowship, Green Papers.

41 PEG to Hugh Green, 8 August 1929; see correspondence with Couch and Clark, summer and fall 1929, Green Papers.

42 Ibid.; PEG to GAL, 14 June 1929; PEG to Clark, 21 June 1929; PEG to Koch, 27 October 1929, Green Papers.

43 PEG, "Thomas Hardy and the Theatre: Some Random Travel Notes," ms. evidently completed in 1930, Green Papers; "Some Notes on a Trip to Hardy Country," scrapbook, typescript, 1929, North Carolina Collection; PEG to Koch, notes to Koch revised and printed, "G.B.S. the Mystic," *Tomorrow* 8 (1949): 29–35; these notes revised again and printed, "The Mystical Bernard Shaw," in PEG, *Dramatic Heritage: Essays* (New York: Samuel French, 1953), 112–31. On Shaw's favorable impressions of PEG, see Blanch Patch to PEG, 17 October 1929, and Florya Sobieniowski to PEG, [after 17 October but before 1 November 1929]; also see PEG retrospective entries on Shaw, diary, vol. 6, 27–31 January 1937, Green Papers.

44 PEG to GAL, 14 June 1929, Green Papers.

45 Hortense Oudesluys to PEG, 22 December 1930; PEG to ELG, [late December] 1930, Green Papers.

46 PEG to Frank J. Shiel, 4 January 1931; H. R. Bankhage to PEG, 18 September 1931; PEG to EGG, 25 June 1932; PEG to Dottie and Marvin Stahl, 9 October 1950; Josiah W. Bailey to PEG, 4 August 1924; Bailey to PEG, 22 January 1931; clipping, enclosure, *Raleigh News and Observer,* 11 November 1931; Bailey to PEG, [November 1931], Green Papers. *North Carolina Government, 1585–1974* (Raleigh, N.C.: Department of State, 1975), s.v. "Josiah W. Bailey."

CHAPTER 9. HARD TIMES AND HOLLYWOOD

1 Edith J. R. Isaacs to PEG, 6 March 1930, Green Papers.

2 Samuel French [unidentified secretary of Frank J. Shiel] to PEG, 18 March 1930; Hugh Green to PEG, 18 February 1930; PEG to Clark, 9 January 1930, in which PEG says that he expects to become chair of the Department of Philosophy and that he feels deep pity for the aspiring writers trying to make a profession of creative writing in the era of the Great Depression, Green Papers. See also correspondence and diary, 1930, esp. correspondence with Theodore Dreiser and Clark; "Mater Dolorosa," unpublished poem in "Harvey Easom," Poems, folder, 1928; Oliver M. Sayler to PEG, 22 May 1930, Green Papers. *Sherwood Anderson's Diaries,* ed. Campbell, Anderson-Wright Papers, Sherwood Anderson Archive, Smyth-Bland Regional Library, Marion, Va. Robert B. House to PEG, 7 September 1929, and Katherine Boyd to PEG, 11 December 1929, Green Papers.

3 See correspondence with Leo Bulgakov, esp. September and October 1930; see diary, 1930, esp. October, Green Papers.

4 See correspondence with Ross, January–November 1930, but esp. PEG to Ross, 23 October 1930, Green Papers. See also *Potter's Field* folders, Hedgerow Collection.

5 *Tread the Green Grass,* in *"The House of Connelly" and Other Plays* (New York: Samuel French, 1931), 225–308 (this is the text and pagination referred to hereinafter); diary, vol. 6, 26 October and 21 November 1928; PEG to Clark, 9 October 1929; "Notes on 'Tread the Green Grass,'" July 1932, Green Papers.

6 See correspondence with Clark, Lamar Stringfellow, and William Dorsey Blake, but esp. Blake to PEG, 26 February 1930, Mary Dunbeyer to Proff [Koch], 2 March 1930 (in which a former Carolina Playmaker documents Blake's incompetence and insincerity), Rachel Foreman to PEG, 17 March 1930 (alleging crookedness as well as incompetence and insincerity in Blake); Clark to PEG, 20, 21, and 26 February 1930, 15 October 1930, and 6 March 1930, Green Papers.

7 *Tread the Green Grass,* passim; "Notes on 'Tread the Green Grass,'" July 1932, Green Papers.

8 "Notes on 'Tread the Green Grass.'"

9 Ibid.; Wolfe, *Look Homeward, Angel,* 596.

10 Correspondence with Eleanor M. Fitzgerald, 1929–32, but esp. Fitzgerald to PEG, 27 July 1932, Green Papers.

11 PEG to Vassili Kouchita, 17 October 1930; Kouchita to PEG, 24 October 1930; Kouchita to PEG, [early November] 1930; Kouchita to PEG, [late November–early Decem-

ber] 1930; PEG to Clark, 8 December 1930; PEG to Clark, 1 April 1931; Clark to PEG, 13 May 1931; Frank J. Shiel to PEG, 8 January 1931, Green Papers.

12 PEG to E. C. Mabie, 4 September 1930; correspondence with Mabie, 1931–32; diary, summer 1932, Green Papers; *"House of Connelly" and Other Plays.*

13 PEG to Tyre Taylor, 23 November 1931, Green Papers.

14 Correspondence, esp. with Miriam Bonner in 1931, 1932, and 1933 indicates that PEG voted for Thomas, 1931–33, Green Papers.

15 Ibid. Cf. correspondence, Elizabeth MacAllister Green and other family members of Paul Green Foundation, "Errata," 1993 for *Paul Green's War Songs* ms., Roper Papers. Family members in particular insist that PEG was never particularly left of center.

16 The careful scholar Avery also takes this position in an early draft of his introduction to the edited letters, copy shown to me and discussed with me. The final draft as published, *A Southern Life,* does not address the issue as such but instead emphasizes the "sane" quality of Green's contemporaneous responses to political disputes.

17 Oliver M. Sayler to PEG, 22 May 1930; note PEG's emphatic sign of assent in his own hand on the letter, much as his namesake Saint Paul deliberately made his own signature on certain documents, Green Papers.

18 Oliver M. Sayler, ed., *Revolt in the Arts: A Survey of the Creation, Distribution, and Appreciation of the Arts in America* (New York: Brentano's, 1930).

19 Ibid.; Sayler to PEG, 22 May 1930, Green Papers.

20 PEG to Russell Sedgwick, 30 August 1930; PEG to Sedgwick, 14 September 1930; Sedgwick to PEG, [September 1930], with enclosure "At the Play" by St. John Ervine; PEG to Sedgwick, 26 September 1930; Sedgwick to PEG, 14 December 1930, Green Papers.

21 John Reed Club to "Dear Friend," 4 March 1930, with PEG's handwritten note that he was going to join the protest; Club to "Dear Friend," 2 May 1930, Green Papers.

22 Club to "Dear Friend," 4 March and 2 May 1930, Green Papers.

23 Ibid.

24 Ibid.; Richard Crossman, ed., *The God That Failed* (New York: Grossett and Dunlap, Bantam Books, 1950).

25 Anthony J. Buttitta, *After the Good Gay Times* (New York: Viking, 1974); interviews, C. Vann Woodward, Guy and Guion Johnson, William Terry Couch, Roper Papers; Roper, *C. Vann Woodward,* 93–94, 109; *Contempo,* vols. 1–3, 1931–33, North Carolina Collection.

26 Dan T. Carter, *Scottsboro: A Tragedy of the American South* (Baton Rouge: Louisiana State University Press, 1969); James E. Goodman, *Stories of Scottsboro* (New York: Pantheon, 1994); *Judge Horton and the Scottsboro Boys* (Tomorrow E Electronics, 1976), motion picture.

27 Anthony J. Buttitta to PEG, 3 November 1931, Green Papers; *Contempo,* vol. 1 (December 1931), North Carolina Collection.

28 John Dos Passos to PEG, [January] 1932; Henry R. Fuller to PEG, 30 December 1932; Miriam Bonner to PEG, 6 November 1931; Bonner to PEG, 13 December 1931; PEG to Bonner, 5 May 1931, Green Papers.

29 Diary, vol. 6, 1932; correspondence with Buttitta, Clark, and Sherwood Anderson, but esp. PEG to Clark, 8 December 1931, Green Papers; interviews, C. Vann Woodward, Glenn Weddington Rainey, and Herbert Aptheker, Roper Papers; Roper, *C. Vann Woodward,* 55–60.

30 Questionaire, *Modern Quarterly,* August 1932, Green Papers.

31 Ibid.; B. P. Gentry to PEG, with clipping from *Harnett County News,* [April] 1931,

Green Papers; Twelve Southerners, *I'll Take My Stand: The South and the Agrarian Tradition* (1931; reprint, New York: Harper and Row, Torchbooks, 1962).

32 Diary, vol. 6, 7 November 1928, Green Papers.

33 Bakshy, "Film: Class War," *Nation,* 26 October 1932, p. 409.

34 PEG to Clark, 7 January 1932; James K. Boyd to PEG, 20 March 1932, Green Papers.

35 Henry Harrison Kroll, *The Cabin in the Cotton* (New York: Long and Smith, 1931).

36 Bakshy, "Class War," p. 409; Mordaunt Hall, "The Screen: A Southern Dirge," *New York Times,* 30 September 1932, p. 17; *The Motion Picture Guide,* ed. Jay Robert Nash and Stanley Ralph Ross, vol. 2 (Chicago: Cinebooks, 1985, 1987), s.v. "Cabin in the Cotton"; Kroll, *The Cabin in the Cotton.*

37 Diary, vol. 6, 1932; telegram, PEG to Florence Bowers, 23 September 1932; Miriam Bonner to PEG, 3 February 1932; Bonner to PEG, 27 October 1932; PEG to MGJ, 22 April 1932, Green Papers.

38 PEG, memorandum, "The Silver Dollar," 21 May 1932, Green Papers.

39 Ibid.; Bonner to PEG, 3 February 1932; diary, vol. 6, spring entries, 1932; Lucien Hubbard to PEG, interoffice memorandum, 23 May 1932, Green Papers.

40 PEG to Louis Graves, 19 March 1932, Green Papers.

41 Ibid.; diary, vol. 6, spring 1932; PEG to ELG, [March] 1932; PEG to ELG, 6 March 1932, Green Papers.

42 PEG to Graves, 19 March 1932, Green Papers.

43 Ibid.

CHAPTER 10. ACTUALIZING ART

1 Odum Papers, 1922–35; Harry Woodburn Chase Papers, 1928–30, Presidential Papers, UNC Archives; on Odum, see Brazil, "Howard W. Odum," and "Social Forces." On Graham, the late Augustus Burns shared the ms. of a planned biography of the UNC president; he talked with me at length, and it was his interpretation that Graham was essentially a "windbag," very shrewd politically and with good instincts, but lacking the courage to engage in the most difficult fights and lacking the tenacity to finish some of his most important campaigns; Readers' Reports notes from Gus Burns's review of this study, ca. 1998, and personal notes on Gus Burns's remarks, October 1998, Roper Papers. On the other hand, the longtime student of educational reform and civil rights Joseph A. Herzenberg finds Graham to be a sincere and courageous reformist, as does the historian C. Vann Woodward. On the contrast between PEG and most—if not every other one—of the UNC characters in 1935–37, see interviews, Woodward and Joseph A. Herzenberg, Roper Papers.

2 See correspondence between James Spencer Love (styled "B" for "Brother") and his sister (styled "Si" for "Sister"), James Spencer Love Papers, Southern Historical Collection; see esp. Si to B, 22 January 1935; B to Si, 21 January 1935. Annette Cox Wright, who is preparing a biography of the industrialist Love, pointed out this correspondence to me and discussed it with me.

3 Phillips Russell and PEG often took road trips to collect folktales and folksongs, and they enjoyed each other's company immensely. Russell later married PEG's sister Caro Mae. B to Si, 25 January 1935, Love Papers.

4 Diary, vol. 6, 6 June, 11 July, 15 September, and 19 September 1935, Green Papers.

5 See Roper, *C. Vann Woodward,* 95–96; interviews, Woodward and Glenn Weddington Rainey, Roper Papers; correspondence, Woodward and Rainey, Glenn Weddington Rainey Papers, Special Collections, Emory University Library, Atlanta.

6 See esp. Woodward, letter to the editor and editorial clipping, 1935, from *Chapel Hill Tar Heel,* enclosures, in Woodward to Rainey, 3 March 1935, Rainey Papers.

7 Ibid. See also *Southern Textile Bulletin,* North Carolina Collection.

8 Diary, vol. 6, 18 September 1935, Green Papers. On chauvinistic rhetoric among the era's socialists, see W. A. Swanberg, *Norman Thomas: The Last Idealist* (New York: Charles Scribner's Sons, 1976).

9 Looking back on the first half of the 1930s, PEG declared that Hollywood work was so stultifying that it diminished his other work; the Group Theater came with opportunities at just the right time, he announced, as quoted in *Sherwood Anderson's Diaries,* ed. Campbell, 68–69. Diary, vol. 5, esp. years 1930 and 1931, and vol. 6, esp. years 1935 and 1936, Green Papers; Harold Clurman, *The Fervent Years: The Story of the Group Theatre and the Thirties* (New York: Alfred A. Knopf, 1945); Wendy Smith, *Real Life Drama: The Group Theatre in America, 1931–1946* (New York: Alfred A. Knopf, 1990).

10 See esp. Smith on the racist treatment of actresses Fannie Bell De Knight and Rose McClendon, in *Real Life Drama,* 36.

11 Ibid.; PEG to Clark, 8 December 1930, Green Papers.

12 PEG to ELG, 1 July 1926; PEG to Nell Battle Lewis, 16 March 1927; diary, vol. 5, 15 and 17 June, 10 October, and 1 and 6 November 1928; Clark to PEG, 6 March 1929, Green Papers; Moses to PEG, 29 December 1932, and ms. "The American Theatre, 1932," Moses Papers.

13 See esp. diary, vol. 5, fall 1930 and correspondence with Clark and Shiel, 1929–30, esp. Clark to PEG, 29 November 1929; Clark to PEG, 9 December 1929; PEG to Theresa Helburn, 1 March 1930; Clark to PEG, 8 April 1930; Clark to PEG, 29 November 1930; Frank J. Shiel to PEG, 6 December 1930, Green Papers.

14 Clurman, *Fervent Years;* Smith, *Real Life Drama;* diary, vol. 5, December 1930, January 1931; correspondence with Clark and Shiel, December 1930–February 1931; Clark to PEG, quoting Crawford, 8 December 1930, Green Papers.

15 Clurman, *Fervent Years,* 43, 44; Smith, *Real Life Drama,* 16, 17, 32, 36, 52–57. Cheryl Crawford to PEG, 27 July 1929, Green Papers.

16 *"The House of Connelly" and Other Plays.*

17 Ibid.

18 Ibid. Actually, PEG's understanding of Jesse Tate evolved: in early versions Jesse Tate was an idealist so enraged with his daughter that he disowned her, but subsequent revisions made him more practical and took away his anger; PEG to ELG, 1 July 1926; PEG to Nell Battle Lewis, 16 March 1927; diary, vol. 5, 15 and 17 June 1928; diary, vol. 6, 11 October, 1 and 6 November 1928; Cheryl Crawford to PEG, 27 July 1929; PEG to Clark, 8 December 1931, Green Papers.

19 Diary, vol. 5, 15 and 17 June 1928, Green Papers.

20 Moses was not permitted to buy the rights because of a ruling by Samuel French's Frank J. Shiel. Shiel's decision was a great frustration to Moses and at the time a considerably greater frustration for the playwright, Moses to Alfred R. McIntyre, 25 January 1933, Moses Papers; Smith, *Real Life Drama,* 52.

21 Smith, *Real Life Drama,* 36, 52.

22 Ibid., 60.

23 Ibid., 62.

24 See reviews and notes kept by Moses, "American Drama" Scrapbook, Moses Papers. Correspondence with Shiel, 1931–33, Green Papers.

25 Clurman, *Fervent Years;* Smith, *Real Life Drama,* 261–67.

26 Smith, *Real Life Drama,* 261–67.

27 Ibid., 261–77; H. Margaret Berry to files, blind copy of solicitation letter, 17 October 1918, Pratt Papers.

28 Smith, *Real Life Drama,* 258–61.

29 Ibid., 261–77. See also Weill and Lenya, *Speak Low.*

30 Weill and Lenya, *Speak Low,* 194 and editor's note.

31 "Paul Green," in *Speak Low,* by Weill and Lenya; see esp. 194.

32 Smith, *Real Life Drama,* 261–77.

33 Ibid.; Jaroslav Hasek, a Central Powers veteran of World War I, wrote short stories in his native Czech language about the soldier Svejk, and he wrote the uncompleted multivolume *Good Soldier Svejk,* translated by Paul Selver as *The Good Soldier: Schweik* (1930); playscript in German, *The Good Soldier Schweik,* by Erwin Piscator, 1928; "Jaroslav Hasek," in *European Writers: The Twentieth Century,* ed. George Stade, vol. 9 (New York: Charles Scribner's Sons, 1983), s.v.; [Robert] Burns Mantle, ed., *The Best Plays of 1936–1937* (New York: Dodd, Mead, 1946), 96–141; Robert Benchley, "Johnny Johnson," *New Yorker,* November 1936, p. 26.

34 Diary, vol. 6, 3 January and 9 August 1936, 22 June 1939, Green Papers.

35 Diary, vol. 6, 1934 passim, and esp. 24 September 1934, Green Papers.

36 Diary, vol. 6, 3–6 April 1935, Green Papers.

37 Diary, vol. 6, 12 July 1935, Green Papers.

38 Ibid.; diary, vol. 6, 15 September 1935, Green Papers. See also Glenda E. Gill interview with PEG, cited in Gill, *White Grease Paint,* 14.

39 Gill, *White Grease Paint,* 14; notes, 1936, "Metamorphosis"; notes [ca. 1935–36] attached, "Notes on Paris," 1918–19, Green Papers.

40 PEG, *Hymn to the Rising Sun* (New York: Samuel French, 1936). All citations to the text of the play are from this edition of the published script.

41 On irony stripping away delusion, see Lester G. Crocker, "Introduction" to Voltaire's *Candide* (1759; reprint, New York: Simon and Schuster, Pocket Books, 1962). On the turning of irony back upon the ironist, see A. Alvarez, "The Noble Poet," *New York Review of Books,* 18 July 1985, 7–10; Roper, *C. Vann Woodward,* 232–67.

42 Diary, vol. 6, 14 and 18 October 1935; Richard Wright, *American Hunger,* rev. ed., with afterword by Michel Fabre (New York: Harper and Row, 1977), 113–26.

43 PEG letter to Percival Wilde, quoted in full in the introduction to *Hymn to the Rising Sun,* in *Contemporary One-Act Plays from Nine Countries,* ed. Percival Wilde (Boston: Little, Brown, 1936).

44 For good, brief, and accessible descriptions of such reader-response theory, see Linda Hutcheon, *The Politics of Postmodernism* (London: Routledge, 1989) and *A Poetics of Postmodernism: History, Theory, and Fiction* (London: Routledge, 1988). Cf. PEG's virulent response to news that Samuel Beckett had won the Nobel Prize, letters to his daughters: PEG to Jan[et] and Jack [Catlin], 30 October 1969 and PEG to Bets[y] and Bill [Moyers], 31 October 1969, Green Papers.

45 See Roper, "Actualizing Art: Paul Green's *Hymn to the Rising Sun* and the Campaign against Capital Punishment in the Old North State, 1934–37," *North Carolina English Teacher* 52 (1994): 11–13.

46 Ibid.; Wilde, *Contemporary One-Act Plays;* diary, vol. 6, October entries, 1935, Green Papers.

47 See program and clippings, esp. Brooks Atkinson's favorable retrospective review, "The Play," clipping, January 1937, Green Papers.

48 Correspondence, 1936–37, Green Papers. See also Avery, *A Southern Life,* introduction and explanatory notes. Avery arranged a dramatic reading of *Hymn* for North Car-

olina Writers Conference, 30 July 1988, brochure and notes, North Carolian Writers Conference Papers, 1988, North Carolina Collection.

49 See Wright, *American Hunger.*

50 Crossman, *The God That Failed.*

51 Wright's ellipsis in quote. Correspondence, 1936–1937, Green Papers; Avery, *A Southern Life;* Wright, *American Hunger,* 113–26. See also John Herbert Roper, "On Richard Wright and Paul Eliot Green," *Richard Wright Newsletter* 5 (spring/summer 1997): 1, 7.

52 See Gill, *White Grease Paint,* 14.

53 Ibid.

CHAPTER 11. NEW DIRECTIONS

1 UNC *Catalogue,* 1938–39; PEG folder, 1937–38, UNC Archives; Glenn Blackburn has shown me a ms. concerning the life and thought of E. Maynard Adams in the philosophy department at UNC, and he has talked with me about PEG's influence on Adams and the direction in which Adams took the philosophy department at UNC, that is, the department had an old-fashioned and somewhat eccentric focus on holistic and world-view moral philosophy, all brought off professionally and with full academic trimmings but in no way in the new "mainstream" analytical philosophy. See also Glen Blackburn, "Three Chapel Hill Liberals: E. Maynard Adams," and "E. Maynard Adams," address, 16 August 2000, St. George Tucker Society, Nashville.

2 Hallie Flanagan to PEG, 13 July 1939, with enclosure "Production Record of the FTP," Green Papers. U.S. Congress, Senate, *Congressional Record,* 76th Cong., 1st sess., 1939, 84, 8088–8104; U.S., Congress, House, *Congressional Record,* 76th Cong., 1st sess., 1939, 84, pt. 7, 7223–35; Clifton A. Woodrum, "Extended Remarks," *Appendix to the Congressional Record,* 76th Cong., 1st sess., 1939, 84, pt. 13.

3 Flanagan, "Production Record" and "Letter to Congress," enclosure, Flanagan to PEG, 13 July 1939, Green Papers; U.S. Congress, Senate, *Congressional Record,* 76th Cong., 1st sess., 1939, 84, pt. 8, 8088–8104.

4 See correspondence with Flanagan, with Brooks Atkinson, and with Clark, 1939; and see diary, vol. 6, 1939, Green Papers.

5 Diary, vol. 6, passim, but esp. 2 October 1934 and 5 July 1935, Green Papers. *Sherwood Anderson's Diaries,* ed. Campbell, esp. 5 December 1936.

6 PEG to ELG, "Sunday Night" [fall 1921]; n.d. "Thursday night" [spring 1921]; [December 1921; "Tuesday night" [spring 1922], written during an on-site inspection of Ocracoke; newspaper clipping, 1926, about Ocracoke and history and legends, Green Papers.

7 James Branch Cabell, *Let Me Lie* (New York: Farrar, Straus, 1947).

8 See earlier discussion of prejudice, antisemitism, and PEG's growth and development during World War I and 1920s, as set in context by Langmuir, *Definition of Antisemitism;* see also in 1941 and 1942 examples of continuing prejudice, but prejudice well short of antisemitism.

9 PEG, diary, vol. 6, 6 January 1934, Green Papers.

10 Hoke Norris, "Negro Novelist at Chapel Hill," Associated Press feature, 1941, clipping in Green Papers; notes on discussions with William Terry Couch, Koch, and ELG, before full meeting with committee about Raleigh celebration, diary, vol. 6, 16 January 1937; other notes, diary, vol. 6, 23 April–4 July 1937, and esp. 22 July 1937, Green Papers.

11 Ibid. See esp. diary, vol. 6, 23 July 1937, Green Papers, for extended notes and discussion of Wagnerian theory for opera in context of this Hegelianism.

12 Auden, "Introduction," *Selected Poetry and Prose of Byron.*

13 See correspondence with Clark, 1931–41.

14 Diary, vol. 6, 5–17 July 1937, Green Papers.

15 See diary, vol. 6, 1937, passim, but esp. 5–17 July 1937, Green Papers.

16 "Dialogue at Evening," *Lost Colony Souvenir and Program,* Green Papers.

17 Ibid.

18 See correspondence with Nell Battle Lewis, 1937; see also diary, 1937, Green Papers.

19 *The Lost Colony,* esp. 2.5. James H. Merrill, *The Indians' New World: Catawbas and Their Neighbors from European Contact through the Era of Removal* (Chapel Hill: University of North Carolina Press for the Institute of Early American History and Culture, 1989).

20 *Lost Colony Souvenir and Program,* 1939, pp. 15–17; PEG, *The Lost Colony* (Chapel Hill: University of North Carolina Press, 1946), "Dialogue at Evening," xvi; "Dialogue at Evening," in *The Hawthorn Tree: Essays* (Chapel Hill: University of North Carolina Press, 1943), 27–36; PEG, *Dramatic Heritage,* 42–48.

21 Gill, *White Grease Paint;* on Robeson, Clark to PEG, 16 December 1925; 20 January 1926; Clark to PEG, with enclosure from Mrs. Paul Robeson, 8 February and 9 November 1926; Russell Sedgwick to PEG, 14 September 1930; PEG to ELG, [January?] 1942, about Robeson and roles in Hollywood, Green Papers. See also Duberman, *Paul Robeson.*

22 Wright, *American Hunger.*

23 Richard Wright, *Native Son* (New York: Harper, 1940).

24 Correspondence, Richard Wright and PEG, Richard Wright folder, 1934–42; correspondence, 1924–25, Benjamin Brawley and PEG, Benjamin Brawley folder, *Reviewer* folder, Green Papers. Interviews, John Hope Franklin and Aurelia Franklin, 10 November 1978, Roper Papers. On Regionalist skittishness, see Daniel T. Rodgers, "Regionalism and the Burdens of Progress," in *Region, Race, and Reconstruction: Essays in Honor of C. Vann Woodward,* ed. J. Morgan Kousser and James M. McPherson (New York: Oxford University Press, 1982), 3–26. However, for spirited defense of Regionalist courage by three who were certainly courageous in their own right, cf. interviews, Guy Johnson and Guion Johnson, 10 January 1980, and William Terry Couch, 10–11 January 1980, Roper Papers.

25 Interviews, Guy Johnson and Guion Johnson, 10 January 1980, and William Terry Couch, 10–11 January 1980, Roper Papers. See Benjamin Franklin Bullock, *Practical Farming for the South* (Chapel Hill: University of North Carolina Press, 1936).

26 Interviews, Johnson and Johnson, 10 January 1980, and Couch, 10–11 January 1980, Roper Papers; see also Charles W. Eagles, *Jonathan Daniels and Race Relations: The Evolution of a Southern Liberal* (Knoxville: University of Tennessee Press, 1982).

27 Hoke Norris, "Negro Novelist in Chapel Hill," [summer 1941], Associated Press clipping, Green Papers. Joseph F. Steelman, "Comments: Strange Careers Indeed!" paper presented at the meeting of the Association of Historians of Eastern North Carolina, October 1979.

28 Frances Saunders, "Responses," PEG Centennial/UNC Bicentennial, UNC Humanities Extension, March 1994.

29 James Halstead, "Photographic Timeline," *Sandhills Review* 46 (1994): 9.

30 Long years later, PEG put the image into essay form, collecting a number of essays and addresses, including some from the 1930s and early 1940s: PEG, *Plough and Furrow: Essays* (New York: Samuel French, 1963).

31 See correspondence between PEG, Houseman, and Wright in Green Papers; see this correspondence collected and arranged in Avery, *A Southern Life;* see also Wright, *American Hunger.*

32 For useful discussions of finances and critical debates, see Axel Storm, "Broadway Nights," King features, 3 April 1941. See also clippings arranged in PEG, 1941: Burns Mantle, in 1941 very much the acknowledged dean of theater critics, announced his vote for the New York Theater Critics Prize and made the connection between PEG's symphonic-drama theories and this play: Mantle, *"Native Son," New York Daily News;* also, Mark Barron (Associated Press critic) described *Native Son* as "pinnacle of the season" and had special praise for PEG's "expert hands," in Barron, *"Native Son* Hits Pinnacle"; Arthur Pollock reported that he himself voted for *Native Son* in the early rounds of voting, but finally switched his vote to *Watch on the Rhine* when it became apparent that Hellman's play would win (comparing the two, Pollock says, *Native Son* is "sharper, surer, more lucid"), Pollock, *"Watch on the Rhine* Wins Critics' Award"; others include Ralph W. Carey, "Among New York Theaters: *Native Son*"; John Hobart, "John Hobart Goes to the Opening of a Play," *San Francisco Chronicle;* "Native Son," *New Yorker,* 5 April 1941; Hoke Norris, "Negro Novelist in Chapel Hill," Associated Press feature; Hart Schaaf, *"Native Son* Hailed," *Richmond Times-Dispatch;* Arthur Spaeth, "The Play: *Native Son," Cleveland News;* Ashton Stevens, "Thrills, Chills, and Canada Lee," *Chicago Herald-American;* Ira Wolfert, "Orson Makes Native Son," *Cleveland Plain Dealer;* Theodore Strauss of *New York Times* drama department in an address praised *Native Son* as *the* exception to a bad season, "Poor Broadway Season," *Long Branch (N.J.) Record,* 15 April 1941; "Richard Wright's Play *Native Son* Acclaimed," *Tampa Bulletin,* 5 April 1941; Richard Peters, "Hanna's *Native Son,"* unidentified Cleveland newspaper, 4 November 1941; Sidney Whipple, "Welles Strives Only for Effect," unknown newspaper; George Ross, "So This Is Broadway," unknown newspaper, clippings in Green Papers.

   There were some negative responses, led by the Hearst publications and by critic John Anderson, who had resisted PEG's Pulitzer recognition back in 1927; *New York Journal-American,* 1 April 1941, p. 1. Others were unhappy with aspects of PEG's writing, though not as sharply so as was Anderson: Stark Young, *"Native Son," New Republic,* 7 April 1941; Kaspar Monahn, "Welles's *Native Son* a Lurid Melodrama"; William F. McDermott, "Canada Lee Gives a Moving Peformance," *Cleveland Plain Dealer;* Lloyd Lewis, *"Native Son* a Blend of Horror," unidentified Chicago newspaper; Charles Gentry, *"Native Son* is Grim Fare," unidentified newspaper, clippings in Green Papers; Jack Gaven, "Orson Welles' New Play," United Press International, 3 April 1941. There were also some quirky responders, not least PEG's own sister Caro Mae Green Russell, who in a regionally syndicated column, "Literary Lantern," announced that her brother had written many things "to which *Native Son* cannot hold a candle"; and the Communist Party's critic, who somehow failed to mention PEG or Welles in a very long piece, Ralph Warner, "The Critics Have Their Say about *Native Son,"* unidentified but apparently *New York Daily Worker,* clippings in Green Papers.

33 *The Lone Star* continued in production in Galveston, Texas, until 1989, and *Trumpet in the Land* continued in production in Dover, Ohio, until 1993. Other symphonic dramas have had more occasional performances.

CHAPTER 12. THE GOOD WAR TESTS THE IDEALS

1 Eric J. Hobsbawm, *The Age of Extremes: A History of the World, 1914–1994* (New York: Pantheon, 1994), for recent textbook treatment, with useful bibliography; on PEG's

evolving reactions, see diary, vols. 6–8, 1939–42, esp. vol. 6, 30 August 1939; vol. 8, [1942?], program proposal for radio show with James Boyd; see correspondence, 1939–42, esp. PEG to ELG, [December?] 1941; PEG to ELG, 25 December 1941; PEG to ELG, January 1942; PEG to MGJ, 19 April 1942; PEG to George R. Coffman, 8 October 1942, Green Papers; also, "A Christmas Prayer," 25 December 1943, program litany for services at Chapel of the Cross, Green Papers.

2 Phrase "chilling shadow of evil" is in PEG to Coffman, 8 October 1942, words reprinted in Avery, *A Southern Life,* 369–70.

3 PEG to ELG, 25 December 1941; PEG to ELG, January 1942. PEG never blamed Woodrow Wilson for the failure of such negotiations, and Avery told me that PEG's favorite president remained Wilson, something that is borne out in PEG diaries, vols. 5–8, 1937–43, Green Papers.

4 Interviews, Frank Winkler Ryan, 15 July 1989 and 18 September 1996, Roper Papers.

5 See diary, vols. 6–8, 1939–41; see correspondence, esp. with ELG, Green Papers.

6 PEG to MGJ, 1941, PEG, quoted phrases from reprinted version, Avery, *A Southern Life,* 365–68; PEG to ELG, January 1942, Green Papers. MGJ's son William "Billy" Johnson was diagnosed with lesions on his lungs shortly after he began his training at Fort Jackson in Columbia, S.C., and he was dismissed from the army for medical reasons. He returned to Chapel Hill, finished school, and also earned a law degree, eventually becoming an important trustee for UNC; in fact, he signed my graduate diploma as chairman of the university's board of governors. Robert "Bobby" Koch had completed the master's degree in art at UNC before enlisting; the younger Koch served out his tour, surviving combat and earning rank of lieutenant colonel. After resigning his commission in 1946, Koch began a lengthy career teaching art at Princeton University. On YMCA, see *Daily Tar Heel* student newspaper files, 1938–42, and also William S. Powell, *The First State University: A Pictorial History of the University of North Carolina* (Chapel Hill: University of North Carolina Press, 1972), 143, 211–36; interviews, Ryan, 1989, 1996. On Howard Kennedy Beale, History Department Papers, 1937–43, UNC Archives; Roper, *C. Vann Woodward,* 130; Woodward to Rainey, 4 December 1942, 19 October 1942, Rainey Papers.

7 PEG to MGJ, 1941, Green Papers; quoted phrases are reprinted in Avery, *A Southern Life.*

8 PEG to MGJ, 1941, Green Papers; quoted phrases reprinted in Avery, *A Southern Life.* See diary, vol. 6, 30 August 1939, Green Papers.

9 PEG, "Johnny and this War," *Raleigh News and Observer,* 12 April 1942; PEG, "A Christmas Prayer," 25 December 1943, Green Papers; verses printed, Church Service Bulletin, Chapel of the Cross, 25 December 1943, bulletin shared with author by parishoner.

10 PEG to ELG, January 1942, Green Papers; PEG was especially upset over reports of war profiteering by munitions makers and other manufacturers in the Burma campaigns.

11 Ibid.

12 Burns, *Soldier of Freedom;* Philip Taft, *Organizing Dixie,* ed. Gary M. Fink, Contributions in Labor History, no. 9 (Westport, Conn.: Greenwood Press, 1981); Gary Brown Tindall, *The Emergence of the New South, 1913–1945,* History of the South Series, ed. Ellis Merton Coulter and Wendell Holmes, vol. 10 (Baton Rouge: Louisiana State University Press, 1967).

13 Roper, *C. Vann Woodward,* 95–96; Woodward to Rainey, 3 March 1935, Rainey Papers. *The* scholar of these piedmont episodes is Liston Pope, author of *Millhands and Preachers: A Study of Gastonia* (New Haven: Yale University Press, 1942).

14 Quoted words are in Woodward to Rainey, 3 March 1935, Rainey Papers. See also PEG, diary, vol. 7, 14 April 1940, Green Papers.

15 "Fred Erwin Beal Gains Freedom under Parole," *Raleigh News and Observer,* 9 January 1942, pp. 1, 2.

16 Ibid. See also Pope, *Millhands and Preachers;* and Avery, *A Southern Life,* 317ff.

17 PEG, "Preface for Professors," May 1942, address distributed to members of faculty and reprinted in PEG, *The Hawthorn Tree,* 1–16. The essay in the latter is the one cited here.

18 Ibid., 9.

19 Ibid, 13.

20 Italics mark words from Episcopal litany, "Burial of the Dead," *Book of Common Prayer* (1927), 324; language from King James translation of the Gospel according to Saint John. In another possible reading, PEG may be speaking about all of his most inspiriting teachers, starting with Hubbard Fulton Page at the Buies Creek Academy and including Carolina's Proff Koch, Greenlaw, and others; but even in such a reading, Williams would stand out as the *primus inter pares.* In any case, the essayist is quite particular with number and gender: "I can still see him as he looked out over his class, his eyes full of vigor and joy"; and he is quite clear when the inspiring believer taught, "twenty one years ago," too late to be referring to Page: *The Hawthorn Tree,* 11.

21 "'Teachers Kill Students' Enthusiasm,' Says Green," *Chapel Hill Daily Tar Heel,* 26 May 1942, p. 1. Copy also in Green Papers. Frank Porter Graham's brand of Christianity and liberalism is well documented in John Ehle, *Dr. Frank: Life with Frank Porter Graham* (Chapel Hill, N.C.: Franklin Street Books, 1994). I rented a garage apartment next door to Robert B. House in academic year 1971–72 and spoke with him often; I found him to be fully as committed to this combination of Protestant reformism and liberalism as Graham and PEG.

22 George R. Coffman to PEG, 6 October 1942; PEG to Coffman, 8 October 1942, Green Papers; PEG letter reprinted in Avery, *A Southern Life,* 369–70; see esp. Avery's careful notes, 369ff.

23 PEG, *The Hawthorn Tree,* and *Forever Growing: Some Notes on a Credo for Teachers* (Chapel Hill: University of North Carolina Press, 1945); interviews, Couch, 10–11 January 1980, Roper Papers.

24 PEG, *Forever Growing,* 93–95.

25 PEG, "That Evening Sun Go Down," in *The Hawthorn Tree,* esp. 152.

26 Ted Robinson of the *Cleveland Plain Dealer* contributed a blurb for this volume's dust jacket and for the dust jacket of *Forever Growing.* See also clippings, *Hawthorn Tree* folder, PEG, 1944, esp. *Chicago Sun,* 30 April 1944; *Christian Science Monitor,* 6 May 1944, p. 12; W. P. Eaton, *Weekly Book Review,* 30 April 1944, p. 17; Gilbert Chase, *Saturday Review of Literature,* 14 February 1944, p. 34.

27 Diana Trilling was virtually alone in her unhappiness with the novel: "I am a little bewildered by so much response to so conventional a little book." See other reviews: *Nation,* 4 September 1943, 274; *Yale Review* 8 (1943): 33; *Social Forces* 22 (1943): 240; *Library Journal* 68 (1943): 363; *Atlantic,* October 1943, p. 131; *Commonweal,* 17 September 1943, 543; Rosemary Dawson, *New Yorker,* 6 September 1943, p. 109; *New York Times,* 22 August 1943, p. 4.

28 Ehle, "Paul Green"; conversation with Ehle, 17 March 1994, strongly reinforces his remarks of that day, notes taken and filed after the fact, Roper Papers.

29 PEG, *Forever Growing;* PEG, *Salvation on a String: Stories* (New York: Harper and Brothers, 1946). On the latter, see Harvey Easom Diaries, 1922–27, Green Papers.

30 Quotations, PEG, *Forever Growing,* 20; Jesus' words about stone and bread, Matt. 7:9; Luke 11:11.

31 PEG, *Forever Growing,* 42. PEG draws self-consciously from Saint Paul's Epistle to the Romans, Rom. 3, 4. The quotation is from Ps. 1:3; and the imagery of the tree fed and nourished by the true stream is prophet Isaiah, Isa. 35, 41, 44, 54, 55, and 58. Finally, he draws self-consciously on Jesus' words concerning living water as quoted by Saint John the Evangelist in John 7:38 (a quoting of Isa. 55) and John 4:14 (a quoting of Isa. 58). All quotations as translated in King James version, the only version that PEG used.

32 PEG, *Salvation on a String;* see folder, "Salvation on a String," 1946, and Harvey Easom Diaries, 1919–22, Green Papers.

33 Telegram, PEG to Harry S. Truman, 18 October 1945, Green Papers; fully reprinted in Avery, *A Southern Life,* 418–19. Avery also provides useful context in his footnotes, including Senator Bailey's negative and even disdainful response to PEG's telegram, 419ff. On Truman's decision and statement, *New York Times,* 9 October 1945, p. 1, also cited by Avery, 418ff.

34 The diaries, 1944–46, Green Papers, confirm Avery's careful work; see esp. Avery, *A Southern Life,* 391–96 ff.

CHAPTER 13. VICTORY IN CIVIL RIGHTS

1 Marion Fitz-Simons, "A Different Path," *Sandhills Review* 46 (1994): 1–2.

2 Richard Sennett, *The Fall of Public Man* (New York: Alfred A. Knopf, 1977), esp. introduction.

3 See correspondence with family members, 1946–65, Green Papers; see also interviews, Betsy Green Moyer, Laurence Green Avery, and EGG, Roper Papers. See also tax records, 1946–65, Green Papers. See Ehle, "Paul Green."

4 See interviews, Betsy Green Moyer, Laurence Green Avery, and EGG, Roper Papers.

5 Ehle, "Paul Green."

6 See correspondence, Paul Eliot Green Jr., Byrd Green, JGC, Elizabeth Green Moyer, 1946–65, and diary entries, 1946–65, Green Papers.

7 PEG, *The Common Glory* (1948) playscript; also, *The Common Glory* (1947, 1950), book, and other versions and songbooks, 1947–76, Green Papers; PEG, *Faith of Our Fathers* (1949); other versions and songbooks, 1949–50, Green Papers.

8 See observations by Kurt Weill in *Speak Low,* by Weill and Lenya; extensive observations and documentation by Avery, *A Southern Life,* esp. nn. on 282, 285–86; 459–60; diary, esp. 16–20 December 1937, Green Papers.

9 See diary, 1937–50, Green Papers. See also Avery, *A Southern Life.*

10 PEG, diary, 16–20 December 1937, Green Papers; quotation is used by Avery, *A Southern Life,* 286n.; see other notations and correspondence collected by Avery; Robert Mason, "Lee's Second Surrender," *Sandhills Review* 46 (1994): 57–64; quotation on 59.

11 Mason, "Lee's Second Surrender," p. 57.

12 PEG, *Dog on the Sun: Stories* (Chapel Hill: University of North Carolina Press, 1949); "*Dog on the Sun*" folder with clippings, 1949, Green Papers; see photograph, *Sandhills Review* 46 (1994): 10; "Collards and Culture" folder, 1949, Green Papers; also "Collards and Culture" folder, 1949, North Carolina Collection.

13 On Reynolds, see earlier discussion about his career in U.S. House and his effects on arts and theater funding. The hog farmer was Olla Ray Boyd, and his wife was quoted widely, but see esp. Ehle, *Dr. Frank,* 162.

14 See August M. Burns III and Julian M. Pleasants, *Frank Porter Graham and the 1950 Senate Race in North Carolina* (Chapel Hill: University of North Carolina Press, 1990); and Ehle, *Dr. Frank.*

15 Burns and Pleasants, *Frank Porter Graham;* and Ehle, *Dr. Frank.*

16 Interview, Woodward, 18 July 1978, Roper Papers; flyer quoted in Ehle, *Dr. Frank,* and Burns and Pleasants, *Frank Porter Graham.*

17 On race-baiting and "Mr. Nigger," see John Charles McNeill, "Mr. Nigger," in *The Pocket McNeill,* 62–63; Burns and Pleasants, *Frank Porter Graham;* Ehle, *Dr. Frank,* 175 and 176, and passim. Frank Porter Graham Papers, 1950 Senate campaign, Southern Historical Collection, University of North Carolina, Chapel Hill.

18 Joseph A. Herzenberg, onetime Chapel Hill town council member and once a graduate student at UNC, studied Frank Porter Graham's career intensively, interviewing Graham often and thoroughly examining the Graham Papers. Herzenberg indicates that Burns and Pleasants are correct on this score; see interviews, Herzenberg, 18 July 2001 and 28 May 2002, Roper Papers.

19 Ehle, *Dr. Frank,* suggests as much; Burns and Pleasants, *Frank Porter Green,* pound home the point; and the late Burns shared a partially completed biography of Graham in which Graham's "windbag qualities" and chatty ineffectuality emerge as an even larger issue throughout his career than in this one campaign. Herzenberg disagrees with the above but concedes that Graham did miss many appointments and did not speak effectively in the runoff campaign; interviews, Joseph A. Herzenberg, 18 July 2001 and 28 May 2002, Roper Papers.

20 On this point, all authorities agree: Grahamn was financially, emotionally, professionally, and to some degree even physically overwhelmed by the political rejection handed him by North Carolina voters in the 1950 runoff. He attempted with no success at all to pretend that he was unaffected.

21 See folder, "Peer Gynt," 1950–51; and diary entries, January–April 1951, Green Papers. *Ibsen's Peer Gynt: An American Version,* trans. PEG (1950). *The Best Plays of 1950–1951, and the Yearbook of Drama* ed. John Chapman (New York: Dodd, Mead, 1951), esp. p. 3.

22 Margaret Marshall, "Drama," *Nation,* 10 February 1951), pp. 139–40; *Theatre Arts* 35 (April 1951): 14; Arthur Diener, communication, *New York Times,* 4 February 1951, sec. 2, p. 1; Atkinson, "On Broadway," *New York Times,* 4 February 1951, sec. 2, p. 3; notices and features, *New York Times,* 21 January 1951, sec. 2, p. 3; and *New York Times,* 29 January 1951, p. 15. Also, Chapman, *Best Plays.*

23 Quote is from Marshall, "Drama." Observation about music is in *New York Times* features, but esp. Atkinson, "On Broadway."

24 Atkinson, "On Broadway"; Chapman, *Best Plays,* 3, 334; Gibbs, "Around Town," *New Yorker,* 10 February 1951, 61. See also *Catholic World* 172 (March 1951): 464; *Commonweal* 53 (February 1951): 468–69; *New Republic,* 5 March 1951, 22–23; *New York Theatre Critics' Reviews,* 1951, 373; *School and Society* 73 (March 1951): 184; *Theatre Arts* 35 (April 1951): 14.

25 Interviews, Couch, 9–10 January 1980; Ehle, 17 March 1994, Roper Papers. Ragan talked often with me about these issues and these personalities when we worked together on two books of his poetry that my St. Andrews Press published. I served as an executive officer for PEG's North Carolina Writers Conference between 1987

and 1989, and in that capacity came to know many of the prominent literary figures who had been active in the 1950s; there I came to know Walter Spearman and Betty Hodges. James K. Boyd, Thad Stem, and Betty Smith I knew only by reputation, by their writings, and by Ragan's reminiscences. John Ehle I came to know while working on the PEG project of his wartime poetry and this biography.

26 On Truman's social policies and his liberal advisors, see esp. Alonzo L. Hamby, *Beyond the New Deal: Harry S. Truman and American Liberalism* (New York: Columbia University Press, 1976), *Man of the People: A Life of Harry S. Truman,* rev. ed. (New York: Oxford University Press, 1998), and *Liberalism and Its Challenges, from* FDR *to Bush* (New York: Oxford University Press, 1992); see also John Bartlow Martin, *Adlai Stevenson* (New York: Harper and Brothers, 1952), and *Adlai Stevenson and His World: The Life of Adlai Stevenson* (Garden City, N.Y.: Doubleday, 1977), for discussion of those Truman liberals who remained active in Stevenson's failed campaign of 1952. See diary, 1950–51, correspondence 1950–51, including photographs, esp. one of PEG at Temple of Epidaurus, Green Papers.

27 PEG, *Dramatic Heritage, Serenata* (1953), "The Seventeenth Star" (1953), *Wilderness Road* (New York: Samuel French, 1955), and *The Founders* (New York: Samuel French, 1955). See folders "Serenata," 1953; "Seventeenth Star," 1953; "Wilderness Road," 1955; and "The Founders," 1955, Green Papers. Laurence Green Avery, "Paul Green Stories (Biographical and Fictional)," *Sandhills Review* 46 (1994): 15.

28 PEG, *The Confederacy* (New York: Samuel French, 1959); Mason, "Lee's Second Surrender," 57; The drama critic was Warner Twyford of *Norfolk Virginian-Pilot.* See also PEG, diary, 1957–58, Green Papers.

29 Ibid.

30 Mason, "Lee's Second Surrender"; Ed Devaney, "Serving in the Confederacy," *Sandhills Review* 46 (1994): 65–70.

31 Devaney, "Serving in the Confederacy," 67.

32 Mason, "Lee's Second Surrender," 63–64.

33 John Howard Griffin, *Black like Me* (Boston: Houghton Mifflin, 1961).

34 Heb. 11:25, 26.

35 Avery has carefully preserved the story, *A Southern Life,* 617–18; 621. See also PEG diary, October–November 1961, and correspondence between PEG and John Howard Griffin, esp. 3 December 1962, and PEG and Julius Tannenbaum, Norman Kantor, and Carl Lerner, 1962, Green Papers.

36 See reviews and notices collected in "Black like Me" folder, 1962–64, Green Papers. See esp. the harsh criticism of *New York Times* and *New Republic* critics, who blame Carl Lerner and his wife, Gerda Lerner, for what they regard as a very poor script: Bosley Crowther, "Screen: 'Black like Me,'" *New York Times,* 31 May 1964, p. 42; Stanley Kaufman, "The Fire This Time," *New Republic,* 23 May 1964, pp. 24, 26–27. Kaufman specifically credits PEG for his earlier dramatic works on behalf of justice for "Negroes," but seems unaware that PEG had much to do with the writing of the film, which he calls "slickly made, preachy, false." Crowther also seems unaware that PEG worked on the script and says scathingly of the Lerners that their script is "artificially sincere."

37 William C. Friday participated with me in a panel discussion about Chapel Hill liberals at a meeting of the Southern Historical Association, 12 November 1998. He took the position, as did I on the occasion, that there were many Chapel Hill liberals in the 1960s, enough to make them almost a folkloric type. Joining us on the panel was the late Augustus Merrimon "Gus" Burns, then working on a biography of Graham.

Burns doubted the substance of Graham's liberalism and on this panel spoke vigorously to the effect that we were exaggerating the extent of and power of liberalism in the campus and community of the era. Many other historians in attendance came forward to indicate that we were wrong, if not crazy. Burns did indicate that PEG was the real thing, even and especially if Graham was not. I now suspect that Burns and his legions of supporters were more right than wrong; but the point here is that Friday very much appreciated and even celebrated the label Chapel Hill liberal for himself—and for me.

38 A very negative portrayal of ineffective teaching is in the memoir "Shabby Genteel by Denham." A much more sympathethic observer who taught in RTVMP noted ruefully that PEG was not very effective in this post, and that some students had to be steered away from him; interview to be released along with his identity after his death and my death, Roper Papers.

39 Interview, Ragan, 31 July 1986, Roper Papers; Ragan covered the controversies in the state capital for the *Raleigh News and Observer,* and he also had a management position with Associated Press for the period and the place. By contrast, William Billingsley gives a much more negative view of Governor Terry Sanford, and of all the higher officials at the University of North Carolina, in "The Anti-Communist Crusade at the University of North Carolina" (Ph.D. diss., University of California at Irvine, 1996), and *The Anti-Communist Crusade at the University of North Carolina* (Athens: University of Georgia Press, 2000).

40 On this point, namely, that UNC figures essentially got around the ban between 1962 and 1968, all authorities are in agreement, including Billingsley, *Anti-Communist Crusade;* interviews, Ragan, 31 July 1986; Herbert Aptheker, 23 March 1985, Roper Papers. See also copy of unpublished ms. shared by Henry Mayer, 1999, Roper Papers; Mayer was student body president at a time when the ban was still in effect, and he was able to defy the letter and the spirit of the ban with full cooperation of UNC officials; Aptheker, then the most prominent Communist in the United States, relates a humorous story of speaking to a very large crowd, "several hundred" he remembered, of students and faculty members who stood on the campus while he himself spoke from a city street a few yards "off-campus."

41 PEG, University Day Address, 12 October 1963, Green Papers, and University Day Address, 12 October 1963, UNC Archives.

42 Jesse Helms, "WRAL Viewpoint Number 710," 15 October 1963, copy in Green Papers; copy also in "WRAL Viewpoint" files, North Carolina Collection.

43 See diary, October and November 1963; see correspondence between PEG, A. J. Fletcher, and Sam Beard, and Federal Communications Commission, October and November 1963; see correspondence collected, arranged, and carefully discussed by Avery, *A Southern Life.*

44 PEG, *Plough and Furrow,* and *Cross and Sword* (New York: Samuel French, 1965); "Cross and Sword" folder, 1965, Green Papers.

45 Ehle, *The Free Men,* passim. So identified with this phase of the civil rights movement was the community of Chapel Hill and the University of North Carolina that the community and the university were even objects of some resentment by those who still supported segregation, as I did in high school, as noted, John Herbert Roper, "Confessions of a Chapel Hill Liberal," *Southern Cultures* 6 (2000): 112–18.

CHAPTER 14. A TIME OF TROUBLES

1 Mims, *The Advancing South.*

2 See PEG, diary, 1941, and correspondence with principals, including Houseman, 1941, "Native Son" folder, Green Papers. See also the full annotation and ample explanations marked as "Houseman" and "Wright" and *"Native Son"* by Avery in *A Southern Life.*

3 Reed has made this point repeatedly, but most tellingly in *Surveying the South: Studies in Regional Sociology* (Columbia: University of Missouri Press, 1993); see also *The Enduring South: Subcultural Persistence in Mass Society,* rev. ed. (Chapel Hill: University of North Carolina Press, 1986), and *Kicking Back: Further Dispatches from the South* (Columbia: University of Missouri Press, 1995). PEG spoke gloomily about the Nixon strategies and their successes in North Carolina in interview with Joe Herzenberg in which I also participated: interview, PEG with Joseph A. Herzenberg, Southern Historical Collection.

4 Acts 14:1–10.

5 These data are redundantly collected and communicated by PEG's own group, North Carolinians against the Death Penalty, and were disseminated widely by reformist and activist reporters in certain North Carolina daily newspapers, esp. *Raleigh News and Observer, Durham Herald,* and the socialist weekly *Anvil* (Durham), published and edited by Joel Bulkley and Robert Brown in the 1970s. I served the latter as a writer for selected political controversies, and in those processes I came to know the Chapel Hill attorney and local politician Gerry Cohen, who gathered much data on these issues and wrote the column "Rim Shots" about southern regional injustices for the *Anvil.* See the full collection of North Carolina daily press coverage of capital punishment in file "Capital Punishment," 1941 to the present, North Carolina Collection. John White, archivist at the Southern Historical Collection, showed me this very full and carefully organized collection of newspaper clippings.

6 See news coverage, "NCIC Defends Bittings," *Raleigh News and Observer,* 5 March 1934, p. 5, and "Bittings Case," *Raleigh News and Observer,* 20 April 1934, p. 1. See diary, March–June 1934, and correspondence, March–June 1934, esp. PEG to Harriet Herring, 28 June 1934, Green Papers; see also full annotation and explanatory remarks, "Capital Punishment," in Avery, *A Southern Life,* esp. chap. 3.

7 PEG to the editor, *Raleigh News and Observer,* 18 November 1947, p. 12; PEG correspondence, 1947–1963 but esp. PEG to Ruby E. McArthur, 25 January 1963, PEG, full text printed in Avery, *A Southern Life,* 618–19. McArthur's husband was viciously murdered in a planned attack at his store, and she wrote to PEG describing the nature of the killing. He wrote back sympathetically and offered to come visit her, but he continued to insist that Jesus Christ did not condone vengeance killing, no matter what the crime of the guilty.

8 Finlator, "Sacred Memories of a Secular Saint," *Sandhills Review* 46 (1994): 110. Marion Wright was not unwilling to give to the cause; he was a distinguished civil rights attorney active in his native western North Carolina hills. Finlator makes the point that PEG distrusted organized religion and disbelieved in a heaven or a hell, but used biblical language and invoked the name and teachings of Jesus Christ as passionately, and as effectively, as any of the Baptist ministers whose churches he had rejected.

9 Ibid.

10 *Furman v. Georgia,* 408 U.S. 238 (1972) USSC. PEG apparently thought the fight was over, as did most liberals of the day, diary, 1972, Green Papers. He did not, however,

proclaim victory forever, and remained politically active in case conservative forces in North Carolina began a campaign to write a new statute.

11 *Woodson v. North Carolina*, 428 U.S. 280 (1976) USSC.

12 See press clippings, "Capital Punishment," 1976–77, North Carolina Collection.

13 "Death Penalty, State by State," *New York Public Library Desk Reference*, s.v.

14 PEG published playscripts: *Texas* (1966, 1967); *Trumpet in the Land* (1970, 1971); *Drumbeats in Georgia* (1973); PEG playbills and programs: *Texas,* playbill and program, Palo Duro Canyon, Texas, 1966, "Texas," 1965–66, folder, Green Papers; *Trumpet in the Land,* playbill and program, New Philadelphia, Ohio, 1970, Green Papers; "Trumpet in the Land," folder, 1969–70, Green Papers; *Drumbeats in Georgia,* playbill and program, Jekyll Island, 1973, Green Papers; and "Drumbeats in Georgia," folder, 1973, Green Papers.

15 PEG, *Words and Ways* (1968), and *Home to My Valley: Short Stories* (1970). See diary, esp. 1966–75, Green Papers.

16 John Ehle recalls a fascinating discussion with the critic Dwight McDonald in which PEG effectively critiqued postmodernism in a reasoned and scholarly way, using essentially classical assumptions, Ehle, "Paul Green," address, 1994. Cf. the correspondence of October 1969, esp. PEG to Janet and Jack Catlin, 30 October 1969, and PEG to Bets [Elizabeth] and Bill [William] Moyer, 31 October 1969, Green Papers. In the letters to these two daughters, PEG says that he was then intensively reading and rereading Plato and Aristotle as a reaction against Beckett's recognition and recent literary trends.

17 Diary, 1920 and 1932, and esp. February 1975, describes the difficulty sleeping during "blue" moods and "funk."

18 Ibid. See esp. JGC to PEG, 12 and 16 February 1975, Green Papers.

19 His occasionally harsh criticism of JGC's poetry is especially noted in JGC to PEG, 14 and 23 June 1975. The halting and apologetic tone of her advice is particularly obvious in JGC to PEG, 12 February 1975, Green Papers. EGG notes that PEG did not easily take criticism or advice from his family, especially women: interviews, EGG, 1990; and Avery notes that few of the young literati—some of whom were more hangers-on than literati—dared to offer serious criticism to PEG about his late work: interview, 10 July 1990, Roper Papers.

20 Interview, Avery, 10 July 1990, Roper Papers.

21 Ibid.

22 Interview, EGG, 1990.

23 PEG published playscripts and published stories: *"The Land of Nod" and Other Stories* (1976); *The Louisiana Cavalier* (1976); *We the People* (1976); *The Lone Star* (1977, 1988); PEG programs and playbills: *The Louisiana Cavalier,* program and playbill, 1976, and "The Louisiana Cavalier," 1975–77, folder, Green Papers; *We the People,* program and playbill, 1976, and "We the People," 1975–77, folder, Green Papers; "Lone Star," folder, 1977–86, Green Papers.

24 Shakespeare, *King Lear,* 5.3. See correspondence between Jesse Helms and PEG, esp. for 1980, in Green Papers. The discussion at the PEG home of Windy Oaks took place on 10 May 1980 and is narrated fully and authoritatively by Avery in *A Southern Life,* 701–4.

BIBLIOGRAPHY

The Works of Paul Eliot Green

Books

This Body the Earth: A Novel. New York: Harper and Brothers, 1935.
The Common Glory Songbook. Williamsburg, Va.: n.p., n.d.
Contemporary American Literature: A Study of Fourteen Outstanding American Writers. With Elizabeth Lay Green. Chapel Hill: University of North Carolina Press, 1925.
Dog on the Sun: Stories. Chapel Hill: University of North Carolina Press, 1949.
Drama and the Weather: Essays. New York: Samuel French, 1958.
Dramatic Heritage: Essays. New York: Samuel French, 1954.
"The Field God" and "In Abraham's Bosom." New York: Robert M. McBride, 1927.
Five Plays of the South. Introduction by John Gassner. New York: Hill and Wang, 1963.
Forever Growing: Some Notes on a Credo for Teachers. Chapel Hill: University of North Carolina Press, 1945.
The Hawthorne Tree: Essays. Chapel Hill: University of North Carolina Press, 1943.
The Highland Call. Chapel Hill: University of North Carolina Press, 1941.
Home to My Valley. Chapel Hill: University of North Carolina Press, 1970.
"The House of Connelly" and Other Plays. New York: Samuel French, 1931.
In Abraham's Bosom. London: Allen and Unwin, 1930.
In the Valley: Eleven One-Act Plays. New York: Samuel French, 1928.
"Land of Nod" and Other Stories. Chapel Hill: University of North Carolina Press, 1976.
The Laughing Pioneer: A Novel. New York: Robert McBride, 1932.
Lonesome Road: Six Plays for the Negro Theatre. New York: Robert M. McBride, 1926.
"The Lord's Will" and Other Carolina Plays. Foreword by Frederick Henry Koch. New York: Henry Holt, 1925. Reprint, New York: Samuel French, 1928.
Mr. Mac: The Folk-History of a Neighborhood. Chapel Hill: n.p., [1944]. North Carolina Collection, Louis Round Wilson Library, University of North Carolina, Chapel Hill.
Native Son. With Richard Wright. New York: Harper, 1941.
Out of the South: The Life of a People in Dramatic Form. Fifteen Selected Plays and Revised Plays. New York: Harper, 1939.
Paul Green's War Songs: A Southerner Looks at the Great War. Edited, with an introduction, by John Herbert Roper. Rocky Mount: North Carolina Wesleyan College Press, 1984.
Paul Green's Wordbook—An Alphabet of Reminiscence. Edited by Rhoda Wynn, foreword by John Ehle. 2 vols. Boone, N.C.: Appalachian Consortium Press, 1990.
Plough and Furrow: Essays. New York: Samuel French, 1963.
Salvation on a String: Stories. New York: Harper and Brothers, 1946.
Six Plays for the Negro Theatre. London: Allen and Unwin, 1930.
Trifles of Thought. Greenville, S.C.: Paul Green, 1918.
Wide Fields: Stories. New York: Robert McBride, 1928.

Wings for to Fly: Three Plays of Negro Life—Mostly for the Ear but Also for the Eye. New York: Samuel French, 1959.

Words and Ways: Stories and Incidents from My Cape Fear Valley Folklore Collection. Raleigh: North Carolina Folklore Society, 1968.

Published Plays and Other Scripts

Plays

Alma Mater. New York: Samuel French, 1938.

Blue Thunder. New York: Samuel French, 1928.

Bread and Butter Come to Supper. New York: McBride, 1928.

The Common Glory. New York: Samuel French, 1948. Rev. Bicentennial ed., New York: Samuel French, 1975.

The Confederacy. New York: Samuel French, 1959.

The Critical Year. New York: Samuel French, 1939.

Cross and Sword. New York: Samuel French, 1966.

The Enchanted Maze. New York: Samuel French, 1939.

The End of the Row. In *Lonesome Road.* New York: Robert McBride, 1926.

The Field God. 1927. In *"Field God" and "In Abraham's Bosom."* New York: Robert M. McBride, 1927.

Fixin's: The Tragedy of a Tenant-Farm Woman. With Erma Green. In *Carolina Folk-Plays,* 2d ser., edited by Frederick H. Koch. New York: Holt, 1924.

The Founders. New York: Samuel French, 1957.

Franklin and the King. New York: Dramatists Play Service, 1939.

The Goodbye. In *"In the Valley" and Other Carolina Plays.* New York: Samuel French, 1928.

Granny Boling. Drama 11 (1921): 389–94.

The Highland Call. Chapel Hill: University of North Carolina Press, 1941.

Honeycomb. New York: Samuel French, 1972.

The Hot Iron. Poet Lore 35 (1924): 48–57.

The House of Connelly. New York: Samuel French, 1931.

Hymn to the Rising Sun. New York: Samuel French, 1936.

In Abraham's Bosom. New York: Samuel French, 1927.

In Aunt Mahaly's Cabin. Reviewer 4 (1924): 190–218.

In the Valley. In *In the Valley.* New York: Samuel French, 1928.

Johnny Johnson. Music composed with Kurt Weill. New York: Samuel French, 1937.

The Last of the Lowries. In *Carolina Folk-Plays,* edited by Frederick H. Koch. New York: Holt, 1922.

The Lone Star. New York: Samuel French, 1986.

The Long Night. Carolina Magazine, n.s., 39 (1922): 10–13.

The Lord's Will. In *The Lord's Will.* New York: Samuel French, 1925.

Lost Colony. Chapel Hill: University of North Carolina Press, 1937.

The Man on the House. Archive 39 (1926): 4–22.

The Man Who Died at Twelve O'Clock. In *One Act Plays for Stage and Study.* New York: Samuel French, 1925.

Native Son. Adaptation, with Richard Wright. New York: Harper, 1941.

The No 'Count Boy. Theatre Arts Monthly 8 (1924): 773–84. Reprinted in *The Lord's Will.* New York: Henry Holt, 1925.

Old Christmas. New York: McBride, 1928.

The Old Man of Edenton. In *The Lord's Will.* New York: Henry Holt, 1925.

Old Wash Lucas. Poet Lore 35 (1924): 254–70. Reprinted in *The Lord's Will*. New York: Henry Holt, 1925.

On the Road One Day, Lord. In *Ebony and Topaz*, edited by Charles Spurgeon Johnson. New York: Opportunity, National Urban League, 1927.

Ibsen's Peer Gynt: An American Version. 1951.

Potter's Field. In *The House of Connelly*. New York: Samuel French, 1936.

The Prayer-Meeting. Poet Lore 35 (1924): 232–53.

Quare Medicine. In *In the Valley*, Carolina Folk-Plays, 3d ser., edited by Frederick H. Koch. New York: Holt, 1928.

Roll Sweet Chariot. New York: Samuel French, 1935.

Roses for Johnny Johnson. One-Act Play Magazine 1 (1938): 963–79. Reprinted in *Best One-Act Plays of 1938*, edited by Margaret Gardner Mayorga. New York: Dodd, Mead, 1939. [Comic scene from *Johnny Johnson* not published with that play.]

Sam Tucker. Poet Lore 34 (1923): 220–46.

Saturday Evening: A Sketch. Archive 40 (1927): 4–10. Reprinted as *Saturday Night* in *In the Valley*. New York: Samuel French, 1928.

The Sheltering Plaid: A Drama in One Act. New York: Samuel French, 1965.

Shroud My Body Down. Carolina Play-Book 7 (1934): 99–111.

The Southern Cross: A Play in One Act. New York: Samuel French, 1938.

A Start in Life: A Radio Play for the Free Company. Carolina Play-Book 14 (1941): 35–47.

The Stephen Foster Story: A Symphonic Drama Based on the Life and Music of the Composer. New York: Samuel French, 1960.

Supper for the Dead. Carolina Magazine, o.s., 57 (1926): 3–13. Reprinted in *The American Caravan*, edited by Van Wyck Brooks et al. New York: Macaulay, 1927. Reprinted in *The Guild Annual*. New York: Literary Guild of America, 1928. Reprinted in *In the Valley*. New York: Samuel French, 1928. Reprinted in *Out of the South*. New York: Harper, 1939.

Texas: A Symphonic Drama. New York: Samuel French, 1967.

This Declaration: A Play in One Act. New York: Samuel French, 1954.

Tread the Green Grass: A Folk Fantasy in Two Parts with Interludes, Music, Dumb Show and Cinema. In *The New American Caravan*, edited by Alfred Kreymborg et al. New York: Macaulay, 1929. Reprinted in *The House of Connelly*. New York: Samuel French, 1931.

Trumpet in the Land: A Symphonic Drama of Brotherhood and Peace. New York: Samuel French, 1972.

Unto Such Glory. In *One-Act Plays for Stage and Study*, 3d ser., preface by Percival Wilde. New York: Samuel French, 1927. Reprinted in *In the Valley*. New York: Samuel French, 1928. Reprinted in *Nelson's College Caravan*, edited by Arthur Palmer Hudson et al. New York: Nelson, 1939. Reprinted in *Representative One-Act Plays by American Authors*, rev. ed., edited by Margaret Mayorga. Boston: Little, Brown, 1937. Reprinted in *Out of the South*. New York: Harper, 1939. Reprinted in *Folklore in American Literature*, edited by John T. Flanagan and Arthur Palmer Hudson. Evanston, Ill.: Row, Peterson, 1958.

We the People: A Symphonic Drama of George Washington and the Establishment of the United States Government. N.p.: Maryland Outdoor Drama Association, 1976.

White Dresses. In *Contemporary One-Act Plays with Outline Study of the One-Act Play and Bibliographies*, edited by B. Roland Lewis. New York: Scribner's, 1922. Reprinted in *Carolina Magazine*, n.s., 40 (1923): 8–12. Reprinted in *Lonesome Road*. New York: Robert McBride, 1926. Reprinted in *Plays of Negro Life: A Source-Book of Native American Drama*, edited by Alain Locke and Montgomery Gregory. New York: Harper, 1927. Reprinted in *Out of the South*. New York: Harper, 1939. Reprinted in *Twenty-five Best Plays of the Modern American Theatre*, early ser., edited by John Gassner. New York: Crown, 1949.

Wilderness Road. New York: Samuel French, 1956.
Your Fiery Furnace. In *Lonesome Road.* New York: Robert McBride, 1926.

Unpublished Plays

"As a Flower." 1925. North Carolina Collection, Louis Round Wilson Library, University of North Carolina, Chapel Hill.

"Banners in the Valley." N.d. North Carolina Collection, Louis Round Wilson Library, University of North Carolina, Chapel Hill.

"A Beginning." N.d. North Carolina Collection, Louis Round Wilson Library, University of North Carolina, Chapel Hill.

"Blackbeard." With Elizabeth Lay Green. 1921. North Carolina Collection, Louis Round Wilson Library, University of North Carolina, Chapel Hill.

"The Cup of Fury." 1923. Manuscript lost.

"Day by Day: A Comedy of Farm Life." N.d. [ca. 1923]. Department of Rural Social Organization, Cornell University, Ithaca, N.Y.

"The Dry Tree." 1925. Manuscript lost.

"The God on the Hill: Poetic Drama of Mood." 1919. Manuscript lost, supposedly destroyed by Green.

"The Immortality of Robert Burns." 1919. Fragment, Paul Eliot Green Papers, Southern Historical Collection, Louis Round Wilson Library, University of North Carolina, Chapel Hill.

"Round and Round: Experimental Tragedy." 1921. Manuscript lost.

"Souvenir: Tragedy of the War." 1919. Manuscript lost, supposedly destroyed by Green.

"Surrender to the Enemy." 1917. Manuscript lost, supposedly destroyed by Green.

Films and Screenplays

Black like Me. Film Features, 1964. Based on John Howard Griffin's autobiography. Green helped with script.

Cabin in the Cotton. Warner Brothers, First National, 1932. Based on novel by Harry Harrison Kroll. Screenplay by Green.

Captain Eddie. Twentieth-Century Fox, 1945. Screenplay by Green, Harold Clurman possibly collaborating.

David Harum. Fox Film, 1933. Based on novel by Edward Noyes Westcott. Screenplay by Walter Woods, Green assisting.

Doctor Bull. Fox Film, 1933. Based on novel by James Gould Cozzens. Screenplay by Green.

Green Light. Warner Brothers and Vitaphone, 1937. Screenplay by Milton Krims, Green assisting.

The Green Years. Metro-Goldwyn-Mayer, 1946. Screenplay by Robert Ardrey and Sonya Levien, Green assisting.

Music in America. U.S. Office of War Information, Bureau of Overseas Motion Pictures, Allied and Psychological Warfare Services, 1944. Screenplay by Green.

Roseanna McCoy. Samuel Goldwyn, 1949. Based on novel by Alberta Hannum. Screenplay by John Collier, Green assisting.

State Fair. Fox Film, 1933. Based on novel by Philip Strong. Screenplay by Sonya Levien and Green.

Time out of Mind. Universal-International, 1947. Based on novel by Rachel Lyman Field. Screenplay by several writers, Green assisting.

Voltaire. Warner Brothers, 1933. Based on novel by George Gibbs and E. Lawrence Dudley. Screenplay by Green and Maude T. Howell.

The Wedding Night. Goldwyn, 1935. Based on story by Edwin Knoph. Screenplay probably by Green.

Work of Art. Fox Film, 1934. Based on novel by Sinclair Lewis. Screenplay by Green.

Unpublished Symphonic Dramas

"Drumbeats in Georgia." Summer-long productions, Jekyll Island, Ga., 1973, 1974.

"Faith of Our Fathers." Summer-long productions, Washington, D.C., 1950, 1951.

"The Golden Isle." Summer-long production, Jekyll Island, Ga., 1971.

"Louisiana Cavalier." Summer-long productions, Natchitoches, La., 1976–80.

"Palo Duro." Production, Palo Duro Canyon State Park, Tex., 1978.

"The Seventeenth Star." Summer-long production, Columbus, Ohio, 1953.

"We, the People." Summer-long production, Columbia, Md., 1976.

Unpublished Play in Tribute Based on Green's Words

Listen to My Song. Production directed by Lee Yopp, Cape Fear Regional Theater, Carrboro, N.C., 1987.

PRIMARY SOURCES

Manuscript and Archival Collections

Libraries, Boston University, Boston
Hedgerow Theatre Collection
Sherwood Anderson Papers

Manuscript Department, Perkins Library, Duke University, Durham, N.C.
Frank Clyde Brown Papers
G. Hope (Summerell) Chamberlain Papers
Hugh Gladney Grant Papers
William Stanley Hoole Papers
Jay Broadus Hubbell Papers
Montrose Jonas Moses Papers

Manuscript Department, Special Collections, Emory University, Atlanta
Glenn Weddington Rainey Papers

Enoch Pratt Free Library, Baltimore
H. L. Mencken Papers
Mencken Scrapbook

Manuscript Department, Moorland-Spingarn Research Center, Howard University, Washington, D.C.
Edward Franklin Frazier Papers

Smyth-Bland Regional Library, Marion, Va.
Sherwood Anderson Archive
Anderson-Wright Papers

Louis Round Wilson Library, University of North Carolina, Chapel Hill
SOUTHERN HISTORICAL COLLECTION
Eugene Cunningham Branson Papers

Paul Eliot Green Papers (The Paul Elliot Green Papers are property of Paul Green Foundation and are deposited with the Southern Historical Collection on the basis of a
restricted-use loan. They are cited here in accordance with Paul Green Foundation and
Southern Historical Collection procedures.)
Bernice Kelly Harris Papers
Clarence Addison Hibbard Papers, 1927–30
James Spencer Love Papers, 1935
Joseph Hyde Pratt Papers
Charles Phillips Russell Papers
Henry Horace Williams Papers
NORTH CAROLINA AUTHORS' MANUSCRIPTS COLLECTION, NORTH CAROLINA ROOM
Elizabeth Lay Green
Paul Eliot Green
Phillips Russell
NORTH CAROLINA COLLECTION
Contempo, 1931–33
The Reviewer, 1925
Southern Textile Bulletin, 1925
UNIVERSITY OF NORTH CAROLINA ARCHIVES
Dean of College of Liberal Arts, 1926–30
University of North Carolina Press Papers, 1927

Interviews

Laurence Green Avery. Typescript. Roper Papers, Southern Historical Collection, Louis
Round Wilson Library, University of North Carolina, Chapel Hill.
Erma Green Gold. Typescript. Roper Papers, Southern Historical Collection, Louis Round
Wilson Library, University of North Carolina, Chapel Hill.
Paul Eliot Green with Jacqueline Dowd Hall. Tape recording. Southern Oral History
Project, Southern Historical Collection, Louis Round Wilson Library, University of
North Carolina, Chapel Hill.
Paul Eliot Green with Joseph A. Herzenberg. Typescript. Southern Oral History Project,
Southern Historical Collection, Louis Round Wilson Library, University of North Carolina, Chapel Hill.
Mary Green Johnson with Laurence Green Avery. Typescript. In the possession of Laurence Green Avery.
Mary Green Johnson with Paul Eliot Green Jr. Typescript. In the possession of Betsy Green
Moyer.
Betsy Green Moyer. Typescript. Roper Papers, Southern Historical Collection, Louis
Round Wilson Library, University of North Carolina, Chapel Hill.
Samuel Talmadge Ragan. Tape recording and manuscript in the possession of John Herbert
Roper.
Richard Shrader. Typescript. Roper Papers, Southern Historical Collection, Louis Round
Wilson Library, University of North Carolina, Chapel Hill.
Daniel Stewart with Laurence Green Avery. In the possession of Laurence Green Avery.

Secondary Sources

Adams, Henry. *Chapters of Erie, and Other Essays.* 1886. Reprint, New York: A. M. Kelly, 1967.

"Again a Serious Study of Negroes in Fiction." *New York Times Book Review,* 28 September 1924, p. 8.

Albee, Ernest. *The History of English Utilitarianism.* Library of Philosophy. New York: Macmillan, 1902.

Albright, Alex. "On Reading Paul Green's Mail: A Conversation with Laurence G. Avery." *Sandhills Review* 46 (1994): 33–50.

Allen, Frederick Lewis. *Only Yesterday: An Informal History of the Nineteen-Twenties.* New York: Harper and Brothers, 1931.

Allsbrook, Raleigh. "South Has Furnished Most Significant Literature in Past Ten Years: Paul Green." *Burlington (N.C.) Daily Times-News,* 17 February 1938, p. 12.

Amott, Teresa L., and Julie A. Matthaei. *Race, Gender, and Work: A Multicultural Economic History of Women in the United States.* Boston: South End Press, 1992.

Anderson, James D. *Black Public Education in the South, 1865–1935.* Chapel Hill: University of North Carolina Press, 1988.

Anderson, John. "Button, Button, Who's Got the Pulitzer Prize?" *New York Evening Post,* 19 February 1927, p. 8.

———. " . . . Look Away, Dixieland." *Theatre Magazine,* December 1930, pp. 47, 64.

Anderson, Maxwell, James Boyd, and Paul Green. *The Free Company Presents—.* New York: Dodd, Mead, 1941.

Anderson, Sherwood. *Sherwood Anderson's Diaries, 1936–1941.* Edited by Hilbert H. Campbell. Athens: University of Georgia Press, 1987.

———. *Sherwood Anderson's Memoirs: A Critical Edition.* 1942. Rev. ed., edited by Ray Lewis White. Chapel Hill: University of North Carolina Press, 1973.

———. *Sherwood Anderson: Selected Letters.* Edited by Charles E. Modlin. Knoxville: University of Tennessee Press, 1984.

Atkinson, Brooks. "Paul Green's Drama." *New York Times,* 19 October 1930.

———. "Ten Free Authors" [review]. *New York Times,* 25 May 1941, sec. 9, p. x.

Auden, Wystan Hugh. *Collected Poems.* Edited by Edward Mendelson. New York: Random House, 1976.

Avery, Laurence Green. "Paul Green Stories (Biographical and Fictional)." *Sandhills Review* 46 (1994): 15–32.

———, ed. *A Southern Life: Letters of Paul Green, 1916–1981.* Chapel Hill: University of North Carolina Press, 1994.

Bailey, Loretto Carroll, and J. O. Bailey. "The Making of 'Strike Song.'" *Carolina Play-Book* 5 (1932): 38–41.

Bailyn, Bernard. *The Ideological Origins of the American Revolution.* Cambridge: Harvard University Press, Belknap Press, 1972.

Baritz, Loren. *The Culture of the 1920s.* American Heritage Series. Indianapolis: Bobbs-Merrill, 1970.

Barron, Mark. " 'Native Son' Hits Pinnacle of This Theatrical Season." *New Bedford (Mass.) Standard-Times,* 6 April 1941.

Battle, Kemp Plummer. *History of the University of North Carolina,* vol. 2, *1868–1912.* Raleigh, N.C.: Edwards and Broughton, 1912.

Beebe, Lucius. "Native Son" [review]. "This New York." *Chicago Herald and American,* 22 April 1941.

Belasco, David [with Montrose Jonas Moses]. "My Life's Story." *Hearst's Magazine* 27 (April 1915): 353–54; 393–94.

Benchley, Robert. "Good Material." Review of *Johnny Johnson*. *New Yorker,* 28 November 1936, p. 26.

Bird, Thomas E. "Yiddish Literature." In *Encyclopedia of World Literature in Twentieth Century* (1984), s.v.

"Black Boy." *New Yorker,* 5 April 1941.

Blackburn, Charles, Jr. "Paul Green's Pulitzer Prize and the N.C. Press." *Sandhills Review* 46 (1994): 113–34.

Bloch, Marc. *Feudal Society.* Translated by L. A. Manyon. Chicago: University of Chicago Press, 1961.

Blythe, LeGette. "Man Will Surely Triumph, Avers Philosopher Green." *Charlotte Observer,* 2 November 1941, sec. 3, p. 5.

Booker, John Manning. "Edwin Almiron Greenlaw." In *Dictionary of American Biography,* supp. 1, *To 1935,* edited by Harris E. Starr, 355–56. New York: Charles Scribner's Sons, 1944.

Bradbury, John M. *Renaissance in the South.* Chapel Hill: University of North Carolina Press, 1963.

Braunlich, Phyllis Cole. *Haunted by Home: The Life and Letters of Lynn Riggs.* Norman: University of Oklahoma Press, 1985.

Brawley, Benjamin. *A New Survey of English Literature.* New York: Alfred A. Knopf, 1925.

Brazil, Wayne Douglas. "Howard W. Odum: The Building Years, 1884–1930." Ph.D. diss., Harvard University, 1975.

———. *Howard W. Odum: The Formative Years.* New York: Garland, 1987.

———. "Social Forces and Sectional Self-Scrutiny." In *Perspectives on the American South: An Annual Review of Society, Politics, and Culture,* edited by Merle Black and John Shelton Reed, 2:73–104. London: Gordon and Breach for the University of North Carolina, 1984.

Bridenbaugh, Carl. *Myths and Realities: Societies of the Colonial South.* Walter Lynwood Fleming Lectures in Southern History. 1952. Reprint, Baton Rouge: Louisiana State University Press, 1980.

Brooke, Rupert. *The Collected Poems, 1887–1915.* 4th rev. ed. London: Sidgewick and Jackson, 1987.

Brooks, Cleanth. *The Language of the American South.* Athens: University of Georgia Press, 1985.

Brown, John Mason. "Drama and the South." *New York Evening Post,* 29 November 1930, pp. 1, 2.

Buckner, Sally. "The Spirit of Learning: Paul Green's Involvement with Education." *North Carolina English Teacher* 52 (1994): 3–8.

Burke, Fielding [Olive Tilford Dargan]. *Call Home the Heart.* 1932. Reprint, with introduction by Alice Kessler-Harris and Paul Lauter, Old Westbury, N.Y.: Feminist Press, 1983.

Burns, Augustus M., III, and Pleasants, Julian M. *Frank Porter Graham and the 1950 Senate Race in North Carolina.* Fred W. Morrison Series in Southern Studies. Chapel Hill: University of North Carolina Press, 1990.

Buttitta, Anthony J. *After the Good Gay Times.* New York: Viking Press, 1974.

Cabell, James Branch. *Let Me Lie.* New York: Farrar, Straus, 1947.

"Calls Dramatic Instinct Inborn." *Chautauquan Daily,* 12 August 1932, pp. 1, 4.

Campbell, Hilbert H., and Charles E. Modlin, eds. *Sherwood Anderson: Centennial Studies.* Troy, N.Y.: Whitston, 1976.

Carey, Ralph W. "Among New York Theaters." *Hartford (Conn.) Courant,* 6 April 1941.

Carter, Dan T. *Scottsboro: A Tragedy of the American South.* Baton Rouge: Louisiana State University Press, 1969.

Clark, Barrett Harper. "Paul Green." *Drama,* January 1926.

———. *Paul Green.* New York: R. M. McBride, 1928.

———. " 'Tread the Green Grass' Turns Up in Iowa." *New York Times,* 24 July 1932.

Clark, David. " 'Strike Song'—Editorial." *Southern Textile Bulletin,* 7 January 1932.

Clark, Emily. *Innocence Abroad.* New York: Alfred A. Knopf, 1931.

Clark, Victor, ed. and comp. *Colorful Heritage, Documented: The Story of Barbecue, Bluff, and Longstreet Presbyterian Churches by the Rev. James D. MacKenzie et al.* 1969. Rev. ed., Lillington, N.C.: Friends of the Harnett County Library, 1990.

Clayton, Bruce. *The Savage Ideal: Intolerance and Intellectual Leadership in the South, 1890–1914.* Baltimore: Johns Hopkins University Press, 1972.

———. *W. J. Cash: A Life.* 1991. Rev. ed., Baton Rouge: Louisiana State University Press, 1997.

Coates, Albert. *Edward Kidder Graham, Harry Woodburn Chase, Frank Porter Graham: Three Men in the Transition of the University of North Carolina at Chapel Hill from a Small College to a Great University.* [Chapel Hill]: [Albert Coates], 1988.

Cochran, Robert. *Vance Randolph: An Ozark Life.* Urbana: University of Illinois Press, 1985.

Contempo, Vols. 1–3, 1931–33.

Cook, Sylvia J. *From Tobacco Road to Route 66: the Southern Poor White in Fiction.* Chapel Hill: University of North Carolina Press, 1976.

Corbitt, David Leroy. *The Formation of North Carolina Counties, 1663–1943.* Raleigh: State Department of Archives and History, 1950.

Cott, Nancy F. *The Grounding of Modern Feminism.* New Haven: Yale University Press, 1987.

Couch, William Terry, ed. *Culture in the South.* Chapel Hill: University of North Carolina Press, 1934.

Crawford, John. "Hound Dogs and Bible Shooting." *New York Times Book Review,* 6 March 1927, p. 5.

Creighton, James Edwin. *An Introductory Logic.* 1898. 4th rev. ed., New York: Macmillan, 1920.

———. *Studies in Speculative Philosophy.* Edited, with an introduction, by H. R. Smart. New York: Macmillan, 1925.

———. *The Will: Its Structure and Mode of Action.* New York: Macmillan, 1898.

Crossman, Richard, ed. *The God That Failed.* 1949. Reprint, New York: Grossett and Dunlap, Bantam Books, 1950.

Crowe, Charles. *Slavery, Race, and American Scholarship: Essays in Historiography.* Needham Heights, Mass.: Ginn, 1988.

Cunningham, G. Watts. "Frank Thilly." *Dictionary of American Biography,* vol. 21, supp. 1 (1944), s.v.

———. "In Memoriam: J. E. Creighton." *International Journal of Ethics* (1925).

Daniels, Jonathan Worth. "American Antaeus." *Pembroke Magazine* 10 (1978).

———. *Clash of Angels.* New York: Brewer and Warren, 1930.

de Nissoff, Mary Evelyn. "A Look at State Literature Given to Men's Fellowship." *Southern Pines Pilot,* 21 April 1988, p. C1.

Devany, Ed. "Paul Green: Documentarian." *North Carolina Literary Review* 2 (1994): 47–56.

————. "Serving in *The Confederacy.*" *Sandhills Review* 46 (1994): 65–70.

Dos Passos, John. *U.S.A.* 3 vols. Boston: Houghton-Mifflin, 1960.

Duberman, Martin Bauml. *Paul Robeson: A Biography.* New York: Random House, Ballantine Press, 1989.

Dudley, Bide. "Bide Dudley Tells the World." *Leavenworth (Kans.) Times,* 30 March 1941.

Durham, Frank. Introduction to *Collected Short Stories of Julia Peterkin.* Columbia: University of South Carolina Press, 1970.

"Dynamite." *Burlington (N.C.) Daily Times-News,* 30 December 1935, p. 4.

Ehle, John. *Dr. Frank: Life with Frank Porter Graham.* Chapel Hill, N.C.: Franklin Street Books, 1994.

Ekirch, A. Roger. *"Poor Carolina": Politics and Society in Colonial North Carolina, 1729–1776.* Chapel Hill: University of North Carolina Press, 1981.

"Ernest Albee." *Dictionary of American Biography* (1928), s.v.

"Ernest Albee [obituary]." *New York Times,* 27 May 1927.

Erskine, John. "At the Play." *Observer* (London), 14 September 1930.

————. "Edward Alexander Mac Dowell." *Dictionary of American Biography* (1946), s.v.

Fass, Paula S. *The Damned and the Beautiful: American Youth in the 1920s.* New York: Oxford University Press, 1977.

Faust, Drew Gilpin. *A Sacred Cirlce: The Dilemma of the Intellectual in the Old South, 1840–1860.* Baltimore: Johns Hopkins University Press, 1977.

Finlator, W. W. "Sacred Memories of a Secular Saint." *Sandhills Review* 46 (1994): 109–12.

Fischer, David Hackett. *Albion's Seed: Four British Folkways in America.* New York: Oxford University Press, 1989.

————. "The Braided Narrative: Substance and Form in Social History." In *The Literature of Fact,* edited, with foreword, by Angus Fletcher, 109–33 New York: Columbia University Press, 1976.

Fitzpatrick, Vincent. *H. L. Mencken.* Literature and Life: American Writers. New York: Frederick Ungar, 1989.

Fitz-Simons, Marion. "A Different Path." *Sandhills Review* 46 (1994): 1–2.

Foner, Eric. *Reconstruction: America's Unfinished Revolution, 1863–1877.* New American Nation Series, eds. Henry Steele Commager and Richard B. Morris. New York: Harper and Row, 1987.

Fox-Genovese, Elizabeth, and Eugene D. Genovese. *Fruits of Merchant Capital: Slavery and Bourgeois Property in the Rise and Expansion of Capitalism.* New York: Oxford University Press, 1983.

"Frank Thilly." In *National Cyclopaedia of American Biography* (1956), s.v.

"Frank Thilly." In *Who Was Who in America* (1943), s.v.

"Frank Thilly [obituary]." *New York Times,* 29 December 1934.

Fried, Michael. *Realism, Writing, Disfiguration: On Thomas Eakins and Stephen Crane.* Chicago: University of Chicago Press, 1987.

Gaston, Paul M. *The New South Creed.* 1970. Reprint, Baton Rouge: Louisiana State University Press, 1976.

Gaven, Jack. "Orson Welles' New Play Strengthens Serious Side of Current Rialto." *Hollywood Citizen-News,* 4 April 1941.

Gentry, Charles. " 'Native Son' Is Grim Fare at Cass." *Detroit Times,* 7 October 1941, p. 22.

Gilbert, Katherine. "Jas. E. Creighton as Writer and Editor." In *Journal of Philosophy* (1925), s.v.

Glasgow, Ellen. "Review of Recent Literature," *Books,* 22 March 1931.

Goodman, James E. *Stories of Scottsboro.* New York: Pantheon, 1994.

Goodwyn, Lawrence. *Democratic Promise: The Populist Moment in America*. New York: Oxford University Press, 1976.

Graves, Robert. *Good-bye to All That: An Autobiography*. New York: Jonathan Cape and Harrison Smith, 1930.

Green, Elizabeth Lay. *The Paul Green I Know*. Preface by Jonathan Worth Daniels. North Caroliniana Society Imprints, ed. H. G. Jones, no. 2. Chapel Hill: North Caroliniana Society, 1978.

Gussow, Melvin. *"Real Life Drama"* [review]. *New York Times Book Review*, January 1991, p. 11.

Haardt, Sara. "Paradox." *Reviewer* 5 (January 1925): 64–70.

———. "The Southern Lady Says Grace." *Reviewer* 5 (January 1925): 57–63.

Hall, Jacquelyn Dowd. *The Revolt against Chivalry: Jessie Daniel Ames and the Women's Campaign against Lynching*. 1979. Rev. ed., New York: Columbia University Press, 1993.

Halstead, James. "Photographic Timeline." *Sandhills Review* 46 (1994): 3–14.

Hammond, W. A. "Jas. Edwin Creighton." *Journal of Philosophy* (1925), s.v.

Hawley, Ellis W. *The Great War and the Search for Modern Order: A History of the American People and their Institutions, 1917–1933*. St. Martin's Series in Twentieth Century United States History. New York: St. Martin's, 1979.

Henderson, Archibald. *The Changing Drama*. New York: Henry Holt, 1915.

Herbstruth, Grant M. "An Analysis of the Plays of Paul Green." Master's thesis, Iowa State University, 1949.

Hibbard, Addison, ed. *Stories of the South*. Chapel Hill: University of North Carolina Press, 1931.

Hobert, John. "John Hobert Goes to the Opening of a Welles Play." *San Francisco Chronicle*, 28 March 1941.

Hobson, Fred C., Jr. *Serpent in Eden: H. L. Mencken and the South*. Chapel Hill: University of North Carolina Press, 1974.

"In Memoriam, Edwin Greenlaw. A Memorial Resolution Adopted . . . by the University of North Carolina." N.d. Reprinted in *University of North Carolina Alumni Review* (November 1931).

"In Their Own Backyard." *Burlington (N.C.) Daily Times-News*, 18 May 1935, p. 4.

James, William. *Pragmatism*. 1907. Reprint, Cleveland, Ohio: Meridian Paper, 1961.

———. *The Will to Believe and Other Essays in Popular Philosophy*. Rev. ed. New York: Longman, Green, 1916.

Johnson, James Weldon. *Black Manhattan*. 1930. Reprint, New York: New York Times and Arno Press, 1968.

Johnson, Thomas L. "South Carolina Academy of Authors: Elizabeth Boatwright Coker, Benjamin Brawley, and Samuel Galliard Stoney." *Carologue* 7 (1991): 11–14.

Jones, Anne Goodwyn. *Tomorrow Is Another Day: The Woman Writer in the South, 1859–1936*. Baton Rouge: Louisiana State University Press, 1981.

Jones, Lewis Pinckney. *South Carolina: A Synoptic History for Laymen*. 1971. Reprint, Columbia, S.C: Sandlapper Press, 1972.

Kallen, Horace Meyer. "Cults." In *Encyclopedia of the Social Sciences*, ed. Edwin R. A. Seligman and Alvin Johnson, 3–4:619–21. 1930. Reprint, New York: Macmillan, 1944.

———. *Why Religion?* New York: Boni and Liveright, 1927.

Key, Valdimer Orlando, Jr., with Alexander Heard. *Southern Politics in State and Nation*. New York: Alfred A. Knopf, 1949.

Kimball, Sue, and Lynn Veach Sadler, eds. *Paul Green's Celebration of Man, with a Bibliography*. Sanford, N.C.: Human Technology Interface, 1994.

King, Richard Harvey. *A Southern Renaissance: The Cultural Awakening of the American South, 1930–1955.* New York: Oxford University Press, 1980.

Koch, Frederick. "Adventures in American Folk Drama." Address. Chautauqua Society of New York, 11 August 1932.

―――. "American Regional Drama." *Carolina Play-book* 5 (1932): 42.

―――. "Making an American Folk Drama." Address. Chautauqua Society of New York, 11 August 1932.

―――. " 'Strike Song'—Editorial." *Carolina Play-book* 5 (1932): 35–37.

―――, ed. *Carolina Folk-Plays.* New York: Henry Holt, 1922.

Langmuir, Gavin I. *Toward a Definition of Antisemitism.* Berkeley and Los Angeles: University of California Press, 1990.

Leed, Eric J. *No Man's Land: Combat and Identity in World War I.* Cambridge: Cambridge University Press, 1979.

Leuchtenburg, William Edward. *The Perils of Prosperity, 1914–1932.* Chicago History of American Civilization Series. Chicago: University of Chicago Press, 1958.

Lewis, Lloyd. " 'Native Son' Blend of Horror, Pathos, and Stump Speeches." *Chicago Daily News,* 11 November 1941, p. 12.

Link, Arthur Stanley, and William Bruce Catton. *American Epoch: A History of the United States since 1900.* 1955. 4th rev. ed., New York: Knopf, 1973, 1974.

Logan, Rayford Whittingham. *The Betrayal of the Negro, from Rutherford B. Hayes to Woodrow Wilson.* Rev. ed. New York: Collier, 1965.

"The Lost Colony: A Play." Broadcast, National Public Radio, 22 June 1997.

Luker, Ralph. *A Southern Tradition in Theology and Social Criticism, 1830–1930: The Conservatism of James Worley Miles, William Porcher Dubose, and Edgar Gardner Murphy.* New York: Edward Mellen Press, 1984.

McDermott, William F. "Canada Lee Gives a Moving Performance in a Raw and Powerful Melodrama." *Cleveland Plain Dealer,* 4 November 1941, p. 6.

McIlwaine, Shields. *The Southern Poor White: From Lubberland to Tobacco Road.* Norman: University of Oklahoma Press, 1939.

MacIntyre, Alasdair. *After Virtue.* Notre Dame, Ind.: University of Notre Dame Press, 1981.

McMath, Robert, Jr. *Populist Vanguard: A History of the Southern Farmers Alliance.* Chapel Hill: University of North Carolina Press, 1975.

Malcolm, Janet. "The Purloined Critic." *New Yorker,* 5 October 1987, pp. 121–25.

Malone, E. Theodore. "The Literary Lantern." *Southern Pines (N.C.) Pilot,* 23 April 1987, pp. 2-B, 3-B.

Mantle, [Robert] Burns. *The Best Plays of 1936–1937.* New York: Dodd, Mead, 1946.

―――. *The Best Plays of 1940–1941.* New York: Dodd, Mead, 1946.

―――. "Native Son." *Buffalo Courier Express,* 6 April 1941.

"Mantle, [Robert] Burns." In *Oxford Companion to American Theatre,* ed. Gerald Bordman. New York: Oxford University Press, 1994.

Martin, Edward A. "H. L. Mencken and Equal Rights for Women." *Georgia Review* 35 (spring 1981): 65–76.

―――. *H. L. Mencken and the Debunkers.* Athens: University of Georgia Press, 1984.

―――. "The Literary Lantern." *Southern Pines (N.C.) Pilot,* 9 November 1987, p. 2-B.

Martin, John Bartlow. *Adlai Stevenson.* New York: Harper and Brothers, 1952.

―――. *Adlai Stevenson and His World: The Life of Adlai Stevenson.* Garden City, N.Y.: Doubleday, 1977.

Mason, Robert. "Lee's Second Surrender." *Sandhills Review* 46 (1994): 57–64.

May, Henry Farnham. *The End of American Innocence: A Study of the First Years of Our Own Time, 1912–1917.* New York: Alfred A. Knopf, 1959.

Mencken and Sara, a Life in Letters: The Private Correspondence of H. L. Mencken and Sara Haardt. Edited, with introduction, by Marion Elizabeth Rodgers. New York: McGraw-Hill, 1987.

Mencken, H. L. *Americana.* 2 vols. New York: Alfred A. Knopf, 1928.

Merrill, James H. *The Indians' New World: Catawbas and Their Neighbors from European Contact through the Era of Removal.* Chapel Hill: University of North Carolina Press for the Institute of Early American History and Culture, 1987.

————. "The Indians' New World: The Catawba Experience." *William and Mary Quarterly,* 3d ser., 41 (1984): 537–65.

Mims, Edwin. *The Advancing South: Stories of Progress and Reaction.* Garden City, N.Y.: Doubleday, Page, 1926.

Moses, Montrose Jonas. "The American Note in Drama." *Current History* 39 (1933): 63–68.

————. "The American Theatre and International Vistas." 1932. Manuscript, Montrose Jonas Moses Papers, Manuscript Department, Duke University Library, Durham, N.C.

————. "Eyes toward the Altar." *Carolina Play-book,* September 1932.

————. "Playhouse Progress: What Granville Barker and Winthrop Ames Have Done for the Art of the Theater." *Independent,* 3 May 1915, pp. 194–97.

————. "Shaw's Friends, the Doctors." *Bellman,* 10 April 1915, pp. 461–64.

————. "Social Forces in American Drama." *Bellman,* 4 December 1915, p. 637.

————. "The Theatre in America." *North American Review* 219 (1924): 82–90.

————. "The Theatre in America." *North American Review* 234 (1932): 528–35.

————. "With William Butler Yeats." *Theatre Art Monthly* 8 (1924): 383–88.

Nathan, George Jean. "Roll, Sweet Chariot" [review]. *Vanity Fair,* December 1934, pp. 45, 46, 68.

Newman, Frances. "Georgia Vindicated." *Reviewer* 4 (1923–24): 234–35.

————. *The Hard-Boiled Virgin.* 1926. Reprint, with foreword by Anne Firor Scott, Athens: University of Georgia Press, 1980.

————. "Immorality in a Library." *Reviewer* 5 (April 1925): 55–58.

————. "Literary Independence." *Saturday Review of Literature* 4 April 1925, pp. 641–42, 645.

————. "Open All Night (Paul Marand)." *Reviewer* 4 (1924): 143–44.

————. *Short Story's Mutations: From Petronius to Paul Marand.* New York: Viking, 1925.

————. "The State of Literature in the Late Confederacy." *New York Herald-Tribune Book Review,* 16 August 1925, pp. 1–2.

————. "Three Episodes from *The Hard-Boiled Virgin.*" *Reviewer* 4 (1923–24): 341–43.

Norris, Hoke. "Negro Novelist at Chapel Hill." Clipping, 30 July 1941, *Native Son* file, Paul Eliot Green Papers, Southern Historical Collection, Louis Round Wilson Library, University of North Carolina, Chapel Hill.

O'Brien, Edward, ed. *The Best Short Stories of 1925.* Boston: Small, Maynard, 1926.

O'Brien, Michael. "C. Vann Woodward and the Burden of Southern Liberalism." *American Historical Review* 78 (1973): 589–604.

————. "From a Chase to a View: C. Vann Woodward." In *Rethinking the South: Essays in Intellectual History,* 190–206. Baltimore: Johns Hopkins University Press, 1988.

"Open Forum Meeting Held at Chapel Hill." *Burlington (N.C.) Daily Times-News,* 23 February 1935, p. 8.

Orr, Oliver Hamilton. *Charles Brantley Aycock.* 1961. Reprint, Chapel Hill: University of North Carolina Press, 1975.

Owens, Wilfred. *War Poems and Others.* London: Chatto and Windus, 1973.

Palmer, Bruce. *"Man over Money": The Southern Populist Critique of American Capitalism.* Chapel Hill: University of North Carolina Press, 1980.

Parker, Roy, Jr. "Paul Green: Apostle of Light." *Fayetteville (N.C.) Times,* 6 May 1981, p. 10E.

———. "Paul Green's Literary Landscape: Harnett County." *Sandhills Review* 46 (1994): 75–78.

Patterson, Daniel W. "A Woman of the Hills: The Works of Maude Minnish Sutton." *Southern Exposure* 5 (1977): 105–10.

"Paul Green: Cotton Picker, Professor, and Pulitzer Winner." *New York Evening Post,* 7 May 1927, p. 1.

Peacock, James L., and A. Thomas Kirsch. *The Human Direction: An Evolutionary Approach to Social and Cultural Anthropology.* New York: Appleton-Century-Crofts, 1970.

Peirce, Charles Santiago Sanders. *Values in a Universe of Chance: Selected Writings of Charles S. Peirce.* Edited, with an introduction, by Philip P. Wiener. Garden City, N.Y.: Doubleday, 1958.

Percy, William Alexander. *Lanterns on the Levee: Recollections of a Planter's Son.* 1941. Reprint, Baton Rouge: Louisiana State University Press, 1973.

Peterkin, Julia. *Black April.* New York: Grosset and Dunlap, 1927.

———. *Bright Skin.* Indianapolis: Bobbs-Merrill, 1932.

———. *Collected Short Stories of Julia Peterkin.* Edited, with an introduction, by Frank Durham. Columbia: University of South Carolina Press, 1970.

———. *Green Thursday.* New York: Alfred A. Knopf, 1924.

———. *Roll, Jordan, Roll.* London: Jonathan Cape, 1934.

———. *Scarlet Sister Mary.* Indianapolis: Bobbs-Merrill, 1928.

Peters, Richard. "Hanna's 'Native Son' Is Powerful Negro Drama." *Cleveland Press,* 4 November 1941, p. 20.

Pettigrew, Thomas F. *A Profile of the Negro American.* University Series in Psychology, ed. David C. McClelland. Princeton, N.J.: D. Van Nostrand, 1964.

Phifer, Mary H. "Southern Personalities: Paul Green—Philosopher and Playwright." *Holland's* 50, no. 10 (October 1931): 11, 73.

Phillips, Ulrich Bonnell. *Life and Labor in the Old South.* Boston: Little, Brown, 1919.

Plesur, Milton. *The 1920s: Problems and Paradoxes: Selected Readings.* Boston: Allyn and Bacon, 1969.

Pocock, J. G. A. "Machiavelli, Harrington, and English Political Ideologies in the Eighteenth Century." *William and Mary Quarterly,* 3d ser., 22 (1965): 549–83.

Pollock, Arthur. "'Watch on the Rhine' Wins Critics' Award." *Brooklyn Eagle,* 23 April 1941.

Powell, William S. *The North Carolina Gazetteer.* Chapel Hill: University of North Carolina Press, 1968.

Prather, H. Leon, Sr. *Resurgent Politics and Educational Progressivism in the New South: North Carolina, 1890–1912.* Rutherford, N.J.: Fairleigh Dickinson University Press, 1975.

———. *"We Have Taken a City": the Wilmington Racial Massacre and Coup of 1898.* Rutherford, N.J.: Fairleigh Dickinson University Press, 1984.

Ragan, Samuel Talmadge. "A Literary Look at North Carolina." Address, 12 April 1988, Southern Pines, N.C.

———. "A Reverence for Writers." *North Carolina English Teacher* 52 (1994): 9–10.

———. "The Truth Seeker." *Sandhills Review* 46 (1994): 71–74.

Reed, John Shelton. *The Enduring South: Subcultural Persistence in Mass Society.* 1971. Rev. ed., Chapel Hill: University of North Carolina Press, 1986.

———. *Kicking Back: Further Dispatches from the South.* Columbia: University of Missouri Press, 1995.

——. *One South: An Ethnic Approach to Regional Culture.* Baton Rouge: Louisiana State University Press, 1982.

——. *Southern Folk, Plain and Fancy.* Athens: University of Georgia Press, 1986.

——. *Surveying the South: Studies in Regional Sociology.* Columbia: University of Missouri Press, 1993.

Rodgers, Marion Elizabeth, ed. *Mencken and Sara, a Life in Letters: The Private Correspondence of H. L. Mencken and Sara Haardt.* 2d paperback ed. New York: Doubleday, 1992.

Roper, John Herbert. "Actualizing Art: Paul Green's *Hymn to the Rising Sun* and the Campaign against Capital Punishment in the Old North State, 1934–37." *North Carolina English Teacher* 52 (1994): 11–13.

——. "Charles Brantley Aycock: A Study in Limitation and Possibility." *Southern Studies* 16 (fall 1977): 277–92.

——. *C. Vann Woodward, Southerner.* Athens: University of Georgia Press, 1987.

——. "Paul Green and the Southern Literary Renaissance." *Southern Cultures* 1 (1994): 75–90.

——. "Paul Green's War Songs." *North Carolina Literary Review* 2 (1994): 22–46.

——. "Paul Turns Pro: 1926." *Sandhills Review* 46 (1994): 85–108.

——, ed. *Paul Green's War Songs: A Southern Poet Looks at the Great War, 1917–1920.* Rocky Mount: North Carolina Wesleyan College Press, 1994.

Ross, George. "So This Is Broadway." *New York World-Telegraph,* 23 April 1941.

Russell, Caro Mae Green. "Native Son" [review]. "The Literary Lantern." *Greensboro News,* 6 April 1941.

Sandrow, Nahma. *Vagabond Stars.* New York: Harper, 1977.

Sassoon, Siegfried. *Siegfried Sassoon Diaries, 1915–1918.* London: Faber and Faber, 1983.

——. *The War Poems of Siegfried Sassoon.* London: Faber and Faber, 1983.

Sayler, Oliver M., ed. *Revolt in the Arts: A Survey of the Creation, Distribution, and Appreciation of the Arts in America.* New York: Brentano's, 1930.

"Says Universal Art Also Local." *Chautauquan Daily,* 12 August 1932, p. 5.

Schaaf, Hart. " 'Native Son' Hailed as Strong Play." *Richmond Times-Dispatch,* 20 April 1941.

Schorske, Carl E. *Fin de Siecle Vienna: Politics and Culture.* New York: Alfred A. Knopf, 1980.

Scott, Anne Firor. *The Southern Lady: From Pedestal to Politics, 1830–1930.* Chicago: University of Chicago Press, 1970.

Seidel, Kathryn Lee. *The Southern Belle in the American Novel.* Tampa: University Presses of Florida, University of South Florida Press, 1985.

Selden, Samuel. "Frederick Henry Koch." In *Dictionary of American Biography,* supp. 3, *1941–1945,* ed. Edward T. James, 526–27. New York: Charles Scribner's Sons, 1973.

——. *Frederick Henry Koch: Pioneer Playmaker.* Chapel Hill: University of North Carolina Library Extension Services, 1954.

"Shall the South Go Industrial?" *Textile World,* 21 February 1931, p. 22.

Shannon, Anna W. "Biographical Afterword [Olive Tilford Dargan]." In *Call Home the Heart,* 433–46. 1932. Reprint, Old Westbury, N.Y: Feminist Press, 1983.

Shaw, Barton C. *Wool-Hat Boys: Georgia's Populist Party.* Baton Rouge: Louisiana State University Press, 1984.

Singal, Daniel Joseph. *The War Within: From Victorian to Modernist Thought in the South, 1919–1945.* Chapel Hill: University of North Carolina Press, 1982.

Spaeth, Arthur. "The Play: 'Native Son' Is Dark Drama." *Cleveland News,* 22 April 1941, p. 16.

Spearman, Walter. *The Carolina Playmakers: The First Fifty Years.* Chapel Hill: University of North Carolina Press, 1970.

Spencer, Cornelia Phillips. *Selected Papers of Cornelia Phillips Spencer.* Edited, with an introduction, by Louis Round Wilson. Chapel Hill: University of North Carolina Press, 1953.

"State Aid for 'Lost Colony' a Tribute to Paul Green." *Detroit Free Press,* 6 April 1941.

Stephenson, Shelby. "Paul Green: An Appreciation." *Sandhills Review* 46 (1994): 79–84.

Stevens, Ashton. "Thrills, Lulls, and Canada Lee." *Chicago Herald-American,* 11 November 1941, p. 10.

Storm, Axel. "Broadway Nights." *Bradford (Pa.) Era,* 3 April 1941.

Sumner, Mark. "Memories of Paul." *Sandhills Review* (1994): 51–56.

Sundquist, Eric J. *Faulkner: The House Divided.* Baltimore: Johns Hopkins University Press, 1983.

Swanberg, W. A. *Norman Thomas: The Last Idealist.* New York: Charles Scribner's Sons, 1976.

Symonette, Lys, and Kim H. Kowalke, eds. *Speak Low (When You Speak Love): The Letters of Kurt Weill and Lotte Lenya.* Berkeley and Los Angeles: University of California Press, 1996.

Thilly, Frank. *A History of Philosophy.* New York: Holt, 1914.

———. *Introduction to the Study of Ethics.* New York: Scribner, 1900.

———. "James Edwin Creighton." *Dictionary of American Biography,* vol. 3 (1929), s.v.

Tindall, George Brown. *The Emergence of the New South, 1913–1945.* History of the South Series, ed., Ellis Merton Coulter and Wendell Holmes Stephenson, vol. 10. Baton Rouge: Louisiana State University Press, 1967.

Tobin, James E., and Charles B. Hale, eds. *One-Act Plays for Stage and Study.* 4th ser. Preface by Green. New York: Samuel French, 1928.

"Treading upon Dangerous Ground." *Burlington (N.C.) Daily Times-News,* 23 February 1935, p. 4.

Tucker, S. M., ed. *Modern American and British Plays.* New York: Harper and Brothers, 1930.

Twelve Southerners. *I'll Take My Stand: The South and the Agrarian Tradition.* 1930. Reprint, with a preface by Louis Decimus Rubin, Jr., New York: Harper and Row, Torchbooks, 1962.

Upton, Dell, ed. *America's Architectural Roots: Ethnic Groups That Built America.* Washington, D.C.: Preservation Press of the National Historic Trust for Historic Preservation, 1986.

Voltaire. *Candide.* 1759. Reprint, with introduction by Lester G. Crocker, New York: Simon and Schuster, Pocket Books, 1962.

Warner, Ralph. "The Critics Have Their Say about 'Native Son.'" *New York City Sunday Worker,* 13 April 1941.

Warren, Robert Penn. "Cowley's Faulkner, Part I." *New Republic,* 12 August 1946, pp. 176–80.

———. "Cowley's Faulkner, Part II." *New Republic,* 26 August 1946, pp. 234–37.

———. "Faulkner: Past and Future." In *Faulkner: A Collection of Critical Essays,* 1–5. Englewood Cliffs, N.J.: Prentice-Hall, 1966.

Wells, Herbert George. *Mr. Britling Sees It Through.* New York: Macmillan, 1917.

Welter, Barbara. *Dimity Convictions.* Athens: Ohio University Press, 1976.

Whipple, Sidney. "Welles Strives Only for Effects." *Denver Rocky Mountain News,* 6 April 1941.

White, Walter Francis. *Rope and Faggot: The Biography of Judge Lynch*. 1929. Reprint, New York: Arno Press, 1969.

Williamson, Joel Randolph. *The Crucible of Race: Black-White Relations in the American South since Emancipation*. New York: Oxford University Press, 1984.

Wolfe, Thomas. *Look Homeward, Angel*. New York: Charles Scribner and Sons, 1929.

Wolfert, Ira. "Orson Makes 'Native Son' Season's Best Melodrama." *Cleveland Plain Dealer,* 30 March 1941.

Wood, Gordon S. *The Creation of the American Republic, 1776–1787*. New York: W. W. Norton for the University of North Carolina Press, 1969.

Woodward, Comer Vann. *Origins of the New South, 1877–1913*. History of the South Series, ed. Ellis Merton Coulter and Wendell Holmes Stephenson, vol. 9. Baton Rouge: Louisiana State University Press, 1951.

Wright, Richard. *American Hunger.* 1944. Rev. ed., with afterword by Michel Fabre, New York: Harper and Row, 1977.

———. *Native Son*. New York: Harper, 1940.

Wynn, Rhoda H. "Paul Green, Storyteller—Humorist." *Sandhills Review* 46 (1994): 135–37.

Yeats, William Butler. *Selected Poems and Two Plays of William Butler Yeats*. Edited, with an introduction, by M. L. Rosenthal. 1962. Rev. ed., New York: Macmillan, Collier Books, 1975.

Young, Stark. "Native Son" [review]. *New Republic,* 7 April 1941.

INDEX

Abernathy, Milton, 141–43, 154. *See also* Communist Party; Marxism; proletariat literature

Ab's bookstore: attracts famous authors, 142; as center of aesthetic radicalism, 141–43, 154. *See also* Marxism; proletariat literature

Adams, E. Maynard, 174–75, 274 (n. 1)

Adler, Stella, 155

Aeschylus, 33

African Americans: in Abramic family patterns, 86, 87; abuse of, in Scottsboro, Ala., 142–43; as cast of *Potter's Field,* 126, 127, 128; as comic subjects in poems and plays, 27, 84; experience of, on chain gangs, 163, 164; and "Negro dialect" stories, 91, 92, 126; as observed by Harvey Easom, 83, 84; and PEG as part of Harlem Renaissance, 108, 109, 265 (n. 28); PEG's theatrical protests against mistreatment of, 213–33; PEG's views on poverty of, 151; portrayal of, in *Hymn to the Rising Sun,* 163–73; —, in *In Abraham's Bosom,* 83, 84, 86–89, 99, 100, 103–5, 108; as protagonists with agency and power, 89, 126; reaction of, to *House of Connelly,* 159; as tragic subjects in poems and plays, 27, 76, 83; in World War I, 34, 38, 40–41, 42, 43, 44, 176, 259 (n. 37)

Africans, in World War I, 34

agency: in *In Abraham's Bosom,* 89; in *Potter's Field,* 126, 127, 128

Albee, Ernest, 73, 74

Almond, Lindsay, 227

American Expeditionary Forces, World War I, 31

American National Theater and Academy (ANTA): produces *Peer Gynt,* 222–24; troupe of, led by Crawford, 221

American Philosophical Association, rejection of, by PEG, 74

Anderson, John, 108, 265 (n. 29)

Anderson, Maxwell, 47, 48. *See also* University of North Dakota Theater

Anderson, Sherwood, 126, 142

antisemitism: as defined by Langmuir, 114–15, 266 (n. 9); of PEG, 113–15, 178, 194, 265–66 (n. 8)

antiwar: PEG's response to atomic bombs, 209–11; PEG's response to Vietnam War, 32; PEG's response to World War II, 195, 197–98; PEG's telegram to Truman, 210–11

arete, 250

Aristotle: and actualization, 113; and PEG's concept of "actualizing art," 152–73

Atkinson, Brooks: praises *House of Connelly,* 160; supports Federal Theater Program (FTP), 176; supports *In Abraham's Bosom* for Pulitzer, 108; supports PEG and southern literary renaissance, 96; visits Chapel Hill, 142

Auden, Wystan Hugh, on satire and humor, 181

Aurelius, Marcus, 133

Australia, troops of, in World War I, 38

"Autumn" (McNeill), 26, 256–57 (n. 24). *See also* McNeill, John Charles

Avery, Laurence Green, 1

Azarkh, Avrom. *See* Granovsky, Alexander

Badlands, as subject for Koch folk drama, 47

Bailey, Josiah: as aspiring poet, 131; as fellow student at Buies Creek Academy, 9, 19; helps Lamprecht escape Germany, 130, 131; as Raleigh attorney and state senator, 130; and work on *The Lost Colony,* 131

Bailey, Pou, 220, 221

Baker, George Pierce: folk dramatist at Harvard, 46–47; and support of prole lit, 139; and Yale University, 123, 124

Bakshy, Alexander, 146, 271 (n. 33)

Balche family, 51. *See also* Green, Elizabeth Lay; Lay, George Atkinson; Lay family

Balzac, Honoré de, 75

Baptists, 5, 9

Barthelmess, Richard, in *Cabin in the Cotton,* 146, 148

World War I (*continued*)
Parade, 30. *See also* African Americans; Belgium; Flanders; France; Harnett Boys
World War II: and antiwar sentiment in Chapel Hill, 195; and character Johnny Johnson as propaganda for, 199; PEG writes "Christmas Prayer" during, 199; PEG's activity in United Front during, 198–212; and PEG's response to dropping of atomic bombs, 209–11; PEG's support of, xii, 32; and Popular Front and United Front, 198, 199
Wright, Richard, xii; and collaboration with PEG on *Native Son,* 173, 186–93; and FTP, 171–72, 176–77; leaves Communist Party, 141
Wyatt-Brown, Bertram, quoted on Abramic fathers, 86, 263 (n. 10)

Yale University: and Baker, 123, 124; and Pratt, 29; and Williams, 15–16, 256 (n. 5)

Yeats, William Butler: influence of, on Koch, 48; and PEG's approach to writing, 77, 262 (n. 23). *See also* Carolina Playmakers; Koch, Frederick Henry
Yiddish culture: in Eastern and Central Europe, 112, 113, 117; and folk drama of, 113, 116–18, 119, 178; and Granovsky, 116–18, 130. *See also* Germany; Granovsky, Alexander; Guggenheim Fellowship; proletariat literature; Russia, people's theater of
Young Men's Christian Association (YMCA): as center of antiwar movement at UNC, 195; in Paris, 41, 42; on ship returning from World War I, 43–44, 259 (n. 37); stateside, during World War I, 35
Ypres, 36, 38
Ypres Asylum, 38

Zimmermann, Ambassador, 28–29